D1189580

T E X T

T E X T

Transactions of the Society
for Textual Scholarship

1

FOR 1981

Edited by

D. C. GREETHAM

and

W. SPEED HILL

AMS PRESS
NEW YORK

T E X T

Transactions of the Society
for Textual Scholarship

COPYRIGHT © 1984 by AMS PRESS, INC.

All rights reserved.

INTERNATIONAL STANDARD BOOK NUMBER

Set: 0–404–62550–9
Volume 1:   0–404–62551–7

INTERNATIONAL STANDARD SERIALS NUMBER

0736–3974

Manufactured in the United States of America

Contents

Notes on Contributors

DR. CLAIRE BADARACCO is Assistant Professor of English at the University of Maryland.

ROBERT STEPHEN BECKER is Assistant Professor of English at Oxford College, Emory University. He is editing *George Moore: Collected Letters* in three volumes, and is writing a biography of the composer Augusta Holmes.

STANLEY BOORMAN, Acting Director of the Center for Early Music at New York University, previously taught at London and Cambridge. His special interests are in late medieval and renaissance music, particularly with the nature of its sources and notation and with related problems of performance practice for early music.

FREDSON BOWERS is Linden Kent Memorial Professor of English Emeritus at the University of Virginia, and editor of the annual *Studies in Bibliography*. In addition to writing two books on editorial theory—*Textual and Literary Criticism* and *Bibliography and Textual Criticism*—he has edited the texts of Thomas Dekker, Christopher Marlowe, Nathaniel Hawthorne, Stephen Crane, and selected texts of Shakespeare, Dryden, Fielding, Walt Whitman, and (as general editor) Beaumont and Fletcher. He is at present textual editor of the ongoing *The Works of William James* in the ACLS–Harvard University Press edition.

A. R. BRAUNMULLER has written extensively about both renaissance and modern drama and has edited several works by Bertolt Brecht. The University of Delaware Press has published his *A Seventeenth-Century Letter-Book: A Facsimile Edition of Folger MS V. a. 321*, and the Malone Society has published his edition of *The Captive Lady*, an anonymous seventeenth-century play until now available only in manuscript.

Born and bred in Switzerland, ULLA DYDO thinks in many languages and likes words in any language. A former editor and publisher of *Odyssey Review*, member Advisory Board, *TEXT*, General Editor, *Index of Middle New York*, and has been an N. E. H. Fellow. She is writing a book on Gertrude Stein's poetry.

A. S. G. EDWARDS is Associate Professor of English, University of Victoria. He is Advisory Editor, *Analytical & Enumerative Bibliography* and *Review*, member Advisory Board *TEXT*, General Editor, *Index of Middle English Prose* and Garland Medieval Texts, and Secretary, Renaissance English Text Society. Currently he is editing *The House of Fame* for the

Chaucer Variorum and a study of the Lydgate tradition in the fifteenth and sixteenth centuries.

JOHN L. I. FENNELL, Professor of Russian, Oxford University, has taught at Harvard, Berkeley, Virginia, and Stanford, and is the author of many books on Russian history and literature. He is the joint editor of the *Oxford Slavonic Papers*, *Russia Mediaevalis*, and *The Cambridge Encyclopaedia of Russia*.

JOHN MILES FOLEY, Professor of English at the University of Missouri, Columbia, specializes in ancient Greek, medieval English, and Serbo-Croatian oral literature. He has published extensively in these areas, has carried on field work on oral culture in Yugoslavia, and has received numerous grants to carry out his researches. Presently he is working on a book on structure and aesthetics in oral epic poetry.

HANS WALTER GABLER pursued post-doctoral research in bibliography and textual criticism at the University of Virginia and subsequently taught there. Now professor in the Department of English, University of Munich, Germany, he is General Editor of the critical edition of James Joyce in progress and volume editor of the recently published *Ulysses*.

DAVID S. HEWITT is Lecturer in English at the University of Aberdeen, Scotland, and is a specialist in Scottish and Romantic literature with a particular interest in editing Scottish texts. His selection of Scott's autobiographical writings, *Scott on Himself*, appeared in 1981.

GUNILLA IVERSEN teaches classical Latin prose and poetry at the University of Stockholm, Sweden, and is co-editor of the anthology, *Latin Poetry from Twenty Centuries*. As a member of the Corpus Troporum research team, she has edited Volumes III and IV of this continuing series.

PAUL OSKAR KRISTELLER is Woodbridge Professor of Philosophy Emeritus at Columbia University. He is author of many books and articles dealing with the history of philosophy, especially with the intellectual history of the Renaissance. As an editor of renaissance Latin and Italian texts, he has been confronted with the question whether and to what extent the textual method developed by classical scholars may be applied to the texts of a different period.

JOHN McCLELLAND was a student of Bernard Weinberg at the University of Chicago. He has published a critical edition of the *Erreurs amoureuses* of Pontus de Tyard (1521–1605) and was for several years a member of the managing committee of the Toronto Conference on Editorial Problems. He is currently Professor of French at the University of Toronto.

JEROME J. McGANN is the Doris and Henry Dreyfuss Professor of Humanities at the California Institute of Technology. His most recent books are *The Romantic Ideology* and *A Critique of Modern Textual Criticism*, both published in 1983 by the University of Chicago Press.

DONALD H. REIMAN is Editor of *Shelley and his Circle*, the multi-volume catalogue-edition of the MSS of Shelley, Byron, and their circles in the collections of The Carl H. Pforzheimer Library, New York. He has edited Shelley's poems for *The Norton Anthology of English Literature*, is co-editor of *Shelley's Poetry and Prose*, and has written and edited several other volumes on the British Romantics.

G. THOMAS TANSELLE, Vice President of the John Simon Guggenheim Memorial Foundation and Adjunct Professor of English at Columbia University, has written on textual and bibliographical matters and is one of the editors of the Northwestern-Newberry Edition of *The Writings of Herman Melville*.

PAUL F. WATSON teaches Italian renaissance art at the University of Pennsylvania, where he is an associate professor. As well as a series of articles on Florentine and Venetian painting from 1350 to 1570, he has written *The Garden of Love in Tuscan Art of the Early Renaissance*, which deals with the *locus amoenus* in Italian art and literature. At present he is completing a book on illustrations of Boccaccio's Italian fiction in Italian art of the fifteenth century.

MARJORIE CURRY WOODS, Assistant Professor of English at the University of Rochester, has published articles on Milton and on medieval literary criticism. She is working on an edition and translation of an early commentary on the *Poetria Nova*, a book of essays on "Chaucer the Rhetorician," a volume on *Troilus and Criseyde*, and a section on "Chaucer and the Rhetoricians" for the Annotated Chaucer Bibliographies.

Introduction

Why *TEXT*? Why a new journal and why a new interdisciplinary society in these days of too many periodicals and too many conferences? The questions are inevitable and quite proper, but there will be only a partial answer here in this brief editorial preface to our first volume. The most eloquent and practical answer to the questions (since it was written specifically to commemorate the first meeting of the Society for Textual Scholarship) can be found in the introductory essay to this collection, G. Thomas Tanselle's Presidential Address given at the 1981 conference. In this essay, Dr. Tanselle confronts the questions that we have assumed any reader of *TEXT* will ask, and an attempt by the *TEXT* editors to answer the same questions here would in large part duplicate his careful advice and his *caveats*. But one major point can be made: *TEXT* exists, and the STS exists, because until now there has been no genuinely interdisciplinary forum—in publication or conference—where textual scholars could speak not only to those with similar interests and experience but also to those whose background, because it was *different*, might provide new information, new methodologies, even new inspiration, for the tasks of textual scholarship. By "textual scholars" we mean all those who are concerned with the basic problem of the transmission of communication through a text, whether that "text" occurs on an inscribed stone, a papyrus roll, a vellum codex, a printed book, a film, a computer tape, a canvas, or even as pure sound (music or words); by "textual scholars" we also mean all those who might otherwise call themselves palaeographers and epigraphers, codicologists and enumerative, descriptive, and analytical bibliographers, literary and historical editors, biblicists, classicists, historians of film, art, and science, musicologists and textual critics, and so on. What these scholars have in common is the fact that texts are subject to change as they are transmitted, but unfortunately, what they have also had in common is a tendency to speak only to their fellows in the same discipline. Such specialization is clearly valuable, and *TEXT* does not seek to disparage the special skills (or even the special vocabularies) that have been developed in dealing with texts in the several disciplines represented here. But we do believe that there are valuable experiences to be shared, perhaps battle-wounds to be displayed, which will serve both to enlighten and to instruct.

The complete answer to that question, Why? resides, of course, in the pages that follow, in the series of articles on textual theories and principles, methodologies and procedures, in fields as diverse as Russian history, fourteenth-century painting, mediaeval and renaissance music, modern correspondence, and Yugoslav epic. For if this book cannot finally speak for itself and justify its existence, then no special pleading by its editors will help its cause. We believe that the articles in this first volume of *TEXT* represent, as a group, both the problems we are confronting and some of the possible solutions, and that if read both as individual statements and as a cumulative response to the interdisciplinary purposes of STS, the articles will explain and elucidate the nature of *TEXT*, now and to come.

The arrangement of this first volume of *TEXT* reflects this interdisciplinary purpose. The first section comprises five essays written especially for *TEXT* and dealing with problems in interdisciplinary textual scholarship. In his Presidential Address, G. Thomas Tanselle defines the principles and procedures of interdisciplinary study, and makes a number of suggestions about possibly fruitful areas of research. Then Paul Oskar Kristeller, whose essay printed here was the closing address at the 1981 conference, discusses the Lachmann system of stemmatic analysis, using the occasion to give a spirited call to arms to scholars in various disciplines. Jerome J. McGann's essay begins by examining the likely academic territory to be staked out by "textual scholarship" and then proceeds to relate some current critical theories to the traditional practice of philological research. Finally, in this section, Claire Badaracco and Fredson Bowers debate the interrelationship of literary and historical editing, with Dr. Badaracco offering a reappraisal of terminology and concepts, and Professor Bowers responding with a detailed defence of the discipline of textual criticism. All five essays, then, are committed to an interdisciplinary approach to textual studies, and all seek to define and elucidate the purposes of textual scholarship.

To some extent, these features also characterize the fourteen essays following, which are arranged in rough chronological order of their subject-matter. For although the essays *are* arranged along an historical line from mediaeval to modern, this chronological pattern is possibly misleading. That is, the essays were not chosen in order to illustrate textual problems in each of the several periods (if we have covered materials from Old English epic to Robert Graves, we are well pleased, but this periodic balance was not our prime purpose)—rather, we sought to publish essays which offered more than a specific examination of a specific local problem of interest only to scholars in the same field. Thus, a number of the essays deal with the textual characteristics of an entire genre or sub-genre or with a general approach to editing (e.g., John Foley on oral literature, Marjorie Woods on mediaeval commentaries, Gunilla Iversen on tropes, A. R. Braunmuller on Elizabethan letters, A. S. G. Edwards on modern enumerative bibliography). Some offer broad historical surveys arising out of a consideration of a specific field of study (Donald H. Reiman on Anglo-American bibliographical theory and practice in relation to the editing of Romantic literature, John McClelland on theories of editing in the modern languages, and John Fennell on the textological school in Russian history and literature). Some combine the first two methods (Robert S. Becker by studying the genre of letter-writing *and* surveying current practices in editing correspondence, Paul Watson by dealing with attribution in art history, and Stanley Boorman by analyzing filiation techniques in the editing of music). Even those essays which focus on one particular author offer a new methodology which, while developing from the specific idiosyncracies of the text studied, have ramifications for the editing of other, similarly idiosyncratic texts (Ulla Dydo on Gertrude Stein, Hans Walter Gabler on Joyce, and David Hewitt on Burns). In all, therefore, the chronologically-arranged essays have, as a group, the same interdisciplinary implications as the first five essays in this volume. It is our intention that this will be the major feature of all subsequent volumes of *TEXT*.

A brief word on our editorial principles: because of the interdisciplinary nature of *TEXT*, we have made no attempt, as editors, to impose a single documentary style on our contributors. We have tried to ensure that each essay has its own internal consistency, but have not invented or appropriated a *TEXT* house-style which all disciplines must obey. Similarly, because the essays (and, we hope, the readership) are international, we have accepted the use of either British or American spelling and punctuation conventions. Finally, because *TEXT* is the "Transactions of the Society for Textual Scholarship," several articles are given as originally presented at an STS conference (i.e., without footnotes or other concessions to the written form). As

noted above, some essays were specifically composed for a conference, others directly for *TEXT*. As this present volume suggests,
we clearly welcome articles with a broad methodological or
theoretical scope, but more limited essays are acceptable if they
describe or exemplify new textual principles or practices that are likely
to be of interest to scholars in other disciplines. See pages 337–338 for
details of submission.

A new interdisciplinary journal and society must obviously owe
their existence and success to a great many people and institutions. If
we were simply to list them all here, *TEXT* would become even more
bulky than it is already; but there are those who must be recognized,
albeit briefly, in this introduction. To our colleagues who served and
serve on the original STS Steering Committee (Allan Atlas and Mal-
colm Brown) and its successor the STS Executive Committee (Elizabeth A. R. Brown, Madeleine Morris, John Moyne, Barbara Oberg,
Thomas Palaima, Donald H. Reiman, Mary B. Speer, Martin
Stevens, G. Thomas Tanselle, and John Van Sickle), we are particularly grateful for having had faith in the organization and publication
(especially in those early days when neither showed signs of a short
gestation period). From the first two Presidents of STS (G. Thomas
Tanselle and Paul Oskar Kristeller), the society and the editors of
TEXT have received inestimably valuable advice, support, and direction. For the indulgence and advice of the now more than eighty-mem-
ber STS Advisory Board, we are particularly grateful. In editing a
journal with such a wide interdisciplinary range, we are obviously very
dependent upon the judgements and criticism of the advisors, and (after the contributions of the authors themselves) the responsibility for
any scholarly virtues this volume might possess lies largely with our
Advisory Board. From many City University of New York administrators we have received enthusiasm for our project and (particularly
difficult in these years of fiscal constraints) the generous use of CUNY
facilities and the investment of college funds in the conferences from
which *TEXT* grows. These administrators include, from the CUNY
Graduate Center, Executive Officers Allen Mandelbaum, Morton N.
Cohen, and Lillian Feder, Deans Norma S. Rees, Sydel Silverman,
Richard A. Styskal, and Solomon Goldstein, and the Center's publici-
ty and graphic arts and design staff, especially Amy Green and Barry
Disman; from Queensborough Community College, President Kurt
R. Schmeller, Deans George Alterman and Michael C. T. Brookes,

English Department Chair Sheena Gillespie, and the printing staff of Joseph Felician; and from Herbert H. Lehman College, President Leonard Lief and Dean Ira Bloom. STS has been generously supported by grants from several institutions—the University of Washington (Seattle), Columbia University (Department of English and Comparative Literature, and the Friends of the Book Arts Press of the School of Library Service), and The Carl and Lily Pforzheimer Foundation, Inc. To all we are extremely grateful. To a legion of willing graduate students (far too many to be mentioned individually here), we are indebted for their having stuffed thousands of envelopes, for having manned registration desks at the conferences, and for having handled a good deal of the clerical work in getting STS and *TEXT* on their respective feet. Susan Gowing, Dolores DeLuise, Gale Sigal, Walter Stiller, Anne Simpson, and Katherine Yates (the latter three having served as Executive Assistants), and Keith Walters (formerly an Executive Assistant, now Secretary of STS) deserve special mention. To our editor at AMS Press, William B. Long, we are grateful for his enthusiasm for *TEXT* and his patience with our interdisciplinary peculiarities, and finally, to the members of STS, for whom this volume is in many cases the first concrete testimony to the existence of the society, we owe a special thanks for having demonstrated to us that *TEXT* had an interested, articulate, and responsive audience already waiting for it. We hope they will find their expectations fulfilled in the following pages.

D. C. Greetham
W. Speed Hill

The Society for Textual Scholarship
April 10, 1981

G. Thomas Tanselle

At the risk of sounding like Emerson writing to Whitman, let me say that I am pleased to greet you at the beginning of what promises to be an influential career for the Society for Textual Scholarship. One is likely to have misgivings these days about the formation of any new organization or the announcement of any new periodical, because we already have too many of both, and we all find ourselves attending too many meetings. What generally happens, of course, when learned societies and journals proliferate is that they focus on more and more specialized subjects and help to accelerate the fragmentation of scholarly endeavor. To some extent this movement is inevitable as knowledge increases; but whenever an organization is established that moves in the other direction and seeks to promote communication across the boundaries of what have become compartments of scholarly activity, one can only rejoice.

The Society for Textual Scholarship is such an organization, for it aims at nothing less than to bring together in fruitful discussion persons concerned with textual matters of all kinds. This goal encompasses, in effect, every conceivable field, since all fields involve communication of some sort; and where there is communication, there is a medium of communication, a means of transmission, the operation of which may produce distortions in what is communicated. Textual problems are not limited to literature, or even to all verbal communication in written or printed form. Problems of textual transmission arise in oral literature, in music, in sound recordings, in films, in engravings and etchings. The images of visual art, the sounds of aural art, are texts, just as the written and printed words and punctuation of manuscripts and books are texts. Investigating the relationships among versions of what purports to be the same work or among

1

attempted reproductions of what purports to be the same version is the task of textual scholarship in all fields; and what this Society can usefully provide is a forum where common croblems—and, at a basic level, there *are* common problems, however diverse their manifestation—can be discussed (indeed, perhaps, discovered) by persons representing a great diversity of experience in textual study.

Recognition of the need for textual study goes back at least to the Alexandrian scholars of the third century B.C., and a long tradition of what is usually called "textual criticism" exists, concerned primarily with the texts of classical and biblical writings, and more recently, with medieval manuscripts. The word "criticism" in "textual criticism" suggests the important role that individual judgment plays in the process of evaluating textual authority and deciding on emendations. This Society has chosen the term "textual scholarship" rather than "textual criticism" not in any sense as a rejection of the latter term but only because the former is the more encompassing term. The great tradition of classical and biblical criticism forms but one branch of textual scholarship as a whole. Another branch is the English-language tradition in the editing of Renaissance and post-Renaissance literature, which has developed largely within the last century—and, one may add, developed for the most part independently of the earlier tradition of textual criticism. Although there are certain points of contact between the two, and although a few scholars, such as W. W. Greg and Vinton Dearing, have worked in both areas, the two remain today almost completely separate: a scholar editing a classic Greek text, say, and one editing a nineteenth-century American novelist do not as a rule have much knowledge of one another's editorial rationale and methods or of the tradition from which those principles and procedures emerged. What is worse, they may even think there is no reason why they should, assuming the materials and objectives to be so different that there is no significant overlapping between the two fields. This attitude results from a failure to think through the basic questions that textual work involves and from a tendency simply to follow procedures that seem to be well established within a given field. That a great distance exists even between editors of literatures in the modern languages is one of the meanings implicit in the title of Conor Fahy's 1976 Oldman Lecture, which comments on the lack of recognition of analytical bibliography by editors of sixteenth-century Italian texts: the title is "The View from Another Planet." Disciplines drift apart and inevitably develop their own ways of dealing with problems that are common to them all; but looking beneath those divergent procedures to the underlying rationale provides a common ground for bringing scholars from a number of fields together again.

As an organization pledged to bringing textual scholars from various fields together, both in person and in print, this Society must confront certain difficulties. The most serious, perhaps, is that the existence of such a society may seem to confirm the mistaken, but widely held, notion that editing and textual work are merely matters of technique, of methodology, and not of content. If scholars who know little about the subject matter of each other's labors can get together to talk about editorial problems, then some observers may be led to conclude that editing is simply a particular kind of technical proficiency and that, once one attains a satisfactory level in this skill, one can set about editing anything. The truth is, of course, that textual and editorial scholarship, like other forms of scholarship, is not a mechanical process but rather a critical investigation that continually demands informed judgment. One may have thought carefully about editorial rationale and principles of emendation; but one is still not prepared to edit the works of a writer about whom one is not otherwise fully informed or a document from a place and period with which one is not fully acquainted. It is possible to be a textual expert in the sense that one has given particular attention to the theoretical issues that textual scholarship entails; but such a person is not equally competent to edit every piece of writing that comes along. One can no more be a successful textual scholar than any other kind of scholar without a firm historical understanding of the period, the figures, and the material one is dealing with; textual work, regardless of the field, continually requires decisions that are dependent on a sensitivity to the language and thought of a given person, time, or place. This is a point that cannot be overemphasized, and we must keep it before us at all times.

To say that, however, does not mean that a society of this kind must be reduced to small groups in which specialists talk only to their colleagues in the same specialty. If that were so, the Society would have no reason for existence. There are certainly basic issues that we can all profitably discuss together, both at these meetings and in our publication. The question is, on what level? I think the first answer to that question must point out that productive discussion consists of more than collections of examples or illustrations, for another of the difficulties a society like this faces—the opposite one from the temptation of specialists to talk only to each other—is the tendency for interdisciplinary papers to state very general (even obvious or superficial) points and to support them with examples drawn from the specialties of the writers. If all that a paper accomplishes is to provide us with further illustrations of a point that we already understood or one that is self-evident, it does not accomplish very much; and a collection of such papers can be particularly tedious. Examples have their place in rational discourse, obviously, and I am not suggesting that they should be totally banished. But I think it is important to see the distinction between examples that are in effect nothing more than decoration and examples that are integral to the establishment of a point. I am always impatient with persons who ask, upon hearing a theoretical statement that is clearly undeniable, how often it proves to be relevant in practice—as if the quantity of such occurrences has anything to do with the validity of the statement. In textual matters, when one calls attention to the significance of punctuation and spelling, for instance, or to the fact that scholars (or anyone else) when quoting should check into the accuracy of the texts from which they are drawing their quotations, someone is almost certain to ask how often it really makes a difference whether one pays heed to these points. Although the answer is that it makes a difference very often indeed, the answer is irrelevant. It would not matter whether one could think of a single example; the validity of the points would not be lessened. In the same way, some textual discussions consist of examples that are totally unnecessary for supporting the general observations made. Those examples may be of some interest in their own right—certainly to scholars of the authors and fields represented—but for a broader audience they do little more than demonstrate how widespread certain problems are. For persons who require such demonstration, a purpose is no doubt served by the examples, and it may be that a certain amount of exchanging of illustrations is inevitable in the early stages of an interdisciplinary organization. But if the organization is to have intellectual validity, it must move beyond that level of discussion. Its members must begin to discuss real issues—and discuss them as co-workers, not as students of one field speaking to students of another.

A dilution of substance is a real danger for any interdisciplinary group, as long as members feel that to make themselves understood they must address their fellows on an elementary level. But if they can take for granted that their concerns are indeed mutual, they do not need to waste time citing examples of the fact. They can move on to see what progress can be made by thinking together. In this process illustrations are obviously of use, when a point is more readily demonstrated by certain situations that arise in one field than it could be by drawing on another field. A diverse group of scholars has at its collective command an enormous range of information and experience; and it is to be expected that insights will have occurred to certain of them, based on the nature of the materials they have worked with, that have not yet been carefully thought about by others, for whom the points are nevertheless relevant. This kind of interchange can result in a true advance in thinking about a subject, and the rationale of an organization like the Society for Textual Scholarship is of course to facilitate such exchanges and foster such advances. As a group we must prevent the Society from becoming simply a forum for watered-down versions of what we are already doing in our individual fields and make it instead a place where new developments occur.

It is not difficult to suggest some of the basic issues that we should consider from an interdisciplinary perspective. A fundamental question that deserves further discussion in a broad context is whether scholarly texts should be exact transcriptions or reproductions of individual documents or printings, or whether they should be eclectic, drawing readings from various sources, including the editor. Should certain materials be handled in one of these ways and other kinds of materials in the other way? What does "exact" transcription mean: how does one define which characteristics of a document—whether handwritten or printed—are parts of the text and therefore worthy of retention in a transcription? When editors construct eclectic texts, what should be their guiding principle for making choices among variant readings? Is the attempt to follow the author's intention an appropriate goal for scholarly editing in all fields? In any case, how is intention to be defined (does it differ from "expectation"?), and how does one handle situations where an author's intention can be seen to shift? Is modernization or regularizing ever justifiable? Is "literature" something that can be segregated and treated editorially in a different way from other writings, or should all writings be approached in the same way?

This list is only a beginning, but it is enough to suggest another of the difficulties facing us. Whenever issues of this kind are brought up with the suggestion that something can be said about them applicable to all fields, one is sure to hear the objection that whatever is said will amount to inflexible rules that will stand in the way of treating diverse situations on their own terms. During the last two decades, for instance, a number of editors of nineteenth-century literary texts, following the lead of Fredson Bowers, have extended Greg's rationale for selecting and emending a copy-text to cover the materials they were dealing with. The merits of this procedure and of the resulting work have been the subject of considerable controversy, and one of the criticisms often made is that Greg's observations derived from his work on English Renaissance printed drama and cannot be appropriately extended to texts such as nineteenth-century novels, emerging from very different printing and publishing conditions. In my view many of the arguments along these lines have been uninformed and illogical, but the point here is not who is right in this particular instance. I cite it only to suggest one kind of difficulty attendant on the effort to find common ground between editorial problems from different periods.

It has become a cliché among some commentators on textual matters to say that every situation is unique and that general guidelines will prove unsatisfactory in handling individual cases. Statements of this kind are made frequently and, in my opinion, rather thoughtlessly. A moment's reflection would surely make it clear that there is a difference between restrictive rules and a logical framework for thinking about a problem. Reasonable people can presumably agree that inflexible rules, not adaptable to specific situations, are undesirable; certainly the proponents of the extension of Greg's rationale have not, so far as I am aware, ever suggested that an editor should follow any rule of thumb that goes against the preserved evidence in any situation. What is sometimes perceived as an effort to propound arbitrary rules is actually more often than not an attempt to find a conceptual framework that encompasses diverse cases—and this activity is one to be encouraged. It is all very well to say that situations must be handled on their own terms; but one is not in the best position to do an effective job by just plunging into the task, without having thought about the whole range of textual situations and their appropriate treatments. There is a long-standing dream in textual criticism for a system that will enable one routinely and objectively to delineate all transmissional histories. Whether such a system can be found, the urge to find it is a constructive one, a seeking for connections rather than divisions. If we proceed in this spirit and look for connections between the textual problems faced in diverse fields, we shall not be moving away from flexibility and toward restrictive rules but shall be gaining insight that can only facilitate the sensitive handling of specific textual problems.

And connections are to be found everywhere we turn. Historians, for instance, have generally given less thought to the problem of selecting a copy-text than have literary scholars, because their editorial work frequently is concerned with unpublished manuscript materials, whereas literary scholars have been faced with poems and novels published in a succession of editions. It is understandable, therefore, that thinking about copy-text is more advanced in the literary field; but historians do, of course, encounter pieces of writing that exist in variant texts with some claim to authority, and an understanding of what rationale has been developed in other fields for dealing with such matters is certainly relevant to their work. Similarly, classical scholars often draw on more sophisticated techniques than editors of later literature for working out the relationships among variant manuscripts, because they customarily deal with scribal copies many steps removed from the authors; but scholars of later literature do at times have to deal with multiple texts the relationships among which are not readily apparent, and they are not fully prepared for the task unless they are acquainted with the work of the classicists. Persons dealing with oral literature or folk materials must read what has been written about authorial intention, for the concept of intention manifested in a text is applicable to anonymous or traditional works as well as to those by single identifiable authors. The techniques of analytical bibliography (techniques for learning the printing history of books from the physical evidence in them, which in turn adds to one's knowledge about the nature of the copy used in setting the texts of those books) should be known and used more than they have been by editors of printed texts in all fields, not just belles-lettres—and, indeed, by editors of manuscript texts as well, for the general approach and some of the techniques can be extended to manuscripts. The recent writings about Greg's rationale of copy-text are, in the issues they raise and their methods of treating them, relevant to classicists, just as editors of later material cannot be excused for failing to be acquainted with the classicists' tradition. Our ignorance of related fields serves only to cut us off from much-needed help. We all face the same questions—whether to reproduce the text of a given document or to alter a documentary text according to certain guidelines, what those guidelines should say about such matters as authorial intention and regularization, what the rationale should be for choosing among indifferent variant readings, and so on. We should answer those questions as thoughtfully as possible, and to do that requires the cooperation of all of us.

When Howard Mumford Jones addressed the American Academy of Arts and Sciences in 1944, he declared, "Our problem is not whether a common language can be artificially reinstituted among learned men, but whether this academy is not charged with the duty of creating a common climate of opinion." These words seem to me equally applicable to our new organization. Its role is not to force us all to speak the same language but to help us to speak our various languages more effectively by making us more fully aware of the larger community of shared interests in which we are speaking. Our duty as a group is two-stranded, like Father Mapple's sermon in *Moby-Dick*. One strand, he said, was a lesson for everyone; the other was a lesson for him as "a pilot of the living God." We may not wish to think of ourselves as clergymen upholding the faith of textual purity, but our program is a similarly double one. As textual scholars we have an obligation to each other and the cause of editing to think through the basic principles of our work and to uphold certain standards in what we do. We also have an obligation to everyone else, to that much larger world of people who read, people who use texts in one way or another without being editors or textual scholars themselves: we can help make clear to them the relevance of textual study to their understanding of whatever it is they are reading or listening to or looking at, and we can encourage them to approach every text in every field in a critical spirit. Intelligent people normally react to the ideas of others with an independent mind, but they often naively take for granted that the text of the language in which they encountered those ideas was accurate and that they therefore do understand what was being said. Textual specialists are fully cognizant of how often texts of all kinds are corrupt, and they can play a role in acquainting the reading public with the fact that responsible reading—the effort to comprehend what someone else is saying—must include an awareness of the ways in which any text may have been affected by the process of transmission.

The universality of this fact is finally what justifies our joining together in this Society, and it underscores the fundamental significance of our undertaking. The present moment is a propitious one for our beginning, for in recent years textual scholarship has begun to achieve in a number of fields the prominence it long ago reached in classical studies. Organized efforts like the Center for Editions of American Authors (now the Center for Scholarly Editions) of the Modern Language Association have been influential in this trend, and interdisciplinary discussion has recently begun between historians and literary scholars in the Association for Documentary Editing. There is no doubt that a great deal of editing and editorial discussion is taking place. Let us see to it that this age of scholarship will be regarded not only as one of industry in textual studies but as one of insight as well.

The Lachmann Method: Merits and Limitations

PAUL OSKAR KRISTELLER

I should like to express first of all my genuine satisfaction with the founding of this Society and with the program of this conference which for the first time brings together many scholars from different disciplines (and especially from literature) who are concerned with textual problems, and more specifically with textual criticism and with other techniques of editing. Such scholars reaffirm in their work what should be the core and foundation of all historical and literary scholarship, but what is now widely attacked or dismissed as irrelevant or oldfashioned, namely the careful study of the texts and documents which form the source material and in a way the content of all our study of the past. I am especially grateful to Professor David Greetham for having invited and encouraged me to talk to you about some problems that have occupied and worried me for most of my scholarly life which now extends over more than half a century. I have been concerned with the study of philosophical texts from Greek and Roman antiquity, have published a number of unpublished or poorly printed philosophical and other texts of the Renaissance and also of the later Middle Ages, most of them in Latin and a few in Italian, and have supervised and edited many similar text editions prepared by my students or younger colleagues. I also conducted for many years at Columbia, and more recently once at the Folger Library, a doctoral seminar on techniques of research in medieval and renaissance philosophy, at first jointly with my late friend Ernest Moody and later alone. Along with other topics such as bibliography, palaeography and manuscript research, the seminar also covered some of the basic problems of editing and of textual criticism.

In my distant days as a student in Germany, I studied mainly philosophy and its history, but also classical philology and medieval history where textual criticism was considered part of our training.

When I later became involved with the study of philosophical and other texts of the Middle Ages and of the Renaissance, I had to face, from the beginning and ever afterwards, the question whether and to what extent the methods of textual criticism as developed by classical scholars (and to a lesser extent by medieval historians) may be applied to the editing of these later texts. I have always felt rather isolated in this enterprise, in spite of the help and encouragement I received from many younger friends and students, for the field of medieval and early modern Latin has been a thinly populated no man's land despised alike (though for different reasons) by classical scholars and by historians of the modern vernacular literatures. Few people seem to realize that the NeoLatin language up to the eighteenth century was a strong competitor of the vernacular in the literature of the various European countries that had in fact a bilingual culture, and that in philosophy, in the sciences, and in the other branches of learning, Latin ruled supreme during the same period. In recent years, the knowledge of Latin has greatly declined among students and younger scholars, and also the concern for texts has become less popular with the rise of neo-romantic and radical attitudes and of various literary and intellectual fads that are fundamentally opposed to reason, to history, and to scholarship. I am pleased to note that textual and other scholarly problems again receive wide and diverse attention from younger scholars, and I greatly welcome the opportunity to explain to you some of the problems I have encountered in my own field and experience, and to learn from the discussion how my views may be corrected or supplemented by the different experiences of scholars in other fields.

The Lachmann method which will serve as the focus of this paper is the standard method of textual criticism formulated by Karl Lachmann in the early nineteenth century and consistently applied to the editing of classical Greek and Latin texts by Lachmann himself and by many other scholars in Germany and elsewhere for most of the nineteenth century and beyond. By the late nineteenth century, classical scholars began to update and revise the method; but they have never completely abandoned it, whereas students of medieval and modern literature have often criticized it or even rejected or ignored it completely. My own position, due to my training and experience, is somewhat intermediary, and I shall try to show, as briefly as I can and in the light of my own experience, that the method, at least in my field, is basically sound but requires a number of important and very specific modifications.

It is necessary to remind ourselves that textual criticism was not invented by Lachmann or his generation of German scholars. Any attentive reader who corrects the misprints of a book or article and any proofreader is practising textual criticism even though he may be unaware of it or at least unfamiliar with the developed methods and techniques of the discipline. Any editor who mediates between the author and the reader and tries to prepare a text that is accurate and makes sense is practising textual criticism, whether he knows it or not, and he will do a better job if he does know it. For there is a tested technique, and it has had a long and respectable history. It was developed and practised by the Alexandrian grammarians in their editions of the Greek classical authors, and by more modest grammarians of late antiquity in their editions of the classical Roman authors. Medieval copyists were on the whole reasonably accurate, but with few exceptions not critical; and it was the great merit of the renaissance humanists and philologists, first in Italy and then in France and the Low Countries, to have revived and developed the skills of textual criticism, both in collating several (especially older) manuscripts and in applying conjectural criticism to Greek and Latin classical texts, and subsequently to the Bible and the Church Fathers, and to the texts of the Roman Law. In the seventeenth and eighteenth centuries, the leading Dutch scholars collated large numbers of classical manuscripts and recorded their variants; and their collations have remained the basis for many text editions down to recent times. During the same period, students of history, such as Mabillon and his successors in France, Muratori in Italy and others, developed similar techniques in editing historical documents and chronicles from the Middle Ages and early modern times, and they were followed in the nineteenth century by the editors of the Monumenta Germaniae Historica in Germany and by those of similar collections in other countries.

As compared with these earlier practices, the Lachmann method made several novel contributions. Earlier scholars had collated many different manuscripts of the same text and selected in each instance the variant reading that they found preferable and that seemed to have the largest manuscript support. Lachmann's crucial change was the separation of two phases in the preparation of the critical text: *recensio* and *emendatio*. Before establishing his text, he subjected all variant readings obtained through collation to a critical analysis and attempted to establish through a calculus of common and individual errors the different groups or families of manuscripts into which the tradition was divided, and the place which each manuscript occupied within the family to which it belonged, summing up his analysis with a so-called *stemma* that derived all extant manuscripts and families from a single archetype. This procedure allowed him to eliminate from consideration all manuscripts copied from extant manuscripts (*eliminatio codicum descriptorum*) and to evaluate both individual manuscripts and entire families in inverse proportion to the number and gravity of their errors. Some sceptics have objected that there may be a difference of opinion as to what constitutes an error, but I am inclined to reply that many errors are obvious, and that the method works if we focus our attention on the obvious errors, and forget about those other variants that may be considered as reasonable alternatives. Once this *recensio* has been completed, the editor may proceed to the *emendatio* and establish his critical text, selecting his variants on the basis of the breadth and quality, rather than of the sheer quantity, of their manuscript support, and limiting his conjectural criticism to those cases where the consensus of all manuscripts and hence their archetype offer a corrupt text that is in need of correction. The editor will tend, in case of doubt, to prefer the more unusual reading (*lectio difficilior*) to the more common ones; will balance the criteria of *recta ratio* and *usus auctoris* (in view of the consistent grammar, style and thought of his author); and will keep in mind the major types of scribal errors, such as repetition, omission, transposition, and substitution of words, interpolation, and the misreading of letters, words and abbreviations in an earlier model. The editor will record in his apparatus all essential variants, making it possible for his critical reader to recognize, criticize and even reverse his decisions. He will not hesitate to correct the archetype but never venture to correct the author. And he will constantly apply his knowledge of author, of subject, of style and of language and his common sense to supplement and occasionally to overrule the merely mechanical and statistical aspects of the method he follows.

This method has its obvious merits, and it is recommended by its clarity and simplicity. It works best in the case of those authors who are preserved by a small number of authoritative manuscripts which permit us to disregard all other manuscripts. This is the case for a number of classical Greek texts, and for the work of Lucretius, which survives in two or three Carolingian manuscripts on which all others depend. It is no coincidence that Lachmann's edition of Lucretius provides one of the chief models of his method. The method has been far less successful in many other cases, especially of Latin authors with a continuous, rich and complicated textual tradition. Here the modern editors often claim to follow only the best out of a large number of manuscripts, but on closer examination it turns out that the best manuscripts are merely the oldest manuscripts, or even worse, the manuscripts that have been best known to scholars over several centuries. In recent decades we have learned, thanks to the greater facilities for traveling and the progress of palaeography, that many of the best manuscripts that form the basis of our editions were badly collated in the past and yield different readings when recollated, and the continuing progress in the cataloguing of manuscript collections has brought forth many manuscripts previously unknown and unused that must at least be recorded and examined, if not collated, before they can be dismissed as unimportant. Also the conjectures credited to modern editors and their friends have often been anticipated by their Italian or Dutch predecessors in earlier centuries.

The fact that the Lachmann method has been poorly applied in many instances is not as important as the way it has been openly revised even within the tradition of classical scholarship. The discovery of classical texts in papyri that are centuries older than the earliest extant manuscripts has led especially Greek scholars to admit that there is a long textual history between the time of the author and that of the archetype of his extant manuscripts, and this modification is reflected in the basically Lachmannian manual of textual criticism by Paul Maas. The earlier prejudice against later manuscripts in favor of the earliest manuscripts was gradually overcome, and Giorgio Pasquali in his classic book on textual criticism proclaims the maxim *recentiores non deteriores* as a major principle. More extensive collating has led to the uncomfortable conclusion that there are many contaminated manuscripts that borrow variants from different families of manuscripts and hence cannot be assigned to any single family. This has led, in the case of texts with a very rich and complex manuscript tradition, to a complicated statistics of variants and has undermined the faith in a simple stemma. Understandably, computers have been used to classify and group the variant readings in such a complex tradition, and this is certainly desirable. Yet the often-heard claim that the computer can collate manuscripts is deceptive or at least premature. Whenever I have asked how a computer can collate, I have received the answer that the manuscript in question must first be transcribed in a special way before the computer can collate it, and one must be a very faithful believer in the computer cult to overlook the simple fact that the real collation is contained in this transcription that precedes the computer, and if errors are committed in this transcription, the computer will repeat them.

Computers apart, the task of the critical editor has been greatly complicated by the need for fresh collations and by the increased number of manuscripts to be collated, as we have seen. Moreover, new methods of manuscript research have been developed that tend to treat each manuscript not merely as a statistical unit for variants, but as a concrete and individual book, which has a unique physiognomy to which the other texts contained in it belong and a personal history, as it were, that extends from its copyist and first owner through all later owners, collectors, librarians and scholars who had access to it, down to its current location in some institutional or private, accessible or inaccessible, well or badly catalogued library.

If the Lachmann method has thus encountered serious problems even within the area of classical scholarship, we should not be surprised to find that it faces even greater and more serious problems when applied to medieval, renaissance and modern texts. For this later period, we have to cope with types of manuscripts that simply do not exist for the classical scholar. We have autograph manuscripts or drafts, manuscripts corrected by the author, dedication copies, copies owned by the author's friends, and after the mid-fifteenth century, we have printed editions proofread or corrected by the author. We have different redactions of the same work by the same author, and we have different redactions of the same work by different authors. We have the fluctuating text of oral performances recorded in writing by different copyists, such as university lectures and disputations (*reportata*, in Latin), speeches (Latin or vernacular), lyrical, epical, and theatrical compositions (mostly in the vernacular languages). We have to cope with entirely new genres of literary composition that follow different rules from those of classical literature. Finally we have to cope with the different vernacular languages that are still fluid and unregulated in their vowels and suffixes, in spelling, punctuation and word division, in syntax and even grammar, as well as the varying dialect habits of authors and copyists. Even NeoLatin often differs in vocabulary, syntax, prosody and style (though hardly in grammar) from classical Latin.

All this is hard and sometimes impossible to handle with the Lachmann method, and a basic alternative has been offered to it in the form of the diplomatic, that is, literal, transcription of a single manuscript source. This procedure is obviously indicated when we have a unique manuscript source or an original document or an autograph or corrected manuscript from which all extant copies are derived. There are exceptions even in these cases, for there may be errors of the copyist or slips of the pen of the author that should be corrected by the editor at least in his apparatus, and I know the case of an edition based on the author's autograph which is still inadequate because it ignores a number of author's additions found in other manuscripts. In the case of different redactions, whether by the same author or by several authors, it is obviously a mistake to conflate them, and the variants of different redactions should be separately recorded in a separate apparatus or in parallel columns or in appendices. Yet it is in my opinion a mistake to follow only one manuscript where the same redaction is found in several independent manuscripts. It is quite sound to edit a single redaction from all manuscripts containing it, according to the Lachmann method, and minor scribal errors should be corrected, not only from the manuscripts of the same redaction, but also from other redactions that contain the same passage. In the case of single redactions that appear in a very large and unmanageable number of manuscripts, we may be forced to give up the ideal solution of a critical edition, and choose a compromise, at least for the time being—collating a small number of judiciously selected manuscripts, and making but a brief sampling of the other mss., just sufficient to determine their family and their individual quality. In the selection of the best manuscripts, priority should be given to manuscripts that demonstrably originate with the author or with his circle of friends.

As we move down beyond the fifteenth and sixteenth centuries, the manuscript copy gradually disappears, except for university lectures, clandestine and occult literature and other special types of writing; the textual tradition rests more and more on autographs and on printed editions contemporary with the author. For a long time, the assumption was held by most scholars, including myself, that all different copies of the same printed edition contain the same text. It was also assumed on fairly good evidence that the first edition of a text, especially when supervised by the author, contained the most correct text, and that all later editions, whether reissued or newly printed, differed from it only by printer's errors, except for editions demonstrably revised by the author himself. Therefore, it seemed sufficient to collate only one copy of the first edition of a text. This comfortable belief has been shattered by recent experiences. Beginning with Shakespeare and a few other writers, it was discovered that different copies of the same edition may contain variant readings, and gradually many scholars have come to believe that each printed copy has a different text from each other copy and must be separately collated. Most such instances have been recorded for English texts after the sixteenth century, but apparently there are a few similar instances concerning Neo-Latin texts of the sixteenth century. We certainly have to accept the evidence where presented, disturbing and uncomfortable as it may be. Yet the task of collating every single copy of an edition is formidable even in the case of Shakespeare, and hardly feasible when it involves less important authors. I may be incorrigibly old-fashioned, but I still tend to think that the variants involved are mostly orthographical or minor, and that the variant readings are not found in individual copies, but rather in families of copies so that it will be sufficient to collate one copy of each family and to determine by sampling to which family each other copy belongs. But I must leave this problem and its solution to the specialists in English and other modern literatures, and cheerfully assert that it rarely or never occurs in Latin texts of the Middle Ages or Renaissance with which I have been concerned. What does occur is the continuing revision of a text on the part of the editors of later reprints, but this is of interest only for the influence and not for the original text of an author, and it strengthens the importance of the first edition when it comes to establish the original text of an author contemporary with that edition.

Summing up my remarks, I should like to draw the following conclusions: the Lachmann method, when first formulated in the early nineteenth century, marked a great and decisive progress over earlier methods of textual criticism, and it was essentially successful in the treatment of Greek and Latin classical authors and in other authors that had a comparable manuscript or printed tradition (Lachmann himself made respectable editions of medieval and modern German authors). The principles involved in his method are basically sound and should be maintained, although with significant modifications that depend on the nature and condition of the texts and on the facts and circumstances of their manuscript tradition. The method must be modified even for classical texts when their tradition is rich and continuous, and when we are confronted with numerous and especially with contaminated manuscripts. It requires even more modifications for non-classical texts when we have to cope with author's variants, different redactions, the fluidity and irregularity of non-classical languages including NeoLatin, and with printed texts contemporary with the author. What remains valid in the Lachmann method is the separation of *recensio* and *emendatio*, the calculus of errors and the grouping of manuscripts according to their errors, at least for single redactions, and the task of emending the text on the basis of *recta ratio* and *usus auctoris* (I trust that even for the sloppy or obscure texts of our own time there is at least an *usus auctoris*, if not a *recta ratio*.) The attempts to abandon the method altogether lead to dilettantism and chaos and should be dismissed, for I have the impression that those who advocate this course are not familiar with the method and with the results it is able to achieve.

I should like to conclude by stating again that I am extremely pleased with the attention given in this conference and by the members of this Society to textual problems in a variety of fields. I hope this discussion and our continued efforts will lead to a renewed rigor of method in such fields as literary and intellectual history, the history of philosophy and of the sciences and other related disciplines that are all threatened by the current waves of narrow techniques and of an amateurish romanticism, not to speak of the cult of the relevant and the total hostility to history and to historical studies which has also become a fact of life in recent years. Our effort may also lead, and I hope it will lead, to a greater awareness of the common premises and methods shared by all the disciplines which are now called the humanities, and to a greater concern for their common philosophical and cultural principles. There will always be problems, textual and otherwise, that escape easy solutions and that continue to be controversial. Yet there are tested methods of textual and other scholarship that allow us to solve at least some problems, to correct some errors and to establish the truth at least on a number of specific points. We should resist the temptation to think that no problems can be solved because some problems cannot be solved, or that the problems we can solve are trivial and only the problems we cannot solve are important. We rather should share the faith of those who put together a puzzle and who know that they may reach their goal slowly and by unexpected detours after they have failed with their first straight attempts. The tested methods of textual criticism, just as other tested skills, should be transmitted, and constantly refined and critically transformed through our actual study of the texts and of their manuscript and printed sources. Our effort will put a limit to any arbitrary interpretation of our texts, of the thought and intent of their authors, and of the historical context in which they wrote their works. The discipline of a valid method will free us from the wrong opinions to which people cling out of preference, fashion, convention, laziness or simple whims and which have no real ground to stand on, and it will help us in our quest for that part of truth which in our area is attainable.

Textual criticism is a skill, it is for the scholar what a tool is for a craftsman. The scholar as a craftsman arrives at a product that is neat and subtle, and this is the aesthetic dimension of our work, and it aims at accuracy in every step, and this is the moral dimension of our work. For a scholar should care, not only for his own original ideas which may after all be wrong, but above all for the authentic meaning of the past author whom he is trying to understand. Our past author may be difficult to understand, but we are trying to understand and to interpret him for our own benefit and for that of our students, colleagues and readers. We shall enrich all of them if we do not try to impose our own ideas on the authors whom we study, but more modestly try to let them speak their own thoughts and learn from them what we did not know before. For the whole enterprise of history, and especially of intellectual history, rests on the belief, or rather the conviction, that the texts of the past contain a substance and a quality, philosophical, literary, and historical, that still speak to us if properly understood and that should not be reduced to the limits of our contemporary understanding, but should in turn help us to extend and overcome these limits.

Shall These Bones Live?

Jerome J. McGann

A professional society launches itself in 1981 under the aegis of "textual studies" and proposes to issue scholarly papers in a journal called *TEXT*. These are notable events, all the more so because their initial impression belies their actual significance. For such a society and such a journal, in an academic world currently dominated by structuralist and post-structuralist theory and practice, necessarily suggest an interest in the semiological and Derridean "text" and in the entire critical enterprise which goes under the heading of "textuality."

One has only to cast a glance at the editorial and advisory board of this society, however, to see that its interests must be very different indeed. Riffaterre, Said, Derrida, DeMan: none of these famous men are part of this project. Instead we find other names—equally famous, perhaps, but residents of another planet—like Orgel, Litz, Vieth, and Bowers. So an illumination grows. *TEXT*, and the Society for Textual Scholarship, is a revisionist action created by philologists, scholars, and "textual critics" in the traditional sense.

The creation of such a society and such a journal at this particular historical moment is, in other words, a bold—even an aggressive— move. It will bring not peace but a sword. Yet when the inevitable conflict is engaged, what will be the issues at stake? Is *TEXT* to be a sort of Vendéean Uprising, a center of reaction where editors, bibliographers, and philologists can meet and agreeably deplore all that is new-fangled, French, and transitory?

I raise these matters here partly because I want to explain my own purpose in associating with this new venture, and partly because I want to make a polemic for a revisionist policy which will not be a reactionary one. In order to make my position clear, I shall have to rehearse some familiar matters relating to the present state of literary studies. Although this narrative is necessary, I shall make it as brief as possible.

Textual criticism, in the traditional sense, is an analytic discipline separated into two provinces, the so-called Lower and Higher Criticism. Its practitioners are those guardians of our dry bones, the editors, bibliographers, and philologists of various sorts who are best known to the ordinary student of literature for the work they do *not* do: that is, interpretation and literary criticism.

It is an historical irony of some magnitude that twentieth-century stylistics and hermeneutics, or literary criticism and interpretation, emerged directly from the traditions of critical philology which developed over the course of the eighteenth and nineteenth centuries. From F. A. Wolf to Wilamowitz, philological analysis was intimately connected, not merely to the elucidation of the text, but to what James Thorpe once (and forever) denominated "the aesthetics of textual criticism."[1] The New Criticism's devotion to "the poem itself," as well as the more recent fascination with texts not as specific objects but as "methodological fields"[2] (or *foci* for interpretive strategies), descend to us through the mediation of various form critics, linguists, and philologists, and most immediately through people like Saussure, Sapir, and Jakobson. In this descent, however, a gap opened up between the work of the scholar and the work of the critic. This gap confronts us today as almost unbridgeable, a gulf we locate by that ultimate sign of contradiction, The Text.

The problem with this polarization in literary studies is not at all that differences should exist between the methods and interests of scholars on the one hand and critics on the other, or between so-called extrinsic and intrinsic studies. One might well recall here those famous words of William Blake, for they seem especially pertinent: "These two classes of men are always upon earth, & they should be enemies. Whoever tries to reconcile them seeks to destroy existence." Blake's view was that "Without Contraries is no progression," and his proverb holds equally well on our tight little island of literary studies.[3] The problem is that these two classes of men (and women) tend to carry on their work in entire isolation from each other, not that they engage in those struggles and intellectual combats which Blake called "Mental Fight." These struggles must begin, and I propose to aid the event by examining some of the positions and fault-lines which appear on either side.

I

The enemies of traditional philology, from its early antagonists like

Leavis to its most recent critics like Barthes, recurrently charge it with various sorts of dehumanization. Philologists murder to dissect, and where are the pleasures of the text for the editor and the bibliographer? Over and over again the literary critic struggles to tear the poetic work from the hands of the Casaubons of the world and to deliver it over to the Dorotheas.

One of the most eloquent, and influential, pleas for such a delivery was made in 1971 by Roland Barthes in his essay "From Work to Text."[4] In this exemplary paper Barthes distinguished sharply between the "work" of traditional literary studies, both critical and scholarly, and the "text" of a new type of hermeneutics. The distinction means to separate "the work," which "is concrete, occupying a portion of book-space," from "the text," which, because "it exists only as discourse" and never as concrete object, is in reality "a methodological field," a locus for the continuous production of literary signification. Barthes spoke for a whole generation of new literary readers and interpreters when he said that *"the text is experienced only as an activity, a production."* This famous dictum announces a renewed method for dealing with the polysemous aspects of literary productions. They are not "works," which Barthes called "objects of consumption," but "texts," which "ask the reader for an active collaboration."

Those of us who have worked with the dead letters of our literary pasts, whether as editors, bibliographers, or whatever, understand all too well the force of Barthes's polemic. William Todd's essay "On the Use of Advertisements in Bibliographical Studies"[6] is a model of its kind, even a brilliant work, but one does not value it—or consult it—because it generates textual pleasure, any more than Todd wrote it to collaborate in an intertextual activity. Todd's essay treats literary works as concrete objects and—worse still—seems uninterested in aesthetic pleasures altogether. The essay merely (merely?) shows us a peculiarly reliable method for establishing accurate dates of publication.

Todd's is a piece of Dryasdust scholarship, sure enough, and those of us who—like myself—admire it are faced with the need to justify it as a fine piece of work. Nor will it do merely to launch a tit-for-tat rejoinder, and ask how much pleasure gets generated through a Derridean text like *Grammatology,* or through the turgid academese one repeatedly confronts in journals like *Glyph* and *Diacritics.* But such journals merely represent the tactical failures of an impressive general strategy; to locate these failures is, at the most, to uncover the symptoms of what ought to be our true objects of investigation.

In fact, these contemporary textual strategies have no more strength than their limits permit, and to use them well one must understand those limits. Barthes, for example, speaks for a large number of influential contemporary critics when he sets a premium upon literature as a process of production rather than consumption, and when he disvalues a critical method which tries to treat artistic works as objects. In each case he appeals to that powerful tradition of aesthetic criticism which emerges with Kant and Coleridge and continues into our own day. Coleridge declared that objects as objects are fixed and dead, and he elevated the activities of the so-called "creative imagination." Reason and what the Enlightenment termed "the critical faculties" are suspect powers in this tradition, which has developed that ideology of process and production—"something evermore about to be"—that is perpetuated in post-structuralist criticism.

The great strength of this tradition lies in the freedom it can give to the critic-as-reader. Authority for literary creativity emerges from the dead past to a living present. In such a situation the function of criticism becomes, avowedly, the sustaining of its own productivity, and its object becomes the process of that productivity. But such a procedure will succeed only when it accepts the limits of its own method. One of those fundamental limits is that such a method can generate literary experience only, not literary knowledge.[7] Such criticism should not mean but be, and as it yearns to embrace its own aesthesis, it also tends to abandon knowledge and science.

We must not mistake the character of this limitation, however. It is not a weakness or a fault in the method; it is simply one of its defining conditions. It appears in the method's lack of concern for historical studies, for philological pursuits of all sorts, for the *physique* and for the memory of artistic creations. These repudiations remind us that textual strategies carried out in a Barthesian mode have a definite, and antithetical, position throughout the modern periods. The function of such criticism is not to examine the newspaper advertisements of published books, or to assemble a bibliography of early printings, or to resurrect those historical references in a literary work which the passage of time has erased from our memories or altered circumstances have concealed from view. This is a methodology which does not aim to study the text of the critic but to generate the text of the reader.

The post-structuralist text and the philological text represent, then, that fundamental opposition in the field of literary studies which used to be called "criticism" vs. "appreciation," but which we now term analysis vs. reading. The one aspires toward a science, the other toward an art, one toward knowledge, the other toward experience. These two classes of men are always upon the earth of humane letters, and whoever seeks to reconcile them seeks to destroy the existence of their shared world.

Blake's proverb does not mean to sanction peaceful co-existence, however. The refusal to seek reconciliation ought to entail a tension and struggle between these opposing interests, rather than an agreement to let each go its own way. This last option has been the road most often taken, and it has generally led to the even-handed excesses of Dryasdust and Skimpole—between whom there is, I think, little to choose.

Problems arise in each case when either method fails to take its own powers and methods into account. In the case of the critic-as-artist, this problem takes the form of an *anamnesis*, sometimes even a deliberate attempt to obliterate that aspect of an immediate experience which has necessarily recuperated the past. For there can be no production process, no continuous act of generation, except within the limits of those specific means and relations of production which the present must accept as its continuing inheritance. This necessity exists because all literary products descend into immediate experience; that is, they come to the reader in determinate forms. The most elemental of these determinate forms is the physical object—normally, a bound and printed "text" (in the traditional sense) which established the conditions for every particular experience of the "text" (in the contemporary sense). Even the critical attempt to erase (or deconstruct) the traditional text depends upon an acknowledgment of its presence and relative authority. Such a text may come to us in forms that appear fairly well fixed, like *Mansfield Park*, or in forms that aspire to greater indeterminacy, like Cortazar's *Hopscotch*, or a play by Shakespeare.[8] These differences are, of course, crucial both for the experience and for the understanding of literary products. In every case, however, we must deal with the specific determinations. The texts, in the traditional sense, of *Macbeth* are defined in very particular ways.

Human beings are not angels. Part of what it means to be human is to have a body, to occupy physical space and to move in real time. In the same way the products of literature, which are in all cases human products, are not disembodied processes. When Barthes says that literature "exists only as discourse," we must forcefully remind ourselves that discourse always takes place in specific and concrete forms and that those forms are by no means comprehended by the limits of language. The aesthetic field of literary productions is neither an unheard melody nor a linguistic event, as one can (literally) *see* by merely glancing at Trollope's *The Way We Live Now* either in its first printing, or in some subsequent edition, like Robert Tracy's recent critical text.[9] If such productions are events in language, as of course they are, their eventualities are experienced in concrete and observable forms and under specific circumstances of time and place. Nor are these concrete particulars merely "accidental" aspects of literary productions. Just as the human body in its particular socio-historical environment establishes certain fundamental and defining human particulars, the concrete forms and specific moments in which literary works emerge and re-emerge are defining constituents of their modes of aesthetic existence.

Thus, if we are to understand how poems mean—if we are to gain knowledge of literary productions—we must pay attention to a variety of concrete historical particulars and not merely to "the poem itself" or its linguistic determination. Many literary critics, even many post-structuralist critics, would not disagree with such a view. But I would urge a further proposition and say that an encounter with the concrete particulars of an aesthetic object—an experience of the objectivity of "the text" in all its rich and various determinations—is fundamental to the *experience* of literary texts (or works) as well.

This proposition asks the critic-as-artist to understand that if the experience of art is an aesthetic process (i.e., a subjective encounter), the process gets carried through in specific sets of objective differentials. The generation of texts, whether philological or aesthetic, is a finite act which in every instance (and it is a process which takes place in particular instances) appears in some exemplary and specific case. It is crucial for the critic-as-artist to remind himself of this—to subject his own acts to the interrogation and critique of that model of otherness which is the philologist's text—if he is not to lapse into ventriloquism. The generation of the text is, even for the aesthetic critic, a perpetually renewed historical process of specific and concrete events.

The "discourse" of literature is not an undifferentiated linguistic stream, but a continuing set of finite relationships that develop in a Valley of Dry Bones between an author, printers, publishers, readers of various sorts, reviewers, academicians, and—ultimately—of society at all its levels, and perhaps even of international society. Every time a work of literature is encountered, the reader places himself in a position where he is able to experience, and join with, that complex human endeavor. Great literary works are valuable to us precisely because they exist to foster and reproduce such discourse. Critics like Barthes aim principally to put us into contact with the *idea* of this discourse. The philologist, on the other hand, aims—or should aim—to put us into contact with such a discourse in a more concrete and experiential way. We can glimpse how this aim is fulfilled even in a passage like the following, which deals with its materials at a relatively high level of generality. Most of you will, I suppose, recognize the voice of James Thorpe.

> Various forces are always at work thwarting or modifying the author's intentions. The process of preparing the work for dissemination to a public (whether that process leads to publication in printed form or production in the theatre or preparation of scribal copies) puts the work in the hands of persons who are professionals in the execution of the process. Similarly, the effort to recover a work puts it in the hands of professionals known as textual critics, or editors. In all of these cases, the process must be adapted to the work at hand, and the work to the process. Sometimes through misunderstandings and sometimes through an effort to improve the work, these professionals substitute their own intentions for those of the author, who is frequently ignorant of their craft. Sometimes the author hbjects and sometimes not, sometimes he is pleased, sometimes he acquiesces, and sometimes he does not notice what has happened. The work of art is thus always tending toward a collaborative status, and the task of the textual critic is always to recover and preserve its integrity at that point where the authorial intentions seem to have been fulfilled.[10]

In the field of literary production and reproduction, differentials are established through the elaboration of critical knowledge: specific details of (traditional) literary texts and their interacting historical contexts. Such knowledge is furnished by the normal "methodological fields" of our discipline, that is, in philological investigations carried out through the Lower and Higher Criticisms.

It is not the possession of such knowledge—in Barthes's terms, its "consumption"—which the critic-as-scholar must have as his object, however. It is the discovery, the repossession, and the use of such knowledge which matters. For knowledge in literary studies must be developed as a function of the aesthetic experience. If it is not, the knowledge is not literary knowledge; it is historical, and only potentially literary. Bibliographers, philologists, literary historians, and traditional textual critics grow ridiculous figures in the eyes of many literate persons because of this passion they have for details that seem ancillary to the experience of literary works. This ridicule is understandable, but it is also deeply misconceived; for the development and elucidation of a work's "minute particulars" are, finally, the *sine qua non* of any aesthetic experience. This is so because all art, by its very character as a symbolic mode, operates in a medium of uniqueness.

A sure grasp of this fact is a distinctive mark of all the great textual critics of the eighteenth and nineteenth centuries, and it equally explains why their legacy continues to dominate their polarized heirs in the twentieth. Their acts of revival, performed on classical, biblical, and national scriptures alike, were primarily attempts to define and sharpen the special character of the literary works they examined. The method entailed a massive program of rigorous and creative antiquarianism: literary works were made distinctive in and for the present by an immediate act of alienation and distancing. Art, which Time seemed bent upon reducing to obscure ruins, or rendering invisible through familiarity, was led across the Red Sea of the past and the deserts of the present to the Promised Land of History. The Ruins of Time, past and present, were overcome by agreeing to cooperate with its passages. Time thereby became History, and Art seemed reborn out of its losses, its otherness, its very distance.

Eichhorn, writing on the book of Genesis, exemplifies such purposes and achievements very well. When you read this book, he tells us you must

> Read it as two historical works of high antiquity, and thus breathe the air of its age and land. Forget the century you are living in and the knowledge it offers you; if you cannot, do not dream that you are reading the book in the spirit of its origin. The youth of the world, which it describes, requires that one sink into its depths. The first beams of dawning intelligence will not bear the bright light of the intellect. The herdsman speaks only to the herdsman, and the Oriental of gray antiquity only to the Oriental. Without intimate acquaintance with the customs of pastoral life, without acquaintance with the manner of thinking and imagining among uncultivated peoples gained through the study of the ancient

world, especially Greece of the earliest times, and of untutored nations of modern times, one easily becomes the betrayer of the Book, when one tries to be its rescuer and interpreter.[11]

This magnificent passage will not abide any irrelevant questions about intentionality, authority, or the general "mode of existence of a literary work of art." The passage shows us why Eichhorn's scholarly "hours when the mind is watchful not to miss the slightest similarities or dissimilarities"[12] between the *E* and the *J* strands in Genesis, are an integral part of his aesthetic experience of that work.

Eichhorn's scholastic drudgery is not merely another part of the "discourse" which the book of Genesis *is*; his scholarship defines the medium and the terms in which every aesthetic experience must take place. By specifying the distinctiveness of past forms of human life, the scholarship cooperates in and reduplicates the object (in both senses) of art, which can only exist in the media of its uniqueness. Reading Eichhorn we understand how the dead will live again.

II

So far this mild polemic has maintained itself at a rather cool and distanced level. It is time for specifics, illustrations, a few hard instances.

I mentioned earlier a celebrated paper by William Todd on the use of newspaper advertisements for establishing dates of publication. That paper focuses one of the recurrent preoccupations of bibliographers: their attempts to define precise details of place, date, and circumstances of publication, and even more the attempt to establish dependable methods for developing the information. The paper's fame rests on its procedural and methodological innovativeness.

His essay is not, of course, an act of immediate criticism. Its purposes are larger and more general—as, for example, Barthes's purposes were in *his* paper, which is also not a piece of literary criticism as such. Nevertheless, what Todd does in his essay indicates the importance he attaches to precision in matters of publication facts. He makes no plea for the aesthetic importance of such facts—scholars rarely do any more—but he might and could have done so. For one can make that demonstration in the case of *all* literary works, whose bibliographical histories are always, and necessarily, crucial to their literary and artistic character.

It makes a great difference, for example, that Byron's noble lyric "On This Day I Complete My Thirty-Sixth Year" first appeared posthumously. Moreover, the character of the poem is decisively marked by its early process of dissemination. The pathos of its heroism and its hopelessness is fixed and critically defined in the way he wrote it in his private journal of 22 January 1824, and in the way he then gave a copy of it, as an afterthought, to Pietro Gamba later that same day. "You were complaining, the other day, that I never write any poetry now:—this is my birthday, and I have just finished something, which, I think, is better than what I usually write."[13] The poem projects itself directly in the emotional conflict which these remarks also call attention to. For we must remember—as, in fact, the poem scarcely allows us to forget—that it was written shortly after Byron had arrived in Greece to support the latest Greek effort to throw off the Ottoman Empire. It is a peculiarly Byronic poem, fully conscious of its immediate circumstances and of its author's entire history in life and letters. Indeed, that history is the fundamental subject of the poem, which reflects upon its author's past under the clarifying pressure of Byron's special immediate circumstances. The poem fairly epitomizes how the emotional force of a literary work is a function of the most specific and precise matters of fact.

The artistic process which Byron had begun on 22 January only receives its complete definition in the early history of the poem's transmission and publication. Here are equally crucial matters of fact in the emotional nexus which the poem has called into being.

Byron wrote and forgot about his journal poem, and by 19 April he was dead. When this news reached England in mid-May it fell like a thunderbolt. Byron's body and his effects were brought back to England along with his journal and arrived early in July. Throughout this period, and for many months afterwards, the periodical press remained hypnotically fixed upon Byron, his career, and his final, haunting days in Greece.[14]

At the same time, some of those who were with Byron in Greece made copies of the poem given to Gamba, who also sent a transcript to Mary Shelley, at her request. One of these copies was used by the (unknown) author of "Lord Byron in Greece," a long essay which appeared in the July 1824 *Westminster Review* and which contained a narrative of Byron's last months. Four lines of the poem were first printed in this essay. The complete poem finally appeared in the *Morning Chronicle* of 29 October 1824, printed from one of the many manuscript copies which were now at circulation. The poem was then reprinted in various other newspapers.

That the poem should have been transmitted and finally published in this way is in perfect keeping with every other aspect of its text and context. A poem about noble causes and the ephemeral, if willing, agents of those causes, "On This Day" properly (we must say) makes its first public speech through the newspapers, and not through Byron directly, but posthumously, through the devotion of those several intermediaries who were with him in Greece when he wrote the verses and met his immortal death. That the actual copy-text for the *Morning Chronicle* printing should have disappeared in the complex network of the poem's early transmission history seems especially appropriate, for Byron's entire audience was in some way complicit in the process which brought this poem to be.

The more we pursue the poem's early bibliographical history, the more sharply do we experience the fragility of such a work and the special human character of the circumstances which it defines and perpetuates. The scholarly reconstruction of that text and its context is no more than a correspondent effort to provide the work with a yet further range of response, one that will eventually meet it on its own terms.

Or take another, less Romantic, but no less eloquent example: Poe's hoaxing tale "Von Kempelen and His Discovery."[15] In this case, if we reconstruct the context of the work's initial publication, we permit ourselves to regain access to the original, outrageous, and even highly significant wittiness of the narrative.

Poe published the work on 14 April 1849 in *The Flag of Our Union*. After his death, when his letters became generally available, readers learned from Poe's own words his initial intentions as he revealed them at the time in a letter to Evert A. Duyckinck, editor of *The Literary World*, the publication which was first offered, but which refused, Poe's narrative.

> I mean it as a kind of "exercise," or experiment, in the plausible or verisimilar style. Of course, there is *not one* word of truth in it from beginning to end. I thought that such a style, applied to the gold-excitement, could not fail of effect. My sincere opinion is that nine persons out of ten (even among the

best-informed) will *believe* the quiz (provided the design does not leak out before publication) and that *thus*, acting as a sudden, although of course a very temporary, *check* to the gold-fever, it will create a *stir* to some purpose.[16]

A number of scholars, most notably Burton R. Pollin, have elaborated the specific relevance of "Von Kempelen" in relation to the California Gold Rush, as well as its filiations with the hoax genre which emerged through the British magazine tradition in the nineteenth century, and they have elucidated as well the tale's numerous coded references to more detailed topical matters of various sorts.[17] The development of this scholarly material lays bare the fundamental textual and contextual matrix of the narrative. Specifically, the scholarship reveals—though not all of the scholarship is aware of this revelation—that "Von Kempelen" is a kind of witty demonstration of the old proverb "All that glitters is not gold."

Briefly, the narrative purports to correct and augment the prevalent accounts of the life and work of August Von Kempelen, the scientist who, according to Poe's narrative, developed a process for turning lead into gold. I do not wish to give a detailed commentary upon this, one of Poe's greatest tales, but to augment on my own part the important work of scholars like Pollin, Kabbot, and Allen. For whereas these men have developed all the necessary materials for revealing the secret of "Von Kempelen"—which is, finally, the secret of how to turn lead into gold—they remain, like the police who broke into Von Kempelen's workshop, in possession of the facts but behindhand in their understanding of those facts.

Pollin, for example, performs a masterful elucidation of the story's many details, which constantly make reference to actual matters of significant fact in Poe's life. What Poe does is so to operate on these common and everyday facts that they emerge, transmuted, into the true "realms of gold" which Keats and all literary persons are familiar with. The fundamental wit of the tale means to say that the California Gold Rush is an idiotic quest after Fool's Gold, that Eldorado is a place existing in imagination, and that its treasures are works of art, like "Von Kempelen." "I shall be a *littérateur*, at least, all my life," Poe told Frederick W. Thomas at the time he was writing "Von Kempelen," "nor would I abandon the hopes which still lead me on for all the gold in California."[18]

Poe's letter to Duyckinck shows that he hoped his tale would produce a "temporary check to the gold fever." He wanted the hoax to work *in fact*, so that it would "create a *stir*" among his readers—and, of course, lead eventually to the elucidation of the narrative's hidden secrets and treasure. The scholarly exploration of "Von Kempelen" shows how the tale has transmuted certain important facts in his personal and literary life and turned them into gold. The narrative involves an extensive and elaborate send-up of contemporary journalism, which seems always to get its stories wrong (though it means to deal in "matters of fact") and to misunderstand what it reports (and especially what it reports about Poe).

When Poe says, in his tale, that he and Von Kempelen "were fellow sojourners for a week, about six weeks ago, at Earl's Hotel," this is a coded reference to his public reading of "The Poetic Principle" at the Earl's House on 20 December 1848, just "about six weeks" previous to the writing of "Von Kempelen." The point of the reference in the fiction is to correct the journalistic "misapprehension" about Von Kempelen, which is to say (in transmuted form) to correct the bad journalistic reports about that notorious event. To correct the journalistic narrative with this "fictional" one is to substitute truth for error and reality for "pure imagination"; it is to turn leaden accounts into golden ones.

For the reader (or scholar) to decode such material is equally to transmute something ordinary and apparently insignificant into something valuable. Indeed, the act of decoding is a replication of the artist's original act of transmutation. In each case, something leaden finds its golden echo. "Von Kempelen" as a fiction thus demonstrates, in actual historical fact, what Poe's invented scientist revealed in the narrative. In the words of the tale, quoted by Poe from an unrevealed source: "pure gold can be made at will, and very readily, from lead, in connection with certain other substances, in kind and in proportions, unknown."[19] In the end the narrative shows us (it does not tell us) how this is done: by writing and then printing stories like "Von Kempelen" in specific journals like *The Flag of Our Union*. Imagination is not enough, nor is the solitary artist. The artist needs the lead of the printer's workshop "in connection with certain other substances," like paper and all the materials and systems of printing and publication, which allow a writer to bring his work into its necessary contact with the world of readers. That entire social nexus constitutes what Poe called—in the poem he published in *The Flag of Our Union* a week after "Von Kempelen"—"Eldorado." That Poe's entire career as writer was dominated by his longing for this Eldorado —specifically, his desire to have, like Dickens, his own publication resources so that his works would never lack for their necessary social component—is a fact about his career which hardly needs even to be mentioned.

I do not wish to derogate from Pollin's excellent work, but his failure to grasp the significance of his own scholarship leads him to certain important misconstructions, and especially to his general conclusion that "Von Kempelen" is "a 'tired' kind of hoax, which defeats its purpose by presenting too much of the familiar from which readers could check on its authenticity."[20] Pollin here misconstrues the nature of the narrative, and of hoaxes in general. For Poe certainly meant his tale to be decoded by his readers; its purpose is only fulfilled when such a decoding begins to operate. Of course, this purpose necessitates an initial secrecy or "quizzing,"[21] but the quizzing must be done in such a way that the reader is also encouraged to elucidate the story's hidden treasures. So Pollin calls the following reference to "Presburg" a piece of "inept humour":

> "The Literary World" speaks of him, confidently, as a *native* of Presburg (misled, perhaps, by the account in the "Home Journal,") but I am pleased to be able to state *positively*, since I have it from his own lips, that he was born in Utica . . . although both his parents, I believe, are of Presburg descent.[22]

The humour is called "inept," presumably, because the pun on "Presburg" seems so obvious—as indeed it is. But the wit of the passage turns on its second pun (which is by no means obvious), not this first one. The obviousness of the first play on words signals the reader to be alert to the possible presence of such devices; the second, on the other hand, is a test, an experiment to see if the reader is capable of reading Poe's story properly, unlocking its secrets and transmuting its lead into gold.

The second pun involves the word "Utica," Von Kempelen's birthplace, according to Poe's narrative. Poe's choice of this city is a cunning device for telling us that the narrative is a hoax. Von Kempelen is from a city whose verbal root is related to that famous Ulyssesean self-characterization, Oútis, No Man. Utica is, in its Greek form, Oútíxn, and Poe is slyly telling those who have ears to hear that Von Kempelen is from No Man's Town.[23] In the end, the passage works its multiple-language puns in order to fashion a general indictment of the journalistic world of the day. It delivers an extremely witty slap at people like Duyckinck, the editor of *The Literary World* who was offered "Von Kempelen" but whose editorial inepititude brought him to reject it, an act which only revealed (as Poe's story itself says) how little he understood about Von Kempelen (and "Von Kempelen").

But if the artistic significance of Poe's wit has not always been fully grasped by scholars, I suspect that the full range of the story's tricks and surprises also remains to be explored. Too many of its passages have passed without scholarly comment, and seem to exist in the tale for no good aesthetic reason. Consider the following paragraph, for example:

> In the brief account of Von Kempelen which appeared in the 'Home Journal', and has since been extensively copied, several misapprehensions of the German original seem to have been made by the translator, who professes to have taken the passage from a late number of the Presburg 'Schnellpost'. *'Viele'* has evidently been misconceived (as it often is,) and what the translator renders by 'sorrows', is probably *'Leiden'*, which, in its true version, 'sufferings', would give a totally different complexion to the whole account; but, of course, much of this is merely guess, on my part.[24]

Pollin says that "In relation to the gold-making achievement this insertion [about the '*Viele . . . Leiden*'] makes no sense at all," [25] and he goes on to to explain the passage in other (and quite relevant) terms. Nonetheless, I think he goes wrong in his remarks quoted above, and I suspect he does so because he has not seen the general set of literary references in the basic alchemical metaphor. In this instance, Poe draws our attention to the clumsy way that Americans deal with passages from German by suggesting a mistranslation by the editors of the *Home Journal* and an emendation on his own part. But the words he chooses to throw before us, and especially *"Leiden,"* may well lead us to suspect that it is this word, and not *"Viele,"* which "has evidently been misconceived (as it often is)." For "Viele" is by no means a word that is often misconceived, whereas "Leid" (sorrow, or suffering)—as anyone who has taught elementary German can attest—is frequently confused by the neophyte with "Lied" (lyric, ballad, song). The passage seems to be an extremely clever and oblique witticism connecting Poe's Von Kempelen not with "misanthropy"—which is the *Home Journal's* construction, as Poe's next paragraph shows—but with poetic creation. And once again we find ourselves at the heart of the story's principal subjects: the nature of poetry and the poetic principle, and the trials of a creative writer like Poe in a journalistic world (Presburg) whose ignorance threatens to destroy the enitre social enterprise which we call artistic creation.

III

Poets and the guardians of poetry have always insisted that the products of imagination transcend time and circumstances. Art may appear in time, but its being's heart and home is with infinitude. It is a product of history, but an inhabitant of eternity. Yet we must sometimes wonder what such claims could possibly mean to Dryasdust, or to any scholar who repeatedly draws his transcendent subject back to its mortal and circumstantial condition.

As the passage from Eichhorn, quoted earlier, suggests, such claims can and should mean a great deal, even to the pedant digging patiently in his Valley of Dry Bones. Nevertheless, when we reflect upon the transcendent character of art, we do not normally find an image of that transcendence in the dead letters of the past, or in the scholar's obsession with what is ancient and completed. Rather, we are generally inclined to consider how ancient works find a contemporary relevance, a continuing ("general") application. In this Battle of the Books, the philologian, like Eichhorn, cries out, "Make it old," whereas the Modernist cries out, after W. C. Williams, "Make it new."

It is time to remind ourselves that "Making it new" can involve not the rebirth of art but its assassination, and that "Making it old" may establish the essential conditions for the resurrection of past achievement. For the special privilege of past human products, especially artistic ones, is that they come to us in finished and completed forms which, by their very finishedness, are able to judge the incompleteness of our present lives and works. They speak to the present precisely because they speak in other tongues, saying what we cannot say and criticizing what we can. Literary works transcend their historical alienation by virture of their definitive otherness, by their sharp and peculiar differentials with their later, contemporary audiences.

Because criticism must articulate a system of differentials, then, a special demand is placed upon it to elucidate literary works at their point of origin, where the initial and determining sets of differentials are permanently established. This concentration upon origins has been traditional in the field of criticism, and for good reason, but it should not be taken to mean that historical criticism fetishizes the archaic object. The purpose of an historical approach is to deal with the literary work as a dynamic event in human experience rather than as an object of analysis, linguistic or otherwise.[26] *Paradise Lost* as read in the seventeenth and eighteenth centuries succeeded to a very different event in the Romantic Age, especially with people like Blake, Shelley, and Byron. Our own experiences with that poem today have been indelibly marked by those earlier ones and by our awareness of the differences between them. To remain ignorant of those human events which constitute literary works like *Paradise Lost* throughout their periodic and continuing lives is to immortalize the present. For all knowledge and experience is historical, including our present knowledge and experience of the literary works we inherit and pass on.

The analytic methodologies necessarily adopted by philologists have produced, even among historical critics, recurrent misconceptions about the aims and purposes of such a critical approach. Thus, in a lengthy, if sometimes naive, recent attack upon philology, John M. Ellis argues that historical criticism is destructive because it pretends to offer the reader privileged and prepared solutions to the literary works we read: "Since literary texts are inherently challenging and often even puzzling, the critic's pose of supplying essential information and the key to the text have proved as tempting to the reader as it has to the critic. It has given him the illusion of understanding complex works with minimum effort."[27] Of course, one has only to pick up any of the great critical works from Wolf, Herder, and Eichhorn to our own day to see how far this characterization strays from the truth. Nevertheless, what Ellis argues seems to me an accurate picture of the work of the philologian who has failed to grasp the soul of his great method, the spirit of his life in letters.

I have tried in this essay to call that spirit back, to rouse it from its slumbers. Let me quote once again from John Ellis since his challenge may recall to our minds the truth about historical criticism and scholarship which we have sometimes forgotten, and hence which Ellis, our contemoporary, has never properly learned from those who should have taught him.

> The context of a work of literature is that of the whole society for which it is a literary text, and which has made it such; its purpose is precisely that use; and its relation to life is to the life the whole community. If we insist on relating the text primarily to the context of its composition and to the life and social context of its author, we are cutting it off from that relation to life which is the relevant one, and substituting for it another that is greatly restricted. Far from stressing the social importance of literature, this approach undervalues the social importance of literature by construing its relation to society in too limited a way. The result is a simplification of the issues of the text down to those relevant to one particular social situation only; but the literary value of the text resides precisely in the fact that this limited social situation was outgrown. Such a view of literature might with some justice be described as a "static" one.[28]

When Ellis says that the context of literature is the use to which it is put by society at large, surely we all would agree. But when he speaks of one (originary) context of use being "outgrown" by a later (present) one, we immediatley recognize the poverty of his sense of "society at large" and the root of his misconception about historical criticism. We do not, we must not, seek merely to reconstitute literary works in archaic forms; rather we try, in the full consciousness of our present circumstances, to raise up the past life of literary works in order to clarify and reveal the nature of our own present experience, including its dynamic relations of continuity and antithesis with all that has brought it to be.

We read literary works in the present, but we have no way of judging such experiences—of testing their limits, their promises, and their ignorances—without an objective standard, a measure of absolute difference which will not submit to the absorption and manipulation of immediacy. That measure always, and necessarily, comes to us from the past. To study literature in the contexts of its origins and its later historical development is to free the reader from the ignorance of his presentness, to alienate him from himself and make him a pilgrim, if not *of* eternity, then at least *with* all "the noble living and the noble dead."

Shall these bones live? Surely if they do not—surely if we neglect the dynamic relation which exists between past and present—the dead will bury the dead. There can be no present or future, in life or in art, if the past is not a living reality *in its pastness*. You, therefore—editors, bibliographers, textual critics and pedants of all sorts—you hold the keys in your hands. The keys to the kingdom. The keys to the kingdom not merely of literature, but of all human culture.

NOTES

1. James Thorpe, "The Aesthetics of Textual Criticism," reprinted in *Bibliography and Textual Criticism*, ed. O M Brack, Jr. and Warner Barnes (Chicago: Univ. of Chicago Press, 1969), pp. 102–138.

2. The phrase is Roland Barthes's. See below, n. 4.

3. See *The Marriage of Heaven and Hell*, plates 16–17 and 3.

4. The essay is reprinted in an excellent survey-anthology of post-structuralist criticism, *Textual Strategies*, ed. with an Introduction by Josué Harari (Ithaca, N.Y.: Cornell Univ. Press, 1979), pp. 73–81.

5. See Barthes, *ibid.*, pp. 74, 75, 79, 80.

6. The essay is reprinted in Brack and Barnes, *op.cit.*, pp. 154–172.

7. Another limit has been explored by Jean Baudrillard in *The Mirror of Production*, trans. with an Introduction by Mark Poster (St. Louis: Telos Press, 1975), where Baudrillard shows the capitalist and bourgeois ideological formations which are imbedded in every production-based approach to the study of social forms.

8. The texts of most plays are notoriously indeterminate and variable because they are written primarily for performance and gain their printed forms in relation to that primary (unprinted) event.

9. That is to say, the printed numbers of Trollope's novel—their size, their format, their schedule of appearance—are all relevant aesthetic matters, as are the physical characteristics of any edition. Books with decorated covers and bindings—like those we see in Hardy's *Wessex Poems* or in Rossetti's various early editions—forcibly remind us of this important aesthetic aspect of all literary works, even of those which are not "beautiful," even mass-produced books. For an excellent discussion of these and related matters see Morris Eaves, "What Is The 'History of Publishing'?", *Publishing History,* 2 (1977), 57–77.

10. Thorpe, *op.cit.*, pp. 136–137.

11. Johann Gottfried Eichhorn, *Einleitung ins Alte Testament*, translated by Emery Neff in *The Poetry of History* (New York: Columbia Univ. Press, 1947), p. 57.

12. *Ibid.*

13. See *The Works of Lord Byron*, ed. E. H. Coleridge (London: John Murray, 1904), VII, 86–88 and nn.

14. For a good survey of these matters see Samuel C. Chew, *Byron in England* (London: John Murray, 1924), pp. 194–219.

15. All citations are from the text of *The Flag of Our Union* as reprinted in the *The Science Fiction of Edgar Allen Poe*, ed. Harold Beaver (London: Penguin, 1976), pp. 324–332.

16. *The Letters of Edgar Allen Poe*, ed. John Ward Ostrom (Cambridge, Mass.: Harvard Univ. Press, 1948), II, 433.

17. See Burton R. Pollin, "Poe's *Von Kempelen and His Discovery*: Sources and Significance," *Études Anglaises*, 20 (1967), 12–23; Michael Allen, *Poe and the British Magazine Tradition* (New York: Oxford Univ. Press, 1969); *The Collected Works of Edgar Allen Poe*, ed. Thomas Ollive Mabbott (Cambridge, Mass.: Belknap Press, Harvard Univ. Press, 1978), III, 135–137. Another recent essay which should be consulted is Jonathan Auerbach's "Poe's Other Double: The Reader in the Fiction," *Criticism*, 24 (1982), 341–361.

18. *Letters, op.cit.*, p. 27.

19. Beaver text, p. 330.

20. Pollin, *op.cit.*, p. 14.

21. See Poe's letter cited in n. 16 above.

22. See Pollin, *op.cit.*, p. 15, and Beaver text, 327.

23. See Paulys *Realencyclopädie* (Stuttgart, 1962), Supplement IX, 1875: "Man findt Oútíxn nur bei den Schriftstellern, die den Namen latinisieren."

24. Beaver text, pp. 326–327.

25. Pollin, *op.cit.*, p. 21.

26. These remarks are made in the context of the recent scholarship which has emphasized literary reception and the theory of literary reception.

27. John M. Ellis, *The Theory of Literary Criticism* (Berkeley and Los Angeles: Univ. of California Press, 1974), p. 154.

28. *Ibid.*, pp. 136–137.

The Editor and the Question of Value: Proposal

CLAIRE BADARACCO

Among American editors in recent years, it has been said that the literary and historical editors have something in common. It would seem they share some fundamental philosophical assumptions: a belief in events as history. They believe that "something happened" and that abstractions are approachable through the fact, which is made up of a discoverable, namable—and for some, tangible—element called "definition." They might be said to believe that the truth, or definition of the fact, can be distorted by incompleteness, invention, lack of judgement or proportion and that understanding, which is their common goal, through methods of research and inquiry, diminishes the possibility for distortion of the fact by their having represented the purest state of the detail. Given that literary and historical editors do have some bases for agreement, they have proceeded to disagree. Their discussion has focussed upon the thesis advanced by G. Thomas Tanselle, specifically his 1978 article critical of the accuracy of reporting in certain literary and historical editions.

The center of my discussion here is the editorial problem of VALUE, the determination made by every editor about the relative value of text and document. On the basis of how an editor solves the problem, he or she might be said to belong to a "textual" or "documentary" school of editorial thinking. This proposal is an attempt to

EDITORIAL NOTE: These two items by Claire Badaracco and Fredson Bowers derive from a session on "The Editor and the Question of Value" held at the 1981 STS conference in New York. Dr. Badaracco submitted the proposal in the form printed here, to which Professor Bowers responded, in both a conference paper and in the study now published in the following pages. The STS Advisory Board considered Dr. Badaracco's expanded conference paper philosophically inappropriate for TEXT, but since her original proposal had provoked such an important discussion, the editors felt that both the proposal and the response should be published, with the understanding that the proposal might not fully represent Dr. Badaracco's current position on the issues at debate.

move beyond Thomas Tanselle's thesis, by arguing that the distinction made between literary and historical is insufficient and bears elaboration. Clearly most editors work from somewhere between the polarities I shall describe. How an editor approaches the problem of value precedes questions of principle, and it is upon the basis of the solution to the problem of value that principles and procedures are enacted.

Generally, the textual editor works with a body of language which was intended by the author to have an audience. If the text has not had an audience in its own time, it is either *flawed* or *found*. The editor's role is to ascertain the author's intention with regard to the semantically autonomous text (which may be constructed from several printed impressions valued on the basis of their relation to authorial time), and to relate the outcome to the author's latter-day audience who are the editor's contemporaries. The textual editor relates the authorial time to the present. Because the editor and hypothetical audience are contemporary, sharing cultural assumptions about the importance of the overall myth or general Story within which the edited text occupies a proportionate position like plot, the textual editor's work can be described as canonical. The editor relates the plot (or text) to the overall Story, acting as talebearer within the culture, by virtue of having presented the text. Both author and text are *other* to editor and audience, and this admits the necessity for interpretation, elevating the role of the editor to that of a critic.

For the documentary editor, it is not the text but the document itself which is of the greatest value. The documentary editor proceeds from the assumption that only the document is knowable, that the tale or Story which can be constructed or based upon the Story is variable and determined by forces which are *other*, such as invention, prevailing myth, politics, whimsy and critical taste. The documentary editor may be a skeptic. The evidence which is contained in the document being edited may challenge or deny the prevailing cultural myth or Story. The editor acts as scribe, reporter, cultural archeologist, and does not interpret or introduce the editorial persona in the edition. The documentary editor's audience is contemporaneous with the document. Less important than who wrote the document is when it was written. Time is more important than character to the documentary editor.

While the textual editor values the art of constructing the text, he or she assumes that the text is greater than the evidence; in every case evidence serves art. For the documentary editor, connoisseurship of documents is valuable, the art is in the evidence; the business of editing is the art of evidentiary reporting. The textual editor is ultimately a cultural conservative; the documentary editor may be challenging cultural assumptions, or regard the editorial role as being other than talebearer. I think a categorical description of the schools of "textual" and "documentary" editing, and editorial decisions which one makes upon principles emerging from one's philosophical stance in relation to the problem of VALUE, is of greater use than the terms "Literary" and "Historical," if our eventual goal is to describe distinctions in methodology. Literary and historical editors take their place within the spectrum of approaches to text and document, and though my description in this proposal is in terms of polarities, their stance is not so clear-cut as I have suggested, but more various.

The Editor and the Question
of Value: Another View

FREDSON BOWERS

Dr. Badaracco is following a current and interesting trend in attempting to evaluate the role in present-day scholarship of the historical documentary editor and the humanities textual editor. The recently formed Association for Documentary Editing takes its members
from both disciplines and in its annual meetings has held significant
discussions in search of a delineation of the valid differences as well as
of the common ground between the two. The process of definition
and of an agreement on methodology is not likely to be completed
very soon, however. Each discipline endures ideological and methodological tugs of war within its own ranks. It is only slightly less difficult to speak of a 'school of documentary editing' than it is to bind
together into one group for analysis the fragmented ranks of literary
editors, at least of works of the nineteenth and twentieth centuries.[1]
Until these internal disputes are better resolved than they are at present, any comparison between documentary and literary editing must
remain a highly personal occupation since there are too many generals
and two few privates within each discipline. My attempt to analyze
Dr. Badaracco's position and to relate it to editorial tradition as well
as to the present situation in theory and practice must therefore reflect
only my own notions. I am very far from attempting to lay down the
law, no matter how positive my convictions.

It would seem that the arguments in this proposal are philosophically and deductively based, not practically and inductively as has
always been the guiding principle of textual criticism. There also
seems to be an appeal to aesthetic considerations which have ordinarily been excluded from discussions of textual-critical theory.

As I follow the argument, 'value' and the scale on which an editor
views it, is taken to be so powerful a determinant that it can even
displace the terms 'literary' and 'historical' as descriptions of
editorial approaches. For the moment let us pass over the practicality

of applying such a subjective scale and try to clarify matters a bit by in-
quiring just *what* is of value, *to whom* it is valuable, and finally *why* it
should be of value.

An historian documentary editor has traditionally been concerned
with making available in accurate and comprehensive reprints the raw
materials of history. In the form of state papers, letters to and from
the subject, memoranda, reports, miscellaneous documents of all
descriptions, these manuscripts (chiefly) are assembled, dated, different versions are assessed, and finally what is judged to be the
definitive form of each document is methodically transcribed and provided with an appropriate commentary not necessarily by the hand of
the text editor. Students of history may read these texts to gain a
firsthand acquaintance with the undigested material, but at higher
reaches these documents provide professional scholars with the
necessary data from which formal eclectic interpretation can be made
in written histories and biographies. Documentary editing, then,
assembles and makes public the building blocks of history. Interpretation of its significance may make one block seem more valuable to certain users than another, but in their constitution all blocks are equal as
factual records on which interpretation must depend. Among the
users of a documentary edition, then, value in a popular sense may
differ widely according to the significance that they may choose to
draw from the records.

However, it does not seem to be this kind of value from the point of
view of the user that Dr. Badaracco has in mind. Instead, she seems to
refer to what I should rather call the *attitude* of the editor to his
material as a criterion of the way in which he handles these
documents. The documentary editor, she says, acts as a scribe,
reporter, and cultural archeologist who does not introduce his
editorial persona into the texts (documents) he is transcribing. This is
accurate as a description insofar as it applies to the physical act of
reproducing the documents, provided the editor has heeded Dr.
Tanselle's strictures on modernizing the texts and other such tinkering
in the act of transcription that in the past has certainly put the impress
of editorial persona on the printed results.[2]

But if we take a larger view of documentary editing and do not con-
fine it to the texts only but consider the total treatment of the texts
within what may be called the edition as a whole, then of course the introduction, but particularly the commentary, may indeed clothe the

skeleton of the documents with the flesh of outside intervention so that the total is by no means so impersonal as its textual base is intended to be. Such intervention may introduce into the *edition* whatever invention, prevailing myth, politics, whimsy, or cultural taste (to use Dr. Badaracco's phrases) commentary editors may possess. Nevertheless, if we distinguish the text itself from its interpretive appurtenances, and if we accept the doubtful effects of the choice for transcription without apparatus of only one among similar documents as well as the effects of the transcriptional methods variously employed, we find that historians believe that they require documentary texts to be offered through a clear, non-reactive and neutral agent. It follows that if we want to know why a documentary editor has a particular attitude toward the text that he produces, we must analyze the reasons for the requirements of historians who are his customers and who have therefore dictated his values to insure that they coincide with their own.

When Dr. Badaracco states that "for the documentary editor it is not the text but the document itself which is of the greatest value," she will not be understood unless one comprehends that she is beginning the use of the term 'text' in a special and not in its ordinary sense. When she speaks of 'document' she means what I should call the text of the document in the concrete terms of a transcription. This latter is a perfectly accepted use. However, to her philosophical mind 'the text' is a conceptual abstraction that exists in its own right, independently of the inscription on the piece of material that we call a document. (Obviously this concept has had no place in documentary editing to date, which takes a very literal view of the subject.) I gather her meaning to be, then, that a documentary editor places the highest value on the document as an inscribed piece of paper that is to be exposed, or made public, viewed as a complete fact in itself. The duty of an editor is to discover the document, date it, arrange it in proper order or category, and then transcribe it accurately. In his ultimate relation to the editorial presentation of the document he is, as Dr. Badaracco says, a scribe.

This seems to be the way the historians want it. In the past, it appears, some have relied too heavily on faultily transcribed and even doctored versions of these building blocks, and they have been burned. Now they wish to be certain of the fact of the inscription of the documents whose texts they require. Indeed, if it were not much more convenient for use and for reference to have transcripts that have been put into readable form in type, photofacsimiles of the documents would have become the authorities instead.

If we consider the text alone, and disregard the commentary and other appurtenances within a documentary edition, we find that differences of opinion about editorial methodology have centered almost exclusively on questions of what, if any, procedures should be adopted to make the text readable for ordinary use. These are mechanical, not critical questions. Although they may touch peripherally on problems of value and to what it may be attached, they do not materially affect Dr. Badaracco's position which, I take it, is that the ultimate consumers set no value on what the editorial process has done to the document (outside of its producing a trustworthy result) because in fact it is required to do practically nothing. Instead, historians place their value wholly on a particular inscribed piece of paper that comprises the document. It follows that the attitude of the users determines the attitude of the text's editor.[3]

Whereas in literature and its allied humanities the modern editors are, in a manner of speaking, in process of training the ultimate consumers of their product in the sophisticated uses that may be made of the textual information contained in a full critical edition of a text, in history the dictation of the consumer to the editor appears to be complete. The historian who must piece together some hundreds and even thousands of documents to make a coherent interpretive pattern falls into the habit, quite easily it seems, of ignoring the fine points of his material, such as what may be learned not only in the internal growth of a document's text through stages of composition or at least through alteration and revision during the process of single composition but also in its textual transmission. Since he must deal with such a mass of material, he must be in a hurry and thus he puts the responsibility on the documentary editor to assess what seems to be the most complete and authoritative physical inscription and then to serve that document up in its final form. He does not have time to study what may have been the writer's veerings of thought, the changes of mind, betrayed by alterations and revisions within the inscription. Nor, save perhaps in exceptional circumstances, is he willing to study the same dynamic changes that can take place between a series of drafts and the final result.[4] However, the determination not to be misled seems to have caused the historians to tighten the rules. You are not the interpreters, we are, the editors are in effect told. Keep your evaluating hands off this material and serve it up to us in its pure documentary form. The dangers to the user of the unrecorded editorial predigestion, chiefly in the selection of one document to reproduce without apparatus from multiple authorities, do not seem to be recognized.

It is curious that the attitudes of the editors, who must deal with these building blocks of matter at first hand, have gone along with this imposed methodology even though as historians they themselves must often have known better.[5] One can understand the fear of misleading which encourages editors to put the responsibility for use (interpretation) completely on the reader and therefore their disinclination— since by a dubious custom no apparatus of variants is provided—to risk an emended or eclectic text instead of the transcription of a single authority. But even if one were to accept this principle of selected transcription without conflation or emendation, it is still difficult to understand why editors have not insisted on providing the maximum of documentary evidence by, primarily, at least, printing an apparatus of variation and alteration occurring within the transcribed text; in any scrupulous sense alterations are as much an integral part of the document as the final form of its inscription.[6] Or, perhaps secondarily, in cases of multiple witnesses why verbal variants in these from the chosen transcribed text have not been thought sufficiently evidential to be worth recording on a consistent basis.

It may be that, like their customers, editors feel nearly overwhelmed by the mass of material they must deal with and hence feel it necessary to omit the apparatus record of what in the social sciences might be miscalled refinements, or matters that seem to be of stylistic interest merely and thus removed from historical concern. When substantive matters are involved, however, this is throwing out the baby with the bath.[7] It is too easy, I grant, for a literary editor—who has a much more limited number of documents to deal with and can fine-tool his product accordingly—to denigrate the mass-production quality which characterizes the documentary editing of historical texts. Nevertheless, as we shall see, historical or documentary editing, with its attitude that the fixed document constitutes the only real essential, has turned a blind eye to the superior possibilities for the transmission of information that have come to characterize the new school of editing making its way in the humanities.[8]

We turn now to the transition from documentary to what this proposal calls 'textual' editing. I am not happy with either term, but I acknowledge that we seem to be stuck by the historians with *documentary editing* and that we are not likely to reform them. Moreover, the term is capable of more or less precise definition and its general signification is well understood. On the other hand, *textual editing* is not a customary phrase, its accuracy depends upon a specialized philosophical use of 'text' that is useless as a definition of a school of editing, and I am not prepared to be stuck with it.[9] As I have remarked, Dr. Badaracco seems to have used 'text' not materially as the sum total of an inscription or printed impression of patterned words or their signs on some substance; instead she seems to have employed it conceptually as an entity that may exist independent of any one set of inscribed words on a precisely identified and handleable piece of paper or vellum. Now this distinction between fact and fiction, reality and ideal, is a valid and indeed a commonplace one in textual criticism but with an important application that differs from Dr. Badaracco's. I am concerned, thus, to get our terms straight according to conventional practice, because we can scarcely agree on definitions until we have agreed on terms.

First, I suggest that 'evidence' is neither an exclusive nor a particularly viable overall term for the unique pattern of words inscribed in a document. Convenient as it may be on occasion to use as a substitute, it has too many other denotations wholly to replace 'text' as denominating the inscription on any identified document. 'Document' itself is a circumscribing word, so that no possible ambiguity can result from our speaking of the text of a document, or even of the text of a particular printing of an edition.[10] The context will ordinarily clarify without difficulty whether 'document' is being used to describe the physical material itself without reference to the inscription on this material, or else both together as a unique and identifiable object. On the other hand, nothing but imprecision and possible ambiguity can result from our taking a common and flexible word like 'text' and restricting it to a highly technical and special set of circumstances involved in the results of the editorial choice and sequence of words in an ideal pattern.

At its simplest this ideal form consists in nothing more than the result of the editorial emendation inserted to improve the correctness or consistency of the text of a particular document that is the only preserved authoritative witness. At its more complex the ideal text is one that has been editorially reconstructed by conflation of two or more different documents, each representing the text in a state, or pattern, that differs by reason of its transmissional history and its relation (whether derived one from the other or independent) to a lost authorial original, or by reason of authorial revision of some sort within this framework of relationship. Whatever the circumstances, this ideal text is an editorial reconstruction of assumed authorial intention.[11] It can have no existence as an entity in any form of original document but only as presented in the critical edition itself, from which it will differ in another edition. Perhaps the most commonly quoted definition is that of R. B. McKerrow, although it has specific reference to his proposed edition of Shakespeare, which is that an ideal text comes as close as the evidence permits to what might have been a fair copy of the final form of his work made by the author.[12]

In the use of the term 'text' in its common and flexible form, the context should make quite clear whether a precise or a general sense is intended. For example, a textual critic may feel quite free to write that the *text* of the third 1749 edition of Fielding's *Tom Jones* is unauthoritative, whereas it would seem quite strained if he were required to write that the *evidence* of the third edition was unauthoritative.[13] On the other hand, he could also write that the fourth edition of 1750, even though revised by Fielding, does not contain a wholly acceptable text of *Tom Jones*. Here quite definitely there is an elevation in the use of the term 'text' and the appearance of a concept of text that transcends the forms in any one of its specific documents. Since criticism guided by textual bibliography is the distinctive force in this process of constructing a new text from the evidence of variant readings, it is proper to call the art that of 'critical editing.' A documentary editor would faithfully reprint the fourth edition of *Tom Jones* with all its blemishes since he would be concerned only with reproducing that singular and overall most authoritative documentary witness to the text. A critical editor selects and emends so that his final text, although always based on some one or more documents according to the circumstances, seeks to present a version closer to the assumed authorial original than any preserved document (even the revised fourth edition of *Tom Jones*) can offer.[14]

We have here what at first sight appear to be Dr. Badaracco's polarities of value, for manifestly the users of a documentary edition place all their value on the text of a single document, such as the fourth edition.[15] On the other hand, the users of a complex critical edition such as the Wesleyan-Clarendon *Tom Jones* value its synthetic ideal text above such limiting fidelity. But various difficulties arise when we thereupon attempt to follow her conclusions that "a categorical description of the schools of 'textual' and 'documentary' editing, and editorial decisions which one makes on principles emerging from one's philosophical stance in relation to the problem of VALUE, is of greater use than the terms 'Literary' and 'Historical,' if our eventual goal is to describe distinctions in methodology."

I should certainly agree, at the start, that the terms 'historical' and 'literary' editing are practically meaningless, although in the end I adduce somewhat different reasons from those given. I suggest they are meaningless because they have been and are being misused as primary instead of what they actually are, that is, derivative and secondary terms that are inaccurate to describe or to substitute for simple methodologies that have a pragmatic and by no means a philosophical basis. These simple methodologies have their own technical distinctions and are quite independent of any philosophical attempt to grade them on the degree of involvement of the editor with textual material and its 'otherness.' I call these terms inaccurate and inadequate as a means of categorizing methods of editing (and I think here Dr. Badaracco would agree) because the so-called documentary method is by no means confined to the presentation of historical documents but is as prevalent in the editing of literature and of other disciplines within the humanities, like philosophy, as it is in the editing of history viewed as social science.

For example, when a work exists in only one authoritative text, which is to say one document whether it be a manuscript or copies of a single printed edition, the text may appear to be so free from error that an editor may find himself unable to bring his critical powers to bear to formulate any permissible improvement toward authorial intention. As a result, his text and that of a documentary editor's would be identical. As an illustration, William James's learned-journal articles on psychology were printed with some care and James customarily read proofs. So far as the only available evidence goes (these are single-text works), they are letter-perfect and an editor can perform few editorial tasks in presenting them other than to copy the journal texts as faithfully as any documentary editor, even though in general the ACLS James edition adopts a critical attitude toward the editing of James's works. The same was true, in general, for the single-text essays in the collection that the ACLS edition made of his philosophical essays, or his essays on religion and morality. If one wants an example from pure literature, the same situation obtained with the poems of Stephen Crane. These pieces existed either in authorially supervised single texts, or else a study of the transmission of multiple documents revealed quite clearly that in most cases only one among them could be considered as authoritative and therefore could represent the document that had to be faithfully reproduced, verbatim.

This kind of non-interventional editing textual critics call a 'diplomatic reprint'—diplomatic from *diploma* or document. This differs from what critics also know as a facsimile reprint, which is a facsimile in modern typeface of the document, line for line and page for page, in books complete with running-titles, catchwords, signatures, press-figures and what not. A diplomatic reprint is as faithful to the original as a facsimile (except for a few recognized mechanical details), but it ignores the line-for-line and page-for-page convention as well as omitting all the appurtenances external to the text. In fact it is more faithful than the usual documentary text since it does not permit the liberties of small changes for readability in which most documentary editors have indulged.[16]

In the editing of strictly historical material according to present documentary standards, it is the lack of an apparatus to record substantive variation in non-copy-text documents containing a version of the same text that troubles Dr. Tanselle most of all. Perhaps the most important difference between the developed editing procedures (whether diplomatic or critical) found in the humanities and the more elementary procedures of historical documentary editing is this question of apparatus. With apparatus, the different texts of the document (for which only one selected example has been reproduced) can be reconstructed and evaluated. Without such apparatus the reader and also any scholar quoting from the documentary edition in lieu of the original manuscript are completely at the mercy of the editor's choice of copy-text (which substitutes for what in the editing of a similarly situated humanities text would be called the 'ideal text') without the comfort and convenience of knowing anything of the contents of the other copies of the document.[17]

Moreover, it would seem that documentary editors departing from fairly strict diplomatic transcription are not always conscious of two important factors that should affect their methodology. I have touched on one: whether a professional or non-professional will be the major audience addressed. Short of modernization, which is completely unscholarly, it may be that editors can eventually come to agree on some ground rules for transcribing documents for perhaps a mixed audience of scholars and more general but informed readers, stated rules affecting mechanical features—one hopes—and with a wary eye to the alteration of features that in an offensive way rip a document out of its time-scheme or verge on fairly minor questions of meaning, as is always possible when tinkering with punctuation. Secondly, if a scholarly audience is addressed, one factor bulks rather large in my mind. That is, the need for quotation by writers and scholars from the editions of the transcribed documents. In a work of scholarship when one quotes from an edited text instead of a photo- or type-facsimile, one likes to know where one stands, and so does the reader. Both need to know with some particularity whether the transcript does or does not represent the original with all exactitude save for whatever mechanical matters may be waived by common consent. The quoter's reference note sometimes enables a reader to avoid possible misunderstandings. If an article quotes Shakespeare in a modernized text and names the edition used, fair warning, at least, is given the reader that more than mere differences in spelling, punctuation, capitalization, and the like may be involved: even the sense may have been altered sometimes significantly by verbal emendation unbeknownst to quoter and to reader, for the standard one-volume Shakespeare texts seldom print lists of emendations. One is certainly better off quoting from scholarly unmodernized texts, even those that have been critically edited and thus emended in some places. In such editions the apparatus of variants which discloses every alteration made in the edited text of anything other than typographical and other mechanical matters would have been available to the quoter who thus could have checked not only the copy-text utilized but also any changes in that copy-text edition or manuscript. The reader, it follows, ought to be able to trust the quoter not to have passed on unwittingly any substantive change affecting the quoted text.

In the lexicon of textual criticism there is, ordinarily, no such thing as an 'ideal text' without critical editing, or at least the application of critical methods in all circumstances where they are appropriate and would prove efficacious. Nevertheless, some texts are not susceptible of critical editing because—in the lack of any other authoritative witness—their apparent consistency and correctness as found in the only preserved document imposes a ban on editorial intervention.[18] However, I have always argued, perhaps very narrowly, that conflation with some other witness is not at all necessary and that any editorial emendation of a single document's text in other than mechanical matters makes the result a critical text that strives toward the ideal. Indeed, this is the usual form of single-text editing. For instance, if in a single-text William James essay a comma in the print needs to be transposed to correct the modification and to make the sense conform to what seems the logic of the statement and what must have been by rational standards James's intention, a critical text of the essay has been formed. Such an emendation would have been made without the evidence of anything except the editor's critical estimate of the necessary and authorially desired sense.

But the presence or absence of evidence is not a requirement affecting the principle. In the critical text of James's *Principles of Psychology* (Cambridge: Harvard University Press, 1981, 3 vols.) the considerable number of revisions that he made in the plates of the copy-text first printing when these were reprinted in subsequent years are incorporated as a matter of course. This operation is critical in chief because it was analysis that permitted the editor to accept these as authorial and not as resulting from the attentions of a publisher's reader.[19] The critical text is then carried one step farther when it incorporates as well the autograph changes James made by annotating his private copy in anticipation of a revised edition that he never completed. This is conflation of authorities even though it occurs within the major authority of the single typesetting of the first edition alone and its series of printings from the same set of plates.

The more common kind of conflation usually joins two or more authorities, or texts. For example, in the Centenary edition of Hawthorne's *House of the Seven Gables* (Columbus: Ohio State University Press, 1965) the copy-text was Hawthorne's holograph printer's-copy manuscript, but some readings were substituted from the first edition, using it not only as a convenient source for minor corrections but also as a source for a few substantive revisions that Hawthorne was judged to have made in the lost proofs. Here one authority (the print) was directly derived from the other in its transmission. Fortunately rare are the most highly conflated texts of all, like *Othello, Hamlet,* and *Troilus and Cressida* (or the special case of a few plays like *King Lear*), where two independent non-derived authorities are preserved,[20] neither perfect in every detail, and each representing (so far as the printing as well as an unknown stage of possible anterior scribal transmission permit) what the author wrote. Textual bibliography is occasionally of some assistance but in the main the problem in these plays is a critical one: to distinguish and hence to adopt Shakespeare's fullest intentions in their final form by reasoned selection from the two authorities.

One may readily sum up this question of 'ideal text' and 'critical edition' by the multiple-witness example of *Tom Jones*. For the fourth edition of 1750 Fielding made his only revision of the text by marking up a copy of the third edition, which had been set from the first of 1749. Following W. W. Greg's principle of copy-text, an editor chooses the first edition as his basis because of its more authoritative 'accidentals' of spelling, punctuation, and so on, which are transmissionally closest of any edition to the lost manuscript. Into this copy-text he then inserts or substitutes all of the revisions in the fourth edition that he persuades himself are authorial and not printer's variants, in the process removing the third-edition corruptions passed on to the fourth which Fielding had not recognized and so permitted to stand in his copy. For the verbal, or substantive, part of his text what the editor is actually doing is reconstructing to his best ability the wording of the marked copy of the third edition that Fielding had sent to the printer, minus its corruptions, and then clothing this most authoritative wording with the most authoritative accidentals of the first edition. The resulting critical text never existed as a whole in this form of double authority in any single document, lost or preserved. But obviously it is superior to an exact reconstruction of the marked-up third edition, and it is also superior to the revised fourth edition since it has weeded out textual corruptions and has substituted a more authoritative form of the accidentals. Although much more complex examples may be found in Shakespeare's *King Lear,* or in *Hamlet,* this is a fair example of a critical text of the conflated kind. Since these eclectic texts are so much less common than single texts, it is perhaps unfortunate that they have attracted an undue attention (because of their interesting problems) and so are generally cited when critical editing is under discussion. This emphasis has undoubtedly led on occasion to a distortion in the recognition of the general nature of edited texts, for the more common critical editions of single texts in the humanities are closer to the usual material with which documentary editors deal.

It is now time to try to apply this analysis to Dr. Badaracco's distinction between what she calls historical or documentary and textual or literary editing, but which I prefer to distinguish in the usual terms as diplomatic (or if necessary, documentary) and critical editing. We are in agreement on what is essentially a commonplace. She writes that "For the documentary editor, connoisseurship of documents is valuable, the art is in the evidence; the business of editing is the art of evidentiary reporting." I take it that this means the editor must evaluate (be a connoisseur of) any documents that exist in more than one version and, having selected the copy, or document, he considers to be superior for his purpose, his only art is then to transcribe it exactly (evidentiary reporting). But history, as I have pointed out, has no monopoly on what historians have learned to call documentary editing (a form of diplomatic reprint). It is not the subject, one must emphasize, that dictates the method but instead the needs of the users.

When it comes to Dr. Badaracco's comments on textual, or critical editing, I am prepared to go along only at the start. "While the textual editor values the art of constructing the text," she writes, "he or she assumes that the text is greater than the evidence; in every case evidence serves art." This is an unexceptionable statement if it means no more than what I hope it means, which is that a properly emended single text or a critical synthesis of multiple authorities will ordinarily produce what is known as an 'ideal text,' or critical reconstruction superior to the evidence (text) of any one document, as exampled in my account of *Tom Jones*. However, there is a catch here, I fancy. It is legitimate for us to inquire what evidence it is that the 'text' is greater than, taking account of Dr. Badaracco's transmutation of these terms so that 'evidence' means inscribed or printed text, and 'text' means some absolute concept of an author's work that exists independently of the documents.

Thus if Dr. Badaracco, as I suspect, has in mind that the critical text as a reconstruction according to an assumption of the author's intention is greater than the sum of its parts, I should agree but only in a purely metaphysical sense. As a textual critic I must disagree that a critical text is greater than the sum total evidence of the various documents on which it is based, because I conceive this to be a practical impossibility.[21] As detailed in the example of *Tom Jones*, an eclectic text cannot remain authoritative if it goes beyond the limits of the combined evidence of its documents and creates a new entity in the realm of pure imagination. I cannot see how an authoritative critical eclectic text can be other than the sum of its documents in different arrangements according as one or the other editor may choose what he regards as superior authority among the variant readings. R. B. McKerrow was tireless in emphasizing the practical limitations that a necessarily narrow view of what constitutes authority places upon textual criticism and its editorial arm.[22] When we go beyond the authority that can reside only in the precise texts of the documents, that is, their readings, we are at another level of criticism. I am perfectly prepared to agree that a soundly emended text will approach nearer to the author's full intention than will a text that never deserts its documentary evidence when it is faulty. To this extent, only, a fully edited text may surpass the evidence by transmitting to the reader another and conjectural level of assumed authorial intention. But by their nature emendations cannot have authority no matter how much they may seem to be an inevitable unraveling of corrupted authorial intention.[23] If we are prepared to recognize the true conjectural nature of emendation, I should gladly grant that one particular well-emended text was in some sense 'greater' than its evidence. But this concession is a double-edged weapon, for I should also insist that another and ill-emended version of the same text was lesser than its evidence.

Nevertheless, emendation is mere opinion that for confirmation can appeal only to the shifting sands of public consensus, itself an opinion.[24] Different editors will produce different texts from the same documents depending upon their standards of selection or of emendation. Thus if authority is considered, there is no such thing as 'the text' of an author apart from its documentary evidence. And even in respect of a documentary foundation for every selected reading, when the material is at all complex there are likely to be as many texts as there are editors. Any possibility of 'the text' fades with each successive edited version. *Hamlet* has no text, edited or otherwise, that can exist as an absolute, but instead myriads of texts derived from varying editorial opinion about the most satisfactory amalgam that can be contrived between the divergent readings of the two basic authorities, with a dollop or two thrown in sometimes from the 'bad' First Quarto, which is an authority of sorts.

Simple observation of what I take to be these truths removes a great deal of the mystique that present-day fashionable critics indulge in about some entity of a text that can exist in its own right apart from and independent of the evidence as well as of the author, the proof of which is taken to be the critical shaping of this 'text' into a legitimate different organ of sensibility by each generation so that the concept of the literary work (its text) is never constant: by the act of publication, or of being edited, this 'text' they assert has removed itself from the control of the author and thus from the chronological and spatial limitations of its documents.[25]

I have no quarrel with this view as literary criticism, but I do quarrel with it as having any relationship at all to textual criticism, least of all any useful relationship. The idea of 'text' in this connection is so vague as to be subject only to the most general application. *What* text of *Hamlet* is it that each generation needs to remake in its own image? The Second Quarto, the First Folio, the Old Cambridge, the Globe, the New Cambridge, Kittredge, Alexander, the Pelican, New Arden, New Penguin, New Riverside? Any answer that merely reiterates 'the text' of *Hamlet* is either so naive as to be absurd or else so generalized in its concept that another word than 'text' should be found to express what it has in mind, on some occasions legitimately.

I am afraid that it is some such idea of 'text' that lies behind what I believe to be the most debatable of Dr. Badaracco's conclusions. That each generation may, as it chooses, find fresh facets in a work and interpret whatever text it reads subjectively to suit its own *autres moeurs* in detail or as a whole is such a self-evident proposition as not to be debatable. I should add, however, that one of the prime virtues of scholarship is to train its practitioners to reach a more sophisticated level by the imaginative transfer of their sensibilities (on a knowledgeable basis) to those of another age so that literature may be comprehended to its fullest in its own time and place as well as in the present. Moreover, objectively, I cannot see that our present rigorous theories of editing the humanities have been affected by any other *Zeitgeist* than that the works of the past should be presented to today's readers—textually—as much as possible in terms of the age in which they were written, whether this was three or three hundred years ago. This view holds for critical editing as it must, of course, for diplomatic. How modern sensibility can replace modern philological resources in the emendation of texts or the selection of readings is scarcely to be envisaged.

Dr. Badaracco correctly states that "the editor's role is to ascertain the author's intention with regard to the semantically autonomous text [I am not sure what this means] (which may be constructed from several printed impressions valued on the basis of their relation to authorial time).'' But I begin to lose her when she continues that this text (which I gather is the 'outcome' of the editorial effort) is related by the editor "to the author's latter-day audience.'' If she means no more than that the edited texts of, say, the sixteenth to the eighteenth centuries can be made more accessible to a present-day audience without modernization by slight adjustment of their original typographical or orthographical conventions, purely mechanical matters like the substitution of short for long 's' and the interchange of 'u–v' and of 'i–j,' then these are not portentous tidings. But I fancy that more is meant, for she thereupon adds: "The textual editor relates the authorial time[26] to the present. Because the editor and hypothetical audience are contemporary, sharing cultural assumptions about the importance of the overall myth or general Story within which the edited text occupies a proportionate position like plot, the textual editor's work can be described as canonical.''

Here I confess I founder, and not simply in the stretched use of 'canonical.' As Gertrude Stein might have said, a text is a text is a text. In constructing a text according to scholarly principles in unmodernized form, I repeat that an editor emends only to correct in its own terms, not to revise. Although he may, for instance, make a few adjustments here and there in the faulty rhetorical punctuation of an Elizabethan play, if his work has been done properly he has not modernized to assist the present-day reader to understand an alien system of pointing: instead, he has corrected the text as needed in its own terms, which are those of the past, and which would have been appropriate and desirable to have been printed in the original for its early audience.[27] True, I can conceive of a distinct relation between audience and the assumptions of editing in some modernized texts of Shakespeare, especially one like J. Dover Wilson's New Cambridge edition with its elaborate, almost Shavian directions fitted to our proscenium-arch, movable-scenery stage and intended to help the user to visualize the text in terms of a modern dramatic representation, not merely of a reading text. But we are not talking about such modernizations extraneous to the text, I trust. Any illustration of this notion of an edited text as a cultural intermediary in its composition or form must apply as well to Hawthorne's *House of the Seven Gables* or even to the forthcoming Cambridge editions of D. H. Lawrence and of Joseph Conrad as it does to Shakespeare.

Except for the platitude that we cannot live in the past except in an evanescent imaginative leap, I cannot conceive how an author and his text are any more "*other* to editor and audience," to use Dr. Badaracco's phrase, than a state paper is to the documentary editor and his audience, a relationship which I gather she considers not to be 'other.' If this otherness does not exist in trained scholarly editors as a significant factor in shaping their work, then the conclusion also does not exist that the conditions under which the critical editor works admit the necessity of interpretation *within the text*, an anomaly that would elevate the role of editor to that of critic in a general literary sense. By definition a critical editor is a critic: we need no ghost come from the grave to tell us this. But he is a critic of *what*? I suggest he is a critic only of the substance of the text, its very words as preserved in the original documents, and the purpose of his critical inquiry is to evaluate this physical evidence in relation to authorial intention (not to the audience's assumptions) and to restore this intention from imperfection or corruption by selection from the evidence or by emendation of the original documents.[28] How this attempt at purification of the text of an author's work makes the editor a 'talebearer' or a critical intermediary between two cultures in any manner that affects the practice of his methodology I do not comprehend.

If the critical text itself is not a consciously contrived tale-bearer that by editorial intervention has in some unspecified way related the cultural assumptions of past and of present in a manner different from the diplomatic representation of a text, then we may inquire how useful is the proposed standard of 'value' to distinguish even the polarities, let alone the middle ground where the two methodologies practically merge in all essentials. How can we apply this subjective concept of 'value' in any concrete intelligible manner comparable to the familiar methodological distinctions that textual criticism makes, ranging from diplomatic through ordinary critical to fully eclectic and synthetic texts like the fortunately rare example of *King Lear* or, for later examples at a much lower and less conjectural level, the University Press of Virginia edition (1975) of Stephen Crane's *Red Badge of Courage* or the ACLS-Harvard edition (1979) of William James's *Some Problems of Philosophy*? The choice of methodology, which I suggest should be our criterion for definition, may be subject to attitudes such as we find at present among historians and their documentary editions. But these attitudes, I suggest, are dictated by the demands of the users of editions for the satisfaction of needs that are not to be defined by disciplines or by subject matter and thus needs that do not necessarily differ between the social sciences and the humanities, between history and literature. If we shift our ground to different users and their requirements, the methodology follows. I suggest that if an historian were to edit Gibbon's *Decline and Fall*, he would forsake documentary for critical editing, just as Professor Nidditch adopted a critical stance in recently editing for Clarendon John Locke's *Essay Concerning Human Understanding*.

Historian or litterateur, for one's specialized purposes does one want a practical substitute for a photo-facsimile? Does one want an unmodernized reading text that has been conservatively corrected in terms of the conventions of its own date and thus is relatively free from the mechanical as well as flawed verbal obstructions posed by a faithful substantially unedited transcript of the original document? Does a scholar object to a talebearer of an editor leading him by the nose and silently conning him into acceptance of this editor's modern cultural concept of the author's intention either in a single-text edition or when special circumstances such as multiple authorities arise? The answer to most of these problems is the scholarly critical edition as presently conceived in a manner not likely to change notably in the foreseeable future. By means of its combined apparatus that lists all editorial emendatory departures from the copy-text, that also records the rejected (that is, unused or passed over) variant readings in any other authorities, and finally that lists all alterations in a manuscript text whether made during composition or on review, the reader may effectively combine the virtues of the exact reprint and the reading text. The scholar can use the reading text provisionally as a convenience. Then, as occasion demands, he can from the apparatus reconstitute the equivalent of a transcript of the original documents.[29]

Let us agree that a critical *edition* comprises not only text (no matter how treated), and possibly commentary, but also apparatus, which one may say fulfills the text and which certainly completes it by enumerating in recoverable form all the evidence on which the editor based his operation. Let us agree, as we necessarily must, I think, that in this sense *edition* is a greater (because more comprehensive) term than *text*. And I conclude, philosophically as well as literally, that in contriving such an edition an editor places no more value on any one aspect of his documents than on another. In such an edition diplomatic (even documentary) and critical editor merge.[30]

A mundane textual critic like me must make it clear that his craft has no connection with and is not influenced by general critical concepts of a supernal text that hovers above his product and is not to be defined by its documents. His sole concern, as I see it, is with *what* these documents provide in the way of evidence as to authorial intention and to its reconstitution. If he is so hubristic as to conceive of himself as a mediator between two cultures, a talebearer in the general history of humanities literature, his text will be infected by an alien virus, as from outer space, and he will fail as a textual critic. Literary and textual criticism are two different breeds of cat, two different disciplines within the *genus* criticism. They have a relationship, indeed, but it is genetic in only one direction, and textual criticism must be kept free from its literary derivative and base itself, instead, on bibliography and philology. Any philosophy that intermingles the two will only promote confused thinking.[31]

NOTES

1. For several decades a general agreement has ruled among literary, or critical, editors of works from the sixteenth through the eighteenth centuries. The editing of medieval manuscript works, I am told, is in the midst of an important split in methodology after many years of peaceful consensus. In the editing of nineteenth- and twentieth-century literature, a break may appear between what one may unkindly describe as the British dilettante school and the American attempt to apply to this later literature the rigorous standards accepted for the earlier. However, the sudden burst of activity in this country that followed on the National Endowment for the Humanities' subsidies for the editing of major American nineteenth-century authors brought into the business a number of scholars without previous editorial experience. Moreover, largely because of the deficiencies in the doctoral programs for American Literature, many of these scholars had an inadequate foundation in the history of English literature and hence no acquaintance with the basic documents of its textual criticism (often centering on Shakespeare) as well as the editorial techniques that had been developed in certain editions to solve common textual problems. With little guidance from tradition, then, and sometimes with a misunderstanding of what study of it has been made, individualistic approaches and even more individualistic editorial theories have evolved that have left the field in some disarray. For a searching and sometimes mordant survey of the history of the attempts of these recent editors to grapple with principles, see G. T. Tanselle, "Recent Editorial

Discussion and the Central Problems of Editing," *Studies in Bibliography*, 34, (1981), 23–65, and its numerous references.

2. "The Editing of Historical Documents," *Studies in Bibliography*, 31 (1978), 1–56; reprinted in Tanselle, *Selected Studies in Bibliography* (Charlottesville: University Press of Virginia, 1979), pp. 451–506. Documentary editions cannot be so objective as they may appear to be at first glance, for the editorial persona is introduced into the texts in various obscure ways. Unless all preserved documents are reprinted complete, the rejection of some on assumed grounds of insignificance derives from a personal decision. No less personal is the editor's decision of which one among multiple documents of the same text is best suited for reprinting as the most authoritative, dependable, comprehensive, or what not. An important, indeed crucial part of the editing is, of course, the accurate transcription (and subsequent proofreading) of the chosen text. However, two different documentary editors of variable paleographical skill can easily decipher a very difficult inscription in different ways and unwittingly introduce an editorial opinion into its wording, or at least its form or texture. All this is in addition to Dr. Tanselle's account of inconsistent editorial interference on a designed or methodological basis.

3. Dr. Badaracco does not explain the reasons for this peculiar value, but we can glimpse it in Don L. Cook's discussion of Tanselle's distinction between works intended for publication and private papers. Tanselle writes: "In the case of notebooks, diaries, letters, and the like, whatever state they are in constitutes their finished form, and the question of whether the writer 'intended' something else is irrelevant" (*Studies in Bibliography*, 31 [1978], 47). Cook comments that intention "becomes irrelevant as soon as one recognizes that the letter, as posted, the journal, as left, warts and all, represents the fullest expression of the author's intention in that document. And we should also note that the authority of that unique document is not increased by its being edited and published" ("The Short Happy Thesis of G. Thomas Tanselle," *Newsletter of the Association for Documentary Editing*, 3 [1981], 2). To this Cook adds, later in the page, "the author's intention with regard to the form and content of a private document resides within, and only within, that document. . . . Would he have clarified his meaning and resolved ambiguities before publishing his own letters or journal? These are irrelevant questions, for what we edit is what he left, not what he did elsewhere nor what he might have done in a longer life."

4. Moreover, since he is presumably unacquainted with classical and biblical textual scholarship and its derivative in the study of medieval manuscripts, he may have little or no idea that when a series of copies is all that is preserved, an overall inferior one may still contain some true readings that are corrupt in what seems to be the best manuscript.

5. However, if one is correct in the general assumption that the principles and methodology of present-day documentary editing go back only a relatively few years to their popularization in Julian Boyd's Susquehanna and then in his Jefferson Papers, one could suggest that it is the editors themselves who have fastened on their own chains, which they are quite prepared to kiss.

6. In his defense of the single-document principle, Robert Taylor of the Adams Papers has recently remarked that the commentary notes are sufficient for pointing out variation in multiple documents that will clarify the writer's intention as expressed in the transcribed document: "Preferably, the editor should choose from among the possibilities the version of an historical document which is closest to finished form, that is, closest to the author's desire at a given time, and then where the author's intention has not been carried out, suggest at those various points with appropriate documentation what that intention was. In this way at least a text is presented that has a real existence" ("Editorial Practices—An Historian's View," *Newsletter of the Association for Documentary Editing*, 3 [1981], 7). Three misconceptions have caused historians to resist the recording of variants. The first is the faith in the adequacy of a selective record at the discretion of the editor. Dr. Taylor, for example, writes: "[Dr. Tanselle] is quite right in stressing that historical editors should examine whatever printed versions are extant, just as one would compare drafts and letterbook copies with finished products and recipients' copies. But, again, I would leave the editor to distinguish between significant and inconsequential differences and to note only the former" (p. 7). This is for multiple authorities, but the same trust in editorial discretion covers the general dislike of noting the internal alterations made by the writer as he was inscribing the document or upon review. "I prefer to leave rather more latitude to editorial judgment than Dr. Tanselle would. Take the matter of deletions. I am convinced that a sensible and sensitive editor can determine whether in the given context a deletion is significant or not. . . . I believe that there is a difference between essential and non-essential, although I cannot draw a precise line. In the interest of precision, Dr. Tanselle would say that it is essential to record every deletion" (p. 5). All one can ask is, Is this documentary? Where is the whole document? The disinclination to record internal alterations has in some part been fostered by earlier elementary methods of indicating authorial changes. Several times Dr. Taylor harps on the theme that readability is seriously impaired by notations within the text: "A multiplicity of devices can be distracting. Within a paragraph a whole succession of angle brackets around deletions can leave a reader to puzzle out just how the final version is to go and cause him to lose the mood of the whole piece, particularly if he finds the editorial apparatus annoying. . . . Aside from the intrusiveness of apparatus, the expense of typesetting a text full of brackets and other devices would greatly increase production costs that are already burdensome" (p. 7). Here I sympathize, for I am no friend of old-fashioned internal methods of recording alterations. They are indeed annoying and almost impossible to read, principally because they give in the main text the earliest version and then proceed to the final form hidden within a thicket of brackets. But this form of nonsense is not necessary. First, a clear text can have all the necessary information about alterations described in footnotes. Second, although there is of course some interpretation and loss of readability when the alterations are inserted in the text for instant appraisal, a new system that reprints the final form of the inscription and describes in shorthand form without angle brackets and the like the earlier versions is available and presents even complicated matter in a relatively painless form. See Bowers, "Transcription of Manu-

scripts: The Record of Variants," *Studies in Bibliography*, 29 (1976), 212–264. This system has been used since 1975 in over ten volumes of the William James edition but seems not to be known by historians.

7. It should be recognized, of course, that once an editor has embarked upon the principle of recording internal alterations made during composition or on review (the two distinguished when possible), no principle of selectivity can be contrived that is scholarly. To attempt to record substantive changes but to omit what were regarded as stylistic would abuse editorial discretion in an intolerable manner, for one could never know what might have been ill-advisedly suppressed. Even incomplete false starts may be of interest if one can extrapolate the intended word. The simple mending of letters for clarity need not be recorded, but mending for alteration must be. Obvious dittography might be omitted; but any list of such options would be very small and subject to debate.

8. This is perhaps as good a place as any to state a purely personal opinion that for the purposes of historical interpreters it may be moot whether an eclectic conflated text made up from multiple authorities is better suited than a transcript of a single document, provided *in both cases* an apparatus records the variants in a manner that allows the substantives of all documents (that is the wording itself) to be recovered. On the other hand I can scarcely feel that it is at all moot whether the record of internal alteration within a transcribed document may be omitted. If an edition of a text is to be taken as complete, fully accurate, and definitive, it constitutes a vital silent suppression of evidence to permit the transcript to be less informative than the original document and thus an inadequate substitute for it.

9. It is not simplistic to inquire what else can a textual editor edit except texts, in which case a documentary editor is also a textual editor. Customarily textual editors have been distinguished from writers of commentary notes or critical introductions as part of a collaborative edition, and certainly they have been distinguished from the 'editors' of paperback editions whose function is to prefix a brief introduction to a reprint of some standard text. But to attempt to distinguish as 'textual' what is merely an attitude toward a text, or the editing of a text with literary subject matter, is to invite confusion. The term 'textual editor' may seem to be an apt contrast to 'documentary editor' but if so it is a case of the tail wagging the dog.

10. This statement needs a caution as applied to printed texts. In modern machine printing from plates or by offset or computer tapes, an edition is the sum total of all printings from the same typesetting. Each time the preserved setting, in whatever form, is run through the press again a new impression or printing results. Experience suggests that in machine printing the copies within any printing are almost certainly going to be textually identical. On the other hand, between printings both authorized and unauthorized variant readings may by manipulation be introduced into the same setting so that copies of any one printing need not be identical with copies of another. In the days of hand printing proofreading might be done and the type altered while the sheet was going through the press with the result that any forme of any sheet may vary as a result of different readings introduced within the printing itself, and some formes may vary more than once if multiple correction was found necessary. As a consequence, in early books one

cannot speak with absolute and detailed but only with general confidence about the text of any single printing. In a lengthy work like the Shakespeare First Folio, for example, it has been estimated that no two preserved copies are textually, or at least mechanically, identical. It follows that scrupulous scholars quoting from hand-printed books feel obliged to specify the provenience of the copy used, for the text might differ in some respect in other unknown copies; hence only an individual copy can be considered to be a textual entity (though within itself of different degrees of correctness, possibly). In machine printing this precaution is transferred to a reference identification of the printing from which the quotation was copied, although it is an unfortunate fact that in earlier machine printing the record of printing is not always listed within the copies and thus may be unidentifiable by the ordinary user. For example, quotation might reproduce rather different texts in some pages of William James's *Principles of Psychology* because of the numerous plate changes made in the early printings, all unidentifiable under the date of 1890. A critical edition, of course, provides the established and therefore the safest text for study or quotation since the editor has performed all necessary collations to identify and evaluate the variant readings introduced during the significant period of the work's printing history.

11. Among critics authorial intention is a slippery and much debated subject that has some consequences for textual criticism. For a study, one should consult G. T. Tanselle, "The Editorial Problem of Final Authorial Intention," *Studies in Bibliography*, 29 (1976), 167–211; reprinted in Tanselle, *Selected Studies in Bibliography* (1979), pp. 309–353.

12. *Prolegomena for the Oxford Shakespeare* (Oxford: At the Clarendon Press, 1939), p. 6: "For scholarly purposes, the ideal text of the works of an early dramatist would be one which, on the positive side, should approach as closely as the extant material allows to a fair copy, made by the author himself, of his plays in the form which he intended finally to give them, and, on the negative side, should not in any way be coloured by the preconceived ideas or interpretations of later times." Since this was written, 'ideal text' has come to be a technical term, and the proviso about the limitations that the preserved evidence sets on the extent of the approach has been inserted.

13. However, he could write that on the evidence of the text the third edition is unauthoritative, using 'evidence' in a quite different manner from Dr. Badaracco's restriction.

14. 'Assumed authorial original' usually means the author's lost original manuscript, but McKerrow's notion of a hypothetical authorial fair copy of the final form of the text covers many situations. As will be seen later, the original manuscript of *Tom Jones*, if it were preserved, would by no means represent the ideal text to reprint in a documentary manner since it would not contain Fielding's final revisions made for the fourth edition. Yet if in a critical manner we distinguish 'accidentals' from 'substantives,' even a purified text of the fourth-edition substantives would not equal the total authority of an authorial fair copy of its text since its accidentals are even farther removed than those of the first from Fielding's characteristics. William James's manuscripts, although used as printer's copy, were usually semi-drafts of his final intentions even in the matter of accidentals.

If he sent an essay to a journal, he would alter the proofs considerably; when the journal text was to be collected in a volume of essays, the substantives (and some few of the accidentals) would undergo a further revision in the marked-up printer's copy of the journal pages; then in turn the resulting proofs would be further worked over. By the time one gets through the successive stages of printing-house styling and authorial correction and revision (which did not always touch the printer's more conventional styling) the full authorial intention in respect both to accidentals and substantives must be sought through a maze composed of the different documents (not all preserved), and an attempt *so far as the evidence permits* to approximate by critical editing to a hypothetical authorial fair copy bears no precise overall relationship to any single document.

15. That is, the present-day documentary editor would reprint the fourth, as in fact has been done in the past. But to illustrate the pitfalls of the documentary method, we should note that for a time the variants in the fourth edition were taken to be unauthorial printer's corruptions and the third edition was wrongly regarded as the true revised edition and in that capacity was actually reprinted in documentary fashion. We now know that Fielding never touched it and that its text is corrupt.

16. A careful facsimile reprint (almost invariably of printed material) has an apparatus that lists doubtful readings owing to bad inking etc., and it may list reprinted misprints as a reassurance to the reader. The more advanced facsimiles, whether type or photo, also list any proof-changes in the text discovered by collation of the chosen copy (its location stated) with as many examples as exist (for rarities) or as many as the editor has time and patience to collate. (In modern works lists of plate-changes in later printings would replace the record of proof-changes necessary for hand-printed books.) The lengthy series of Malone Society Reprints of Elizabethan plays started under the general editorship of W. W. Greg are excellent examples of scholarly type-facsimiles with apparatus, and this series also contains a number of diplomatic transcripts of manuscripts, again with the noting of doubtful readings but more especially with a full listing of alterations within the text when these have not been visually reproduced by typographic means. In this respect a proper diplomatic reprint edition differs notably from what would have been an historian's documentary edition of the same material. With the displacement of expensive collotype by the cheaper fine-screen offset process, photo-facsimiles have at present practically replaced type-facsimiles. Examples of careful photo-facsimile editions with apparatus are the series of Shakespearean quartos started by W. W. Greg for Sidgwick and Jackson and continued for Clarendon by Charlton Hinman. For the same material edited by diplomatic transcript and then critically, the curious may consult the Elizabethan play *The Welsh Ambassador* as reproduced in the Malone Society Reprints (1920) and in *The Dramatic Works of Thomas Dekker*, ed. Bowers, vol. IV (Cambridge University Press, 1961).

17. The closest correspondence to a documentary-edited manuscript text but one treated with greater freedom than a strict diplomatic transcript is the modified form sometimes found in the more scholarly collections of letters of literary and

other folk where the audience is in some considerable part composed of non-professionals and hence readability commands a higher premium. Literary or other manuscripts in the humanities seem to be mostly transcribed for professional scholars and critics in a form closely approximating a diplomatic transcript insofar as the editor understands the concept, but perhaps with some trifling modifications such as the bracketed supplying within the reprinted text of missing letters or required punctuation, although some editors may prefer to enhance readability by adopting various of the silent expansion devices found among historians. So long as a clear statement is made about what has and has not been done, and so long as what has been done is concerned with what might be called paleographical or typographical matters such as the expansion of 'w^{ch}' or of 'y^t', for instance, or in early manuscripts of the special character that stands for final '(e)s', I take a more relaxed view of the problem in editions addressed to a wider audience than does Dr. Tanselle, whose severest strictures, after all, are reserved for the unstated silent changes made in some documentary editions of matters that cannot be automatically recovered such as the simple expansions I have mentioned. Certainly the silent modification of punctuation leaves a reader not knowing where he stands.

18. It may not be a quibble to suggest that by default these must logically also be considered to represent 'ideal' texts since they approach to full authorial intention so far as the evidence warrants such a judgment. However, the term 'ideal' is best restricted to critically edited texts to avoid ambiguity.

19. In fact, critical analysis proceeded one stage beyond this overall decision in the several cases where the printer himself seems to have altered a word or two in order to accommodate a James expansion in the same line of the plates. Such consequential non-authorial changes need to be identified and discarded. Much easier, of course, is the correction of an obvious printer's error elsewhere in the resetting of a revised line or in a line reset only to correct some misprint, discovered and marked, perhaps, by the publisher. Actually, in a printing or two the only alterations in the plates being mechanical and thus differing from other printings where James's corrections and revisions are beyond question, an editor may assume that within those printings the variants are non-authoritative although he may choose to adopt what he considers to be necessary corrections.

20. 'Non-derived' in the sense that two independent manuscripts lie in back of the two authorities. There is partial derivation in the cases where the later edition was set up directly not from its underlying manuscript but instead from a copy of the earlier print which a scribe had brought into general conformity with the manuscript in order to produce a more convenient printer's copy. Sometimes not convenience but necessity seems to have enforced this slightly odd procedure when the manuscript being utilized was a promptbook that would not be permitted to leave the theater for the printing house. Mixed transmission of this kind introduces more serious editorial problems than if both editions had been set up directly from their respective manuscripts, not merely the first.

21. There is the continuing problem, of course, of what exactly is the meaning of 'greater.'

22. This view runs through the whole of his *Prolegomena*, but see especially pp. 12–13.

23. Technically, emendation may mean nothing more than alteration of the copy-text without regard for the origin of the change, whether drawn from some other authority or from conjecture, although as popularly and generally used it is likely to apply to conjectural alteration of a reading present in the authoritative document(s). For example, an editor of *Hamlet* after choosing the Second Quarto as his copy-text might (wrongly in my opinion) emend I.ii.129 "O that this too too sallied flesh would melt" to the Folio's "solid flesh." This would be an alteration within the limits of authority and hence the text could be no 'greater' than the evidence. On the other hand, if he emended the Quarto and Folio "For if the sunne breede maggots in a dead dogge, being a good kissing carrion" (II.ii.181–182) to the traditional reading "being a god kissing carrion," going back to Warburton, he would be making an emendation in the popular sense without authority. Adoption of such a natural emendation, and various others of similar sort, may make an edited text more correct in general critical opinion than the readings permit of any of its documents; and in this respect it may well reconstruct by conjectural critical means what was Shakespeare's intention that had been corrupted in transmission within authoritative documents. But if an emended text is greater, what happens when one editor chooses *sallied* (for *sullied*) and *good*, but another *solid* and *good*, and a third *sallied* and *god*? Which is the greater text, given equal divergence in dozens of other cruces? When one goes beyond authority, gradations of 'greater' depend upon criteria impossible to demonstrate or to apply. I believe we must sharpen our terms to recognize that when in anything but a general sense we talk about 'the text' of a work like *Hamlet* or *Tom Jones* we are setting up an ideal of what the author wrote that no document and no critical edition can encompass. All editions are an attempt at recovery of what the author wrote, but the tolling bell of the minatory *insofar as the evidence permits* must warn us of human inadequacy when dealing with the dead. If, for instance, we say that the text of *Hamlet* must have read "a god kissing carrion," we are appealing to our conjectural conception of what was contained in the lost Shakespearean manuscript as representing 'the text.' This manuscript must remain ultimately unrecoverable in any evidential manner even though within the limits of documentary evidence we can in considerable part reconstruct the major features of its general outline. If we clearly recognize that we have crossed a border, we can then attempt by informed guesswork further to narrow down some details of 'the text' of *Hamlet*, but little common consent can be expected to accompany this individualistic effort. The actual text of *Hamlet*, as Shakespeare wrote and then perhaps revised it in part, is a chimera. By emendation supplementing the selection from documentary evidence editors may do their best to lend some substance to the shadow. But the best that can be achieved is what can be described as 'a working text' which by definition is provisional. Provisional or not, it is at least concrete although itself subject to marked editorial differences of opinion about specific readings, as between *sallied* and *solid*. Moreover, the preserved evidence for the major outline of this provisional working text may be recognized, and textual critics—even without full consensus—can analyze divergences within the evi-

dence as caused by corruption, or transmissional selection or authorial revision. In many respects what 'the text' of *Hamlet* was like (especially Shakespeare's final intention) we shall never know and can never recover as an entity by any process of selection and emendation. The best efforts of textual criticism can only narrow slightly the limits of a mystery. (I am ignoring difficult questions of the mutations of a text within its period of authorial history such as afflict any attempted reconstruction of 'the text' of T. S. Eliot's *Murder in the Cathedral*, for it is probably true that no such *terra firma* as 'the text' of this work can exist but only a series of shifting texts rewritten for different conditions of production. Such a mutation may just possibly lie behind some of the problems of the *Hamlet* text. At another level, in many modern plays there is the pre-rehearsal text which the author wrote and the actual production text after the director, actors, and ushers, possibly, had worked it over with or without the approval of the author. There may be a final intention in respect to the produced text, but this may not wholly agree with the final intention of the author in writing the play before or even after he was forced to accept outside revision. Chronologically we know Dickens' final intention in the altered ending of *Great Expectations*, as produced or published, but do we know whether his secret and critical final intentions coincided? Of course the narrowness of view proper for the language of textual criticism need not prevent a critic, whether literary or textual, from using 'text' as the equivalent of the contents of a work as revealed by the working text with which we are familiar, preferably in a critical edition. What really troubles me is the use of the word 'text' for a philosophical concept that would not, in fact, be satisfied even if the author's ideal fair copy of his final intentions existed.

24. This is not to say that public opinion over the course of time may not stabilize and pronounce certain emendations like *god* in *Hamlet* to be sanctified as authorial intention. The test of time is the best authority we have for such decisions that 'satisfy' our sense of appropriateness. A consensus of this sort may be operative even though incomplete, as in the case of Theobald's classic emendation in *Henry V* of 'a Table of greene fields' to 'a' babbled of green fields' despite the strained glosses that the few defenders of the original adopt. Or no consensus may yet have developed. Since *sullied* is beginning to make its way against *solid flesh*, something of a consensus reversal may be taking place, a not unknown phenomenon.

25. It is assumed that we can never put ourselves in the place of the Athenian watching Sophocles performed in the vast amphitheatre, that we must in some part guess what the Elizabethan playgoer felt about the rejection of Falstaff (if there was in fact any more uniformity in this reaction than there has been in modern times), just as it is proposed that there is difficulty fully to share Trollope's estimate of the moral condemnation the reader should feel at the mother's forgery in *Orly Farm*. The present-day sexual revolution, moreover, has certainly interfered with a modern reader's empathy with the *mores* of Victorian novels. Thus, it is asserted, texts (meaning actually the import of the contents) change their significance and need reinterpretation with the passage of generations. On the other hand, no one can prove that another may not feel like an Athenian. Empathy and understanding are not necessarily similar. Under instruction we can understand

and even empathize with Antigone's peculiarly Greek religious outrage at the exposure of her brother's body. Under instruction an agnostic can read *Paradise Lost* with understanding and sufficient sympathy, perhaps as much as or more than that accorded by some segments of Milton's original audience. The discreet veiling of sexuality in Victorian literature need not obscure from the present generation the facts and implications any more than it did to the original readers who were familiar with the coded allusions and lacunae. That Freudian psychology has revealed to present-day readers a deeper understanding of *Hamlet* than was possible, say, for Pope is admittedly true; but we do not necessarily understand Hamlet better than Shakespeare and the more perspicuous of his audience merely because we can put a technical name to certain human emotions. However, that Freud gives us a new and different 'text' of *Hamlet* is a patent absurdity. Shakespeare's observation of human behavior conveys as much basic understanding to the modern reader as would any clinical report. In fact, the Freudian analyses of Hamlet that have been published—examining him as if he were a real person—sound like parodies.

26. This is a particularly confusing passage, in part because the meaning of 'authorial time' is uncertain. In the passage quoted above, which states that an editor may reconstruct an eclectic text from several witnesses "valued on the basis of their relation to authorial time" I can see no other meaning than the normal one that the nearer or more distant relationship of witnesses to the authorial original may affect their authority, and also that in time (that is, in an ascertainable chronological order) the author may have revised one document from the state of the text of an earlier. But in the present sentence 'authorial time' in this relation makes no sense and one must intepret the same phrase to mean, I suppose, that in some manner the editor relates the past to the present. How this is supposed to be done I am uncertain. One obvious way would, of course, be by means of an edition that makes an early text available to a later audience; but I fancy more than this truism is intended, though obscurely.

27. Indeed, today's editors of unmodernized Elizabethan dramatic literature are so scrupulous in emending according to the terms of the document itself that in substituting a different word or form for the original reading they make sure not only that its spelling is appropriate for the time of original printing but even that it is characteristic of the compositor who set the passage in which the alteration is made. Thus if one were to emend a Shakespeare Folio passage set by Compositor A from 'to' to *do*, an editor would adopt A's characteristic spelling 'doe' and not the 'do' that would have been proper if Compositor B had set the line.

28. It is necessary to repeat that the editor is a textual critic to greater or lesser degree completely dependent upon the nature of the textual material on which he operates; and with some material he is a critic only negatively in that he finds nothing that need or else can be done, in his critical opinion, to bring the document—on the preserved evidence—closer to the author's presumed original or to the author's fullest intentions as manifested in some revised document other than the original. It should be remarked that in this account of the lack of opportunity for critical method afforded by many texts I am speaking exclusively of the 'substantives,' or the words themselves, not of the 'accidentals,' or the texture in which

the words are clothed. The degree of interference with these 'accidentals' permissible for an editor of nineteenth- and twentieth-century unmodernized literary texts is a matter on which various editors today have taken quite opposite sides. A certain amount of the debate, especially among practitioners of American-literature editing, is due to a misunderstanding of W. W. Greg's "Rationale of Copy-Text," one of the key twentieth-century documents in textual criticism. For an attempt at clarification of the intent and import of this essay to editors of works in later periods than the Elizabethan, see Bowers, "Greg's 'Rationale of Copy-Text' Revisited," *Studies in Bibliography*, 31 (1978), 90-161.

29. In some sense, perhaps, more or less in the way a present-day critic for convenience reads some modernized edition of Shakespeare (since no critical old-spelling edition is in existence) as a provisional text for general purposes, but consults photo-facsimiles of Quartos or the Folio for any close work requiring the authority of the original documents.

30. I cannot conceive of a critical *edition* without its necessary apparatus which provides the documentary information required by some users as well as a text that makes a convenient synthesis or correction required by others. Since the respective value placed on the two parts of an edition—text and apparatus—will vary kaleidoscopically according to the individual user and his special needs at the moment, the scholarly editor is no longer the victim of the requirements of only one segment of an audience, and hence he is relieved of the problem of adapting his values to those whom he may be addressing. In my view, then, it follows that the value placed on a document, that is, the editor's attitude toward and treatment of the documents with which he is working, cannot be polarized between diplomatic (or documentary) and critical editing in any meaningful and certainly in no defining way except as their methodology differs. An editor of a critical edition cannot help placing just as much value on the documents as represented in his apparatus as on the documents as represented in his text (sometimes they will differ but sometimes not), even though by their placement as part of text or apparatus he has indicated his opinion of their relative authority or correctness in respect to each of their variant readings. They have all contributed to the formation of his text. Freedom to alter the evidence of a document (that is, its text) is inherent in the definition of critical editing. But that this act of correction (or, but more rarely, of synthesis and ideal reconstruction) in the text-part of an edition implies any definable difference in the attitude toward (or value placed on, except in the sense of authority) the documents an editor must employ other than the attitude (and values) of a diplomatic transcriber toward the evidence of his documents—this is a concept that as a practising editor I feel I must deny. (It may not be evidence, but I cannot resist remarking that I have just finished spending a great deal more time analyzing and listing in a formulaic manner for the apparatus alterations in the manuscript that is preserved of the final two chapters of William James's *Varieties of Religious Experience* than I did in preparing the first-edition copy-text critically.)

31. Some remarks on these two disciplines and their relationship will be found in Bowers, *Textual and Literary Criticism* (Cambridge: At the University Press, 1959).

Editing Oral Epic Texts:
Theory and Practice

John Miles Foley

In beginning this discussion I think it only right to acknowledge a potentially embarrassing conceptual impasse: the task at hand is to present a *written* discussion of the progress of translating *oral* epic texts to *written* editions. I could, in a poor imitation of Plato's rhapsode Iōn, imagine or have imagined for me a natural continuity among a source poem, its recorded and transmitted text, and the many later performances of the poem in different times and places: for this "stitcher" of poetic fragments, the magic of mimesis closed the gap between the *kléos* of Achilles and Odysseus in the mythic time of oral tradition and latter-day presentations from fixed texts; for Iōn and his colleagues, the heroes lived and fought again in each reciter's reenactment of the poems. Each recitation was in this way unique and original, and the distance between performance and text was consequently obviated.[1]

But although the Socratean metaphor of the rings is a handsome notion, I prefer to be less anecdotal and more the doubting realist: for the modern, very literate reader the distance between oral performance and written edition is vast, and it entails a journey over largely uncharted territory. If we are to attempt that journey, we must begin by admitting that the written recension of an oral text—no matter how informed, expert, and nobly serious its editor—is inescapably an exercise in oxymoron. This is not to say that such a typographical facsimile is valueless, or even that it distorts the "original" text beyond critical recognition or aesthetic appreciation; it is to say that the written edition is something entirely different, even distinct, from the text-performance on which it is based. To approach the original text, to restore a fraction of its reality as an oral experience, we must be willing to measure the capabilities of written media and to turn them to best advantage. We must be willing to design a typographical format which goes beyond the usual conventions of editing to take account of the special nature of oral texts, to the extent, of course, that a print medium can accommodate such an undertaking. And, as we shall see, it will at a certain point be desirable and productive to leave Gutenberg's galaxy behind and to enlist the aid of a yet more modern medium, the electronic digital computer, to recover the pre-print and pre-manuscript technology of oral literature. Wherever the search for a faithful edition of an oral work may take us, however, that search starts with a single fundamental premise: the oral text is a text *sui generis* and is not equivalent to a written text.[2]

I base this first premise on the degree of reductionism necessary to render an oral performance as the sort of written edition with which the modern scholar and student are so familiar. The aural reality of the source must of course be entirely discarded, and this is a crippling loss. W. B. Stanford's, Stephen Daitz', and Robert P. Creed's restorations of ancient Greek and Anglo-Saxon epic illustrate how important the dimension of sound can be in poetic traditions whose languages are long dead,[3] and, more immediately, we can sense the startling discrepancy between oral "holograph" and edited oeuvre by listening to, or ideally by participating in, an oral poet's actual performance. At the most general level, then, the experience of hearing and observing a poem in its original form cannot be unthinkingly confined to a one-dimensional script without sacrificing a significant part of the work's reality and, therefore, without seriously compromising its artistic integrity.

More specifically, we can trace the illegitimacy of a simplistic translation of media by considering a number of individual features peculiar to the oral epic text.[4] Apart from the crucial phenomenological disparity between sound and visually apprehendable print, there is the aspect of music: a special melody or rhythm often associated with oral performance, and especially with the epic. Whether or not a poet accompanies himself on an instrument (and the role of that instrument is likewise not to be discounted in assessing a text and presenting an edition), he may well have recourse to one or another group of recurrent vocal melodies or rhythmic phrases which assist in transmitting the work and which are as much a part of its tradition as the phraseology that they support.[5] Shifts from one to another of these phrases may coincide with narrative shifts; modification of a single pattern, perhaps by including an extrametrical interjection, may signal a point of juncture or ramification in the verbal structure of the text.[6] Where possible and profitable, such melodic and rhythmic features deserve to be noted and explained by an editor. If they are ignored or silently deleted from the edition, an entire dimension of textual activity is suppressed.[7] Even within the pattern of recurrent suprasegmental phrases, a poet may use special intonations to particular effect. Although this aural punctuation may be purely personal, a singer's momentary imprint upon the indifferent continuity of a poetic tradition, nonetheless it is unambiguously an aspect of his oral text and should be presented to the reader of a written edition in a convenient and straightforward format.[8]

The passage quoted below illustrates how important the aural dimension can prove in another genre, that of the Serbian healing charm, where it takes the form not of melody or rhythm but of an acoustic pattern, a succession of matched sounds which emerges as a phonetic series. Here the source of the passage is a *basma* (spell) recorded by Barbara Kerewsky-Halpern and myself in a Yugoslav village in 1975.[9] Unlike the epic singer, the *bajalica* (conjurer) uses no instrument to accompany herself; neither does she employ any inventory of musical phrases to articulate her verses. Nevertheless, the acoustic patterns of her magical utterance are prominent and functional.

> *Kako* dodje, *tako* stiže;
> Ovu boljku odmah diže.

These rhyming patterns, along with sequences involving assonance, sound substitution, and other types of euphonic association,[10] ramify throughout the charm texts, lending an aural power to the healing properties of the spells.

Even more fundamental problems can arise concerning the true character of a typographical recension of material such as that exemplified above. Although it may seem puerile to inquire what a "word" is and how it ought to be represented, in the case of the oral epic songs of Yugoslav singers (*guslari*) we may have unexpected difficulty in arriving at answers to these questions. For what the *guslar* conceives of as a *word* is by our print-centered definition a whole *line* or group of lines, a stich or group of stichs, each containing from two to six lexical units. For reasons that the imminent discussion of phraseology will make clearer (and that the foregoing brief mention of whole-line melodic and rhythmic patterns may perhaps have adumbrated), the poet does not atomize his verse into our lexical particles. As an oral entity, the verse line stands on its own; to break it down further would be to rupture the wholeness of a compositional unit.[11]

And yet, although the integrity of the line as a unit was affirmed by the *guslari* who were asked about the matter, these same poets easily modify, truncate, and augment the phraseological entities they call "words" by metathesizing or substituting items within them (our "words" within their "words"), by building non-lexical phonological bridges between or within items to prevent vowel hiatus, by doubling the values of vowels and their syllables in order to eke out a syllabic constraint or otherwise accommodate the demands of prosody, and in general by maintaining a free-flowing and malleable exchange between the narrative movement of the story and its stichic expression. The examples below illustrate these phenomena as they occur in an oral tradition:

Metathesis	Sultan Selim otvorijo rata
	or
	Sultan Selim rata otvorijo
	Sultan Selim waged war
Substitution	Podviknuše lički Mustajbeže
	Podviknuše beg Mustajbeg lički
	Mustajbeg of the Lika shouted
Hiatus bridge	Kad deveto jutro *j*osvanulo
	When the ninth morning dawned
	I *j*Andja mu riječ besjedila
	And Andja spoke a word to him
Vowel doubling	A govori ba*a*nica mlada
	And the young banica spoke

The medium of oral diction is a remarkably plastic one with many levels of structure, only a few of which correspond to conventions developed for and in the written text. To address the second question, then, which concerns the problem of representing the oral as opposed to the written "word" in an edition of an oral text, we can see that the prospective editor is left to design a typographical format which takes account of the particular kind of "words" encountered and the special morphology to which they are subject.

An oral text's aural features deserve to be documented and established as part of the edited text. Along with these *oral* characteristics of the synchronic work, however, we must consider the *traditional* structure of the text as a diachronic document. As Milman Parry first showed in his doctoral theses of 1928,[12] the epic poetry of Homer and the Yugoslav *guslar* emerges from generations upon generations of a poetic tradition, from hundreds of years of tales which were transmitted entirely without the aid of writing. The history of such oral traditional poetry is not a search for stemmata or prescriptions for *termini ad quem*, but rather of the dynamic and essentially timeless shape-shifting of a living, evolving multiform of a tale or cycle of tales. Just as no one performance is "original" or archetypal but only an avatar of an ongoing process, so the structures within the performance are also momentary realizations of multiforms. At the level of the line, traditional structure takes the shape of the *formula*,[13] or substitutable verse increment, which answers the metrical needs of the given line and which the poet can manipulate according to the demands of his tale-telling. Formulas can fossilize into apparent tags, as in the case of so many Homeric epithets, or they may admit more variation. Examples of this sort of multiform are provided below:[14]

EXAMPLES OF FORMULAS

Greek whole-line: ἦμος δ' ἠριγένεια Φάνη ῥοδοδάκτυλος 'Ηώς
When rosy-fingered dawn, daughter of morning, shone,

second
hemistich: εὐρυκρείων 'Αγαμέμνων
wide-ruling Agamemnon

Iliad 1.102: ἥρως 'Ατρείδης εὐρυκρείων 'Αγαμέμνων
the hero Atreus' son, wide-ruling Agamemnon

Iliad 11.238: καὶ τό γε χειρὶ λαβὼν εὐρυκρείων 'Αγαμέμνων
And seizing it in his hand, wide-ruling Agamemnon

Old English Pattern: __ X __   under wolcnum
 __ X __   *under the clouds*

Instances: weorold under wolcnum   *Genesis* 916a
world

wintra under wolcnum   *Genesis* 1231a
winters

wære under wolcnum   *Genesis* 1438a
were

Weox þa under wolcnum   *Genesis* 1702a
Grew up then

wide under wolcnum   *Genesis* 1920a
widely

wand under wolcnum   *Exodus* 80a

wound
wrætlic under wolcnum   *Andreas* 93a
splendid
wann under wolcnum   *Rood* 55a
dark
(partial listing)

Serbo-Croatian second
          hemistich: u pjanoj mehani
                         in a drinking tavern
         Instances: Vino pije u pjanoj mehani
                         He drank wine

                         A da vidiš u pjanoj mehani
                         But you should have seen

                         I sreća mu u pjanoj mehani
                         And his luck

Traditional structure, the flexible story architecture which allows both the oral poet to tell his tale spontaneously and the poetic tradition to maintain itself over time and place without committing its contents to the petrified record of writing, also takes a characteristic form at the level of narrative logic. Here we encounter the *typical scene* or *theme*, as Lord calls the unit,[15] a stereotyped grouping of ideas which epitomizes a narrative event, providing the poet with a conventionalized increment by means of which he can develop the story. Examples of themes include the well-known Homeric feast scene, the Beowulfian monster-fight, the arming of the hero in Serbo-Croatian epic.[16] Each instance of a multiform shares a general structure and verbal complement with the other occurrences, and each fills out the resultant generic sameness with particularized details necessary to the nominal context. Thus Beowulf always speaks his *beot*, or martial boast, before entering combat,[17] although that boast may take somewhat different forms depending on the nature of his adversary, the stage of his own life, and so on. As in the case of the formula, some themes are more consistent in actual verbalization than are others, but there is always a significant amount of verbal correspondence as well as a general idea-pattern shared by all instances. Briefly put, the theme or typical scene is a kind of narrative formula, a pattern whose phraseology consists of ideas and corresponding verse lines or increments.[18]

Although not nearly as much research has yet been done on the larger levels of traditional architecture, Lord and others have begun to describe a structure commonly called "story pattern," or, to continue the analogy, formula at the macrostructural level of the poem as a whole.[19] Thus Lord speaks of the Return Song, essentially the story of Odysseus, as a traditional tale-type multiform which occurs throughout the Balkan literatures. An outline of this pattern is as follows:

A	D	R	Rt	W
Absence	Devastation	Return	Retribution	Wedding

There is evidence that the story of Return may descend from Indo-European tradition:[20] the Serbo-Croatian songs, for example, are filled with examples of long-imprisoned heroes who return as beggars to reclaim wife and wealth, and in fact we meet with striking parallels to Homer's story—Bojičić Alija's *biljeg* (or wound) is recognized by his nurse in one song from Stolac, and the hero's faithful wife whiles away her time weaving in another. Other story patterns emerge from well-collected oral traditions; in the Serbo-Croatian material the Rescue and Wedding songs have been isolated and exemplified.[21] But whatever example one chooses to illustrate the morphology of tale-types, it is clear that the story pattern is a traditional structure and as such participates in the continuing generation of individual performance texts from an oral tradition.

But what then of the individual text which has become separated from its context in the poetic tradition? What does the unique text represent and where and what is the poem?[22] We cannot assume that a single text is "the poem," since it is only a version of the narrative, only one possible recension of a multiform which will forever evade the fossilization of print. No more can we assume that any of its parts— the traditional structures discussed above—is original and archetypal; each instance of formula, theme, and story pattern is by its very nature only an instance. In the case of oral traditional epic, we are always dealing with occurrences of multiforms and never directly with the multiform itself. To establish any one text or textual feature as standard is to mistake the ontology of oral traditional structure. We must find other criteria to apply to the process of editing such material.

If each instance of a formula, theme, or story pattern is equally a version of a multiform which cannot itself be reduced to a finite, individual occurrence, then the sum of all instances or versions—or rather their Gestalt[23]—should amount to a reasonable representation of that multiform. And, in fact, this prescription for indicating an underlying pattern through its concrete occurrences imitates the learning process through which the Yugoslav *guslar* passes in appropriating his craft. As Lord describes it,[24] the singer listens to the performances of mature bards for some time before publicly trying his own hand at oral epic composition; during that time he is absorbing the multiform structures by means of repeated experience with their occurrences, by hearing the range of morphology in phraseological and narrative grammar and syntax. Ideally, then, we might seek to emulate the *guslar*: we might attempt to learn the tradition—the contextualizing matrix for the performance-text—by listening to as many of its text-instances as possible. Theoretically, we could thus become as familiar with the generative multiforms of text and tradition (within limits) as the *guslar* and his audience, and although as literati most of us might wisely stop well short of actual oral performance, we would at least have enough knowledge of context not to misread the poem.

To return to one of the questions posed earlier, under these conditions the text and "the poem" are coincident but not equivalent. This fundamental disparity points up a crucial difference between oral epic and written literature which cannot be underestimated. Although the text contains and instances the poem, it is not itself the poem. In order to apprehend the work faithfully, the reader or auditor must bring to the text a knowledge of the traditional context which is always implicit in any single text but which becomes active only when it is summoned by the reader from his experience with the tradition. To edit a poem rich in this special kind of meaning demands a great deal more than editing a detached, decontextualized text; to edit the oral traditional work is somehow to provide the reader with the background necessary to a faithful extrapolation from text to context and on to the poem by reactivating the poem's traditional resonance. Without such an extension from version to source, without simulating a knowledge of traditional multiforms with which to interpret otherwise apparently unique texts and structures within works, we have reduced the oral epic to—quite literally—a faint echo of its original self. We have, in short, edited the multi-dimensional source poem out of its natural richness and complexity and into a manageable but hopelessly monolithic artifact. This unfortunate process is, as I said at the outset, an exercise in oxymoron.

As one example of the dangers inherent in such a reduction, we may note the continuing critical debate over the "meaning" of noun-epithet formulas, expecially in Homeric studies. The supposed problem of how such standard phrases relate to changing narrative situations has occupied many scholars, some of whom have gone to considerable lengths to try to explain how traditional formulas do or do not contradict the story action which surrounds them.[25] Of course, the dialectic underlying this manufactured problem is a false one: traditional formulas owe their primary allegiance to the continuity of tradition and not to the nominal pattern of a single text. Otherwise they would not be traditional and we would be dealing with a text exactly like a written text. The invariable formulas, as opposed to the substitutable phrases which some have called "formulaic systems,"[26] generate meaning by metonymy or, more exactly, by synecdoche: they conjure their referents *pars pro toto*—not independent of the present text (for the present text is always an avatar of the tradition) but rather primarily dependent on a much larger and older context. Achilles' swift feet are neither appropriate nor inappropriate; they simply instance his total characterization, and the telling detail stands for the whole complex of his identity. To construe the meaning of a formula only in any single occurrence is to misread both text and poem. Yet the typographical recension encourages precisely this kind of misreading.

Likewise, at the other end of the spectrum, we should remember that the narrative progress of oral traditional epic, informed and directed as it is by story pattern, is hardly cut from new cloth in each performance, but rather echoes in some fashion a traditional structure or multiform as ubiquitous in its way as the formula. Thus Odysseus' return, for example, follows a certain traditional logic, a preordained train of events. While the master poet may dextrously manipulate the course of the island adventures or rapprochement with Penelope at this or that juncture, the main outlines of his survival and reascendancy in Ithaka were drawn long before Homer, perhaps even by some Indo-European singer of tales. If we insist upon dissecting the unique text which has survived to our time, poring over it for evidence of an archetypal poem or for what we take as clues to resolve supposed problems of suspense or foreshadowing, we will do the work a great injustice.[27] Just as in the case of formula, the key to understanding the text is to recreate the poem, and for oral traditional epic recreating the poem means reinvesting the text with traditional meaning.

The question for the prospective editor thus becomes how to accomplish that reinvestiture, how to remake the poem from the text. Early collectors and editors of Serbo-Croatian oral epic, concerned as they were with other aspects of what Murko called *la poésie populaire orale*,[28] characteristically assembled what amounted to anthologies constructed along generic lines. Either a focal hero, like Kraljević Marko in the Serbian tradition or Djerdjelez Alija in Moslem epic song, or an area, such as the borderland Krajina, often served as the unifying feature of a published collection.[29] With the appearance of the first two volumes of the Parry-Lord material in 1953–54, the series which has continued under the general title *Serbo-Croatian Heroic Songs,* a first step was taken toward placing the individual text in its traditional context. Here are multiple versions of a poem by the same and by different singers within the local tradition of Novi Pazar: by reading through the volume, one can gain some understanding of the poetic context out of which each song emerges. Later volumes in this series carry on the work of documenting the oral epic tradition in the various regions in Yugoslavia where the collections were made in the 1930s and afterward.[30] As the edition progresses, the effect of increased coverage will be cumulative: as more and more material becomes available, the individual texts modulate more and more toward the poems and the tradition which they collectively instance.

As fine and necessary an editing project as *Serbo-Croatian Heroic Songs* is, and as much of an improvement as it represents over other editions of oral epic, it cannot fully restore traditional meaning to the texts it epitomizes. Even if the series reached to hundreds of volumes in length and its apparatus to thousands of pages documenting every occurrence of every formula, theme, and story pattern, the project could not recreate the oral epic tradition. Apart from this inevitable shortfall between ideal methodology and particular application, the major reason for this inadequacy is the endemic limitations of the typographical recension as a text edition of oral epic. What good can it do to note a thematic analog perhaps thousands of lines away, possibly the work of another poet in another locale, with a simple citation? Should the reader wish to consult the analog, he must put down his edition of the text at hand and go rummaging through a companion volume, trying at once to follow the parallel, to maintain narrative momentum in the text presently being read, and to ascertain the context of the analog in its own field of reference. Alternatively, we could include the analog in our edition of the object text, perhaps in an appendix or even at the bottom of a page; in this case, the question quickly becomes one of admissibility. Where exactly do we draw the line? Do we cite all formulaic relatives for a given line? Do we include as a key index only one line from the analogous text or more than one? And if we choose to include a number of lines, how are they to be set up typographically? Themes will not fit at the bottoms of pages; must they then be relegated to an appendix? And what shall we do about story patterns? Even if all of these logistical problems could be solved, we would be left with a much larger, more serious question: how can the uninitiated reader, untrained as he is in the poetic tradition we are attempting to reconstruct, manage to juggle all of the multiform occurrences in analogous texts at the same time that he is pursuing the narrative development of the tale at hand? The fundamental problem is to sort and then to represent the protean instances of these traditional multiforms in a way that the reader can understand and assimilate. He must be able to find a path through the forbidding maze of object text and analogous material without meeting the Minotaur.

From the point of view of the history of media, it is somewhat ironic that the electronic computer, amanuensis of the modern age, should come to the aid of the editor of preliterate texts. But automatic text-processors such as HEURO I, my system offers, I believe, far the best means now available of extending written text to oral traditional poem, of restoring traditional context to a work. As the name unsubtly implies,[31] HEURO I is a heuristic series of programs which "reads" an object text in terms of its tradition, thus recreating the lost context and revivifying the work. The text-processor recognizes formula, theme, and story pattern elements in an object text and automatically searches its data file of reference texts for other occurrences of the same structures. If correlative patterns are found in the data file, HEURO I reports them and, depending on their size and importance, either prints them out immediately alongside the object text or offers the reader the opportunity to choose whether he wishes to view them or to move on. At every point the reader is able to compare traditional collocations and to interpret the text before him not as an *oeuvre complète* but as one version of a multiform. The single text is no longer unique, no longer cut off from its tradition by the tyranny of the printed edition; rather it becomes again a text contextualized, a poem reinvested with the lifeblood of its tradition.

HEURO I performs these routines hierarchically, proceeding from the macrostructure of tale-type through the narrative texture of themes and on to the microstructure of individual formulas. At each level the system concords and lists all occurrences in the data file and offers the analyst the choice of viewing any or all of them beside the relevant line or passage from the object text. Thus, on encountering element D (Devastation), the second term in the Return Song equation, it locates and prints out the references for all other instances of this element, citing the first verse and the line numbers for the entire passage:

OBJECT TEXT	DATA FILE
122 Pocmilijo Alagić Alija *DEV* *Alagić Alija cried out*	2.42 Pocmilijo tri bijela dana *DEV* 2.79 *He cried out for three white days* 3.55 A cmilijo Ograšćić Alija *DEV* 3.179 *And Ograšćić Alija cried out* 11.91 Pocmilijo sužanj nevoljniče *DEV* 11.201 *The unwilling captive cried out*

Now the reader may decide whether he wishes to have a closer look at any of the analogous passages in texts 2, 3, or 11. If he does, either the entire Devastation element or a specified section of it can be elicited in each case, and he can move from one text to another comparing verbalization of the Devastation multiforms.

When it finishes with this initial stage of the reading process, or if the reader decides to skip over closer examination of the story pattern analogs cited, HEURO I moves on to the next level of traditional structure, that of the theme. Now it happens that the D element opens in most cases with the theme of "A Captive Laments," so line 122 of the object text would have a double label:

THEME 12   122 Pocmilijo Alagić Alija   *DEV*

The designation *THEME 12* refers to a dictionary of typical scenes, abbreviated in the machine-readable texts to save space. When the system exits the story pattern analysis and enters on a thematic search, it identifies and prints out the full descriptive name of the theme below the original line:

THEME 12   122 Pocmilijo Alagić Alija   *DEV*
THEME 12 – A Captive Laments

It then searches the data file for all instances of this narrative unit and reports the first lines and passage citations:

THEME 12	2.42	Pocmilijo tri bijela dana	DEV	2.79
THEME 12	3.55	A cmilijo Ograšćić Alija	DEV	3.176
THEME 12	3.695	Pocmilijo Alagić Alija	DEV	3.781
THEME 12	11.91	Pocmilijo sužanj nevoljniče	DEV	11.201

Just as in the first phase of the heuristic analysis, the reader can now choose on the basis of such a report to view any or all of the passages cited, in whole or in part, moving freely along axes of traditional equivalence from one text to another. In the present example, he may want to focus on the passage beginning at line 695 of text 3, since it seems from the notation that a second Devastation multiform and *THEME 12* occur in that song. This second instance within the same song betokens a double-cycle Return epic, a multiple of the simplex pattern described above, and provides an illustration of how song-types evolve by combination and permutation within an oral tradition.[32]

During the second phase of analysis, HEURO I will locate and concord all themes as it encounters them, whether or not they are coincident with the beginning of a story pattern. Having accomplished that concordance and given the reader the opportunity to contextualize whatever typical scene he meets in the object text, the system then proceeds to a line-by-line formulaic scan, a third level of analysis which continues until the next thematic or story pattern label turns up. During the formulaic phase, the reader is automatically provided with correlative phraseology in other texts in the data file: the system prints out the actual corresponding line or lines in a 2- to 4-line context alongside the object text:

OBJECT TEXT	DATA FILE
	A govori Bojičić Alija:
E ču li me, nerodjena majko.	"Ču li mene, nerodjena majko.
	Ja sam sret'o tvoja Bojičića,

In practice, the formulaic routine operates through a key-word-in-context processor; that is, the program locates related phraseology by matching key words which are chosen for their relative importance by the program itself. As the system evolves, I plan to make the selection mechanism more sophisticated, and eventually to teach the computer enough about the morphology of Serbo-Croatian to enable it to overcome the vagaries of inflection and dialect. As it stands now, however, the basic heuristic algorithms are not language-dependent. Thus HEURO I can be easily adapted to any oral literature whose transliteration can be made machine-readable (that is, put into Latin letters), and this flexibility is a great advantage at the beginning stages of establishing computerized editions.

At each of the three levels, then, HEURO I seeks out analogs for traditional structures, first recognizing the pattern in the object text and then locating other occurrences of that pattern in the data file. The reader or analyst constructs the file of reference texts before analysis begins: it may consist of any combination of texts, from the object text alone through the corpus of texts sung by a single *guslar*'s local tradition or elicited even more widely. The textual referent for the heuristic routines can, in other words, be modified to suit the reader's or analyst's specific purposes. Since the reader has the option of viewing any or all of the thematic and story pattern correspondences, as well as of attenuating the sensitivity of the formulaic search, he can in effect teach himself the poetic tradition at the pace and in the depth necessary to the task at hand.

At present HEURO I operates exclusively on approximately 10,000 lines of Serbo-Croatian oral epic, a group of eight texts chosen from among those I am preparing for a volume of *Serbo-Croatian Heroic Songs* in the Harvard series. The system makes available to the uninitiated reader an edition of any one of these texts in a uniquely active context; according to the selection made for the data file, any of these works is automatically set against the background of its tradition. As the reader proceeds through each work, summoning analogs to the object text to reveal its multiform structure, he begins to revivify the performance record, to transmute text back into poem. For the scholar, HEURO I provides a method of studying multiformity at every level, on a scale and with an accuracy otherwise impossible. The text-processor glosses any line or any passage by charting its traditional identity over the 10,000-line sample. As one learns more about a given traditional structure, he is correspondingly more able to describe the basic processes of oral epic tradition itself. For the reader, HEURO I constructs a uniquely faithful edition, recalling a traditional ambience forever lost from the printed text. For the analyst, it assembles a structural profile of the object text and the tradition of which that text is one momentary example.

Apart from enlarging the data base for Serbo-Croatian oral epic and improving the sensitivity of automatic text-processing routines, I plan in the future to extend the capabilities of HEURO I in interdisciplinary directions. Highest in order of priority is developing editions of selections from certain ancient Greek and medieval English texts, works which are thought to derive from oral traditions. To be able to read the Homeric poems as the oral palimpsest they constitute, especially in the light of encouraging theoretical progress on oral traditional structure made by classicists in recent years,[33] is, it seems to me, of the first importance. And the Old English epic *Beowulf*, whose formulaic and thematic patterns are well documented, should profit from the kind of edition that HEURO I makes possible.[34] Of course, the limited size of the textual samples and our fragmentary knowledge about the actual performance and transmission of the Greek and Old English epics preclude assembling a text and tradition model as faithful as in the case of the Serbo-Croatian material, but these kinds of limitations will always be with us in dealing with dead-language traditions. At the very least, the construction of computerized editions promises to recover more of the poems involved than could the usual typographical recensions. In addition, I plan a series of such editions in modern English translation, so that students in courses like my oral literature seminar at the University of Missouri can have the opportunity to teach themselves poetic traditions whose languages they do not control. As I believe it should, HEURO I thus commands a wide spectrum of possible uses, from original language editions and analytical tools for scholars to pedagogically oriented editions in translation for students. At all points, however, the fundamental premise remains the same: to recontextualize the individual text, to reinvest the epic poem with the richness of its oral tradition.

* * *

I stated at the outset that my task in this paper was an exercise in oxymoron, that conducting a written discussion of how to mediate between oral texts and printed editions posed serious conceptual problems. Notwithstanding that disclaimer, I have plunged straight in, trying to illustrate how oral epic is a very special sort of "literary" form, one which in fact denies the etymology from *littera*. The dimensions of sound, performance, melody and rhythm—even the disparity in the notion of what a "word" is—make it reductive to present as an edition of an oral text only a typographical record of lexical items, the merest libretto stripped of its real identity. The multiform structures of oral epic are another concern; in editing and later in reading, the units of formula, theme, and story pattern must have a dynamic role, just as they have a role in both the synchronic performance of the text and the diachrony of its tradition. In an attempt to recover this multiformity and to remake the traditional poem from the unencumbered record of its performance, I have built a computerized text-processor called HEURO I. This system accomplishes what the reader untrained in an oral epic tradition could never accomplish on his own: it automatically provides a meaningful context of analogous material as a traditional background to the individual text. As the reader moves through the narrative sequence of the object text, the processor searches out corresponding elements of formula, theme, and story pattern, continuously contextualizing the single instance with numerous parallels. In this way the apparently unique structure becomes a multiform and the unique text-version a poem. It is my hope that this computerized system and its more sophisticated progeny will teach the literate reader the pleasures and advantages of preliteracy by recalling what our written, typographical culture has forgotten—the complexity and subtlety of oral epic art.

NOTES

1. See further Eric A. Havelock, *Preface to Plato* (Cambridge, Mass.: Harvard University Press, 1963), Walter J. Ong, *The Presence of the Word* (1967; rpt. New York: Simon and Schuster, 1970), and Ong, *Interfaces of the Word* (Ithaca: Cornell University Press, 1978), and my "Education Before Letters: Oral Epic Paideia," *Denver Quarterly*, 13 (1978), 94–117.

2. The bibliography of oral literature is vast and interdisciplinary; as an indication, see Edward R. Haymes, *A Bibliography of Studies Relating to Parry's and Lord's Oral Theory* (Cambridge, Mass.: Harvard University Printing Office, 1973) and my "Introduction: The Oral Theory in Context," in *Oral Traditional Literature: A Festschrift for Albert Bates Lord*, ed. John Miles Foley (Columbus: Slavica Press, 1980), pp. 24–117. The most important early work in the field, and the foundation upon which all other writings rest, is that of Milman Parry, now available in *The Making of Homeric Verse: The Collected Papers of Milman Parry*, ed. Adam Parry (Oxford: Clarendon Press, 1971), hereafter cited as *MHV*, and that of Albert B. Lord, especially *The Singer of Tales* (1960; rpt. New York: Atheneum, 1968 *et seq.*), "Homer as Oral Poet," *Harvard Studies in Classical Philology*, 72 (1967), 1–46, and "Perspectives on Recent Work on Oral Literature," in *Oral Literature: Seven Essays*, ed. Joseph J. Duggan (Edinburgh: Scottish Academic Press, 1975), pp. 1–24 (a complete review of Lord's writings through 1979 will be found in my "Introduction"). For a brief overview of the

history of the field and new directions, see my "Oral Literature: Premises and Problems," *Choice*, 18, iv (December 1980), 487–496, and my *Oral-Formulaic Theory: An Introduction and Annotated Bibliography* (New York: Garland Publishers, 1983).

3. W. B. Stanford, *The Sound of Greek: Studies in the Greek Theory and Practice of Euphony* (Berkeley: University of California Press, 1967), which includes an illustrative recording; Stephen G. Daitz, *A Recital of Ancient Greek Poetry* (New York: Jeffrey Norton Publishers, 1978); Robert P. Creed and Burton Raffel, *Lyrics From the Old English*, Folkways 9858.

4. In what follows I refer, with the exception of one example drawn from the Serbian octosyllabic charm tradition, only to the genre of epic poetry. On the principles of genre-dependence and tradition-dependence, see my "Tradition-dependent and -independent Features in Oral Literature: A Comparative View of the Formula," in *Oral Traditional Literature*, pp. 236–254; "The Viability of the Comparative Method in Oral Literature Research," *The Comparatist*, 4 (1980), 47–56; and "Formulaic Befuddlement: Traditional Oral Phraseology and Comparative Prosody," in *In Geardagum: Essays on Old English Language and Literature*, vol. 3, ed. by Loren C. Gruber and Dean Loganbill (Denver: Society for New Language Study, 1980), pp. 7–17.

5. On the music associated with epic in the Yugoslav tradition, see Béla Bartók's transcription of parts of Salih Ugljanin's *Ropstvo Djulić Ibrahima* in *Serbo-Croatian Heroic Songs* (*Srpskohrvatske junačke pjesme*), vol. 1 (Novi Pazar: English Translations), coll. Milman Parry, ed. Albert B. Lord (Cambridge, Mass. and Belgrade: Harvard University Press and the Serbian Academy of Sciences, 1953–54), pp. 436–462. In addition to the companion volume (no. 2) of original language texts, this series, hereafter cited as *SCHS*, also includes later additions: *The Wedding of Smailagić Meho* (*Ženidba Smailagina sina*), by Avdo Medjedović, vol. 3 (translation) and 4 (original language), coll. Milman Parry and Albert B. Lord, trans. Lord, ed. David E. Bynum (1974); *Ženidba Vlahinjić Alije* and *Osmanbeg Delibegović i Pavičević Luka*, by Avdo Medjedović, vol. 6, ed. Bynum (1980); and *Bihaćka krajina: Epics from Bihać, Cazin, and Kulen Vakuf*, vol. 14, ed. Bynum (1979). On rhythmic patterns in Old English, see my "Formula and Theme in Old English Poetry," in *Oral Literature and the Formula*, ed. Benjamin A. Stolz and Richard S. Shannon (Ann Arbor: Center for Coordination of Ancient and Modern Studies, 1976), pp. 207–232.

6. At the beginning of his song, for example, a *guslar* often includes the interjection *Ej!* as a kind of cue to the onset of the narrative:

> Ej! Rano rani Djerdjelez Alija
> Ej! Djerdjelez Alija rose early

Unless otherwise noted, all examples drawn from the Yugoslav oral epic tradition are taken from songs collected by Milman Parry, Albert Lord, and David Bynum in the central Hercegovinian region of Stolac, songs which I am preparing for publication in *SCHS*.

7. Compare Bynum's discussion of melody in songs from the Bihać area (*SCHS*, 14:15–43).

8. In practice, it is often impossible to say definitively whether a certain feature of oral style is traditional or the poet's own improvisation.

9. I refer to the field work phase of a project on "Aspects of Serbian Oral Expression," sponsored by the National Endowment for the Humanities. Resulting publications include: John Miles Foley and Barbara Kerewsky-Halpern, "*Udovica Jana*: A Case Study of an Oral Performance," *Slavonic and East European Review*, 54 (1976), 11–23; "The Power of the Word: Healing Charms as an Oral Genre," *Journal of American Folklore*, 91 (1978), 903–924; "*Bajanje*: Healing Magic in Rural Serbia," in *Culture and Curing*, ed. Peter Morley and Roy Wallis (London and Pittsburgh: Peter Owen and the University of Pittsburgh Press, 1978), pp. 40–56; Foley, "Research on Oral Traditional Expression in Šumadija and its Relevance to the Study of Other Oral Traditions," in *Selected Papers on a Serbian Village*, ed. Barbara Kerewsky-Halpern and Joel M. Halpern (Amherst: University of Massachusetts, 1977), pp. 199–236; "Epic and Charm in Old English and Serbo-Croatian Oral Poetry," *Comparative Criticism* (Yearbook of the British Comparative Literature Association), 2 (1980), 71–92; and "Field Research an Oral Literature and Culture in Serbia," *Pacific Quarterly*, 7 (1982), 47–59.

10. On euphonic patterns in oral epic, see especially Lord, "The Role of Sound-Patterns in Serbo-Croatian Oral Epic," in *For Roman Jakobson* (The Hague: Mouton, 1956), pp. 301–305; Berkley Peabody, *The Winged Word: A Study in the Technique of Ancient Greek Oral Composition as Seen Principally through Hesiod's "Works and Days"* (Albany: State University of New York Press, 1975); and Robert P. Creed, "The *Beowulf*-Poet: Master of Sound-Patterning," in *Oral Traditional Literature*, pp. 139–161.

11. Consider this excerpt from a conversation between Parry's assistant Nikola Vujnović and the *guslar* Mujo Kukuruzović (Parry text *6619*):
    Nikola: Let's consider this: "Vino pije lički Mustajbeže"
    ("Mustajbeg of the Lika was drinking wine"). Is this
    a single word?
    Mujo: Yes.
    N: But how? It can't be *one*: "Vino-pije-lički-Mustajbeže."
    M: In writing it can't be one.
    N: There are four words here.
    M: It can't be one in writing. But here, let's say we're
    at my house and I pick up the *gusle*—"Pije vino lički
    Mustajbeže"—that's a single word on the *gusle* for me.
    N: And the second word?
    M: And the second word—"Na Ribniku u pjanoj mehani" ("At
    Ribnik in a drinking tavern")—there.

12. *L'Epithète traditionnelle dans Homère* (Paris, 1928), rpt. in English translation in *MHV*, pp. 1–190; *Les Formules et la métrique d'Homère* (Paris, 1928), rpt. in English translation in *MHV*, pp. 191–239.

13. Parry's original definition is "a group of words which is regularly employed under the same metrical conditions to express a given essential idea" ("Studies in

the Epic Technique of Oral Verse-Making. I. Homer and Homeric Style," rpt. in *MHV*, p. 272).

14. Examples from Homer are taken from Guy L. Prendergast, *A Complete Concordance to the Iliad of Homer*, rev. and enlarged by Benedetto Marzullo (1875; Hildesheim: Georg Olms Verlag, 1971); Old English examples are from Jess B. Bessinger, ed., and Philip H. Smith, progr., *A Concordance to the Anglo-Saxon Poetic Records* (Ithaca: Cornell University Press, 1978).

15. Lord's definition of themes is "groups of ideas regularly used in telling a tale in the formulaic style of traditional song" (*The Singer of Tales*, p. 68); see further pp. 68–98.

16. On the structure of themes in various oral traditions, see Lord, "Perspectives," and my "The Oral Singer in Context: Halil Bajgorić, *Guslar,*" *Canadian-American Slavic Studies*, 12 (1978), 230–246, and "*Beowulf* and Traditional Narrative Song: The Potential and Limits of Comparison," in *Old English Literature in Context: Ten Essays*, ed. John D. Niles (London and Totowa: Boydell and Rowman & Littlefield, 1980), pp. 117–136, 173–178.

17. See further Alain Renoir, "The Heroic Oath in *Beowulf*, the *Chanson de Roland*, and the *Nibelungenlied*," in *Studies in Old English Literature in Honor of Arthur G. Brodeur*, ed. Stanley B. Greenfield (Eugene: University of Oregon Press, 1963), pp. 237–266.

18. See Lord, "Perspectives," and my "*Beowulf* and Traditional Narrative Song."

19. On the story pattern, see, for example, Lord, *The Singer of Tales*, especially pp. 186–197; "The Theme of the Withdrawn Hero in Serbo-Croatian Oral Epic," *Prilozi za književnost, jezik, istoriju i folklor*, 35 (1969), 18–30; Michael N. Nagler, *Spontaneity and Tradition: A Study in the Oral Art of Homer* (Berkeley: University of California Press, 1974), pp. 131–166; and my "The Traditional Structure of Ibro Bašić's 'Alagić Alija and Velagić Selim'," *Slavic and East European Journal*, 22 (1978), 1–14.

20. In addition to Lord's proposals (note 19), see Douglas Frame, *The Myth of Return in Early Greek Epic* (New Haven: Yale University Press, 1978).

21. See Lord, *The Singer of Tales*, pp. 245ff.

22. Compare the inquiries of Robert Kellogg in his "Oral Tradition," *New Literary History*, 5 (1974), 55–66.

23. Compare Nagler's use and development of the term *Gestalt*, in his *Spontaneity and Tradition*, pp. 1–63.

24. See "Singers: Performance and Training," in *The Singer of Tales*, pp. 13–29.

25. An example of this approach is Anne Parry's *Blameless Aegisthus: A Study of* amūmōn *and Other Homeric Epithets* (Leiden: Brill, 1973).

26. After Milman Parry, who defined a formulaic system as "a group of phrases which have the same metrical value and which are enough alike in thought and words to leave no doubt that the poet who used them knew them not only as single formulas, but also as formulas of a certain type" ("Studies I," rpt. in *MHV*, p. 275). Among later studies, see especially Donald K. Fry, "Old English For-

mulas and Systems," *English Studies*, 48 (1967), 193–204, and my "Introduction."

27. With these concerns we confront the foundation of the Analyst-Unitarian debate over one or many Homers, the Homeric Question of the nineteenth and early twentieth centuries; see further Adam Parry's "Introduction" to *MHV*, pp. ix–lxii.

28. Mathias Murko, author of *La Poésie populaire épique en Yougoslavie au début de XXe siècle* (Paris: Librairie Honoré Champion, 1929) and the posthumous *Tragom srpskohrvatske narodne epike (putovanja u godinama 1930–32)*, 2 vols. (Zagreb: Matica Hrvatska, 1951), was present at Milman Parry's *soutenance* and apparently had an important influence on the latter's field work in Yugoslavia.

29. Thus the famous collections of Vuk Karadžić, under the general title *Srpske narodne pjesme*.

30. See note 5 above.

31. HEURO, from εὕρψ, "I find," with an intended pun on he(u)ro, as in "he(u)roic poetry." I take this opportunity to thank the John Simon Guggenheim Memorial Foundation for a 1980–81 Fellowship, the University of Missouri for a 1980 Faculty Research Grant, and the University of Massachusetts at Amherst for a Visiting Adjunct Professorship in Comparative Literature and a Computing Center Grant, all of which underwrote research on HEURO I. I am also extremely grateful to my programmer, Bernate Unger of the Anthropology Department at the University of Massachusetts, for writing the programs which comprise the text-processor.

32. For examples of this kind of evolution, see my "The Traditional Structure," "*Beowulf* and Traditional Narrative Song," pp. 133–136, and "Narrativity in the *Odyssey, Beowulf*, and the Serbo-Croatian Return Song," in *Proceedings of the IXth Congress of the International Comparative Literature Association*, vol. 1, Classical Models in Literature, ed. Zoran Konstantinović, Warren Anderson, and Walter Dietze, Innsbrucker Beiträge zur Kulturwissenschaft, 49 (Innsbruck: University of Innsbruck, 1981), 295–301.

33. Especially Nagler, Peabody, and Gregory Nagy, *Comparative Studies in Greek and Indic Meter* (Cambridge, Mass.: Harvard University Press, 1974).

34. On oral traditional structure in Old English, see my "Introduction" (note 2).

Problems in the Editing of Tropes

GUNILLA IVERSEN

Liturgical tropes flourished during the period from the ninth to the twelfth centuries. This was, as we know, before the time of the universities, and the monasteries were still the natural centres for learned studies, for the creation of book illumination and for sculpture, for literature, philosophy and music, etc.

In Saint Gall, Mainz, Reichenau, Rheinau and Minden in the East, in Winchester, Cambrai, Metz, Saint Evroult in Autun and Fleury in the North West of the former Carolingian Empire, in Saint Martial in Limoges, in Auch, Aurillac and in Apt in the South West, in Nonantola, Monza, Vercelli, Padova, Ivrea, Piacenza and Verona, in Benevento and in Monte Cassino—everywhere there was intense creative activity.

A focal point for this creativity was the Latin Mass, since the performance of the Mass can be considered a great *Gesamtkunstwerk* in honour of God. In spite of the intense efforts of Charlemagne to make the Mass uniform throughout his vast empire, there was still considerable variation between different regions and even more after the division of the Empire. The multiplicity, the great variety, is in fact more striking than the uniformity.

Nonetheless, the chants of the Mass (the Kyrie, the Gloria, the Sanctus and the Agnus Dei and the chants like the Introit, the Alleluia verses, etc.) were sung with basically the same text everywhere. However, every monastery could create its own particular version of the feast by adding new verses to all these obligatory chants. These new verses—the tropes—were sung as introductions, insertions and terminations to the liturgical base-chants. They wind around them as

strands of ivy around a tree trunk. But they were not only adorn-
ments. Far from that, the tropes also explained and deepened the
words of the liturgical base text and today they help us to see how the
medieval participants in the Mass interpreted the specific liturgical situation and the feasts.

The composing of tropes flourished up to the twelfth century and
was already diminishing in the thirteenth century, long before their
condemnation and excision at the Council of Trent in the middle of
the sixteenth century.

Some of the tropes, like the Easter trope *Quem quaeritis*, survived
in- and outside the church, but most of the rich repertory of tropes
was left in peace and forgotten until the end of the last century when
Léon Gauthier[1] revived interest in them through his book *Les Tropes*.
A great number of versified tropes were edited in the *Analecta Hymnica Medii Aevi* at the beginning of the century.[2]

During our century, the tropes have been studied mostly by musicologists trying to define and describe the melodies, to clarify the relationship between the melody of the tropes and that of the base text and
the oral transmission of the melodies.

Since 1970, on the initiative of Dag Norberg and Ritva Jonsson, a
research team of philologists in Stockholm has been studying tropes
and making critical editions of their texts in the series of *Corpus
Troporum, Acta Universitatis Stockholmiensis, Studia Latina Stockholmiensia*.[3]

Let us first recall a few important factors that complicate the editing
of these texts:

1. What we call *tropes* include in fact texts of various types: the
Prosulae, added to a pre-existing melody, the *Proper tropes*, added to
texts changing from feast to feast, and the *Ordinary tropes*, always
combined with essentially the same base text.

2. The way of performing the tropes differed considerably from
one chant to another.

3. The texts in the repertory of one single manuscript reflect different levels of Latinity. Thus the language in the *Prosulae* clearly differs
from that of other tropes and is often very peculiar. One reason for
this is, of course, that these texts were added to a pre-existing melody
and that the phrases had to fit a given number of syllables. Also they
had to coincide at certain points with the words of the base text, as we
will see.

4. The Latin language is not the same in early as in late texts.

5. The standard of the Latin differs from one region to another. A text from Italy, for instance the Beneventan texts, or texts from Aquitania, often offer a very "bad" Latin, while the tropes from Saint Gall are given in a very "good" Latin with few "unclassical" readings.

6. The manuscripts were often originally made up of *libelli*, that is, small collections of anonymous texts, perhaps of only one or two leaves, that were successively gathered and copied into one book during a long period.[4] We must presume that these small *libelli* often contained texts and melodies that had been transmitted orally and written down a long time after they had been included in the local repertory.

7. New chants were added to the repertory but they were used side by side with the old ones.

Thus the repertory of a single manuscript may contain pieces of very different age and provenance but still they constitute together the specific repertory of a living liturgical tradition. In other words, the multiplicity and the variety of this "floating" material is enormous and the editing of this vast body of disparate texts entails at least three main problems:

1. The first is to find a method of presenting what I call the *main structure* of the troped chants. That is, to present all the different combinations of the separate verses, the so-called *trope elements*, that belong to the same trope, and also to demonstrate the way the trope elements and the base liturgical text are linked together.

2. The second main problem is to establish the text in such a way that variants are presented as readings just as valid as the so-called established text. The criterion of authenticity cannot be used in the traditional way on this material, for every text reflecting an actual liturgical practice has to be regarded as an authentic text. Thus it is inappropriate to use a traditional stemmatic method on these texts.

3. And last there is a problem that is always important when making editions to be used by scholars from different disciplines, who will want to use the editions for very disparate purposes. The text editions must be provided with information useful to these scholars; but how much should there be and what kind of information do these scholars need?

I will now illustrate some of these problems and present some of the specific solutions offered by the Corpus Troporum research team in the effort to make adequate editions of these recalcitrant texts. Each one of the volumes edited to date has demanded its own special method.

1. THE MAIN STRUCTURE

The first problem is to provide the *main structure* of the texts. The trope manuscripts edited in the Corpus Troporum date from 900 to the twelfth century and number about 170, with most of them dating from the eleventh century. They all have their own repertory and their own way of combining the parts of the tropes, the trope *elements*, in one chant. Let us look at one of the *Proper* tropes to the Introit antiphon, the *Puer natus* in the Corpus Troporum I.

Tropes to the Proper (the variable songs) of the Mass

Puer natus est nobis,
et filius datus est nobis:
cuius imperium super humerum eius:
et vocabitur nomen eius
magni consilii angelus.

Ps. Cantate domino canticum novum,
quia mirabilia fecit.
V Notum fecit dominus salutare suum
ante conspectum gentium
revelavit iustitiam suam.
V Gloria patri.

This is the antiphon, sung everywhere to basically the same Gregorian melody, as the opening chant of the third Christmas Mass. To this text were added trope texts as introductions, intercalations and terminations. In 63 manuscripts we have found no fewer than 121 different trope elements added to this text (Ex. 1). Confronted with this enormous multiplicity, which made editing by traditional methods impossible—the Corpus Troporum used another solution. The edition is built up not of "full tropes" in the sense of composite wholes but of single elements of tropes given in alphabetical order. Thus the reader may reconstruct the full trope of each particular manuscript by means of the tables.

In Example 2 all the manuscripts are listed and the reader may see which trope elements are combined in a chant in every single manuscript. As we can observe, nearly every manuscript has its very own combination of trope elements. Only two from Saint Gall (SG 376, SG 378), three from Vercelli (Vce 146, Vce 161, Vce 162), two from Monza and two from Nonantola in North Italy (RoC 1741, Bo 2824), have identical repertories in the Nat. III section. A comma indicates the end of a full trope. Let us look at the first trope given in the repertory of the Nonantola manuscripts. It is built up of four elements, 38, 31, 32, and 84. In this way, the complete manuscript reading for a full trope can be reconstructed by comparing the list of numbers given for each manuscript with the incipits in the numerical listing.

In Example 3 we have the elements put together. As we can see, all these trope elements are found in many other manuscripts but only the two Nonantola manuscripts combine just these four elements in one chant. The *apparatus criticus* also provides information on the main structure of the chant, that is, the way trope text and base are combined. (In the Nonantola manuscripts, the base text is divided so that the words of the trope anticipate the words of the base text.) This is not an easy way to reconstruct a text. It is a highly technical system and it does not give the reader an immediate impression of the whole trope as it appears in any individual manuscript. It demands a certain effort to reconstruct the specific version of the trope in each manuscript. Inevitably, we have been criticized for this by some scholars. Others—those who want to study single repertories, to compare different traditions—find this unorthodox method useful and agree that, in spite of the difficulties it involves, it is the only possible way of representing this floating and dispersed material.

In order to complete the edition and to give a more direct picture of the material, we have included in the volume a collection of so-called *tropi selecti* (Ex. 4). These are diplomatic reproductions of a certain number of trope repertories for each feast.

Tropes to the Ordinary of the Mass

The tropes connected with the *Ordinary of the Mass*, such as the *Sanctus* and the *Agnus Dei*, offer a somewhat different picture. Here the tropes are added to a liturgical text that does not vary from feast to feast as the Proper chants do. And even if there are trope elements that "float" from one trope to another, these tropes are definitely more coherent and permit another method for the editing.

As we can see in the *Agnus* trope *Omnipotens aeterne* (Ex. 5), all the elements that belong to this trope are given together and with the base liturgical text. Elements that can occur with the trope are given immediately after the established version. In a table after each trope, the reader finds all the combinations of the trope elements. After that follows the *apparatus criticus* and a commentary. This form of edition does not include all the different ways of combining the trope text and the base text given in every single manuscript. However, the main structure is often an important clue in defining the tradition to which the version belongs. This fact was not given due regard in the *Analecta Hymnica*, where the main structure of the tropes is too often "normalized" in a way that does not correspond to the evidence given by the manuscripts themselves. So, for instance, the trope *Omnipotens aeterne* (AH 49, 385), is presented in a way that does not correspond to its form in any of the manuscripts (Ex. 5).

Some of the tropes are given in two versions, for example, the *Agnus* trope *Fulgida qui regnas* (Ex. 6), which is represented in a South Italian version (I) and in another version found in North Italy and Nevers (II). The text in the first version is structured in short phrases, typical for this South Italian tradition. The Northern version has longer phrases.[5] It has a different melody. In this case as in many others we are, as philologists, grateful to musicologists who by means of the music can help us to confirm a division that we make on textual grounds.

In order to present accurately the methods of combining the parts of troped songs, the *Agnus Dei* volume includes an *aperçu des manuscrits*. As the trope manuscripts are at the same time the earliest sources presenting the *Agnus Dei* chant, which did not become a part of the mass until the eighth century, this *aperçu* also gives important information about the base liturgical chant itself. In fact it shows that the chant had not attained a fixed, standard, threefold form in this period, as has been claimed lately.[6] (Ex. 7, 8, 9). In the *aperçu* the reader also finds the location of the tropes in the manuscripts, whether they are gathered into special fascicles or found among the proper texts for each feast, and the rubrics.

As is shown by the examples, the early tropes in the Western tradition (here represented by MSS from Winchester and St. Martial in

Limoges, the words *Agnus Dei qui tollis peccata mundi*) were sung only once and the trope elements were followed by the prayer *miserere nobis*, "have mercy upon us." In Italy, in the Nonantola manuscript RoC 1741, different structures show influences from different traditions. The later Italian manuscript from Monte Cassino MC 546, presents the specific Italian structure, in which the entire phrase was repeated before every trope element. Finally the late manuscript from Saint Gall of the East-Frankish tradition, shows the structure that came to be representative for the *Agnus Dei* tropes from the end of the eleventh century. In the *Agnus Dei* volume the edition of the texts and the *aperçu des manuscrits* form together the basis for the analytic study of the form and the function of these tropes in different traditions.

Tropes to the Alleluia, the Prosulae

Another method is used in the editing of the *Prosulae* of the Alleluia verses (Ex. 10). The verses are given in alphabetical order. For each verse, the incipits of its trope texts, the *Prosulae*, are indicated in a table. Then follow the established text and its *apparatus criticus*, and a commentary. The performance of the *Prosulae* is extremely intricate and offers special problems for the editor. In this volume italics show where the *Prosulae* coincides with the base text, the base text itself being given in bold type. Thus we see that even within the very frame of the tropes as a genre the special character of the tropes for different liturgical base texts forces us to find different methods to present the main structure.

2. THE ESTABLISHED TEXT

The next level of editorial problems (after the presentation of materials) concerns the question of how to establish the text in the edition. We have seen in the *Puer natus* example how many variants and separate versions there can be of just one trope.

Which version, which variant is to be selected for the established text? The accepted rule in editing literary texts according to the genealogical method is, of course, to try to return to and present the form of the text that can be established from extant documents that putatively comes closest to the final version made by the author himself: that is, the most "authentic" stage of the textual transmission.[7]

But when one deals with medieval liturgical texts, the criterion of "authenticity" cannot be defined in the same terms.[8] For here we have poetry which is for the most part anonymous, although this is not the most important factor. The most important thing is that each different version of a text, as long as it belonged to a liturgical practice, is to be regarded as authentic. The most interesting task for us today is not to come back to and re-establish the first, the earliest text, which may be the natural editorial impulse, but to give as accurate a picture as possible of all the versions that were used in their own right in different regions. One can compare this with the position of the social anthropologist, for whom the most interesting thing to know is not which was the first elephant joke (the one with the elephant footsteps in the butter, the elephant in the matchbox, etc.), but to investigate the different elephant stories being told in different areas.

Thus a variant given in the *apparatus criticus* (and recording such differentiation) can be just as valid and "authentic" in this sense as the so-called "established" version. Still we must choose *one* text or one variant over another to form the *established* text. Should we then choose the earliest, the most widely spread, the one that has the "best Latin"? What criteria should we follow? A text may have been first composed in a version that was then forgotten or reformed in another version which is the one that actually became disseminated and popular. Should the version given in the most manuscripts be the one chosen? An objection to this solution is the fact that the number of manuscripts known to us today may be unrepresentative of actual copying. We have many manuscripts from Saint Martial in Limoges, for instance, and from Saint Gall, but this fact has perhaps exaggerated the importance given to these monasteries. Should we choose the "special" but understandable version of a text that, in its more disseminated version, seems difficult to understand? So for instance the versions in the manuscript Apt 17 from Apt in Provençe often present a revised and clearly corrected version of tropes that are confused and quite difficult to understand but which sometimes reveal a great depth of meaning. What seems to be "bad Latin" in a manuscript may reflect nothing but the poor knowledge of Latin of the individual scribe. It is therefore sometimes impossible to judge between what reflects the status of Latin knowledge of the author and of the scribe.

The text often represents a late copying of a song that had for long been transmitted orally. This oral transmission involves what we could call the "cross-eyed bear phenomenon" (The cross I'd bear for you, o Christ). You misunderstand what you hear, but you have your own very clear meaning of the words. Thus, for example, the singers in Saint Martial might have thought that they were singing the same *Agnus* song that their friends in Winchester sang at Saint Stephen's feast (Ex. 11). It is not until the text is written down that you can see that in Winchester they sang (or at least the scribe heard) *Tu ades corona confitentium*, "Be here with us, you the first of martyrs," whereas in Aquitania they sang *Tuam des coronam*, "you give your martyr crown." Another example of texts that reflect an oral tradition is the *O amnos* (Ex. 12), that is the *Agnus Dei* in Greek transcribed in Latin letters. It is given here in two versions, one East-Frankish, represented in Saint Gall, and one West-Frankish, Aquitanian. Here all the orthographic variants have been noted in the *apparatus criticus*. In none of the manuscripts has the scribe divided the words correctly. Probably this Greek version was like a formula used especially for the Pentecost liturgy and giving to the Pentecost Mass a certain dignity and above all functioning like a sort of speaking-in-tongues, illustrating the Holy Spirit's gift of multilingualism.[9] An especially intricate problem with the Saint Gall version is that it is not in fact easy to decide whether it is here a trope or a variant of the base liturgical text (Ex. 13, 14). On the other hand the Aquitanian *O amnos* quite evidently is a trope and added to the Latin base text *Agnus dei qui tollis peccata mundi* and even followed by *miserere nobis* (Ex. 15).

How shall we treat a text that seems impossible to understand as it appears in the manuscripts? Of course, the editor's natural ambition is to provide the reader with a text that is understandable and correct. But how far shall the editor go in order to provide such a text? There may be a temptation to correct and emend a reading which is not "good" Latin or which seems dubious to us today. In cases where the texts are very corrupt and seem impossible to understand, we might opt for an eclectic method and pick readings from different manuscripts and so construct a text that was evidently never sung in this form.[10] The "established" text becomes a *new* version of the chant. The risk with this method is that we disregard the meaningfulness of the medieval text as it is represented in its documents and instead put ourselves and our knowledge in the centre. What we create is the twentieth-century's version of a text "adapted from an idea in medieval manuscripts." The second temptation is to "correct" too ambitiously according to literary sources. Even if we recognize a possible source, the version of that source known to us may not be exactly the same as was known to the trope composers.[11] On the one hand it is always exciting to find a source that gives a clue to a corrupt text. See for instance the Easter text *Hodie namque Christo* (Ex. 16), where the antiphon text helps to understand the trope text.[12] On the other hand the Easter trope *Ex omni gente* (Ex. 17) illustrates a case where the source has another version and where the reading of the trope, even if it is difficult, can be retained as the form *cogniti* here, "understood by all nations."

An extreme solution being used by the Corpus Troporum V, in treating the Apt manuscripts, is to give a diplomatic version of the problematic and obscure text, just as it stands in the manuscript, and parallel to that to present our own edited version that makes sense to us.[13] But such a method can only be used in editions of one or two manuscripts.

Confronted with many separate variants we have been forced by the character of this text material to follow all the different criteria mentioned. Even though the "best" or the most representative version very often also *seems* to be the original one, it should be stressed again that a different, and less attractive variant might be just as authentic.

On the whole we have more and more come to a stage where, as much as possible, *we avoid altering the text given in the manuscript*, as long as there is the slightest possibility of making some sense of it. We must be aware of the fact that we know only fragments of the literary and scriptural context, the cultural atmosphere in which the tropes were created. We lack clues that could clarify the allusions, quotations, and sources. The meaning of a difficult passage may seem obscure to us today, but will perhaps be evident one day when we find the missing link, the source, the allusion, the manuscript reading that we did not have at the moment of editing the text.

In editing medieval texts of this kind we must be very generous and respect the medieval composer and even the medieval scribe who must be given the credit of at least *intending* something sensible. Except for absolutely obvious scribal errors we should more often retain even a dubious reading. But in doing so we must also be very generous to our readers and supply the texts with commentaries, suggest plausible translations, quote possible sources and even—if the text is extremely difficult—give our own emended version as a parallel text.

3. THE ADDITIONAL INFORMATION

Scholars are only just beginning to study the tropes *as literature*. The first stage has been to provide the text editions. Until now the *Quem quaeritis* has been the trope most studied, since it belongs to the history of drama.[14] Most scholars using our editions today are musicologists, liturgists, paleographers, and theologians. The text editions must therefore be provided with information useful to these scholars. But how much and what kind of information?

We have found that indices of feasts, repertories, surveys of manuscripts as entities, and descriptions of traditions and text analysis are important for most scholars using the trope editions; but we have now abstained from special sections giving melody-examples and dealing with the music. We prefer to give a photographic plate of a trope where the music is important for the understanding of the text and where the relation between text and music is especially intricate. For practical reasons it seems now to be more useful to construct separate editions of music and text, but with mutual references between them. Thus, for example, an edition of the melodies to the *Agnus dei* tropes and the *Sanctus* tropes is being prepared in the German series *Monumenta Monodica Medii Aevi* by Charles M. Atkinson who is one of the musicologists who work in close contact with the Stockholm group.[15] Generally it is important to stress the enormous need for collaboration with scholars from other disciplines that the study of these medieval liturgical chants provokes. And this intense collaboration with liturgists, theologians, literary historians, art historians, musicologists, and other scholars all over the world is one of the factors that make research on tropes such a fascinating adventure.

EXAMPLE 1. CT I, 228–229

(Nat III intr)

1^c	Laudemus omnes dominum	42^a	Quod prisco vates cecinerunt
2	Praeter omnium puerorum	43^a	Daviticae stirpis genuit
3	Ex tempore quidem	44^a	Perdita restaurans et restaurata
4	Crucis videlicet lignum	45	Hodie natus est nobis rex regum
5	Ex se natum sine matre	46	Qui sedebit super thronum
6	Hodie natus est Christus	47	Ecce venit deus et homo
7	Ineffabilis fortis	48	Eo quod futura annuntiabit
8	Ante natus quam mundus	49	Gaudeamus omnes die hodierna
9	Praecipuum sempiternum	50	Quem a patre omnino novimus
10^{a+}	Qui creavit quicquid	51	Admirabilis consiliarius deus
11	Privilegio patris filii	52	Ad aeternae salutis gaudia
12	Iudeis ac gentibus	53^a	Quem nasci mundo docuere
13	Cuius potentissimus	54^a	Visceribus sacris quem gessit
14	Hodie in terra pax	55^a	Et diadema cluens capitis
15	Deus de caelo dedit	56	Qui caelestia simul et terrestria
16	Potestas eius est	57	Rex caeli terrae marisque de virgine
17	Et regnum in manu	58	Arborem mortis vincens
18	Magnus et metuendus	59	Sicut est propheta prophetarum
19	Hodie exultent iusti	60	Puer natus est nobis filius Dei
20	Date gloriam deo nostro	61	Et potestas eius in generatione
21	Notum fecit dominus	62	Quem quaeritis in praesepe
22	Nativitas est hodie	63	Ecce adest de quo prophetae *cf* 33
23	Cuius potestas est	64	Vera dei forma patris
24	Deus fortis pater	65	Gaudeamus hodie quia deus
25	Hodie cantandus est	66	Quem prophetae diu vaticinati sunt
26	Absque nascentium	67	Hunc a patre iam novimus
27	Qui nos filios sui	68	Rex lumen de lumine regnat *cf* 41
28	Deus quod pater suo	69	Fortis et potens deus
29	Nomen quod extat omne	70^c	Gratuletur omnis caro
30	Miro modo cum de virginis	71	In plenitudine temporum
31	Quem virgo Maria genuit	72	Per partum virginis
32	Nomen eius Emmanuel	73	Rex regum solus potens
33	Ecce adest de quo *cf* 63	74	Pater futuri saeculi *cf* 80
34	Deus pater filium	75	Potestas et regnum in manu
35	Fabricator mundi princeps	76	Et regni eius non erit finis
36	Omnium votis sanctorum	77^a	Emmanuel fortis deus rex
37	Praedictus a prophetis	78	Altissimi filius et
38	Hodie salvator mundi per	79	Hodie orta est stella ex Iacob
39	Hic enim est cui	80	Princeps pacis pater futuri *cf* 74
40	Glorietur pater cum filio	81	Dominabitur a mari usque ad mare
41	Rex lumen de lumine eia regnat *cf* 68	82	Christus dominus princeps

EXAMPLE 2. CT I, 226–228

PUER NATUS (Nat III intr)

SG 484	1[c] 2 3 4 5, 6 7 8 9 10[a+] 11 12 13, 14 15 16 17 18, 19 20 21, 22 23 24, 25 26 27 28 29 30
SG 381	1[c] 2 3 4 5, 6 7 8 9 10[a+] 11 12 13, 14 15 16 17 18, 19 20 21, 22 23 24, 25 26 27 28 29 30
SG 376	25 2 3 4 11 12, 30 13, 1[c] 7 8 9 10[a+], 5, 26
SG 378	25 2 3 4 11 12, 30 13, 1[c] 7 8 9 10[a+], 5, 26
SG 380	25 2 3 4 11 12, 30 13, 1[c] 7 8 9 10[a+], 5
SG 382	25 2 3 4 11 12, 30 13
Wi 1609	1[c] 2 3 4 5
Be 11	25 31 32 33, 13, 1[c] 2 3 4, 5, 34
Ba 5	25 31 32 35 18, 19 36, 14, 1[c] 2 3 4 5, 34, 37, 33
Lo 19768	38, 14 15 16 17 18, 19 20 21, 6, 37 35, 33 39 31 32 40 5, 34, 25, 37 31 32 35, 36, 25, 38 34, 33 31 32
Cdg 473	25, 33 31 32 41, 42[a] 43[a] 44[a] 45, 34 46 47 48, 49 50 51 52 53[a] 54[a] 55[a] 56 42, 57 58 59
Ox 775	25, 33 31 32 41, 42[a] 43[a] 44[a] 45 56, 34 46 47 48, 49 50 51 52, 53[a] 54[a] 55[a] 56 42, 57 58 59
Lo 14	25, 33 31 32 41, 49 50 51 52 56, 45 53[a] 54[a] 55[a], 42[a] 43[a] 44[a], 34 46 47 48 60
Cai 75	25, 33 31 32, 42[a] 43[a] 44[a], 34 46 47 48
Cai 78	25
Me 452	25, 34, 33 31 32, 31 32, 42[a] 43[a] 44[a]
Pa 9448	25, 33 31 32 61 51, 34 21, 42[a] 43[a] 44[a]
Pa 10510	25, 33 31 32, 42[a] 43[a] 44[a]
Pa 9449	62, 63 31 32 64, 34 46 47 48, 65 66 67 51, 52 68 56, 25, 53[a] 54[a] 55[a]
Pa 1235	62 63 31 32 64, 34 46 47 48, 65 66 67 51, 52 68 56,, 25, 53[a] 54[a] 55[a]
Pa 13252	62, 25, 65 66 67, 34 53[a] 54[a] 55[a], 33 31 32 42[a] 43[a] 44[a]
PaA 1169	33 31 32 69 70[c] 71 72 73 40, 19, 34
Pa 1084c	42[a] 43[a] 44[a]
Pa 1240	65 66 67 51, 33 31 32 34, 46 47 48, 52 68 56 74, 54[a] 53[a] 55[a] 74
Pa 1121	62, 65 66 67 75 51, 33 31 32 76 74, 34 46 47 48 53[a] 54[a] 55[a] 77[a], 52 68 56 78, 79 80, 81
Pa 909	62, 65 66 67 75 51, 33 31 32 76 74, 34 46 47 48, 53[a] 54[a] 55[a] 77[a], 52 68 56 78. 79 80 81 82
Pa 1119	62, 65 66 67 75 51, 33 31 32 76 74, 34 46 47 48, 53[a] 54[a] 55[a] 77[a], 52 68 56 78, 79 80 81
Pa 1084a	79 80 81
Pa 1084b	62, 65 66 67 75 51, 33 31 32 76 74, 34 46 47 48, 53[a] 54[a] 55[a] 77[a], 52 68 56 78
Pa 887	62, 65 66 67 75 51 83 40, 34 46 47 48, 33 31 32 76 74, 53[a] 54[a] 55[a] 77[a], 52 68 56 78

Apt 17	62, 65 66 67 75 51, 33 31 32 76 74 84, 34 46 47 48, 53ᵃ 54ᵃ 55ᵃ 77ᵃ 85, 52 68 56 78
	42ᵃ 43ᵃ 44ᵃ 86, 87 88 89ᶜ, 60 90 91 92, 93 80 81 94, 79 95 96 97
Pa 903	62, 65 66 67 75 51 83 40, 33 31 32 76 74
Pa 1871	62, 65 66 67 75 51, 33 31 32 76 74, 34 46 47 48, 53ᵃ 54ᵃ 55ᵃ 77ᵃ, 52 68 56 78, 87,
	42ᵃ 43ᵃ 44ᵃ
Pa 779	62, 65 66 67 75 51, 33 31 32 76 74, 34 46 47 48, 53ᵃ 54ᵃ 55ᵃ 77ᵃ, 52 68 56 78
Pa 1118	62 83, 65 66 67 75 51, 33 31 32 76 74, 34 46 47 48, 53ᵃ 54ᵃ 55ᵃ 77ᵃ, 52 68 56 78,
	79 80 81, 90 40 92, 60, 98 95 96 80, 87, 97 91 47, 85, 93 99, 42ᵃ 43ᵃ 44ᵃ 86 100,
	40 91, 101
Apt 18	102ᵃᶜ 83, 33 31 32 40 91, 103 47 79 84 89ᶜ, 34 53ᵃ 54ᵃ 55ᵃ 88, 104ᵃ⁺
Vic 106	62, 65
Ka 15	25, 38 34 43ᵃ 44ᵃ 33 31 32 51, 42ᵃ
Ka 25	25 7 8 9 10ᵃ⁺
Ba 6	105, 106 7 8 9 10ᵃ⁺ 11 12 5, 25
Wi 1845	25
Ox 27	1ᶜ 2 3 4 5, 7 8 9 10ᵃ⁺ 11 12 13. 25, 106, 105
Mü 14083	25 107 108 109 110 111 112, 34 33 31 32, 42ᵃ 43ᵃ 44ᵃ
Mü 14322	25 107 108 109 110 111 112
Ox 222	62, 25, 34, 33 113 114
Vce 146	33 31 32, 62
Vce 161	33 31 32, 62
Vce 162	33 31 32, 62
Vce 186	33 31 115 32 51, 60 93 116 84, 21 117
Mza 75	33 31 115 32 51, 38
Mza 76	33 31 115 32 51, 38
Vro 90	38
Vro 107	25, 33 31 32 84 40 91, 5, 38 115 51 19 62, 118, 53ᵃ 54ᵃ 55ᵃ, 42ᵃ 43ᵃ 44ᵃ
Ivr 60	62 119, 65 66 67 51, 34 88 114, 34 46 47 48, 53ᵃ 54ᵃ 55ᵃ, 33 31 115 32 51 117, 120
	60 93 116, 6 2 8 11
Pia 65	62, 33 31 32 113, 117 121, 53ᵃ 54ᵃ 55ᵃ, 34
To 20	62, 117, 53ᵃ 54ᵃ 55ᵃ, 33 31 32 115 51
Mod 7	62, 117, 33
RoC 1741	38 31 32 84, 19 34 40 91, 33 118
Bo 2824	38 31 32 84, 19 34 40 91, 33 118
RoN 1343	38 31 32, 19 34 40 91, 33 118
RoA 123	38, 33 31 32 115 51, 42ᵃ 43ᵃ 44ᵃ 117, 53ᵃ 54ᵃ 55ᵃ
Pst 121	34, 33 31 32, 60, 117, 62,, 38 42ᵃ 43ᵃ 53ᵃ 54ᵃ 55ᵃ
Ben 34	33 31 32 76 51

EXAMPLE 3. CT I, 112, 175, 144, 134

Hodie salvator mundi per virginem nasci dignatus est
gaudeamus omnes de Christo domino
qui natus est nobis
eia et eia
PUER NATUS   Nat III intr 38

   Ka 15 Lo 19768 Lo 19768 (bis) Mza 75 Mza 76 Vro 90 Vro 107 RoC 1741 Bo 2824
   RoN 1343 RoA 123 Pst 121 (oct)
   salvator: redemptor *Mza 75 Mza 76*   per virginem: de virgine *Mza 75 Mza 76*
   Vro 90 RoA 123   gaudeamus: dicamus *Mza 75 Mza 76* gaudemus *Vro 90*
      domino *om Vro 107*   eia et eia *om Ka 15 Vro 107* deo gratias dicite eia
   Mza 75 Mza 76   PUER *om Mza 76, RoA 123 Pst 121 (oct)*
   s n Lo 19768 (bis) Mza 75 Vro 90
   cf CAO 4,6848,6856,6858

Quem virgo Maria genuit
ET FILIUS   Nat III intr 31

   Be 11 Ba 5 Lo 19768 Lo 19768 (oct) Lo 19768 (bis) Cdg 473 Ox 775 Lo 14 Cai 75
   Me 452 Me 452 (bis) Pa 9448 Pa 10510 Pa 9449 Pa 1235 Pa 13252 PaA 1169 Pa 1240
   Pa 1121 Pa 909 Pa 1119 Pa 1084b Pa 887 Apt 17 Pa 903 Pa 1871 Pa 779 Pa 1118
   Apt 18 Ka 15 Mü 14083 Vce 146 Vce 161 Vce 162 Vce 186 Mza 75 Mza 76 Vro 107
   Ivr 60 Pia 65 To 20 RoC 1741 Bo 2824 RoN 1343 RoA 123 Pst 121 Ben 34
   ET FILIUS: ET VOCABITUR *Lo 19768* CUIUS *Be 11 Pa 10510 PaA 1169 Apt 18*
   Mü 14083 Vro 107 RoC 1741 Bo 2824 RoN 1343 MAGNI CONSILII CANTATE
   Ka 15
   s n Lo 19768 Mza 75

Nomen eius Emmanuel vocabitur
CUIUS   Nat III intr 32

   Be 11 Ba 5 Lo 19768 Lo 19768 (oct) Lo 19768 (bis) Cdg 473 Ox 775 Lo 14 Cai 75
   Me 452 Me 452 (bis) Pa 9448 Pa 10510 Pa 9449 Pa 1235 Pa 13252 PaA 1169 Pa 1240
   Pa 1121 Pa 909 Pa 1119 Pa 1084b Pa 887 Apt 17 Pa 903 Pa 1871 Pa 779 Pa 1118
   Apt 18 Ka 15 Mü 14083 Vce 146 Vce 161 Vce 162 Vce 186 Mza 75 Mza 76 Vro 107
   Ivr 60 Pia 65 To 20 RoC 1741 Bo 2824 RoN 1343 RoA 123 Pst 121 Ben 34
   CUIUS: ET VOCABITUR *Pa 10510 PaA 1169 Mü 14083 Vce 186 Mza 75 Mza 76*
   Vro 107 Ivr 60 RoC 1741 Bo 2824 RoN 1343 MAGNI *Be 11 Lo 19768 Lo 19768 (bis)*
   Apt 18   CANTATE *Ka 15*
   s n Lo 19768 Mza 75
   Is 7,14

Magni consilii angelus eia iste vocabitur
nomen Emmanuel psallite domino jubilate dicentes
MAGNI   Nat III intr 84

   Apt 17 Apt 18 Vce 186 Vro 107 RoC 1741 Bo 2824
   consilii: conscilii *Vro 107 RoC 1741*   nomen ... dicentes: puer eia cantate domino regi magno canentes *Apt 17 Apt 18* puer et eia *Vce 186*   MAGNI: CAN-
   TATE *Apt 17* ET VOCABITUR *Vce 186*
   Is 9,6

EXAMPLE 4. CT I, 323–324; Piacenza, Bibl. Cap. MS 65, fol. 228v

Pia 65   (Nat III intr)

          20
f228v »In natiuitate domini ad missam maiorem»
          »Finita tercia cantore⟨s⟩ uadant retro altare
          excelsa uoce incipiant»
          Ecce adest de quo prophete cecinerunt dicentes
          PUER NATUS EST NOBIS
          »Qui ante fuerint respondeant»
          Quem uirgo Maria genuit
          ET FILIUS DATUS EST NOBIS
          »Item qui retro fuerint respondeant»
          Nomen eius Hemmanuel uocabitur
          CUIUS IMPERIUM SUPER HUMERUM EIUS
          ET UOCABITUR NOMEN EIUS MAGNI CONSILII ANGELUS
          »V̄» Multiplicabitur ei imperium et pacis non erit finis
          »Illi uero qui retro erant ante altare ueniant
          et cum aliis simul cum omni decore dicant»
          Gloria tibi Xpiste gloria tibi sancte
          gloria tibi domine
          quia uenisti omne genus liberare
          omnes gaudentes dicite eia
          PUER NATUS EST GLORIA PATRI EUOUAE
          Ecce agnus dei ecce qui tollit peccata mundi
          quem Ysaias propheta predixit
          PUER NATUS EST

EXAMPLE 5. CT IV, 63–64

Agnus dei qui tollis peccata mundi, miserere nobis.

A Omnipotens aeterna dei sapientia, Christe,
miserere nobis.

B Verum subsistens vero de lumine lumen,
miserere nobis.

C Optima perpetuae concedens gaudia vitae,
miserere nobis.

. . .

I Quem Iohannes in Iordane baptizavit
ovans et dicens :

. . .

D Rex regum, gaudium angelorum, Christe,

. . .

E Agne dei vivi, qui tollis crimina mundi,
dona nos omnes hic vivere pace quieta.

ABC	Cdg 473	Ox 775	Du 6	Pa 10508	Pa 7185	Pa 13252	Lei 60
	Pa 1087	Pa 1240	Pa 1132	Pa 1133	Pa 1134	Pa 1135	Pa 1136
	Pa 1137	Pa 909	Pa 1120	Pa 1119	Pa 1084b	Pa 1871	Apt 18
	Vro 107	Mod 9	Ivr 60	RoC 1741	RoN 1343		
AC	Pa 903	Pa 1118					
BCA	PaA 1169						
IABC	Lo 13						
IBAC	Pa 887						
ABCD	Pa 1177	Pa 1177 sec.					
ABCE	Apt 17	Apt 17 sec.					

I *Introductio vagans, vide* Quem Iohannes (50a)

A aeterna:aeterne *Pa 1240   Pa 1132   Pa 1133   Pa 1134   Pa 1135 Pa 1136   Pa 1137   Pa 909   Pa 1120   Pa 1119   Pa 1084b   Pa 887 Apt 17   Apt 17 sec.   Pa 1118   Apt 18, ex* aeterne *corr. Pa 1871*   dei:et dei *Pa 1118* deus *ex* dei *corr. Pa 887*

B verum:*primam litteram om. Apt 18,* verbum *Pa 1084b*   vero:verum *Pa 1133   Pa 887*

C optima:optimam *Pa 1120*   perpetuae:perpetua *PaA 1169   Pa 1177*
  Pa 1177 sec.   Pa 1240   Pa 1135   Pa 887   Pa 1871   Pa 1118   Vro 107
  Mod 9, perpetuam *Pa 1137   Pa 1120   Pa 1084b*, perspicue *Apt 17   Apt*
  17 sec.   concedens:conced *Pa 1240*, conce *marg. absc. Pa 1136*, con-
  cede *PaA 1169   Pa 1132   Pa 1133   Pa 1134   Pa 1137   Pa 1120   Pa*
  1119   Pa 1871, concedas *Lo 13*, concedat *Pa 1084b   Pa 887*, concedat *ut*
  videtur Pa 1118, concedat ad *Pa 903*, concedens . . . vitae *propter detrimen-*
  tum desunt Lei 60

I dicens:indice prodiit *ut videtur Pa 887*

EXAMPLE 6. CT IV, 51-52

26a versio I
Agnus dei qui tollis peccata mundi, miserere nobis.

A Fulgida qui regnas
in maiestate,
tute nobis tribue
semper laudare.

Agnus dei qui tollis peccata mundi, miserere nobis.

B Alpha et O,
cui tripudiant
agmina sanctorum,
aeterna nobis
largire gaudia.

Agnus dei qui tollis peccata mundi, miserere nobis.

C Ipse ad patriam
nos perduc atque
verae laetitiae
gaudia. Amen.

ABC Vat 602   MC 546   Ben 34   Ben 35

B aeterna ... gaudia:atque omnia *Ben 34*, iocunda tu nobis fac de tuo auxilio
semper gaudere *Ben 35*
C nos:nobis *Ben 34   Ben 35*   perduc atque:perducat *Ben 34*   verae ...
Amen *non legitur Ben 35*, ubi est vera laetitia atque gaudia *Ben 34*

Schildbach *95;* Cf. *Te Deum;* Voir p. 263 s et planche XXXII.

A *tute* peut s'interpréter de trois façons : 1. comme *tu* renforcé; 2. comme
tu te : « Que tu nous donnes de te louer à jamais »; 3. comme un adverbe :
« Que tu nous donnes de faire louange toujours en sécurité. »

B *Alpha et O* cf. *Apc.* 1,8   21,6   22,13 *agmina sanctorum* cf. *ICL 475; CT* II
37,6 et 72,1.

26b versio II

Agnus dei qui tollis peccata mundi, miserere nobis.

D O lucis splendor,
angelorum cui canit concentus,
igne cor nostrum tuo adure, redemptor.

Agnus dei qui tollis peccata mundi, miserere nobis.

A Fulgida qui regnas in maiestate,
tute nobis tribue semper laudare.

Agnus dei qui tollis peccata mundi, miserere nobis.

B Alpha et O,
cui tripudiant agmina sanctorum,
iocundos nos fac de praemio aeterno.

DAB Pa 1235   Vce 161   To 18   Mod 7
ABD Mza 77

D canit:canet *To 18*   concentus:concentu *Vce 161 Mod 7*   redemptor:
red] emptor *non legitur Vce 161*

A maiestate:trinitate *Vce 161*   *Mod 7*   tute . . . semper *non legitur Vce 161*
laudare:laudere *Vce 161*, largire *Mod 7*

B cui . . . aeterno *non legitur Vce 161*   tripudiant:tripudiat *Mod 7*
sanctorum:superna *Mod 7*   nos:nos nos *Mod 7*   fac *om. To 18*
praemio aeterno:praemiis aeternis *Mza 77*, praemiis aeternis *ut videtur To 18*
praemia aeterna *Mod 7*

Schildbach 95 var. 1 Mza 77   Pa 1235   Vce 161   To 18, 96 Mod 7;
Voir planches X et XI.

D Cf. *Lc.* 24, 32.

B Voir 26a; Dans la leçon de Mod 7, *agmina superna* est au singulier, cf. Elf-
ving p. 13.

C Voir 26a.

EXAMPLE 7. CT IV, 110–112: Oxford, Bodl. MS 775; CT IV, 136: Paris, Bibl. Nat.
MS lat. 1121

Ox 775   env. 1050 [1], Winchester

I: En fascicule.
II: Comme addition.

I
f. 74v   INCIPIUNT LAUDES RESONANT QUAE
         DULCITER AGNUM/QUI VENIENS
         PECCATA PIUS TULIT IMPIA MUNDI

         Quem Johannes in deserto . . .

         Agnus – mundi miserere nobis
         Qui sedes . . . .   Miserere nobis
         Rex regum . . . .   Miserere nobis
         Lux indeficiens . . . .   Miserere.

f. 75   MUNUS ABEL PUERI MEMORANT
         HAEC CANTICA SCI

         Cui Abel . . . .
         Agnus dei.
         Qui gratis . . .   Miserere nobis
         Tu ades corona . . .   Miserere.
         Lumen sine nocte . . .   Miserere nobis

ITEM   Agnus – mundi miserere nobis
         Omnipotens aeterna . . .   Miserere nobis
         Verum subsistens . . .   Miserere.
         Optima perpetue . . .   Miserere nobis

ITEMQUE ALIAE   Agnus – mundi miserere nobis
         Qui patris in solio . . .   Miserere.
         Tu pax tu pietas. . . .   Miserere nobis
         Singula discutiens . . . .   Miserere nobis

f. 75v   Agnus – mundi miserere nobis
         Qui es vera . . . .   miserere nobis
         Qui sedes – excelsis   Miserere nobis
         [2] Agnus – mundi dona nobis pacem [2]

[116]

ITEM

Agnus – mundi miserere nobis
Qui sedes in throno ...   Miserere nobis
²Agnus – mundi dona nobis pacem²

f. 76

II
f. 121v

²Agnus – mundi miserere nobis
Qui sedes ad dexteram ...
Agnus dei qui.²

³Agnus – mundi   Lux lucis ...   Miserere nobis
Agnus – mundi   Verus sanctorum ...   Miserere nobis
Agnus – mundi   Nostra salus ...   dona nobis pacem³

¹ Selon Holschneider p. 24, Ox 775 est une copie anachronique d'une source qui date de l'époque 978 à 984.
² Addition au vieux répertoire du ms., contemporaine de la compilation du ms. (?). Voir p. 254 s.
³ Addition du XIIᵉ siècle; Cf. Planchart I p. 284; Voir planche XIV.

Pa 1121   994–1031, Limoges, S. Martial

Parmi les tropes du propre avec des antiennes de fraction.

f. 4   ANTE COMMUNIONEM AN(TIPHONA)   (Emitte spiritum ...)
f. 4v   AD AGNUS DEI   Redemptor mundi ...
(Nat. III)   Agnus – mundi miserere nobis
                                                  Qui sedes ...   Miserere nobis
                                                  Rex regum ...   Miserere.

f. 14   (Venite populi.)
(Resurr.)   TROPHI AD AGNUS DEI   Pro cunctis deductus ...
f. 14v   Agnus – mundi miserere nobis
                                                  Antiquus plastor ...   Miserere.
                                                  Nostrorum criminum ...   Miserere.
                                                  Priorum spes antiqua ...   Miserere.
                                                  Decus angelorum ...   Miserere.

EXAMPLE 8. CT IV, 182–183: Roma, Bibl. Casan. MS 1741; CT IV, 189: Monte Cassino MS 546

RoC 1741   fin du XIe s., Nonantola

En fascicule après le Sanctus avant un fascicule des antiennes de fraction.

f. 41v

Agnus – mundi   *Miserere nobis*
Qui sedes . . . .   *Miserere.*
Rex regum . . .   *Miserere.*
Lux indeficiens . . .   *Dona.*

f. 42

Agnus – mundi   *Miserere nobis*
Omnipotens aeterna . . .   *Miserere.*
Verum subsistens . . . .   *Miserere.*
Optima perpetue . . .   *Dona.*

f. 42v

Agnus – mundi   *Miserere nobis*
Tu deus et dominus . . .   *Miserere.*
In sede aeterea . . . .   *Dona.*

f. 43

Agnus – mundi   *Miserere nobis*
Suscipe deprecationem . . .   *Miserere.*
Qui sedes – patris   *Dona.*

Agnus Dei   *Qui tollis – mundi miserere nobis*
Ad dexteram . . .   *Qui tollis.*
Quos tuo sancto . . .   *Qui tollis.*
Ut te ducente . . . .   *Qui tollis.*

f. 43v

Agnus Dei   *Qui tollis – mundi miserere nobis*
Exaudi domine . . .   *Qui tollis.*
Tuam domine . . .   *Qui tollis.*
Largitor pacis . . . .   *Qui tollis.*

f. 44

Suscipe – filius dei
Agnus.
Qui sedes ad dexteram ...
Agnus.

f. 44v

Agnus – mundi   *Miserere nobis*
Salus et vita ...   *Miserere.*
Supplicum preces ...   *Dona.*

Agnus – mundi miserere nobis
Alleluia alleluia
Agnus – mundi miserere nobis

IN FRAC(TIONE) IN NAT(IVITATE) D(OMINI)   (Emitte angelum tuum ...)

f. 45   IN FRAC(TIONE) IN SABBATO SCO.   (Hic est agnus ...)

f. 46   IN FRAC(TIONE) IN PASCHA   (Corpus Christi ...)

IN FRAC(TIONE) IN S. SILV(ESTR)I   (Angeli circumdederunt ...)

MC 546   fin du XIIe s. – début du XIIIe s., Monte Cassino

En fascicule.

f. 69

Agnus – mundi miserere nobis   Ad dexteram patris ...
Agnus.   Quos tuo sacro ...
Agnus.   Rex regum deus ... Amen

f. 69v[1]

Agnus – mundi miserere nobis   Salus et vita ...
Agnus.   Supplicum preces ...
Agnus.   Conditor mundi ... Amen

Agnus – mundi miserere nobis   Fulgida qui regnas ...
Agnus.   Alpha et O ...
Agnus.   Ipse ad patriam ... Amen

Agnus – mundi miserere nobis

EXAMPLE 9. CT IV, 105–107: Sankt Gallen, Stiftsbibl. MS 382

SG 382¹ début du XIe s. Sankt Gallen

SG 382 add. XIIIe s., Sankt Gallen

Tous les tropes de l'Agnus Dei se trouvent dans la partie plus récente du ms.

I: Comme addition.

II: En fascicule.

I:

p. 54		²Agnus dei.		
		Danielis prophetia . . .	Agnus — mundi	Miserere nobis
		Iam descendit . . .	Agnus — mundi	Miserere nobis
		Vitam confert . . .²	Agnus — tollis	Dona nobis pacem

II:

p. 64	IN SUMMIS FESTIVITATIBUS			
p. 65	VERSUS SUPER			
	AGNUS DEI	Plasmator rerum . . .	Agnus dei mundi	Miserere nobis
		Pro nostris natus . . .	Agnus dei.	Miserere nobis
		Surgens scandisti . . .	Agnus dei.	Dona nobis pacem
	ITEM ALII VERSUS	Qui resides caelis . . .	Agnus — mundi	Miserere nobis
		In nostris festis . . .	Agnus — mundi	Miserere nobis
		In te speranti . . .	Agnus — mundi	Dona nobis pacem
	ITEM ALII VERSUS	Iustus Abel . . .	Agnus — mundi	Miserere nobis
	IN EPIPH(ANIA) ET	Tu quem Johannes . . .	Agnus — mundi	Miserere nobis
	IN NAT(IVITATE) S. IOHANNIS	Christe patris . . .	Agnus — qui.	Dona nobis pacem
p. 66	ITEM ALII VERSUS	Omnipotens pater . . .	Agnus — mundi	Miserere nobis
		Christe redemptor . . .	Agnus dei.	Miserere nobis
		Magnus et magnificus	Agnus — qui.	Dona nobis pacem
	ITEM ALITER	Cuius magnitudinis . . .	Agnus — mundi	Miserere nobis
		Qui dominaris . . .	Agnus — mundi	Miserere nobis
		Qui ultima tempora . . .	Agnus — qui.	Dona nobis pacem
	ITEM ALITER	Patris factus hostia . . .	Agnus — mundi	Miserere nobis
	IN PASCHA	Qui nos tuo sanguine . . .	Agnus — mundi	Miserere nobis
		Nostris cunctis hostibus . . .	Agnus — qui.	Dona nobis pacem

	Agnus dei	Text	
IN PENTECOSTEN	Agnus – mundi	Veni tuos visita . . .	*Miserere nobis*
	Agnus dei.	Veni salus gentium . . .	*Dona nobis pacem*
ITEM ALITER	*Agnus dei.*	Fons indeficiens . . .	*Miserere nobis*
	Agnus dei.	Auctor summe . . .	*Miserere.*
	Agnus dei.	Pax aeterna . . .	*Dona nobis pacem*
	Agnus – mundi miserere nobis		
	Agnus – mundi dona nobis pacem		
p. 68	*Agnus dei mundi*	Maria videns angelum . . .	*Miserere.*
	Agnus dei.	Per virginalem filium . . .	*Miserere.*
	Agnus dei.	Maria Iesum generat . . .	*Dona.*
	[3]*Agnus dei.*	Passio Christe tui . . .	*Miserere.*
	Agnus dei.	Hi sunt salvati . . .	*Miserere nobis*
	Agnus dei.	Fac nos pace frui . . .	*Dona nobis.*[2]
p. 69	[4]*Agnus – mundi*	Iesu summi fili . . .	*Miserere nobis*
	Agnus.	Iesu ductor pie . . .	*Miserere nobis*
	Agnus – qui.	Iesu tuis laudibus . . .	*Dona nobis pacem*[4]
		[5]Vulnere mortis . . .	
		Inviolatae virginis . . .	
		Sanguinis unda . . .[5]	
p. 81	*Agnus dei.*	Mortis dira ferens . . .	
		Ad vitam surgens . . .	
		Caelos ascendens . . .	
	Agnus dei.	Qui de caelis . . .	
	Agnus dei.	Qui Mariam elegisti . . .	
	Agnus dei.	Praesta nobis . . .	

[1] Voir SG 484 note 1.

[2] Insertion faite par une autre main entre le *Sanctus* et l'*Alleluia*.

[4] Suivi du *Sanctus* de « *festi Marie Virg.* »

[5] Ecrit par la même main que *Danielis prophetia?*

EXAMPLE 10. CT II, 19–20

4

V Amauit eum dominus et ornauit eum, stolam gloriae induit eum.

1 Dicat nunc ouans tibi Christe (exordium)   ⎤
2 Amator piorum dominus sanctum (intercalatio) ⎦ Pa 1084 Wo 79 Apt 18

1 Dicat nunc ouans tibi Christe (exordium)   Pa 776

3 Gloriosa dies celebris et sollemnitas (exordium) ⎤
4 Et ornamentis sacris perornauit (intercalatio)   ⎬ Ox 222 Vro 107 Ivr 60
5 Arma tyrannica sanctus (exordium)   ⎦

6a Sol et luna Christo domino seruite (exordium) ⎤ Mod 7
7 Et ornans caritate fide spe (intercalatio)   ⎦

8 Alleuemus domino odas (exordium)   ⎤
9 Et ornans caritate ... inclitae (exordium)   ⎬ RoA 123
10 Laudes concinent deuotae (exordium)   ⎪
6b Sol et luna Christo domino seruite (exordium) ⎦

11 O rex cunctorum salus aeterna (exordium)   ⎤ Ben 34
12 Stolam gloriae Christe tuis fidis (intercalatio) ⎦

1 **Alleluia.**
  Dicat nunc ouans tibi, Christe deus, ecclesia,
  quam tu proprio lauisti sanguine purificans
  quamque semper emundans beatificas,
  fac manere gloriosam   5
  nunc atque in aeterna saecula.
  Pa 1084 Pa 776 Apt 18 Wo 79

2 **Amauit eum dominus**
  *Ama*tor piorum *dominus*
  sanctum istum coronauit, perpetim gloriosum,
  stola quippe sanctitatis ornando,
  tropheoque castitatis comendo,   5
  caelestis eum ueste *gloriae*
  induit iocunditatis atque perpetuae,
  in qua sine fine congaudet
  cum sanctorum agmina,
  quibus ipse deus atque rex,   10
  pater, uerbum atque flamen,
  condonat regnum nunc et in aetern*um*.
  Pa 1084 *Apt 18* Wo 79

ante alleluia *add fort recte* Nunc atque semper canat omnis terra *Wo 79*   2

dicat nunc nunc *Wo 79*, dica *Apt 18*   deus ecclesiae *Pa 1084 Pa 776 Apt 18*

3   quam tu: quanto *Pa 1084 Pa 776*   lauisti: iusti *Pa 776*   sanguinem *Pa 1084*

purificas *Apt 18*   4   quamque semper emundans *om Pa 776*   emundans:

purificans *Pa 1084, om Apt 18*   beatificat *Pa 1084 Pa 776*   5   manere fac

Wo 79   manere: munere *Pa 776*   gloriosa *Pa 776 Apt 18*   6   nunc in

aeternum atque in saecula *Pa 1084*, nunc atque in aeternum in secula *Pa 776*, nunc

quoque in aeterna saecula *Apt 18*, nunc in aeuum et in saecla *Wo 79*

1   *om Pa 1084 Wo 79*   2   amans sancta *ante* amator *add Wo 79*   3   *pro*

hoc versu habet et ornauit eum *Apt 18*   istum: hunc rite *Wo 79*   4   stolam

Apt 18   ornando: commendo *Apt 18*   5   strofioque *ut vid Apt 18*   co-

mendo: ornando *Apt 18*   6   caelestium uirtutum gloriae *Pa 1084 Wo 79*   7

in iocunditatis atque perpetuum et *Pa 1084*, induit iocunditatis quoque perpe-

tua *Apt 18*, in supernis in iocunditatis atque in perpetuum et *Wo 79*   8   congau-

dens *Pa 1084 Wo 79*, gaudet *Apt 18*   9   cum turma sanctarum *Wo 79*   9-10

atque rex pater uerbum *iter Apt 18*   11   atque fagme *Pa 1084*, et suum

Wo 79, adque flamme *Apt 18*   12   condonat: congaudens *Pa 1084*, congaudet

Apt 18   regnans nunc et in aeuum *Apt 18*, regnum et nunc clarum et in aeternum

ubi nos petimus patens ingressum *Wo 79*

EXAMPLE 11. CT IV, 75–76

Ia   Cui Abel iustus atque sanctus
        agno agnum obtulit immaculatum,
        Agnus dei qui tollis peccata mundi, miserere nobis.

A Qui gratis moderaris cuncta,
   semper indeficiens rex,   *miserere nobis.*

B Tu ades corona confitentium, deus, *miserere nobis.*

C Lumen sine nocte, virtus angelorum
   manens semper piissime, eia,   *miserere nobis.*

    . . .

Ib   Quem Iohannes in Iordane baptizavit
        ovans et dicens : ecce

A   Pa 10508 sec.

IaABC Cdg 473   Ox 775   Pa 13252 $\Big\}=\alpha$

IbACB Du 6   Pa 10508

ACB Lo 13   Ma 288   Ma 289

ABC Pa 1084b   Pa 1137   Pa 909   Pa 1120   Pa 887   Pa 903   Pa 1871 $=\beta$

Miserere super nos (36a) *introductio ante* ABC *ut videtur in Pa 1120 Pa 887*

A cuncta ... rex *om Pa 10508 sec.*

B tu ades:tua *vel* tuam des β, quam des *Lo 13*   corona:coronam *Lo 13*   *Pa*
   909   Pa 1120   Pa 887   confitentium:confitentum *Cdg 473   Ox 775*
   Du 6   Pa 10508   Pa 13252   Pa 1084b   Pa 1871, confitentem *Pa 909*
   Pa 1120, confitencium *ex* confitentem *corr. Pa 887,* confitentibus *Lo 13*

C manens:deus β   eia *om.* β, ea *ut videtur Lo 13*

EXAMPLE 12. CT IV, 59–61

38a **versio I**

A O AMNOS TU THEU
   O ERON TAS AMARTIAS TU COSMU ELEYSON IMAS.
   . . .

L *Agnus dei qui tollis peccata mundi, miserere nobis.*

A   SG 484   SG 381   SG 376   SG 378   Pa 9449   Ka 15

AL   Ox 27

ALA Wi 1888   Be 11

LLALL SG 380

A amnos:annos Pa 9449   tu theu:thu theu *Ka 15*   o eron tas amartias:
o erontas amartias *ut vid   SG 484*   oe rontas amartias *SG 376*
SG 378   SG 380, o erontas amarthias *Wi 1888*, o eruntas amarthias *Pa
9449*   to cosmu:tu chosmu *Pa 9449*, thu chosmu *Ka 15*, tu cosmoy *Ox
27*   eleyson:eleison *SG 484   SG 380*   elyson imas:elyso nymas *Ox
27   imas:ymas   Wi 1888*

38 b   versio II

A O AMNOS TU THEU O YO TU PATROS
   O ERON TIN AMARTIAN TU COSMU ELEYSON YMAS.
   . . .
L *Agnus dei*, fili patris, *qui tollis peccata mundi, miserere nobis.*
   . . .
B Lux indeficiens, pax perpetua
   omniumque redemptio, Christe,
   . . .
C AGIOS AGIOS AGIOS KYRRIOS O THEOS SABAOTH
   PLIRIS O URANOS KE I GI TIS DOXIS ⟨SU⟩
   OSANNA EN TIS IPSISTIS.
   EULOGIMENOS O ERCHOMENOS EN ONOMATI KIRRIU
   OSANNA EN TIS IPSISTIS.

AL   Pa 909   Pa 1120   Pa 1834   Pa 1119
LAC   Pa 1871
LAB *et* C   *post rubr.* ITEM *add.* Pa 1084c

A amnos:annos *Pa 1119*, amno *Pa 909*   o yo:o io *Pa 1119*, o hyos *Pa 1084c
Pa 1871*   o eron tin amartian:o eruntin amartian *Pa 1084c*, o erontin
amartian *Pa 1871*, o erontas amartian *Pa 909*   o erontas amarcian *Pa 1120
Pa 1119, Pa 1834*   tu cosmu:tu chosmu *Pa 1834*   eleyson:eleison *Pa
1084c   Pa 1120   Pa 1119*, eleson *Pa 909* ymas:imas *Pa 1084c   Pa 1120   Pa 1119*
L fili:filius   *Pa 1084c   Pa 1871*   qui *detrimento deest Pa 1834*
C kyrrios:kyryo *Pa 1871*   o uranos:oranos *Pa 1084c*   ke i gi tis:keigitis
codd.   su *om. Pa 1084c   Pa 1834*   ipsistis eulogimenos:ypsistis eulogimenos *Pa 1871*   o erchomenos:oerchomenos *codd.*   kirriu:kiriu
Pa 1871

EXAMPLE 13. Sankt Gallen, Stiftsbibl. MS 484, pp. 244–245

Agnus dei miserere nobis ppter

misericordiam tuam

Agnus dei qui tollis peccata

mundi miserere nobis.

Agnus dei miserere nobis eia eia

EXAMPLE 14. Sankt Gallen, Stiftsbibl. MS 381, p. 311

311

Rex regum gaudium angelorum deus. Miserere

Agnus dei qui tollis peccata mundi

Lux indeficiens pax perpetua omnium,

redemptio sancta. Miserere nobis.

QUOMODO

Agnus dei qui tollis peccata mundi

miserere nobis. ALITER

Agnus dei qui tollis peccata mundi

miserere nobis. GRECUM

O ymnos michen deromnas amarius in

cosmu eleyson unus.

Agnus dei qui tollis peccata mundi

miserere nobis.

Agnus dei miserere nobis propter mise-

cordiam tuam.

EXAMPLE 15. Paris, Bibl. Nat. MS lat. 1084, f. 143

EXAMPLE 16. CT III, 112

Hodie namque Christo
cum humana lingua coma servivit arboria
et quamvis fuerit rigida
misit regi spolia arbore flexu
osanna
DOMINE NE LONGE   Palm intr 9

    Pa 1084c Pa 1118
    Christo: Christus *mss*   coma servivit arboria: cum asserviris et armonica *Pa*
    1084c cum aserviris et armonia *Pa 1118*   fuerit: fieri *Pa 1084c* fierit *Pa 1118*
    rigida: frigida *mss*   regi: regis *Pa 1118*   arbore flexu: arbor et fluxu *Pa 1118*
    sn Pa 1084c

EXAMPLE 17. CT III, 99

Ex omni gente cogniti
Graecis Latinis barbaris
cunctisque admirantibus
linguis loquuntur omnibus
SPIRITUS DOMINI   Pent intr 83

    Vol 39 Vat 4770 Ben 35 Ben 38 Ben 39 Ben 40
    omni: omnes *Vat 4770*   gente: gentes *Vat 4770 Ben 38* gentem *Ben 40*
    cogniti: cognoti *Ben 35*   Graecis: Greci *Ben 39* Greciis *Ben 40*   om]nibus
    SPIRITUS DOMINI *deest parte pag absc Vol 39*   SPIRITUS DOMINI: ET
    HOC QUOD *Ben 35 Ben 38*
    sn Vat 4770
    Walpole 116,21–14; *cf* Act 2,7–12; quod est probatum . . .

NOTES

1. Gauthier, L., *Histoire de la poésie liturgique au moyen âge. Les tropes*. Paris (1886), 3rd impression, 1969.

2. *Analecta Hymnica Medii Aevi*, ed. Blume, C., Dreves, G. M., and Bannister, H., Leipzig (1886-1922), *Tropen des Missale im Mittelalter*, Vols. 47 and 49.

3. The following volumes are already published in the series of CORPUS TROPORUM: *Corpus Troporum I, Tropes du propre de la messe, 1, Cycle de Noel*. Acta Universitatis Stockholmiensis, Studia Latina Stockholmiensia XXI. ed. Ritva Jonsson et al. Stockholm 1976.
   Corpus Troporum II, Prosules de la messe 1, Tropes de l'Alleluia, Acta Universitatis Stockholmiensis. Studia Latina Stockholmiensia XXII, ed. Olof Marcusson, Stockholm 1976.
   Corpus Troporum III, Tropes du propre de la messe 2, Cycle de Pâques, Acta Universitatis Stockholmiensis, Studia Latina Stockholmiensia XXV, ed. Gunilla Björkvall. Gunilla Iversen, Ritva Jonsson, Stockholm 1982.
   Corpus Troporum IV, Tropes de l'Agnus Dei, Edition critique d'une étude analytique, Acta Universitatis Stockholmiensis, Studia Latina Stockholmiensia XXVI, ed. Gunilla Iversen, Stockholm 1980.
   The following volumes are now under preparation:
   Corpus Troporum V, Les deux tropaires d'Apt, Inventaire, édition et analyse, G. Björkvall, Studia Latina Stockholmiensia.
   Corpus Troporum VI, Tropes du propre de la messe 3, Les fêtes des Saints, ed. *Ritva Jonsson*.
   Corpus Troporum VII, Tropes du propre de la messe 4, Les fêtes mariales, ed. Ann-Katrin Johansson.
   Corpus Troporum VIII, Tropes du Sanctus, ed. Gunilla Iversen.
   see also: G. Iversen (ed.) *Research on Tropes*, Proceedings of a symposium organized by the Royal Academy of Literature, History and Antiquities and the Corpus Troporum. Stockholm, June 1-3 1981, Stockholm, 1983.

4. Cf. Huglo, M., *Aux origines du Tropaire-Prosaire*, Nordiskt Kollokvium IV i Latinsk Liturgiforskning, Oslo (1978), pp. 53-56, English translation in *The Journal of Plainsong and Medieval Music Society* (London) II (1979), pp. 11-18; Krogh-Rasmussen, N., *Les Pontificaux du Haut Moyen Age. Genèse du libre liturgique de l'Evéque*. Vols. I-III unpublished dissertation, Paris (1977) III, pp. 431-439, to be published in *Spicilegium Sacrum Lovaniense*.

5. In this particular case I am grateful to Professor Leo Treitler, State University of New York at Stony Brook, who has confirmed the division of the phrases by means of the notation.

6. See *CT* IV, pp. 210-224.

7. See e.g. Reynolds, L. D. and Wilson, N. G., *Scribes and Scholars, A Guide to the Transmission of Greek & Latin Literature*, Oxford (1868) 2nd ed. 1974, also offering a brief bibliography of textual criticism.

8. Cf. Vogel, C., *Introduction aux sources de l'histoire du culte chrétien au Moyen-*

Age, Spoleto (1965) 1975, pp. 45f.; *Corpus Troporum I*, p. 19; Ottosen, K. "La Problématique de l'edition des textes liturgiques latins," *Classica et medievalia, Francisco Blatt Septuagenario dedicatá*, Copenhagen (1973), pp. 541-556; Björk, D., "On the Dissemination of Quem quaeritis and the Visitatio sepulchri and the Chronology of Their Early Sources," *Comparative Drama*, vol. 14, nr. 1 (1980), pp. 46-69; Planchart, E. A., "The transmission of medieval Chant," *Cambridge Yearbook, Early Music History*, vol. 7 (1981).

9. See *Corpus Troporum IV*, p. 293f.

10. Cf. Piltz, A., Review of the *Corpus Troporum*, I and II, *Archivum Latinitatis Medii Aevi* (1980), pp. 179-192.

11. Cf. *Corpus Troporum I*, pp. 38-39.

12. Commentary of *Hodie namque Christo* and *Ex omni gente* in *Corpus Troporum*, III:
Hodie namque Christo: Nous nous sommes permis d' "améliorer" le texte de cet élément, visiblement abîmé, d'après ce qui est probablement sa source, l'antienne pour *Dom. in Ramis CAO 3107: Hodie namque Christo cum humana lingua coma servivit arboria et quamvis fuerint rigida miserunt Regi spolia arborum flexus Hosianna* (Pa 17436, l'antiphonaire de Compiègne). *Hodie namque Christus cum humana lingua comam serviret arboria et quamvis fuerit rigida misit Regis spolia arboris flexu, Hosianna* (Verona XCVIII). Nous proposons la traduction suivante: "Aujourd 'hui les chevelures (= feuilles) des arbres ont servi le Christ, avec la langue humaine: et bien qu'elles fussent rigides, elles ont, grâce à une flexion de l'arbre, donné au Roi sa proie."
Ex omni gente: Ce texte est le sixième strophe de *Iam Christus astra ascenderat* dont Walpole donne la version suivante:

> Ex omni gente cogitur
> Graecus, Latinus, Barbarus
> cunctisque admirantibus
> linguis loquuntur omnium.

Pourtant, il donne aussi les variantes *cogniti et omnibus*, et, dans le commentaire, il explique: "The variant *cogniti Graecis* (wherein the ablatives or datives of 22 are in a peculiar kind of apposition with ex o. gente, "men of all nations") would come from Acts II,11 and the thought is expressed in line 23 *cunctisque admirantibus*. *Cogniti* would mean "understood", but this would be a strange use of the word". Cependant, nous n'avons dans nos manuscrits que la forme *cogniti* et nous devons la retenir, puisqu'elle donne un sens acceptable:" compris par toutes les nations".

13. Björkvall, G., *Corpus Troporum V, Les deux tropaires d'Apt*, (in preparation).

14. For a short bibliography see e.g. D. Björk, *op.cit.*

15. The edition of the melodies of the *Agnus Dei* and the *Sanctus* tropes is being prepared by Charles M. Atkinson, of Ohio State University, Columbus; cf. Weiss, G., Die Monumenta Monodica Medii Aevi, *Nordiskt Kollokvium* III i *Latinsk Liturgiforskning*, (Helsingfors) 1975, pp. 111-122.

Editing Medieval Commentaries:
Problems and a Proposed Solution

Marjorie Curry Woods

[The] commentary proves through its very existence that a given author or text was carefully read and studied at a given time and place and, in many instances, that such texts or authors were used as textbooks or readings in some school or university. For the commentary as a literary genre is the product of the class lecture, and in its form, method, and content, it discloses the intellectual interests of the commentator and his approach to his text. Commentaries often indicate the connections in which a given author was read or studied, that is, the branches of learning which he served to illustrate, and the other ancient or medieval authors associated with him. The study of the commentaries will thus throw much light upon the curricula of the schools and universities in which they originated.[1]

Thousands of manuscripts of medieval commentaries have survived; thousands more have been lost. Although some of these were written by individual readers for their own use, most were produced as notes for the study of texts in medieval schools and universities. This group includes commentaries on philosophical, theological, legal, literary, grammatical, astronomical, mathematical, and rhetorical texts.

The relationship between text and commentary was extremely close during the medieval period. Most commentaries were lemmatic: the text was broken up into short phrases for glossing, and these phrases (the lemmata) provide the organizing principle for the commentary. In addition, commentaries often were written around the text, in wide margins which had been left specifically for this purpose. In other manuscripts, the text was written in sections, interrupted by groups of glosses on those particular sections. Thus the text and commentary were read together, with constant reference to each other. (A commentary copied separately, as a text on its own, was usually a particularly important one.) When we realize that the beautiful and unglossed display manuscripts of texts (which have received much modern attention for their aesthetic qualities and legibility) probably had far fewer readers than the unattractive, much-glossed school texts, we can argue that most texts which were commented upon probably were read with a commentary more often than they were read alone. Especially for the twelfth and thirteenth centuries, it is exceptional to find manuscripts of some texts which are not glossed.

Yet, although commentaries have been called "the most important form of scholarly literature of the Middle Ages,"[2] very few of them have been edited or even studied. More than twenty years ago, an international group of scholars began a project called the *Catalogus Translationum et Commentariorum*,[3] with the aim of listing and describing the Latin translations of ancient Greek authors and the Latin commentaries on ancient Greek and Latin authors. A glance at the four volumes so far published reveals both how many medieval commentaries on ancient texts have survived and also how few of them have been examined. The situation is even worse with medieval commentaries on medieval texts, especially literary and rhetorical ones. Ten years ago John Ward could write, "No medieval rhetorical commentary or gloss has yet been fully published,"[4] a statement which is virtually true today. The reasons why medieval commentaries have been neglected may include both the cultural prejudice, stronger in some fields than others, against medieval methods of interpretation and analysis, and the difficulties involved in working with highly abbreviated, technical notes in the margins of manuscripts which, because they were often used as class texts, are worn and generally unattractive. These conditions may indeed have affected attitudes toward commentaries. But there is a more subtle problem which may help to explain why commentaries are more often summarized and described than edited: the uneasy relationship between the kinds of information we may want from an edition of a commentary and the possible methods of editing it.

There are two basic methods of editing texts which have survived in more than one manuscript: the stemmatic method usually associated with the name of Lachmann, and the editing of a single manuscript. Using the stemmatic method,[5] the editor attempts to reconstruct the archetype, the earliest form of the text which can be determined from the extant manuscripts. Reynolds and Wilson have described the theory succinctly:

> Of fundamental importance in stemmatics are the errors which scribes make in copying manuscripts; for these errors provide the most valid means of working out the relationships of the manuscripts. *Special attention is paid to errors of*

omission and transposition [italics mine]. For stemmatic purposes these errors can be divided into (a) those which show that two manuscripts are more closely related to each other than to a third manuscript (conjunctive errors), and (b) those which show that one manuscript is independent of another because the second contains an error or errors from which the first is free (separative errors). . . . On this basis the interrelationships of the various manuscripts and manuscript groups are worked out step by step until, ideally, a stemma [or family tree] of the whole manuscript has been reconstructed.[6]

This stemma illustrates the relationship of the extant manuscripts to the archetype and to each other. Only the readings postulated for the archetype are used in the text of the critical edition; deliberate changes in and corruptions of the text and readings coming from the contamination of one manuscript by another are omitted, although they may be recorded in the critical apparatus.

The stemmatic method of editing assumes that a text as close as possible to the author's original is desired. Editors of classical scholia, which survive in manuscripts chronologically and textually further removed from the original than is commonly the case with medieval commentaries, usually present a critical edition giving the text of the reconstructed archetype.[7] And for some medieval commentaries, such as those with known authors or important places of origin, such an edition would be useful.

But several aspects of the textual transmission of commentaries make the stemmatic method of editing particularly hard to apply to medieval commentaries. 1.) Authorial corrections and revisions make the definition of the original very difficult. "[Medieval] commentaries are lecture notes which their authors are likely to have altered frequently as they repeated their courses before new audiences; they were, moreover, modified by the teachers who made use of them soon after they were published."[8] 2.) Because commentaries are usually written in the margins around the text commented upon, material may be omitted or altered to fit the available space on the page. 3.) A scribe may have deliberately added, altered, or omitted material in a commentary. As Berthe Marti said about Arnulf of Orlean's commentary on Lucan's *Pharsalia*,

> Every *magister* who used or copied Arnulf's commentary felt free to alter it by drawing upon the information which had been accumulated by succeeding generations of interpreters and by them added to the common body of glosses found in the margins of most texts of the poem. He would modify the length and content of the scholia to suit his own purposes. As is the case with most

similar compilations, Arnulf's commentary is found in various forms, some fuller than others. It is impossible to establish with any certainty which ones, among the manuscripts copied almost during his lifetime, may represent the original text, and whether the apparently interpolated texts correspond to revisions made by the author in the course of his teaching career, or again whether other *magistri* or students or scribes are responsible for the additions and omissions.[9]

4.) Because oral transmission is often involved at some stage in the history of a commentary, the use of synonyms and alterations in word order is much more common than in other kinds of texts.

Thus in commentaries the "errors of omission and transposition"[10] so important to the stemmatic method are often deliberate alterations and therefore misleading and unreliable as evidence of textual transmission. As Robert Dale Sweeney has said, ". . . an attempt to construct a stemma based on the presence or absence of various scholia, or to determine, by the mere comparison of manuscripts, whether or not a given passage is 'original,' must fail."[11] These conditions do not in every case preclude the possibility of determining an archetype of a medieval commentary,[12] but they do raise questions about what information and what aspects of the history and development of a text we want from an edition.

When the versions of a commentary vary greatly because of deliberate authorial revision or scribal alteration, when they are in fact "re-edited with almost every transcription,"[13] it is often not possible to construct a stemma, or at least a closed one leading to a single archetype. And if we are interested in how a text was actually taught and interpreted in a classroom, we may be less interested in a reconstructed version which may never have been used in exactly that form than in a specific version from a specific manuscript of the commentary. It has been argued that an edition of a single manuscript is the only way to produce an authentic text of a work which has been affected by deliberate editing or alteration at various stages of its transmission. This argument has, for obvious reasons, seemed more cogent to scholars interested in medieval texts than to those interested in ancient texts whose only surviving versions are medieval.[14]

Reproducing the readings of a single manuscript does provide the modern reader with an authentic medieval text that was written and presumably read in the same form in which we can read it now. And if one manuscript is particularly important (because it was read or owned by an important person, or was copied at or owned by a noted center of learning), the version of the commentary which it contains would be worth editing by itself. Yet those same problems of determining the best manuscripts to use for reconstructing the archetype for a critical edition can also make it difficult to determine what manuscript should be used as the basis for an edition.[15]

But for most of the commentaries which still remain to be edited, neither of these methods will be completely satisfactory. A text constructed by the editor according to the stemmatic method is shorn of the evidence of medieval teaching methods and individual approaches to a text which the more "corrupt" readings provide.[16] On the other hand, an edition of a single manuscript gives us only one version, albeit a superior one. Many modern scholars are interested not just in the original author's commentary or in a particular version, but even more in the general response to a text conveyed by the manuscripts of a commentary studied together as a group, and in the development of attitudes toward the text as they are revealed in the succession of individual manuscripts. It is the discussion of these two aspects of commentaries, general trends and individual readings of particular significance, which makes studies of commentaries so interesting and frustrating.

These problems confronted me when I began working on the commentaries on Geoffrey of Vinsauf's *Poetria Nova*, a text which was written about 1215.[17] Of the almost two hundred surviving manuscripts of this work,[18] about half contain marginal commentaries, and there are other manuscripts containing commentaries copied as separate texts. I decided to begin with an edition of the earliest commentary, an anonymous one surviving in four manuscripts,[19] three from the mid-thirteenth and one from the mid-fourteenth century. Three of the manuscripts contain the commentary written in the margins around a text of the *Poetria Nova*; in one, however, the commentary has been written out separately, as a text in itself.[20]

All four manuscripts contain the same *accessus*, or introduction, and present much the same basic interpretation of the text.[21] The *Poetria Nova* is described as having two structures: first, it is divided into the five parts of rhetoric (invention, disposition, style, memory, and delivery), but it is also itself a rhetorical treatise composed of the necessary parts (*exordium, narratio, divisio, confutatio, conclusio*). The author is described as a rhetor-poet and a teacher; his poem is an-

alyzed as a successful poem and rhetorical treatise as well as a successful teaching text.[22]

But some of the conditions of the composition and transmission of
commentaries which were discussed above have affected each manuscript. Further, although the manuscripts do fall into two groups of
two, each individual manuscript offers unique evidence of different
methods of teaching the *Poetria Nova*. Munich Clm. 4603, for example, concentrates on units of text rather than glosses on individual
words. It is usually fuller in explanation than the other manuscripts
and adds two brief explanatory paragraphs and a short poem on the
Poetria Nova as an epilogue. On the other hand, Vienna MS. 526 gives
only a short introduction to each group of lemmata but devotes more
attention to the specific words in the section. Vienna MS. 2513 is the
most concise of the manuscripts; in its discussion of the tropes and figures it compares the *Poetria Nova* to the *Rhetorica ad Herennium*
more often than do the other manuscripts, a possible indication that
these two rhetorical works were being studied together. The only fourteenth-century manuscript, Vienna MS. 1365, adds important explanatory material and significantly more synonyms and definitions; unfortunately, it breaks off at line 270. In addition, in each manuscript
there are unique statements about different aspects of the *Poetria
Nova* or the nature of poetic discourse.

Since none of the commentaries on this text had ever been edited
and since there was growing controversy about the place of rhetorical
training in the development of medieval literature and criticism, I decided that as much of the manuscript material as possible had to be included in the text of the edition. Munich Clm. 4603 was chosen as the
base text for two reasons: it is one of the earliest manuscripts yet contains one of the fullest commentaries, and its commentary was copied
as a separate text, so that its contents have not been altered because of
limitations of space. There are some readings in the base manuscript
which are clearly misunderstandings or at least less probable readings
than those in some of the other manuscripts. But in order to provide a
text which represents as closely as possible a specific version of the
commentary as it was actually taught, I preserved a reading from the
base manuscript when it represented what the scribe intended, even
when it is clearly contrary to what Geoffrey of Vinsauf intended.

All different or added material found in the other manuscripts is
put in a second column, arranged sequentially when there is material

from more than one other manuscript. Thus all concepts and approaches found in all the manuscripts are included in the text of the edition. Added synonyms have been included when they seem to indicate consistent interest in expanding the students' vocabulary. But summaries and simple changes in choice of words or sentence structure are usually left in the apparatus.

In order that the format be as clear as possible, I have used a double textual apparatus (see illustration): the first part indicates omissions in the other manuscripts of material in the base manuscript and identifies the manuscript sources of the material in the second column;[23] the second part lists variant readings. So that the reader may determine as fully as possible the kinds of changes and errors made in the different manuscripts of the commentary, almost all textual variants are included in the apparatus, except for differences in the order of words or sequence of glosses, unless these affect the sense of the text.[24] To show the fluctuating support in the other manuscripts for readings in the base manuscript, a positive apparatus is used, that is, one which indicates which manuscripts agree with a reading in the base text,[25] as well as which ones disagree.

There are several problems with this method of editing commentaries. Because not all changes in word order are included in the textual apparatus, it is not possible to reconstruct the commentary exactly as it is found in a manuscript other than that used for the base text. Also, the selection of the manuscript to be used as the base will always contain an element of subjective judgement and emphasis. And finally, this method is practical only for commentaries which have survived in a relatively small number of manuscripts, because the second column would become unwieldy if the readings of too many manuscripts had to be included in it.

But the advantages of such an edition outweigh its disadvantages. The reader is given both the complete commentary from a significant manuscript and the textual information needed to construct a stemmatic edition, and much more information as well. For with the interpretive material from all the manuscripts gathered together yet distinct, we can discern both the general approach—the core of the commentary which made it worth copying and adapting—along with the individual variations made for specific purposes, which purposes we may then determine. And because the commentary was useful enough to have been copied, at least partially, a century after it was

Si ex absentia subiecti solius uel solius predicati
imperfecta est oratio, multo magis ex absentia utriusque
sumitur ratio <sicut ibi>: "Principio celum <ac> terras,
camposque liquentes / lucentemque globum <lune Tytaniaque>
5   astra." Hec tota oratio nullam certam habet sententiam
sed respicit ad sequens nomen
       | et uerbum hic, scilicet
"spiritus intus alit." Ut ergo longius sit opus, ponatur
<aliquod> equipollens per circumlocutionem uice nominis
10   et uerbi, ut si <dicendum> esset "Sol oritur," <diceretur>
"Caligo terre scinditur / percussa solis spiculo," et similia.
    <241> TERCIUS EST GRADUUS. Sequitur tercius in
quo agitur de comparatione que duplex est, comparatio
manifesta et oculta.

15   Manifesta comparatio est | Et fit quando, per magnum
quando poeta uolens | notum uel eque notum, res
demonstrare qualitatem rei | minus nota demonstratur, uel
de qua agit conuertitur ad | quando trahitur argumentum
rem similem, ut per partem | a simili uel a maiori uel a
20   notam partem minus notam | minori; comparatio enim est
<demonstret>. Et trahat | rei ad rem collatio et fit
argumentum a simili, | per hec signa: <246> "magis,
                                         | minus, eque";

sicut in Alexandro <ubi> describatur animositas Alexandri
25   quam habuit in pueritia. Inducitur comparatio manifesta
sic: "Qualiter Hircanis si forte leunculus aruis

3-5 Principio...astra et 8 spiritus...alit Verg. Aen.
6.724-26.   26-p. 87.12 dextra Qualiter...effrenus
Gualteri de Castellione Alexandreis 1.49-56 (PL 209.465).

3-10 Principio...esset om. V.   7 et...scilicet PO.   15-
23 dextra Et...eque V.   24-26 ubi...sic om. V.

1-3 Si (Sed P)...sicut ibi (sicut ibi P: sicut in O: om. M)
MPO: uel utrumque V.   absentia M: defectu PO.   uel M:
uel absencia P: uel ex absencia O.   2 ex om. P.   3
sumitur ratio om. PO.   ac O, Verg: et P: om. M.   terras
MO, Verg: -am P.   4 lune Tytaniaque PO, Verg: lucis solis
uibra M.   5 tota om. P.   habet M: demonstrat PO.   7
scilicet om. O.   8 Ut MP: ubi O.   9 aliquod PO: -quid M.
10 dicendum PO: dictum M.   Sol oritur MO: solcantur P.
diceretur P: dicatur M: om. O.   11 spiculo MO: radio V:
speculo P.   11 et similia om. VPO.   12 TERCIUS MPO, Far:
HIC CITIUS V.   EST MVP, Far: HINC O.   GRADUUS MV: -UM
COLLATIO om. O) PO, Far.   12-13 Sequitur...comparatione
MPO: scilicet comparatio V.   12 tercius M: de tercio gradu
P: tercius gradus O.   13 comparatio MP: -ionem O: om. V.
14 manifesta...oculta MV: enim alia oculta alia manifesta PO.
15 comparatio om. O.   17 rei MP: regi O.   19-20 partem...
partem M: rem notam PO.   20-21 minus...demonstret (-strat
M) MP: res que minus est nota demonstretur O.   21 Et trahat
MP: contrahens O.   22 argumentum MP: artem O.   24 sicut
MPO: Vnde V.   ubi PO: ut M.   describatur M: -bitur P:
scribitur O.   animositas MP: audacia O.   25 pueritia sua
P.   26 si MV, Gualt: cum PO.   forte MV, Gualt: fronte PO.

first written, we can see how the presentation of the commentary developed over time. Finally, such an edition allows us to retain and use readings which from a stemmatic perspective are "corrupt," to learn from manuscripts which might otherwise be dismissed as "contaminated," and to go beyond such value judgements to a fuller understanding and appreciation of the intellectual achievement and heritage of an earlier age.[26]

NOTES

1. Paul Oskar Kristeller, ed., *Catalogus Translationum et Commentariorum: Mediaeval and Renaissance Latin Translations and Commentaries; Annotated Lists and Guides* (Washington, D. C.: Catholic University of America Press, 1960—), I, x. For other statements about the importance of commentaries, see Paul M. Clogan, ed., *The Medieval "Achilleid" of Statius* (Leiden: E. J. Brill, 1968), p. x.; B. Bischoff, "Living with the Satirists," in *Classical Influences on European Culture A.D. 500–1500; Proceedings of an International Conference Held at King's College, Cambridge, April 1969*, ed. R. R. Bolgar (Cambridge: Cambridge University Press, 1971), p. 94.

2. Kristeller, "The Scholar and His Public in the Late Middle Ages and the Renaissance," *Medieval Aspects of Renaissance Learning* (Durham, N. C.: Duke University Press, 1974), p. 6.

3. See Note 1.

4. John Oastler Ward, "*Artificiosa Eloquentia* in the Middle Ages: The Study of Cicero's *De Inventione*, the *Ad Herennium* and Quintilian's *De Institutione Oratoria* from the Early Middle Ages to the Thirteenth Century" (Diss. Toronto, 1972), II, 3. In other areas the situation is changing more rapidly; Ward goes on to compare the poor record in the publication of rhetorical commentaries with "the increasing number of published grammatical, dialectical, and theological texts of the Middle Ages" (p. 3); many legal commentaries have been published as well.

5. The standard exposition of this method has been Paul Maas, *Textual Criticism*, tr. Barbara Flower (Oxford: Clarendon Press, 1958), but for a fuller treatment see Martin L. West, *Textual Criticism and Editorial Technique* (Stuttgart: B. G. Teubner, 1973).

6. L. D. Reynolds and N. G. Wilson, "Textual Criticism," *Scribes and Scholars: A Guide to the Transmission of Greek and Latin Literature*, 2nd ed. (Oxford: Clarendon Press, 1974), p. 190.

7. See, for example, the editions of Servius's commentaries on the works of Virgil: G. Thilo and H. Hagan, eds., *Servii Grammatici Qui Feruntur in Vergilii Carmina Commentarii* (Leipzig: Teubner, 1881–1902; rpt. Hildesheim, 1961); E. K. Rand *et al.*, *Servianorum in Vergilii Carmina Commentariorum Editionis Harvardianae* (Lancaster, Pa.: American Philological Association, 1946–65), Vols. II and III; second volume reviewed by Eduard Fraenkel, *Journal of Roman Studies*,

37-38 (1947-48), 131-143; 39-40 (1949-50), 145-154; Paul Charles Burnes, ed., "The Vatican Scholia on Virgil's *Georgics*: Text and Analysis" (Diss. Toronto, 1974). A useful list of editions of commentaries on Latin classical texts is Paul Faider, *Répertoire des éditions de scholies et commentaires d'auteurs latins* (Paris: Société d'Edition "Les Belles Lettres," 1931). Christopher Kleinhenz, in the collection *Medieval Manuscripts and Textual Criticism* (Chapel Hill: Univ. North Carolina Department of Romance Languages, 1976) which he has edited, assumes that for all medieval texts as well, "the intent (generally utopian) of any edition is to recreate or reconstruct the work of the author from existing evidence" ("The Nature of an Edition," p. 273). This volume contains a useful short bibliography.

8. Berthe M. Marti, ed., *Arnulfi Aurelianensis Glosule super Lucanum* (Rome: American Academy in Rome, 1958), p. lx. See also Cora E. Lutz, *Remigii Autissiodorensis Commentum in Martianum Capellam* (Leiden: E. J. Brill, 1962), p. 50; and Clogan, *Medieval "Achilleid,"* p. x. The examples given in these notes are all from editions of commentaries on literary works, but the problems under discussion pertain to commentaries on all kinds of texts.

9. Marti, p. lx.

10. See above pp. 134-135.

11. *Prolegomena to an Edition of the Scholia to Statius* (Leiden: E. J. Brill, 1969), p. 52.

12. As, for example, Sweeney himself has done. See also Louis Holtz's edition of Muridac, *In Donati Artem Maiorem* (Turnhout: Typographi Brepols, 1977).

13. Ludwig Bieler, "The Grammarian's Craft: A Professional Talk," [*Classical*] *Folia*, 10 (1958), p. 8. He is describing medieval school texts in general.

14. The most famous criticism of the stemmatic method is found in Joseph Bédier, "La Tradition manuscrite du *Lai de l'ombre*, Réflexions sur l'art d'éditer les anciens textes," *Romania*, 54 (1928), 161-196; 321-356. Although Bédier was not working with commentaries, he was confronting a similar textual problem in the manuscripts of vernacular poetry: fluid texts. A recent discussion of the two basic approaches to editing is Leonard E. Boyle's "Optimist and Recensionist: 'Common Errors' or 'Common Variations'?" *Latin Script and Letters A.D. 400-900: Festschrift Presented to Ludwig Bieler on the Occasion of His Seventieth Birthday*, eds. John J. O'Meara and Bernard Naumann (Leiden: E. J. Brill, 1976), pp. 264-274.

15. See A. G. Rigg, "Medieval Latin," *Editing Medieval Texts: English, French, and Latin, Written in England: Papers Given at Twelfth Annual Conference on Editorial Problems, University of Toronto, 5-6 November 1976* (New York: Garland Publishing, Inc., 1977), pp. 107-125. The works in the Toronto Medieval Latin Texts series are edited according to these principles; for an unsympathetic reaction see J. B. Hall, "The Editing and Emendation of Medieval Latin Texts: Two Case Histories," *Studi medievali*, ser. 3, 19 (1978), 443-466; and the reply by Rigg, "The Editing of Medieval Latin Texts: A Response," forthcoming in the same journal. For an edition of a single manuscript of both a literary text and the gloss on it, see Clogan, *Medieval "Achilleid"* (also discussed in Hall's article).

Sometimes only one complete manuscript of a medieval commentary has survived; the others are incomplete or in fragments. In such cases the complete manuscript usually becomes the basis for the edition, but corrected by readings from the other manuscripts; see Edmund Taite Silk, ed., *Saeculi Noni Auctoris in Boetii Consolationem Philosophiae Commentarius* (Rome: American Academy in Rome, 1935); and Bengt Löfstedt, ed., *Ars Laureshamensis, Expositio in Donatum Maiorem* (Turnhout: Typographi Brepols, 1977). Of course, some medieval commentaries have survived in only one manuscript: Lutz, ed., *Iohannis Scotti Annotationes in Marcianum* (Cambridge, Mass.: Medieval Academy, 1939); A. K. Clarke and P. M. Giles, eds., *The Commentary of Geoffrey of Vitry on Claudian, "De Raptu Proserpinae"* (Leiden: E. J. Brill, 1973); Haijo Jan Westra, ed., "The Commentary on Martianus Capella's *De Nuptiis* Attributed to Bernardus Silvestris: A Critical Edition" (Diss. Toronto, 1979).

16. An eclectic edition of a medieval commentary, in which "the best readings have been adopted, regardless of their source" (Marti, p. lxxi), gives the reader some of the best information but without its specific contexts.

17. John Pits mentions without date an early edition of this work printed in Vienna by Wolfgang Lazius (*De Illustribus Angliae Scriptoribus* [Paris, 1619], p. 262); cited in *DNB* 20, p. 373. The *Poetria Nova* was published by Polycarp Leyser in *Historia Poetarum et Poematum Medii Aevi* (Magdeburg, 1721), and later separately (Helmstedt, 1724). It was edited next by Edmond Faral in *Les Arts poétiques du XIIe et du XIIIe siècle: Recherches et documents sur la technique littéraire du moyen âge* (Paris: E. Chapman, 1924; rpt. 1962); translated by Margaret F. Nims, "*Poetria Nova*" *of Geoffrey of Vinsauf* (Toronto: Pontifical Institute of Mediaeval Studies, 1967).

18. Based on an unpublished list of the manuscripts of the *Poetria Nova* compiled by Nims while preparing her translation and supplemented by John Conley, University of Illinois at Chicago Circle, who is preparing a critical edition of the *Poetria Nova*. Professor Conley has made available to me his microfilms of a number of the manuscripts. In working on an annotated list of the manuscripts of the commentaries and a study of their contents and manuscript traditions, I have examined approximately a quarter of the manuscripts *in situ*.

19. M: Munich, Bayerische Staatsbibliothek, Clm. 4603, saec. xiii, fols. 130^r–136^r; V: Vienna, Österreichische Nationalbibliothek, MS. 526, saec. xiii, fols. 95^v–111^v; P: Vienna, Österreichische Nationalbibliothek, MS. 2513, saec. xiii, fols. 34^r–62^v; O: Vienna, Österreichische Nationalbibliothek, MS. 1365, saec. xiv, fols. 65^v–75^r. A fifth manuscript, Metz, Bibliothèque Municipale, MS. 516, saec. xiv, was destroyed during World War II. (After preparing this article I discovered another manuscript: Wolfenbüttel, Herzog August Bibliothek Cod. Guelf. 124 Gud. lat., saec. xiii, fols. 1^r–22^r.) The edition of the commentary is available as a dissertation, "The *In principio huius libri* Type A Commentary on Geoffrey of Vinsauf's *Poetria Nova*: Text and Analysis" (Diss. Toronto, 1977); I am finishing a translation of the commentary which will be published with the Latin edition by Garland Publishing, Inc.

20. Munich Clm. 4603 (M).

21. Another manuscript, Paris, Bibliothèque Nationale, MS. Lat. 15135, fols. 163r–200r, contains a shorter version of the *accessus*, but the rest of the commentary is very different.

22. For a fuller discussion of the content of this commentary see Woods, "Literary Criticism in an Early Commentary on Geoffrey of Vinsauf's *Poetria Nova*," forthcoming in *Acta Conventus Neo-Latini Bononiensis*.

23. The concept of this first apparatus is based on Sweeney's insertion of a "running tally of the witnesses for any given passage . . . so as to distinguish carefully between lacunae and omitted scholia and parts of scholia" (p. 96).

24. The word order fluctuates constantly, and indicating these variations would have almost doubled the length of the apparatus. Other variants which are not recorded include orthographical variations, except in proper names and transliterations of Greek words; additional glosses by much later hands; *iste* for *ille* when used as a definite article; careless omissions of letters when they are the only variants; and corrections by the original scribe of careless errors.

25. With the exception of simple omissions and additions in a single manuscript.

26. I would like to thank Virginia Brown, L. E. Boyle, and A. G. Rigg of the University of Toronto and Richard Tarrant of Harvard University for reading and criticizing an earlier draft of this article.

Gatherings of Artists:
The Illustrators of a *Decameron* of 1427

PAUL F. WATSON

MS. Ital. 63 in the Bibliothèque Nationale, Paris, is a text of Boccaccio's *Decameron* copied in Florence during the autumn of 1427 by
Lodovico di Silvestro Ceffini. Ceffini was not a professional scribe
but an amateur, a successful tradesman whose personal copy of the
Decameron this codex was. As Ceffini worked his way through the
text, he left ample room for illustrations. All one hundred stories of
the *Decameron*, the prefatory matter for each of its ten days, and the
narrator's proem, introduction, and conclusion are embellished with
drawings tinted in watercolor. There are one hundred and thirteen of
these. Ceffini's book is thus the only known instance of a *Decameron*
manuscript from Italy with a full complement of illustrations. But its
interest does not stop there. The methods of connoisseurship, as developed by art historians, suggest that many artists labored to illustrate this text. Its physical structure reveals how they organized their
labors. Ceffini's *Decameron* thus offers important insights into the
making of a Quattrocento manuscript, undertaken as a collaborative
enterprise between an amateur scribe and a team of artists.[1]

The illustrations of MS. Ital. 63 speak with one stylistic voice. All
the drawings are characterized by lively but flattened figures, given to
sweeping gesticulations and to grimaces that sometimes verge upon
caricature. Usually the figures dwarf their settings, tiny landscapes
and seascapes, gaily colored buildings, interiors whose scale is that of
a doll's house. The overall effect of Ceffini's manuscript is not unlike
that of the color comics in Sunday morning's newspaper. To illustrate
the *Decameron* the scribe engaged a Florentine draughtsman whose
artistic allegiance lay with the International Gothic style and, in particular, with its local practitioners, Lorenzo Monaco, Gentile da Fab-
riano, and Giovanni Toscani. Of lesser rank than these masters, this
anonimo works in a racy style characteristic of inexpensive Florentine
manuscripts of the early Quattrocento.[2]

Although the illustrations share common conventions for space, figure, and narrative, they vary greatly in quality and in such technical matters as the application of pigment or the modelling of figures. Ceffini's illustrator, therefore, must have been the proprietor of an extensive workshop employing many assistants. Previous scholarship has, in fact, proposed that three artists collaborated on MS. Ital. 63.[3] However, careful examination of the illustrations swells that number to eight.

Some of Ceffini's artists contributed many drawings, some only one or two. The most prolific draughtsman did sixty-three. Throughout he favors quick nervous line and equally swift washes of watercolor, often carelessly applied. Since his drawings begin the program of illustration, he is here designated as Master A (pl. 1). Master B provided eighteen drawings, all framed by yellow borders. Fond of elegant costumes, he attempts to model his figures with rounding strokes of the brush, in distinction to the flatness typical of Master A (pl. 2). The third draughtsman, Master C, tackles crowded compositions, which are further complicated by his fondness for green tapestries introduced whenever the narratives permitted (pl. 3). He contributed a dozen drawings. The same number was executed by Master D, who consistently depicts Boccaccio's characters as dwarfs (pl. 4).

The remaining artists were responsible for only eight illustrations. Three are by Master E, distinguished by heavy-handed modelling and smeared color (pl. 5). Much more delicate are three illustrations by Master F, who models his pretty blonde types with a brush almost dry (pl. 6). Master G contributed only one drawing which stands apart from its companions by virtue of its carefully wrought paint surface and by the artist's predilection for pug noses (pl. 7). Master H does not deserve that professional title; his two drawings are singularly inept, parodies of the manner of Master A (pl. 8).

Connoisseurship paints a picture that is quite untidy. Eight draughtsmen seem excessive and unwieldy, even for a manuscript of the scale of Lodovico Ceffini's *Decameron*. It is not unusual, of course, for many artists to collaborate on the decorations of medieval and renaissance manuscripts. These books, however, tend in the main to be sumptuous works whose fine illumination was spread over long periods of time, artist succeeding artist as the program continued. Ceffini's inexpensive paper volume, however, must have been quickly illustrated as the slapdash character of many of its pictures suggests. Moreover, Master A, the most prolific illustrator, was intermittently active. After working on the first twenty-four folios, he disappears for thirty-six, reappears, disappears again, reappears, in a pattern of seemingly random labor that runs throughout MS. Ital. 63. The quantity of his illustrations, their initial placement, and the authority of his essential conventions, which the others respect, show that he must have been the proprietor of the shop to whom Lodovico Ceffini turned in 1427. How he organized his shop and to what purpose the evidence of artistic style does not show.

The physical structure of MS. Ital. 63 sheds much light on these problems. Measuring 371 by 255 mm., it contains 312 folios. It is divided into twenty-eight gatherings, usually of twelve folios each. Decorated catchwords mark each gathering's end. An examination of the gatherings reveals that each of the four major artists involved was responsible for the illustration of at least one gathering. The relationship of artists and gatherings can be easily tabulated:

Gathering	Artist
1	blank
2	A
3	A
4	H and D
5	D
6	D
7	A
8	A and D
9	A
10	A and D
11	A
12	A
13	A
14	B
15	C
16	C
17	C
18	B
19	A
20	A
21	A
22	A
23	G, F and E
24	A
25	A
26	A
27	B
28	B

The gatherings of MS. Ital. 63 indicate clearly how eight draughts-men, so identified by connoisseurship, were deployed to illustrate Cef-fini's *Decameron* in the fall of 1427. Responsible for fourteen of the gatherings, Master A farmed out the others to shop assistants, and perhaps even to proprietors of other workshops, as he worked with in-creasing haste to complete the task of illustration.

As the explicit inscription on folio 304^r informs us, Lodovico Cef-fini finished copying the text on 9 October 1427. Perhaps he delivered his codex to the shop of Master A unbound, so that the master and his assistants might spread out the gatherings and speed their task. One of the proprietor's closest assistants was Master D, he of the dwarfish im-agination, who collaborated with A on two gatherings. The evidence of placement is confirmed by that of style, since Master D is clearly a follower of the chief illustrator. Master D also subcontracted some of his labor, giving two illustrations in the fourth gathering to inept Mas-ter H, who is also close to Master A's manner. After fol. 28^r, we see no more of Master H; perhaps he was tried and found wanting. Master D retired after fol. 106, to be replaced by Master C, addicted to green hangings, who undertook a cluster of three gatherings. Like his prede-cessors, this craftsman is close to Master A, and presumably was a member of his shop. Master B completed the manuscript, taking on the last two gatherings. His art is so much better than that of A and his satellites that it raises the possibility that he was not part of A's work-shop but rather an independent artist brought in to complete the task of illustration. Further evidence of an autonomous artistic personality is B's habit of framing his pictures in yellow, unlike A and his follow-ers who generally allow their illustrations to invade the page. More-over, the three artists who decorated the twenty-third gathering (Mas-ters G, F, E) are all closer to Master B, especially in their shared fond-ness for richly painted surfaces, than to Master A and his satellites. Perhaps Gathering 28 was subcontracted to Master B, who then gave it to his assistants.

Gathering twenty-three and those preceding it also show signs of mounting haste. Folio 255^v, for example, has Master G's only contri-bution to the manuscript, an illustration of *Decameron*, VIII, 9, set squarely in the space that Ceffini had ruled out for it (pl. 7). Folio 250^v, however, has an illustration by Master A of the same story, in vi-olation of the governing pattern of this program, that each tale receive only a single picture (pl. 1). Perhaps Ceffini simply singled out VIII, 9, as his favorite and demanded two depictions of the discomfiture of Messer Simone. The earlier drawing, however, is squeezed into the *bas-de-page* of folio 250^v, as are several other illustrations, all by Master A, in this gathering. It reads as an afterthought, jotted down by a man working at high speed. It is likely that Master A simply forgot that Ceffini had set a space aside on folio 255^v for a picture in a gathering farmed out to other artists. Slips of this sort, cropping up in the last gatherings of the text, indicate a hectic state of affairs in Master A's shop and suggest that Ceffini must have set a firm deadline, which all hands hurried to meet. Perhaps his deadline could be met only by assembling gatherings of artists.

PLATE 1. Paris, Bibliothèque Nationale, MS. Ital. 63, fol. 250ᵛ by Master A.
Source: Branca, *Decameron*, III, p. 744.

PLATE 2. MS. Ital. 63, fol. 298ʳ, by Master B. *Source:* Branca, III, p. 938.

PLATE 3. MS. Ital. 63, fol. 159ᵛ, by Master C.   *Source:* Branca, II, p. 415.

PLATE 4. MS. Ital. 63, fol. 46ᵛ by Master D.   *Source:* Branca, I, p. 124.

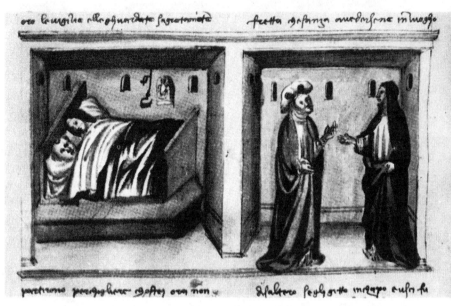

PLATE 5. MS. Ital. 63, fol. 263ᵛ, by Master E.   *Source:* Branca, III, p. 780.

PLATE 6. MS. Ital. 63, fol. 256ᵛ, by Master F.   *Source:* Branca, III, p. 749.

PLATE 7. MS. Ital. 63, fol. 255ᵛ, by Master G. *Source:* Branca, III, p. 742.

PLATE 8. MS. Ital. 63, fol. 25ᵛ, by Master H. *Source:* Branca, I, p. 65.

NOTES

1. The most important studies of the MS. and its scribe are: Tammaro de Marinis, *La biblioteca napoletana dei Re d'Aragona* (Milan, 1947), II, 31–32; Vittore Branca, "La prima diffusione del 'Decameron'," *Studi di filologia italiana*, VIII (1950), 70–71: and Vittore Branca, "Copiste per passione," *Studi e problemi di critica testuale* (Bologna, 1961), p. 72.

2. Most of the illustrations are reproduced in color in Giovanni Boccaccio, *Decameron*, ed. Vittore Branca, 3 vols. (Florence, 1966).

3. Bernhard Degenhart and Annegritt Schmitt, *Corpus der italienischen Zeichnungen* (Berlin, 1968), I, 302–303.

Textology as a Key to the Study of Old Russian Literature and History

JOHN L. I. FENNELL

Before discussing how textology is used by contemporary students of mediaeval Russian literature and history, a word must be said as to what exactly is meant by the term itself. It was first used by the great Pushkinist, Tomashevsky, in 1928 (*Pisatel 'ikniga Ocherk textologii*). He used it, however, simply as a variant of "textual criticism" (*kritika teksta*) and applied it in the main to modern literature as a sort of science of the pre-history of a text from its first MS to its first published version. Nowadays most Russian mediaevalists tend to interpret "textology" somewhat differently.

In nineteenth-century mediaeval Russian studies, textual criticism was used, if at all, simply to recreate the missing prototype of a work by means of an analysis of the surviving MSS. In other words, extant texts were studied in order to find out what the original version, the Ur-text, was like. If of course the original MS. of a work was available, then later versions of it decreased in interest. The results of such textual study may, of course, be extremely useful and important. But it is limited; it is directed at one stage only in the evolution of the work—namely the initial stage. It tends to be synchronic, not diachronic. If Russian literature were static, then this would be fine. But it is not. One must always bear in mind that it is dynamic, permanently on the move, in a state of flux. A work is capable of changing, and does change, from generation to generation, according to the literary tastes or the political inclinations of its copyists, redactors, editors and compilers.

One of the aims of modern textology is to take the study of a work further, to examine it diachronically: in all stages of its development, from its conception to the end of its manuscript tradition. It attempts to trace the history of a literary monument—be it a saint's life, a murder story, a military tale or even a sermon—throughout its numerous redac-

157

tions, and it seeks an explanation not only of *why* the changes took place, but also of how these changes illustrate the mentality of the age or district in which they took place.

Let us assume, for the sake of argument, that a literary monument (*not*, however, a chronicle) has survived in thirty MSS. The first task is of course to establish as nearly as possible the dates of the various MSS. by using specialist knowledge (philology, palaeography, watermarks, etc.). The next stage is to work out the dependence of each copy, or each group of copies, on the others; in other words, to build up a chronological hierarchy of existing MSS. and of hypothetical missing copies of the work. This stage, the purely detective stage, calls for all the expertise of textual criticism: the ability to decide which of two closely similar copies is primary and which secondary—i.e., which is closer to the prototype; it calls for the ability to distinguish between possible types of textual discrepancies: between purely mechanical scribal errors (caused by idleness, ignorance, or physical malaise on the part of the copyist, evidenced by such marginal glosses as "How late and dark it is," "this is a terrible pen," "When will the abbot ring for supper?") and deliberate stylistic or ideological alterations; and—often the hardest of all to identify—semi-involuntary alterations of sense caused by the desire on the part of the scribe to clarify what he fails to understand in the work he is copying. And thirdly, in this stage of his work, the textologist requires the ability to distinguish between interpolations and deliberate omissions: when comparing two similar texts, for example, in which one contains an episode/sentence/word missing in the other, it must be decided whether it was added to the first or subtracted from the second, often a very difficult problem to solve.

The final stage in the textologist's work is perhaps the most important: it is to study the history of the movement of a work throughout the ages—i.e., to study how each successive generation, age or century (and often how different districts) reacted to the work in question or to the events described in it; how the work changed (by adornment, simplification, addition or subtraction), and above all why it was changed. The importance of this stage in the investigation is obvious: it enables one not only to acquire a knowledge of the ideology and literary tastes of successive generations, but also to reconstruct the history of other works which have imperfect or faulty manuscript traditions. By becoming acquainted with the habits and techniques of scribes of different ages and of different political centers, it is possible to recognize patterns peculiar to certain periods, to certain districts, to certain scriptoria and even to certain copyists. For example, the study of the evolution of a number of twelfth- or thirteenth-century literary works during the fourteenth, fifteenth, and sixteenth centuries enables us to discover a pattern in the development of these works; we begin to recognize when certain changes take place, in which periods texts are most likely to be shortened or embellished, when ideological changes occur, etc. Thus in a work written, say, in the thirteenth century but surviving in no MSS. earlier than the fifteenth or sixteenth centuries, it is possible to reconstruct the history of the growth of that work (its "movement," *dvizhenie*, the term used by Russian textologists) with a certain degree of accuracy.

The earliest stage might well be a dry, unemotional narrative typical of the chronicles of the period and virtually restricted to purely technical details (e.g., military details if the work is based on a battle or a siege or a campaign); at a later stage folkloric materials might be added—perhaps a duel fought by semi-mythological *bogatyri*, or some heroic action designed to bolster up the reputation of someone or other's ancestor; and we might also find an overall dramatization and exaggeration of the original account and the heightening of emotional effects—by adding a nought or two to the number of enemy killed, for example, or by introducing new, and completely spurious, personae into the story in order to stress the universality of the event; and finally, if there are any Turkic, Tatar, Moslem, or just plain heathen enemies around, to add a whole string of pejorative epithets and incidents designed to convert them from some sort of divinely protected and protective force sent by God to punish erring Christians (for such was the role attributed to all Pechenegs, Polovtsians, and Tatars from the eleventh through the mid-fourteenth century), and make them into evil, often lecherous, persecutors of Christianity inspired by the Devil: this was the typical literary attitude of the Russians to any easterners in the second half of the fifteenth century, after the fall of Constantinople.

And so, by deduction and patient detective work, it is possible to reconstruct the history of a Tale throughout two or three centuries of its existence. Still more important, it is no longer necessary to accept the more plausible later versions—for they are more plausible in so far as the copyists have gained in skill and technique and editorship—

either as reflecting what in fact happened at the time, or as the reaction of contemporaries to the event.

So far I have been discussing the problems of analyzing the history of finite literary works—i.e., works with a beginning and an end, works which are not being permanently continued in scope and time. In the study of chronicles, however, the problems are far more complex, and textology becomes far more important as a tool to work with. Let me begin my remarks on Russian chronicle-writing by pointing out what I think to be two distinctive features: the first is the somewhat obvious observation that chronicles are continuous works: they have virtually no beginnings—or very rarely beginnings that are traceable to one person, and their ends occur only when there is no one else to continue them or take them a stage further. The chronicle, in other words, is always in a state of flux. The second feature is that the Russian chronicler was not, by and large, just an impartial copying machine who took over his predecessor's work and brought it up to date. He was not Pushkin's majestic figure of Pimen, faithfully copying and recording, "fulfilling the task allocated to [him] by God." The true Russian mediaeval scribe was nothing like this. He was often grossly partial and completely prejudiced. Furthermore, he was, as often as not, an informed and intelligent textual critic in his own right, capable of collating and emending the works of his predecessors. The compiler of the great hypothetical codex of 1448, for example, had at his disposal at least six different chronicles to collate; and his aim was to rewrite history in the spirit of *his* age and to make sense out of what was often contradictory nonsense. The same applies to the compiler of the Moscow codex of 1479. The chronicler worked either independently (though rarely), or in the interest of a politically inclined monastery, or of a lay ruler, or perhaps of a bishop. At most stages of the compilation of a chronicle one can assume tendentious political editing, an attempt to rewrite the history of the past and sometimes deliberately to misinterpret the present.

An example will illustrate this. An event takes place in such and such a principality and is faithfully recorded (or as faithfully as people were capable of recording) by the local prince's own chronicler: twenty years later, when the local prince has been ousted by his brother, the brother's chronicler rewrites the account of the event, reversing the roles of hero and villain; in another twenty years, say, a member of the original princely family manages to come to power, and again the chronicle changes hands and again history is rewritten. And so it goes on. In the end it all has to be disentangled. The only consolation for the modern historian and textologist is that in time the past becomes too remote to interest the contemporary chronicler: the misdeeds of the ruler's great-great-great grandfather may really be of little interest and the distant past may be left in peace. Hence so few editors of the fifteenth or sixteenth centuries bothered to tamper with the earliest Russian chronicle codex, the *Povest' vremennykh let* (Tale of the Bygone Years), and many late chronicle compilations contain identical copies of the history of Kiev up to the beginning of the twelfth century.

The problem of interpreting the chronicles becomes still more acute when there are a number of mutually hostile provincial centers, each with its own chronicle, as is the case in the thirteenth and fourteenth centuries in Russia. Some of these chronicles may have survived, but the majority are merged in the great centralizing historical undertakings of the late fifteenth and sixteenth centuries, when the central Muscovite chronicles simply absorbed the local chronicles of the past, censoring them and altering them where necessary to suit the political purposes of the day.

An example will illustrate just how textology can be used, not only to throw light on the historical event—in this case to discover what actually happened—but also to illustrate contemporary and subsequent reactions to the event in question. In 1327–1328 the first stage of the great conflict between the two most powerful political entities in north-east Russia (the principalities of Tver ' and Moscow) came to a head. After what looks like a spontaneous uprising on the part of the inhabitants of Tver ' and a massacre of all the Tatars who happened to be present in the city at the time, Uzbek, khan of the Golden Horde, sent a punitive force (if not commanded by, then at least advised by, Ivan I of Moscow), which razed Tver ' to the ground and virtually put the principality out of action and off the political map of Russia for the next forty years. Now the fullest and artistically the most satisfying account of the happening, that of the great Moscow codex of 1479, gives the impression of a great organized national struggle, a huge spontaneous patriotic uprising against the Tatars. The Tatars, on the other hand are shown as planning not only to "slaughter all the people of Tver '," but to place their own princes on all the Russian thrones and even to convert the Orthodox Russians to Islam. Ivan I of Moscow, whose actions could hardly be passed over in silence—after all he was the great-great-great grandfather of Ivan III in whose reign the version was compiled—is portrayed as somewhat reluctantly marching with the Tatar reprisal force "on the orders of the khan." Now this is the general picture which has been accepted and repeated by generations of nineteenth-century—and even twentieth-century—historians. Vernadsky, for example, talks about the Tverites being unable to suppress their "anti-Mongol feelings" and Uzbek *ordering* Ivan to lead a punitive expedition against Tver '. The picture is a totally misleading one, but it is precisely the picture which the compiler of the 1479 codex wanted *his* readers to get. However, if one examines the earliest chronicles, some of which are concealed, but fairly clumsily and therefore recognizably, in later compilations, an entirely different picture emerges. The contemporary Tver ' chronicle, for example, shows the Tverites and their prince Aleksandr as completely guiltless, the victims of a huge confidence trick, an act of provocation designed to remove Aleksandr from the scene and to serve as an example for the other principalities—typical, indeed, of Tatar policy in the first half of the fourteenth century. Aleksandr does all he can to calm down the rebellious population and urge moderation. Ivan of Moscow, on the other hand, is shown in the original Tver ' version as cynically exploiting the situation for his own ends. Now the contemporary Muscovite chronicler barely mentions the episode. And not surprisingly, for it hardly reflects to the credit of the house of Moscow. Only the contemporary, and really rather parochial, chronicler of Novgorod, who tends to be more or less impartial where events do not immediately concern the interests of the republic, gives a straightforward and factual account, without apportioning blame to either side. Thus by collating the three contemporary accounts the picture of what happened emerges in quite a different light from that shed by the later work, and it can be reconstructed with reasonable accuracy.

As for the motives of the various protagonists, they are described according to the particular political bias of each district. By studying them we can learn what contemporary reactions were, not only to the massacre and to such questions as who was right, Aleksandr or Ivan, but also towards the Tatars in general. Even the Tver ' source shows a remarkable reluctance to criticize them, an astonishingly neutral attitude to the people who were after all responsible for the destruction of their city; they are treated as a sort of divine punishing force sent by God to chastise the Russians for their sins. The subsequent versions found in many of the later chronicle compilations of the fifteenth and sixteenth centuries show a changing attitude both to the events described and to the Tatars. The later Muscovite sources, as one would expect, justify Ivan and condemn Aleksandr; still later Tver ' sources rehabilitate Aleksandr and obliquely condemn Ivan—obliquely, in order to skirt round the Muscovite censorship. And all show the same hatred of the Tatars as an aggressive, proselytizing, anti-Christian element—all of which is so conspicuous for its absence in the fourteenth century.

In the account of the Mongol invasions of the thirteenth century (1223; 1237–40) one finds the same sort of attitude. The contemporary accounts, which can easily be extricated from the mish-mash of later versions, show a fairly calm approach to what were probably looked upon at the time as steppe invasions on a scale somewhat larger than those of the Polovtsian incursions of the eleventh century. The numbers of troops engaged on either side, the casualties, the towns destroyed, were probably given reasonably soberly: in the initial clash on the Kalka river in 1223, for example, the Russian and Polovtsians numbered probably less than 5000 all told; in 1237–40 the overall numbers were higher, as this time troops from Suzdalia took part. But in any case the numbers were very small indeed. As for losses, it is impossible to make even a rough guess. It looks as though the number of towns captured (not necessarily destroyed) by the Tatars in the major invasion was certainly not more than eighteen, some perhaps little more than villages at the time, and possibly only seven: these are the only ones of which there any details, and certainly they were not all sacked. Indeed, many of the descriptions of the so-called "disasters" employ standard "disaster" clichés which had been used time and again before the earlier crises.

In the subsequent stages all the earliest versions are tidied up and joined together in an attempt to provide a huge picture of universal destruction and misery. All the original petty political animosities of the thirteenth century, which so simplified the Tatars' task, were conveniently forgotten. Instead we are given a false picture of a united heroic Russian people putting up a brave and fierce resistance to the vicious, evil, anti-Christian Tatars. The narrative becomes more and more polished, the sense of shock and horror is increased, and it becomes impossible to sift fact from fiction and imagination. Numbers, of course, are wildly exaggerated: the number of Kievan volunteers killed in 1223, for example, which was probably not more than

100, increases to 1000, to 10,000, to 30,000 and finally, in the early six-teenth century, to 60,000—considerably larger than the total popula-tion of the city itself. The aim of all this was to cover up a murky past. The Russians would have had little to be proud about—especially as far as the aftermath of the invasion was concerned—had they known the true facts of the first half of the thirteenth century. After all, what had been going on? A crude struggle for power. So the whole business was conveniently turned into a holocaust.

In conclusion I would like to suggest some further valid reasons for using textology as an aid to the study of early Russian literature and history.

Firstly, the question of anonymity. The vast majority of mediaeval Russian literature works were anonymous; indeed, early Russian liter-ature is peculiar for its astonishing lack of interest in authorship, for its authorlessness, one might say. The composer of a work was rarely concerned with laying a claim to what he had written or copied, with proclaiming his authorship. Indeed, those humble disclaimers which are found at the beginning of so many Russian and Byzantine Saints' Lives (the humility topoi: "I, the wretched sinful one, am unworthy to write the Life of such a glorious saint, miracle-worker, martyr, etc.") are extended to most other forms of literature, and to such a degree that, however much a writer intends to express his own opinion, he will nevertheless often stress the fact that his work is not original, that it is based on the writings and thoughts of other, greater, writers and thinkers than he. In fact a writer will often ascribe his own thoughts to the fathers of the Church, say, in order to give them weight, to lend them a certain cachet (for example, the early twelfth-century "In-struction" of Vladimir Monomakh to his children), or perhaps to save him from the possibility of being branded as a heretic. "Authorship," then, is not a mediaeval Russian concept at all. The result of this non-authorship is that successive generations of writers had no compunc-tion whatsoever in altering their predecessors' work and treating it in what might seem to us today a completely cavalier manner in order to suit their own purposes. In other words, we are concerned not with an individual author, but with a collective author, not with one compiler, but with generations of compilers—all embroidering on, or simplify-ing, or shortening, or lengthening the same basic work until in the final version we may hardly be able to recognize the original.

In this state of near-anarchy resulting from "authorlessness," textology must be used to make some sense of it all, to restore order. Otherwise one is left with a chaotic situation.

The second reason why I think it is essential to employ textology when studying early Russian sources is because nearly all Old Russian literature is grossly tendentious. The fact that mediaeval writers shunned originality did not mean that they eschewed literary devices or that they were totally unsubtle in their approach and their manner of writing. Of course, they were not. Indeed, some, like Daniil Zatochnik, used highly sophisticated contrivances such as punning and word-play; others, like the author of the *Zadonshchina*, used dazzling imagery; and yet others, like Ivan the Terrible, whom I would call the first truly creative Russian writer, and Avvakum, used deliberate stylistic juxtapositions and contrasts which are startling in their modernity. But all these were only effects. They were only secondary adjuncts to the authors' deeply committed purpose in writing. Daniil did not pun just to amuse: his aim was to convince the prince of the need to employ intelligent men in his service; Sofoniya of Ryazan' was writing not just to lull his readers with the beauty of his imagery, but to glorify the united principality of Moscow in 1380; Ivan IV was not trying to entertain or to amuse, but to pour scorn on his ideological enemies: his caustic wit was subordinated to politics; and Avvakum was writing with the passion of a religious fanatic, determined to save the souls of his wretched fellow-sufferers and followers, whether they liked it or not.

In other words, for the pre-eighteenth-century reader, most Russian literature was something created not necessarily to give pleasure, but to instruct, to teach, to drum home some idea or other, whether religious, or political, or moral. Hence the content of so much early Russian literature is of a didactic, a religious, or a politically doctrinaire nature. You read about a war, about a battle, about a man's life, about a murder, *not* to be entertained or even to learn the truth about some person or event, but in order to become a better person, spiritually or politically. And you write, or copy, or edit, in order to improve your listeners' souls or to instruct them in the correct way to lead their lives.

If, then, mediaeval Russian literature was predominantly didactic and/or tendentious, it is clearly of the greatest importance to study the shifts in the degree of didacticism and tendentiousness from age to age, from district to district, even from scriptorium to scriptorium. And this is precisely where textology, by establishing the time and milieu of each recension of each particular work or chronicle, is of such importance.

The serious student of early Russian literature of history must concern himself with textology if only to investigate the mentality of the age which he is studying. For it enables him to find out not necessarily what actually happened, but how people viewed contemporary events and, more important still, how they reacted to previous literary monuments and past history. It helps him to discover how people's minds worked.

The Uses of Filiation
in Early Music

STANLEY BOORMAN

There is no real reason to believe that the actual, as opposed to the perceived, procedures of transmission of early music differed in any significant manner from those for any other texts of the period before the overwhelming impact of printing. The process seems to have involved the same patterns of memory and copying, of editorial freedom to gloss and of concern for responsible copy that are found in many other fields.[1] But I deliberately limit this statement to a reflection on the manner of copying and not to any discussion of the scribes' view of the material to be copied.

There are certain significant differences between music and almost all other texts. Of these, the most obvious is that of the language used: the musical language would have been as little known as Greek or Arabic to many early scribes, and must have made similar demands on the availability of specialists.[2] For most of the period, these specialists would have been rather different classes of people: those who were able to cope with Greek or Arabic were of necessity literate and probably also learned, whether they were medieval religious or later humanist. The specialist musician and musical scribe need not have been learned, or even well-read: he was often a skilled performer who also could copy with a fair hand.

Some categories of musical document were, admittedly, the work of scribes more like the traditional non-musical copyist—manuscripts of chants copied in monastic or ecclesiastical scriptoria;[3] manuscripts of secular song before the mid-fourteenth century, apparently the work of the same class of scribe that wrote the poetic contents;[4] or the musical treatises that were sometimes written and copied by scholars with skills in other disciplines of the quadrivium or in philosophy.[5] (It is perhaps not surprising that these are just the types of document that were first subjected to Lachmann's or other text-critical procedures.)[6] But the majority of the remaining manuscripts seem to have been the

167

work of professional musicians or of music scribes, neither of whom need have had either the literary talents or knowledge or the pretensions to accuracy in certain areas that are to be found in other fields.[7]

However, that is not a point that I wish to labour. To whatever extent the musical scribe was atypical, he can still be compared with the best of the scholar-scribes simply because he was, of necessity, a professional, fluent in music and its notation. For this reason, if for no other, the actual patterns of transmission of music need not have been intrinsically different from those for any other subject.

Therefore, there is perhaps little to be said about copying *procedures* in the present context. Musicologists have spent considerable time analysing the likely patterns of change that can result from an attempt at copying music thoughtfully.[8] In so doing, we have begun to raise a separate set of issues. In discussing these issues, I want to turn from procedures of transmission to the perceived patterns of transmission, as seen in the light of the peculiar nature of music for the period before *ca.* 1500. As a result, I hope to show that filiation has a rather special role in the editing of music.

It might seem that similar actual patterns of transmission should lead to similar perceived patterns, to similar evidence: that the processes of filiation by which one can move from the perceived to an understanding of a plausible actual pattern should be parallel with those employed in, say, medieval French literature; or that the extent to which filiation and textual criticism will lead towards an understanding of an authentic text is much the same in music as elsewhere.[9]

There are those musicologists who have acted as though this were so: they have attempted to produce stemmata for their editions, and have provided as many dubious and as many plausible genealogies as have appeared in other fields. There are others who have argued that the very nature of the musical language, of the notation by which it is transmitted, precludes any direct comparison of methods or results between fields. There is a grain of truth in both positions. There are, in fact, few features of music manuscripts that can not be found elsewhere, in poetical anthologies for example, or classical literature:[10] yet what we can learn from analysing the texts contained in music manuscripts is entirely different from what may be discovered in examining manuscripts in other disciplines. The pursuit of an "authentic" text for music is almost that of seeking the chimera, and it is also (as I propose to show) essentially irrelevant.

Thus, even if the basic principles of filiation can be applied to musical documents (insofar as there are any basic principles left to us), yet they will reveal, when well applied, completely different levels of information. This is because of the different nature of music itself, as much as that of the language in which it is written (the musical notation), and even to some extent depends upon the characteristics of the manuscripts themselves.

* * *

These manuscripts may be very diverse. It should be reasonably obvious that the music in a typical manuscript fair copy, a presentation copy or a repository is not as accessible to the average lay reader as other classes of material might be.[11] This is particularly true in most early documents, where music to be simultaneously heard is not laid out so that it can be read simultaneously by one person, as is now the custom.[12] Indeed, one can go further, and assert that many manuscripts can hardly be used to read the music at all, even when a separate reader-cum-performer is available for every voice of a piece. This is sometimes a product of the lay-out or the notation, but is more often a result of the errors and variants in the copying.

There are, of course, some variants in most manuscripts that can immediately be classed as errors: this is no less true in music than elsewhere. However, while, in literary sources, there are several classes of errors, masquerading as variants, which could not be detected by even a reasonably careful reader of the text, the range of such variants is much larger in music. This is again a product of the simultaneous nature of music: when two or three parts are meant to be performed together, but are copied out (and therefore checked) separately, many variants in the copying could seem to make absolute sense by themselves while not working with the other parts.[13] This is not meant to excuse such variants: it is no more than a suggested explanation why so many works could not have been performed directly from the surviving documents.

This has raised among musicologists the vision of large numbers of manuscripts copied, apparently *not* to be used.[14] Yet many manuscripts contain performance instructions embedded in the lay-out, in the notation or in additional annotations.[15] These manuscripts, at least, must be presumed to have been of some use to performers. While many manuscripts have no such pretensions (presentation copies survive freely in this, as in any other field), yet others suggest to the modern scholar a situation in which the scribe was writing for a performer who would look at the text, perhaps to refresh his memory or to begin learning a new work, but who would not use it as a dictatorial authority for his performance.[16]

A second level of interest for the musicologist lies in the nature of the notation of early music. I want to make only two particular points here: the first is that the notation changes rapidly, much more so than does either the script or the content of verbal language. The nature of the changes in notation, perhaps, is closer to the way in which cant or slang change: namely, change is rapid; knowledge of the change is essential to the understanding of the musical text; and the obsolete forms can acquire new and contradictory meanings. A fair number of pieces survive in two or more manuscripts where the notation of the music (and hence its visual appearance) is radically different.[17] Even more can be shown to survive in versions that take some cognisance of minor changes in notation.[18] In Example 1, for instance, the upper line shows a notation which is several years earlier than that of the lower. The music contained in the two lines is essentially the same, in that there are no variants in the readings which would force the two manuscripts apart in a filiation. This is, visually, an extreme case: but it would not be impossible to argue that a scribe competent to write in the notation of the lower line would also be expert enough to transliterate accurately from that of the upper.

EXAMPLE 1. Giovanni da Florentia: *Nascoso el viso*

Such a situation will clearly influence our view of the filiation for this piece. Unless we can be aware of the underlying notational rules affecting the copying in a manuscript, we may well place it in the wrong branch of a stemma. Fortunately, in a few cases, a scribal attempt at bringing the notation up-to-date has resulted in a musical nonsense that points to a problem in the notation as its probable cause.

Notation also has a dialect element: English notations were regularly different from those on the other side of the Channel, and different levels of notation can be shown to be operating in Italy during the fourteenth century: there are other major repertories so afflicted.[19] All of these variants in notation and interpretation are susceptible to analysis on the level of local and temporary changes, and reflect to some extent the way in which separate musical institutions existed in isolation: each was able to practise its own modification of general notation and its own interpretation of the various notational symbols, and each imposed this on documents and works that came to it from elsewhere.

But notation is also interesting for another reason. We are accustomed in other fields to the notion that more than one symbol or sequence of symbols can have the same meaning—variant spellings. There is a similar range of notational spellings in music, and Example 2 gives two such notations for a section of a mid-fifteenth-century chanson.

EXAMPLE 2. Ockeghem: *Ma bouche rit*

In this passage, there is only one very minor musical difference between the two manuscripts, consisting of the replacement of a single note by two shorter notes (indicated by an asterisk between the two lines). All the other changes are notational, the equivalent of spelling variants. Such changes appear, almost as if at random, in all the surviving manuscripts of early polyphony: many pieces exist with a remarkably different visual effect in different manuscripts and prints. To some extent, the changes are visually attractive, and seem to have been used by certain scribes for the sake of their appearance—making a page more interesting to look at, in one way or another. But recent research is beginning to suggest that *some* of them had specific meanings for the performance of the music, for accentuation and articulation, for example. Thus, in many manuscripts, and particularly in the early stages of music printing, specific notational spellings were adopted by some copyists, involving conscious decisions and modifications.[20]

This has to imply that different scribes, or copyists working for different institutions, saw the so-called spelling changes as more than just that—as if they carried some level of content, and reflected some local or scribal need in the notation.

There is a further, and major, complication in that the manner in which music is notated has never been detailed enough to carry all the information necessary for performing the work. There are always levels of interpretation that can not be expressed in the notation. In most cases, notation has not grappled with them simply because composers have been content to leave them to the performer, especially if they are part of the normal background and expertise of a competent musician. The earlier the music, the more these levels of performance seem to have been regarded by the composer as unimportant, and therefore are not present in the notation.[21] However, modifications of the notation can be made in order to provide some of this guidance, and these changes seem regularly to have been made by the scribe himself. If this be so, then clearly there are elements of the music (either in the notation or in performance) which could be and were left to the scribe or performer—that is, which the original creator, the composer, did not try to prescribe. Any understanding of the readings that have been preserved has to distinguish between normal major variants and these lesser changes, what one might call "minor substantive" variants.

The more obvious variants need not detain us here for long. Their nature and function will be apparent, for they involve the creation of quite different versions of parts of a work. An excellent example of this is in the transmission of Dufay's *Missa sine nomine*, composed for three voices: it is also preserved in a reduction for two voices, mostly achieved by eliminating one of the three and making some necessary adjustments to the others, in a manuscript written for a Venetian monastic house, and apparently reflecting performance requirements.[22] In Example 3, the upper pair of lines shows the normal three-voiced version, with the lower pair presenting the unique two-voiced arrangement.

EXAMPLE 3. Dufay: *Missa sine nomine – Sanctus*

More normally, the change can not be explained so easily. Example 4, from the same mass, shows two different versions of one voice from a single section, both of which produce good musical results.

EXAMPLE 4. Dufay: *Missa sine nomine - Credo*

This is no different from practices in other fields, except that it seems to have been generally approved of, almost welcomed at times, in music.[23]

The second level of change, which must concern the musical theorists of filiation much more, is the pattern of making minor performing changes to the music—a pattern that is so widespread that it seems to be endemic to the situation: in other words, it appears to be part of the nature of early music, and not only of its transmission.

As I have said, no musical notation has ever needed to include symbols for any part of the music that is solely the province of the performer's expertise and that would have been expected of all performers. For example, there are periods when almost no ornaments were written into the music, simply *because* they were expected of the performer, who would know, from his experience, just what to add.[24] There are similar features in early music, which, while they need to be notated, still leave the same freedom to the performer. But, since *something* has to be written down, (for a space can not be left in the music) the individual scribe is likely to write either what was in his exemplar, or what he himself would perform.

This leads to a startling array of variants at various levels—of ornamentation, of decorative filigree, of changes in accidentals, and so on—spattered across the manuscripts in a very complicated pattern. Any selection of manuscripts of the most popular works reveals that few of the surface elements remain constant in more than two or three manuscripts, even when the manuscripts themselves come from the same branch of a stemma: ". . . the art of transmission itself would almost seem to have been enough to stimulate recomposition or reworking."[25] The sorts of changes involved are illustrated in Examples 5 and 6. The first is a simple decoration and minor change while the

second shows some of the more common types of cadence variation.
Even on purely visual terms, these changes can not have been made by
chance, but require some scribal decision.

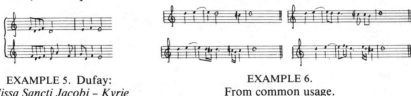

EXAMPLE 5. Dufay: EXAMPLE 6.
Missa Sancti Jacobi – Kyrie   From common usage.

Scholars have thus been forced to recognise not only that the
changeable nature of these early music details is present in all repertoires, but also that it seems to have been entirely acceptable to the
composer. Indeed, we have come to realise that such changes, in detail
or large-scale, could have been made as much by the composer as by
any later scribe. Even they, therefore, need tell us very little about a
stemma. There exist, for example, manuscripts of the music of
Machaut which claim to be fairly close to the composer, but which
contain different versions of the same pieces, as if he himself had approved two different approaches to the work. Indeed, some manuscripts contain two interwoven versions of such works.

In other cases, two versions survive in two different groups of manuscripts, two traditions, both of which can be traced back to early
roots. An example is Machaut's *ballade, De petit po*. One three-
voiced version (employing the first and second lines of the example)
survives in most of the North European manuscripts, among them
some close to the composer; a version with a different third voice (using lines two and three of music) is found in manuscripts principally
with Italian backgrounds. The two additional voices (lines one and
three) are not compatible, yet they are both copied in two manuscripts, one Northern and one Italian, alongside the nucleus, the second line of the example.

EXAMPLE. 7 Guillaume de Machaut: *De petit po*

The presence of both additional parts suggests that neither need be
given precedence over the other, that neither is strictly "correct,"

with the other merely a "later change." It may be that the concept of more than one "author's version" must be accepted as generally valid for music, both because of cases like this, and as a result of a situation in which we can not assume that the composer had a fixed preference for many of the details (or even the larger aspects of his work).

Thus the integrity of an early piece of music does not lie in what appears on the page: it is not even defined by how the music sounded. If it exists at all—that is, if the work has any single identifiable form—that form has to lie behind the audible and visual detail, at some level of underpinning structure.

The problem facing the textual critic of early music is therefore that there is no text to criticise, and no value (*in these terms*) to the surviving variants. In the case of major changes, of different versions, we confront problems that have been discussed outside music.[26] In music, too, we sometimes have to adopt a position in which the two versions are equally valid. In some cases the history of one or the other version cannot be pushed back to the *milieu* of the composer. However, in the context of the present discussion, such versions do not cease to have important value. They are immediate demonstrations of the extent to which major changes to works of music were considered acceptable, as well as indications of how different generations tried to make popular works more up-to-date.

The problem of value is much more acute in dealing with minor changes. These, as I say, abound through the repertoire. Some scholars have argued that they are virtually valueless, that they do not, indeed, can not, tell us more than the way in which random events appear, and that any approach to an Ur-text can only work through establishing the provenance of manuscripts and trying to find a best or earliest text.[27]

However, these changes are more serious than mere spelling changes. The latter, in literary texts, may be no more than a product of habit interacting with memory while copying. In music, minor changes often can not arise in this way. While some changes may imply a process of homogenisation, of relating simple variants to a pattern that the scribe favors, others require an act of will on his part. This can be detected and to some extent measured through examination of two features of music and its sources.

i) One is that the greater proportion of music manuscripts are the equivalent of anthologies, copied from a number of exemplars and arranged by the scribe, either according to some conscious plan, or in the order of acquisition.[28] This has enabled scholars of some chant repertoires to group manuscripts by their contents, by the choice of individual works which scribes made within the confines of liturgical requirements, reflecting the repertoires that were available to them.[29]

It usually can not be applied to most polyphonic anthologies, however, where neither liturgical constraints nor availability of materials are ever so well defined. An anthology manuscript will often contain music from a period of well over thirty years as well as from different parts of Europe. Ideally, therefore, it should yield evidence of different notations, different musical styles and different patterns of scribal alteration. This can make possible a simple, though lengthy analysis of how the patterns of such variants occur throughout the manuscript. Those patterns that recur continually (though not continuously) are likely to be those of the scribe himself, or at least of the institution for which he is writing; those that appear only occasionally or only in small sections will probably reflect the practice of his exemplars.[30]

ii) The second aspect is that the performing resources for music, as well as the manner of performance, varied considerably from one institution to another, and from one area to another. We can trace different practices for the same music in Italy and in Northern Europe, in Florence and in the Veneto. We can also trace different resources and their impact in Padua as opposed to Paris, in England as opposed to Northern Italy. Some of these differences can be recovered from archival evidence and from narrative.[31] Even more can be seen in the manuscripts via a potentially circular line of reasoning. This goes as follows: if all the Italian manuscripts of chansons show a certain characteristic, say, omission of the words for the music, that is perhaps because the Italians did not use the words. That is why the manuscripts omit the words. However, the reasoning is actually sound — for it is based on the presumption that such types of general change in groups of manuscripts must reflect some real change in requirements.[32]

This, in its turn, is a response to the simple aesthetic problem that music could not be preserved (at least until the gramophone was invented) for transmission from one centre to another: all that was possible was the transmission of a short-hand, musical notation, which enabled an approximate reconstruction.[33]

The scribe in the new centre received a version of the composition which, in large scale elements or in detail, differed from the performing practice which he followed. He, having to prepare a copy of the work for local consumption, was faced with two possibilities: one was to create a new version of the music, reflecting his local performing needs, and his own personal taste. The second was not to do this. The latter is at least possible, for we have little evidence, at least before 1500, of manuscripts regularly being used in performance. I have already suggested that they probably acted much more as an *aide memoire*: if this were so, then the performers were certainly as capable of making local adjustments to the music as was the scribe.

Where these patterns of change do exist in the manuscript, they have been measured satisfactorily in a number of repertories between *ca.* 1350 and 1500, and some isolated studies have revealed them in earlier music: they seem to comprise both local (temporal and regional) changes and idiosyncratic changes peculiar to the one scribe.[34]

My argument has been designed to raise the question of just what filiation *can* do for early music. After all, if every manuscript (or even, as is more true, the great majority) demonstrates as much temporary and local influence on the readings as does the original version, there is perhaps little hope for filiation, at least as a means to recovering an authentic text. I believe this to be true. Except in those very rare cases where we suspect a composer's direct influence on a surviving manuscript,[35] we can have no grounds for reconstructing what he may have written. In some of these rare examples (and I have already cited the case of Machaut), there is enough variation between manuscripts for us to doubt that the composer even had a single authentic form in mind. Rather, he, like every later scribe, made a series of choices for those parts of the work where there was no essential version, and reached different decisions under different circumstances if he rewrote the piece later.[36]

Filiation, then, will not provide us with any answer to the question of whether there ever was one version preferred by the musical creator. Usually, it will not even provide limits to the range of acceptable versions. It will, it is true, often give us a few clues: if we have enough manuscripts from the areas in which the composer was working, we can at least limit the number, the almost infinite number, of variations, to those which might have been popular at that place and time.[37]

And this points to the main uses of filiation in music, slowly being recognized among musicologists, the most important of which is this pattern of local taste and custom. As I have said, studies have already begun to show different regional approaches to the text, to ornamentation, and to patterns of texture, as well as some institutional approaches to setting words or to accidentals.

Concurrently, such patterns of evidence will show the lines by which these matters of taste or notation changed. I established some years ago that the patterns of variants in a group of early sixteenth-century manuscripts were responses to a new approach to the notation of tempo: some manuscripts showed the older, some the new, and one shows a copyist grappling with the transition and not fully comprehending what is required: similar things have been done for earlier music.[38]

Twenty years ago two leading scholars[39] attempted to arrange the works of a major fifteenth-century composer, Dufay, in chronological order, on the strength of the notations in which they survive. Today, such a procedure would not be acceptable. Studies of filiation have shown the extent to which notation, in common with other features of the manuscripts, is the product of local and scribal need—indeed, have confirmed that notation is a prime candidate for change. This type of research is turning us more towards an interest in the ways in which music, its notation and its performance, changed over the years in which the same pieces were retained in the repertoire. Once we have a grasp of local performing and notational styles, we will begin to understand something about the form of the music itself before it was subjected to those changes.

Even then, however, we will be no nearer to unearthing the form and detail of an Ur-text, since the earliest manuscripts, or those most proximate to the author, will have been subject to the same processes as are most apparent in the later ones. In other words, the hyparchetype for the earliest may well be the same as the archetype for all sources: the pattern of variants should not be expected to reveal whether or not this is so.

Thus, it is clear that the most valuable uses of filiation in the editing of musical manuscripts will remain for some time in the realm of rediscovering local and scribal habits. However unsatisfactory such a procedure may be in other fields, here, at least, it is the only reflection that we have of how the music was treated by performers, and thus of how it might have been transmitted from one to the next.

SOURCES OF MUSIC EXAMPLES

1. From the Rossi codex (Rome, Biblioteca Apostolica Vaticana, Rossi 215) and from Florence, Biblioteca Nazionale Centrale, Panciatichi 26.
2. From the Mellon chansonnier (New Haven, Yale University Library, 91) and Dijon, Bibliothèque municipale, 517.
3. From Bologna, Civico Museo Bibliografico Municipale, Q15 and Venice, Biblioteca Nazionale Marciana, IX.145.
4. From the two sources for Example 3, and from Bologna, Biblioteca Universitaria, 2216.
5. From Bologna, Civico Museo Bibliografico Musicale, Q15 and from Trent 87.
6. Examples drawn from common usage.
7. Line one in the Machaut manuscripts; line 4 in Chantilly, Musée Condé, 564, Florence, Biblioteca Nazionale Centrale, Panciatichi 26, and Paris, Bibliothèque nationale, f.it.568; both lines in Cambrai, Bibliotheque municipale, 1328 and Modena, Biblioteca Estense. M.5.24; lines 2 and 3 in all manuscripts.

NOTES

1. I do not intend to cite references outside the field of musicology — the methodological studies will presumably be familiar to most of my readers. A brief bibliography of those most relevant to musical problems will be found at the end of S. Boorman, "Limitations and extensions of filiation technique," *Music in medieval and early modern Europe*, edited by I. Fenlon (London: Cambridge University Press, 1981), pp. 319–346. In music, there has (to my knowledge) so far been no study of the role that memory played in the copying process: it is, in any case, difficult to assess, for reasons that will appear below. As for the concern for responsible copy, this occurs even in the earliest polyphonic manuscripts—there are numerous erasures and careful alterations in Florence, Biblioteca Medicea-Laurenziana, Pluteus 29.1 (one of the principal sources of polyphony of the Notre Dame school); similar evidence can be found in the majority of early musical documents, including printed ones, although there is also, of course, the usual evidence for careless and casual scribes.
2. In ecclesiastical institutions, there seems to have been little problem, for most of the singers (in a secular establishment) or monks (in monastic houses) could be made reponsible for the musical books. For examples, see A. Ducroit, "Histoire de la Cappella Giulia depuis sa fondation par Jules II (1513) jusqu'à sa restauration par Grégoire XIII (1578)", *Mélanges d'archéologie et d'histoire*, lxxv (1963), pp. 179–240 and 467–559 (especially pp. 513–525). In court chapel circles, there is evidence for paid music scribes during the Renaissance, occasionally on a semipermanent basis: the work of Jean Michel in the sixteenth century is discussed in J. Rifkin's paper offering "New light on music manuscripts at the court of Fer-

rara in the reigns of Alfonso I and Hercules II," read at the New England Renaissance Conference, 26 October 1974; and that of a group of scribes at the Netherlands court circle, *ca.* 1500, by H. Kellman in "Josquin and the courts of Netherlands and France: the evidence of the sources," *Josquin des Prez*, edited by E. Lowinsky (London: Oxford University Press, 1978), pp. 181–216. The copying of secular manuscripts seems to have been much more haphazard: see the remarks by C. Wright, *Music at the court of Burgundy, 1364–1419: a documentary history* (Henryville: Institute of Medieval Music, 1979), pp. 158–159 and the implications of the studies by C. Hamm, "Manuscript structure in the Dufay era," *Acta Musicologica*, xxxiv (1962), pp. 166–184, and J. Rifkin, "Scribal concordances for some renaissance manuscripts in Florentine libraries," *Journal of the American Musicological Society*, xxvi (1973), pp. 305–326. It is apparent that many musical manuscripts are not integral units, but composite, made up of entirely discrete fascicles copied at several different times, often by different people.

3. We do not have enough evidence for the copying of chant manuscripts: further, the nature of the manuscripts that have survived militates against the easy identification of scribes, for many are relatively stylised and most are likely to be copies of manuscripts prepared in the same or a similar institution a generation earlier. However, occasional references to payment for copying (or illuminating or binding) chant manuscripts do survive: and a number of manuscripts contain an *explicit* in which a scribe identifies himself as a member of the relevant order.

4. The scribe who copied the words in the musical sections of the single manuscript of the *Roman de Fauvel* that contains music (Paris, Bibliothèque nationale, f.fr.146) is probably the same as that for the non-musical sections: the same may be true in some of the Machaut manuscripts. It is usually impossible to tell whether the music scribe also copied the words of the text.

5. Perhaps the most obvious of these is Boethius, whose musical writings were avidly read and abstracted, and were already in print before 1500.

6. See for example, *Le Graduel Romain, édition critique par les moines de Solesmes*, iv: le texte neumatique (Solesmes, 1961–62), where parts 1 and 2 are concerned with the relationship between sources; T. Karp, "The trouvère MS tradition," *The Twenty-fifth Anniversary Festschrift (1937–1962): Queens College of the City University of New York Department of Music* (New York: Queens College, 1964), pp. 25–52; and G. Weiss, "Zum Problem des Gruppierung südfranzösischer Tropars," *Archiv für Musikwissenschaft*, xii (1964), pp. 163–171.

7. Thus the scribe of the *Buxheimer Orgelbuch* (*ca.* 1470: Munich, Bayerische Staatsbibliothek, Cim. 3526) showed no knowledge of French in his transcription of chanson titles, and that of the *Faenza Codex (ca.* 1400: Faenza, Biblioteca Communale, 117) apparently had the same problem.

8. For a recent, straightforward discussion of the position as regards early music, see M. Bent, "Some criteria for establishing relationships between sources of late-medieval polyphony," *Music in medieval and early modern Europe*, pp. 295–317.

9. There are still many musical scholars who appear to believe that we can, in our present state of research, recover an authentic text of early music. For example,

"it has always been my understanding that stemmatics was a tool designed to render all extant sources superfluous by allowing scholars to reconstruct lost original." (R. Sherr reviewing M. Staehelin's *Die Messen Heinrich Isaacs*, in *Journal of the American Musicological Society*, xxxiv [1981] p. 145.)

10. See my brief discussion of this point on pp. 320–321 of the article cited in Note 1.

11. It is of course true to say that no manuscript will make music accessible to the "average reader" (unless it is a phonograph record); yet these classes of manuscript do tend to remove the sounding music further from the musical reader. They have little in common with the additional aids to the performer that are cited below, in Note 15.

12. The patterns of lay-out in early manuscript are discussed, with additional details, in the article "Sources, MS", *The New Grove, Dictionary of Music and Musicians*, edited by S. Sadie (London: Macmillan, 1980), xvii, 590–609.

13. To create an example: in a work for three singers, as copied in most of the normal renaissance lay-outs, a complete musical phrase could be omitted from the part for one of them, without the result seeming to make nonsense to a single reader. The error might well not be detected until three singers tried to fit all the parts together, and produced chaos.

14. This position, dubious as it must seem, can be bolstered by the general lack of evidence in any form for singing polyphony (as opposed to chant) before the fifteenth century; by the strong evidence that polyphony (both sacred and secular) was aimed at solo performers before the end of the fourteenth; and even by the lay-out of choir-stalls and the seating of soloists.

15. Examples would include lines connecting syllables with specific notes (Oxford, Bodleian Library, Can. misc. 213 [*ca.* 1430]; see H. Schoop, *Entstehung und Verwendung der Handschrift Oxford, Bodleian Library, Canonici misc. 213* [Bern: Haupt, 1971], pp. 61–63); indications for solo and choral sections (Bologna, Civico Museo Bibliografico Musicale, Q15 [*ca.* 1430]; indications for the addition of an improvised part (see E. Trumble, *Fauxbourdon: an historical survey* [Brooklyn: Institute for Medieval Music, 1959] for a list of the Continental uses of this technique). See also Note 21, below, and M. Lewis, "Antonio Gardane's early connections with the Willaert circle," *Music in medieval and early modern Europe*, pp. 209–226.

16. Apart from evidence such as that cited in the previous footnote, there are cases like the scrupulous writing out of all text repetitions in Padua, Archivio del Duomo, MS. A17 (1522), written by the *maestro di cappella*, Passetto, for use in the cathedral, or the care in notating cross-rhythms and rhythmic difficulties in some of the manuscripts written for the cathedral at Casale Monferrato during a similar period. It is perhaps hardly necessary to comment here on the evidence for much greater feats of memory among diverse classes of society during the Middle Ages and early Renaissance.

17. In many cases, the music itself is essentially the same: i.e., the notation changes, though not the content. Much of the repertoire of the late twelfth and early thirteenth centuries is transmitted in very diverse forms in different manuscripts due

to the development of organising notational symbols: the transmission of vocal pieces in a notation suitable for lute is another instance. Possibly, the various notations of chant provide a further example, although we can seldom be sure that none of the notational changes do not correspond to musical changes.

18. The most well-known example of this is in the transition from an Italianate notation to a more international, French notation late in the fourteenth century (see Note 20), though there is a series of most interesting modifications during the earlier part of the same century in France, and I am currently finding similar patterns in notational change of *ca.* 1500.

19. At present, the only published study of the former is M. Bent, "A preliminary assessment of the independence of English Trecento notations," *L'Ars Nova italiana del trecento*, iv, pp. 65–83, and the most recent discussion of the latter is by J. Nadás, to appear in *Journal of the American Musicological Society*. Lute and keyboard music had regional notations throughout the Renaissance. The most convenient introduction to these is the article "Tablature," *The New Grove Dictionary of Music and Musicians*, xviii, pp. 506–515.

20. I presented evidence for this being the pattern (*ca.* 1500) in my "Notational spelling and scribal habit," *Formen und Probleme der Überlieferung mehrstimmiger Musik in Zeitalter Josquin Desprez*, Wolfenbütteler Forschungen, VI (Munich: Kraus, 1981), pp. 245–280.

21. Perhaps the best-known change of this sort was the introduction of so-called metronome marks, indicating the number of beats per minute (and hence the precise speed of the music), as a result of an invention by Mälzel (*ca.*) 1816). However, there were no indications of minor changes of speed, of instrumentation, or of dynamics before the very late sixteenth century.

   In some cases, details of performance are not notated because they are a part of normal performing convention—the composer can include them in his conception of the work, but need not write them out. There are many traces of possible conventions of this nature from the medieval and renaissance periods (see, for instance, the articles "Chiavette" or "musica ficta" in *The New Grove*) and a few firm examples (such as *alternatim* singing of those hymns in which the composers have written polyphony only for the alternate, non-chanted verses — or ornamentation and embellishment (for which see H. Brown, *Embellishing 16th century music* (London: Oxford University Press, 1976), which was a normal part of performing almost all music.

22. See G. Cattin, "Il manoscritto Venet. Marc. Ital. IX, 145," *Quadrivium*, iv (1961), pp. 1–61.

23. Thus, a number of fourteenth-century works survive with four simultaneous parts, of which two are essential and may be combined with either of the other two. Many fifteenth-century chansons were modified by having a new *contratenor* composed to replace the original, or by the addition of a later fourth part: a highly speculative theory attempting to assign composers to the added parts has been advanced by A. Atlas, "Conflicting attributions in Italian sources of the Franco-Netherlandish chanson, 1445–*ca.* 1505: a progress report on a new hypothesis," *Music in medieval and early modern Europe*, pp. 249–293.

24. An example is that of Elizabethan keyboard music, when only one or two ornament signs seem to have been used, although probably with several interpretations. The problems that such a habit creates for the modern scholar are best illustrated by the continuing controversies over the practice in the French baroque, involving what are called *notes inégales* and 'double dotting.'

25. E. Roesner, "The problem of chronology in the transmission of organum duplum," *Music in medieval and early modern Europe*, p. 398.

26. For example, in J. Thorpe, *Principles of textual criticism* (San Marino: Huntington Library, 1972), or, more usefully, in F. Brambilla Ageno, *L'edizione critica dei testi volgare* (Padua: Antenore, 1975).

27. D. Hughes, "Further notes on the grouping of Aquitanian tropers," *Journal of the American Musicological Society*, xix (1966), pp. 3–12, while not concerned with seeking an Ur-text, does argue that a study of the variants in his sources would not help in grouping them or the readings.

28. One of the most useful discussions of this latter feature of many renaissance manuscripts is Hamm's article cited in Note 2. A number of recent studies have confused the concept of discrete fascicles within a manuscript with the related concept of the 'fascicle-manuscript,' a small collection (often of only one or two bifolios) deliberately copied as a self-contained unit, perhaps for transmission from one centre to another: examples of the latter are described in Hamm's "Musiche del Quattrocento in S. Petronio," *Rivista italiana di musicologia*, III (1968), pp. 215–232.

29. Some study of this has been undertaken by D. Hughes (see Note 27) and in more detail by the editors of the *Corpus Troporum*. In this context, see especially Gunilla Iversen's study attached to Volume iv of the series, *Tropes de l'Agnus Dei* (Stockholm: Almqvist & Wiksell, i [1980]).

30. I have attempted this form of analysis for a late fifteenth-century chansonnier: see my article cited in Note 1, above.

31. As examples, see C. Wright, "Performance practices at the cathedral of Cambrai, 1475–1550," *The Musical Quarterly*, lxiv (1978), pp. 295–328, and R. Bowers, "Choral institutions within the English church, 1350–1500," Ph.D. dissertation, The University of East Anglia, 1975.

32. This argument, albeit in a much more sophisticated form, has recently been put forward most convincingly by L. Litterick, "Performing Franco-Netherlandish secular music of the late fifteenth century: texted and untexted parts," *Early Music*, viii (1980), 474–485.

33. The only resolution of this problem was, of course, to send the musicians from the first centre to the second, to train the singers there. The earliest recorded attempts at this seem to be the sending of Bishop Chrodegang of Metz (by Pepin in 753) and an anonymous singer (by Charlemagne) to Rome, in order to learn the Roman versions of chant.

34. Thus, A. Planchart, "The transmission of medieval chant," *Music in medieval and early modern Europe*, p. 363, refers to "small variants that may not [be] signs of anything more than the local style of a given center"; and E. Roesner, *op.cit.*,

p. 393, discussing "the 'house-style' of the manuscript." For later sources, see J. Nadás, *op.cit.* and A. Atlas, *The Cappella Giulia Chansonnier (Rome, Biblioteca Apostolica Vatiacana, C.G. XIII. 27)*, (Brooklyn, Institute for Medieval Music, [1975–61]), which groups the Italian manuscripts of the late fifteenth-century chansons into local families in accordance with the range of variants present.

35. Autographs of music are very rare indeed before 1600. The cases that have been advanced for a number of autograph additions to surviving manuscripts are occasionally fairly strong, but there is no sign of an autograph in the sense that a literary scholar might wish.

36. An instructive example of this is in the work of Carpentras: R. Sherr, "Notes on two Roman manuscripts of the early sixteenth century," *The Musical Quarterly*, lxiii (1977), pp. 48-73.

37. But this does not remove the composer's awareness of different performing possibilities, which he knew of as existing in different centres. He can have found no problems in accepting them, or presumably in approving them for his own works, if he took up a new position in a different centre.

38. See Note 20.

39. H. Besseler, *Guillelmi Dufay, Opera Omnia*, Corpus mensurabilis musicae, i (Rome: American Institute of Musicology, 1964), in the introduction to Volume vi; and C. Hamm, *A chronology of the works of Guillaume Dufay based on a study of mensural practice*, (Princeton: Princeton University Press, 1964).

Editing Elizabethan Letters

A. R. BRAUNMULLER

Following the lead of John Lyly's successful court-comedies, many Elizabethan and Jacobean dramatists employed the convention of the young woman disguised as a young man. No matter how well tutored, modern audiences still find the device a little hard to accept. When that convention is combined with others, as it is in Beaumont and Fletcher's *Philaster*, the whole *mélange* verges on the incredible, or the ridiculous, in a way Beaumont and Fletcher would not have appreciated. In that play, Euphrasia disguises herself as the page Bellario in order to be near her love, Philaster. All seems well for a time, but Philaster decides to "prefer" (recommend) Bellario to his own love, the Princess Arethusa, in order to serve as her page and as a go-between. Bellario naturally objects, and complains,

> In that small time that I have seen the world,
> I never knew a man hasty to part
> With a servant he thought trusty; I remember
> My father would prefer the boys he kept
> To greater men than he, but did it not
> Till they were grown too saucy for himself.[1]

As a regular Jacobean theatre-goer might have predicted, Bellario and Arethusa are slandered, and Philaster temporarily believes that his former page and present love have betrayed him. The plot can be unwound only when Bellario proves that she/he is the long-lost Euphrasia, unrecognized by all the court until this moment:

> —It is a woman; let her speak the rest.
> —How? That again.
> —It is a woman.
> —Blessed be you powers that favour innocence.
>
> (5.5.133–35)

The point of recalling this silly plot-complication is not to mock Beaumont and Fletcher, but rather to assert the value of studying Elizabethan letters. Letters and other documents inform us, for example, that Elizabeth Southwell, a foolish court-beauty, did indeed elope in 1605 with Leicester's son, Sir Robert Dudley, and wander through Europe to Rome disguised as Sir Robert's page. Furthermore, the seemingly witless idea that Bellario can satisfactorily be exchanged by the two lovers like some trinket, or Bellario's rather odd objections when she recalls her father preferring other pages "to greater men than he"—these practices, too, can be documented from contemporary letters. For example, Thomas, fifth baron Burgh and a client of Robert Cecil, wrote Sir Robert in 1596:

> If it lay as much in my power to conduct you to the end of your desires, as it abideth with me to satisfy you in this portion of your liking to a musician, I would make you as sensible of being beholden to me, as I am feeling of a great obligation to you for kind favours. Daniel you shall have; three other boys with him are 'mishapned' to me, one of them both plays and sings an excellent treble, but his conditions are not stayed, and one other hath a voice for a very high mean; the last is Jack, of whom I think you have taken best notice. Of these, and whatsoever else is with me, command what you will. The four, with all his instruments, were all by my worthy companion bequeathed me; choose as freely as where your commandments have most interest.[2]

The Daniel of this letter, by the way, was John Daniel, the poet's brother. I mention *Philaster* and these letters not to recall quaint Elizabethan customs, but to suggest that studying (and editing) Elizabethan familiar letters can have literary and even literary critical value.

The number of surviving Elizabethan writings which might legitimately be called "letters" is very great. The new Cambridge Bibliography's list of printed editions of "letters" covers more than five columns, making the section larger than those devoted to Erasmus, or to Webster, or to the Marprelate Controversy. Besides being bulky, these letters have been preserved in many different forms, and that variety has great bearing on how they can be or ought to be edited. I do not intend to discuss the editing of single letters as they have passed into the State Papers or lingered among other kinds of family muniments. Many of the modern collections of Elizabethan letters are in fact collections of such scattered, single exemplars; effectively, the editor defines the collection *post facto* by sender or recipient.[3] These assemblies of letters did not exist before the modern scholar sought them out, and the appropriate editorial issues are very different from, and I think less interesting than, the problems one meets when confronting a manuscript collection of letters formed by an Elizabethan individual somehow involved in writing or reading the original letters. I also set aside pious collections made by the adoring children of famous or loved ancestors (like *Letters to Severall Persons of Honour: Written by John Donne*) or the polemical volumes assembled to prove a religious or political point through individual or collective writings (like Coverdale's *Certain most godly . . . letters of . . . true Saintes and holy Martyrs*). These gatherings are really just early versions of the modern collections of single exemplars: they may be very important for their conten , but as illustrations of editorial problems or even as examples of Elizabethan social customs and ideas about writing they are usually quite uninteresting.[4]

I would like to discuss letter-collections which are coeval with their writing and especially those collections (called ''letter-books'') which represent letters sent and sometimes contain originals or copies of letters received. Since the way these collections came into existence is both interesting in itself and germane to their editing, I would like to survey the most common types of collections, or letter-books.

The easiest to deal with are the numerous surviving collections of diplomatic dispatches. Their subject-matter, of course, principally interests historians unless the ambassador or other envoy happens to mention a literary figure or to describe some literary or dramatic event, but their form is a relatively ''pure'' one. Usually, these collections will consist of duplicate, scribal copies of the diplomat's letters, sometimes interspersed chronologically with the replies or other official communications he received. Depending upon the individual diplomat (or his secretary's diligence), the file copies will sometimes be drafts, often corrected in one or more hands. These collections pose few editorial problems because they immediately circumscribe the editor's hunting ground by date, place, likely (or even named) recipients, and so forth. The editor has then only to find the originals of the copies, flesh out the historical circumstances of the diplomat's mission, and try to identify the secretary or secretaries and find extrinsic examples of their hands.

Mufti or civilian examples of such neatly defined collections are rare, because the ordinary letter-writer has more correspondents and more diverse subjects of correspondence than a professional engaged in lying abroad for his country. The diplomat usually has a defined mission, specific superiors at home and specific foreign opposite numbers. When a civilian collection has similar limits, it is almost always because one half of a pair of letter-writers has preserved the correspondence. Often this half survives without the drafts or duplicate copies of letters sent.[5] Very often, if the letter collection contains more than a single writer's letters to a single recipient, the wandering editor can anticipate the difficult problems associated with early miscellanies and commonplace books. Indeed, the line between letter-books and commonplace books is sometimes so fine that only a mad taxonomist would bother trying to draw it.[6]

The editorial problem appears because such collections tend to be immensely varied. The practice of writing down one's thoughts, or jotting notes of important events, or making a list of memorable sayings and useful hints was still relatively new in the sixteenth century, just as the proper capability (literacy, paper supplies, and so forth) was still not very widespread. The editor, like any other student of Elizabethan life, must be prepared not merely for different concepts of order—intellectual history will have made that idea familiar—but for the extremely chaotic consequences of what usually seems to have been a binary alternative: written or non-written material. An individual's written texts are today carefully separated by function: checkbook, diary, file copies of business letters, copies of personal letters, contracts with house-painters and plumbers, and so on are all docketed (carelessly or otherwise, especially when the Internal Revenue Service becomes interested). The cost of paper, the unfamiliarity of the act of writing, and other facets of Elizabethan life made such separation unlikely in theory and virtually unexampled in practice. Moreover, even the basic modern distinction between first thoughts and final versions may not be observed in early letter-books. The drafting of personal letters seems to have been much more common in Elizabethan than in more recent times, perhaps because even educated letter-writers tended to dictate letters to a professional scribe or secretary rather than set quill to paper themselves. Speech, for so long the only medium of communication, gave way slowly before the written symbol.

All these conditions and more produce the chaotic and demanding editorial problem of the Elizabethan letter-book which, as I said, will often resemble the commonplace book or miscellany as much as it resembles the early equivalent of a file of letter copies. To give a hint of a letter-book's potential range of contents, one might instance John Conybeare's letter-book.[7] Besides copies of his own personal correspondence, the volume includes such items as: letters written for his illiterate neighbors; letters written for his pupils, designed to impress the paying *pater familias* with his son's progress; academic exercises and declamations; sporadic lists of Latin adages with English translations; notes on rhetorical figures from Susenbrotus; a list of medically dangerous days of the year, and recipes for curing any of the consequences. All of this material dates from 1579–1594. Conybeare was a rural school teacher. An urban, especially a London, letter-writer would be apt to add several other kinds of material to his letter-book. For example, he would note down major political, military, and diplomatic events, usually through some narrative focussed on individuals. Thus, the famous description of Sir Richard Grenville and *The Revenge* turns up in a number of collections, despite the fact that it appeared in print within a month of the battle.

Another type of letter often appears in urban collections: the famous letter by the famous letter-writer. These letters gained a strange kind of perpetual existence in Elizabethan manuscript collections. Burghley's advice to his son, Sidney's letter on travel, and many other letters (e.g., the exchange between Essex and Egerton) appear again and again, even generations after their authors have dropped the quill for good.[8] Sometimes these letters carry the privy marks of their origin, but often they have been refashioned either to act as models in general or to serve as some specific individual's communication with some other specific individual. Most amusing of all are occasions when a standard famous letter is successively up-dated with new examples to keep it "current." The precepts remain the same, only the illustrations change. Lord Burghley, for example, wrote a celebrated letter of advice to his son Robert Cecil, and many manuscript collections contain a copy. Since the letter foresees Cecil's marriage as a future possibility, it must date from before 31 August 1589, when he married Elizabeth Brooke. A modern scholar dates it "ca. 1584."[9] Nonetheless, once the text entered manuscript circulation, it became—to some degree—the property of the collector; it left its restricted historical situation and moved towards common currency. Thus, numerous manuscript copies make slight, probably anachronistic, modifications. A paragraph on the necessity for temperate public behavior ends (in one manuscript version):

> Yet do I advise thee, not to affect nor neglect popularitie too muche, Seke not to be .*E.* and shun to be .*R.* /.

The initials clearly stand for "Essex" and "Ralegh," respectively, but they are almost certainly later additions to the original text, meant to up-date (to, say, the later 1590s) the advice.[10] Norman K. Farmer, Jr., has traced the sixty-year-long life of what he calls "a most ubiquitous letter of advice on travels"; having been written, apparently, in the mid-1570s, the letter progresses through various ascriptions until it appears in the first collected edition of Greville's works (1633).[11]

The Elizabethan letter-writer not only used his letter-book as a diary, medicine chest, almanac, or account book; he also used it as an aid to writing letters. Repository and formulary, if you will. Famous letters by famous people were preserved not just as examples of art or morality, but as potential aids in writing one's own letters. At a humbler level, some letter-books contain anonymous model letters on standard topics, precisely parallel to the printed collections of instruction and example which began to appear (in English) with William Fulwood, Angel Day, and the other Elizabethan Emily Posts.[12] A manuscript volume of *ca.* 1635 (Huntington MS. HM 1338), for example, contains an entire series of what appear to be formulaic letters: "An epistle from one freend to another concerning retirednes" (ff. 13v–14r) or another letter "Of ye sorrow not to be repented of: an epistle from a brother to his sister" (ff. 14r–14v). Letter-books will often also contain examples of standard legal documents—warrants, commissions, prorogations of Parliament or summonses to it—for their genealogical interest or to assist the owner in writing or drafting such a document for a less literate friend or to help identify the real article when it appears.[13] These model documents sometimes appear with blanks for the individuating circumstances, but they sometimes have specific names, dates, and circumstances included. In the latter case, of course, it is not always possible to be sure what made the owner keep a copy: its specific application to someone known to the compiler or its general form.[14]

In describing the various ways Elizabethan letters are preserved in letter-books, I have already mentioned some of the problems confronting the editor. The most obvious point to be made about editing letter collections is that they are manuscript rather than print. Consequently, the editor must settle on transcriptional principles and other conventions of presentation: for example, whether to use symbols in the text itself or notes keyed by line number to indicate deletions and interlineations. The editor can treat part of the task as the standard process of editing any Western paper manuscript of the early modern period: identify watermarks, sort out the handwriting(s) as to degree of proficiency, date, and so forth; look for any signs of earlier forms of binding, stabbing, or gathering; examine the MS for unequal staining or wear as a help to hypothesizing its previous form(s); try to develop a theory about the original sequence of writing and especially the arrangement of leaves if the early binding is present or can be reconstructed. In most of these tasks, good library records—especially records of purchase and/or previous sale—can be shortcuts, and the lucky editor may detect the marks of the MS's having belonged to some famous and well-documented collection.

When the essentially factual analysis has been completed, the editor is still not free of the devil which frightens every print-bibliographer's eye: multiple copies. Unlike most other manuscript forms, Elizabethan letters, especially in letter-books, are almost always copies—because they are drafts and therefore not the author's final formulation, or because they are copies made for the sender's information, or because they are duplicates made from originals which for some reason the letter-book's compiler did not preserve. Any number of reasons can be imagined for this last state of affairs. In the case of at least one of Leicester's undiplomatic letters from the Low Countries, the transcriber actually received the original letter back from Walsingham and copied it into the Earl's own collection, complete with a scribbled notation Walsingham had made on the original![15] This last piece of mechanical repetition says little for the copyist's wit, but any editor would be grateful if others were so helpfully bovine. Whenever a cipher or code was involved, too, any plain-language text which greets the modern editor probably has a very odd relation to the letter originally sent.[16] Yet, while we may be able to speculate and even in special circumstances prove why a recipient should preserve a copy rather than the original, it is often a mysterious business. Finally, as we saw in discussing the forms Elizabethan letter-books take, many letters will be copies because in fact they were never addressed to the letter-book's compiler in the first place.

Of course, the chances are that if any given letter-book has a text which appears elsewhere, then the letter-book's version will be a copy . . . and so will the other version because the existence of two versions implies circulation unless one of them can definitely be shown to be a letter sent and received. The larger the number of surviving exemplars (assuming roughly equal textual quality and equally early dates), the less secure the inferences from the hypothetical provenance of any one of them. Naturally, there are vast collections of originals: a very large one exists at Hatfield, and every editor is grateful indeed to find a letter addressed to the Salisbury family (i.e., in the Elizabethan period, Burghley and Cecil) because the "real" letter is likely to be calendared in the Historical Manuscripts Commission's Salisbury volumes. For other writers—Essex is a prime example—many originals have long since disappeared, although numerous manuscript and printed copies survive. When a letter appears to be a draft or copy of an original sent to an identifiable individual, the editor retreats at once to such storehouses of information as the *Dictionary of National Biography*, the British Library manuscript catalogues, and the indices to the Historical Manuscript Commission's publications. If the editor is lucky, he will find some mention of an original. On other occasions, he will discover the letter printed in Thomas Birch's many historical volumes or in Arthur Collins's *Letters and Memorials of State*, or in the other great seventeenth- and eighteenth-century collections of letters. Sometimes a printed text provides clues to the modern existence and whereabouts of an original, but that happy chance is rare.

One feature of English Renaissance letter-books needs more extensive examination than it has received, and it is a feature that strikes at the heart of every definition of the genre. The question is: what is a "letter"? We are all acquainted with Gabriel Harvey's and Edmund Spenser's *Three proper, and wittie familiar Letters: lately passed betwene two Vniversitie men: touching the Earthquake in Aprill last, and our English refourmed Versifying.* (Doubtless the reformed versification was also intended to be an earthquake). These letters were of course printed and there seems little doubt that Spenser and Harvey designed them for publication from the start. Furthermore, Josephine Bennett's investigation of Harvey's so-called letter-book concluded that of the four letters in that document supposedly addressed by Harvey to Spenser, only one is likely—in fact—to be meant for Spenser and all four qualify as "literary fictions" or "literary ventures."[17] A recent book on Francis Bacon shows a wise caution when the author warns that a letter's text comes from a collection made up of "copies of letters—or, perhaps, simply drafts of letters. Hence we cannot assume that they were sent to the addressee, or that if sent they went in the form we have them."[18] In the Elizabethan period, what became with Montaigne's and Bacon's help the English essay was developing very rapidly. One of its major sources was the nominal "letter," often buried in a commonplace book or letter-book.[19] Consequently, an editor who has determined, however tentatively, that the letters he has under study are copies still has, or should have, no assurance that an "original," complete with addressee and signs of having been sent and received, even exists or ever existed.

Our discussion has passed imperceptibly from such potentially knowable "facts" as watermarks, handwriting, binding, and so forth into the area usually considered a form of literary criticism, or in this case literary and historical criticism. In editing an anonymous or semi-anonymous Elizabethan letter-book whose provenance is doubtful or unknown, the editor must constantly shuttle between simple textual study and the study of his text's contents. It is an impure art because the landmarks do not always define the path. Sometimes the path—or hypothesis—will define what may be considered a landmark. Thus, with each letter, the editor tries to discover (or validate) the letter's date and sender, its addressee, its place of origin, and its destination. For dating, he will sometimes rely, cautiously, on internal evidence or the letter's position relative to other datable items in the letter-book. (This latter procedure can be as shaky as the former because Elizabethans tended to ignore either chronological organization or organization by subject-matter, especially if paper were growing scarce. The quickest example of this problem is their frequent habit of inverting and reversing the manuscript volume and writing backwards toward what had already been filled, as Philip Henslowe did in his "Diary," or of dropping back to fill empty spaces with entirely heterodox material.) For senders and recipients, the editor needs the reference volumes of various Elizabethan professions and occupations—Inns of Court and college registers, histories of livery companies, dictionaries of printers, musicians, and physicians, etc.—as well as the indices to the State Papers and the other reference works already mentioned. If a letter appears to concern some legal matter, the Public Record Office's immense and confusing collections may have to be consulted. Sometimes, especially for artisans or domestic retainers, legal documents or the household records of great families are the only possible sources of information.[20] Place-names, either in superscription or within the letter's text, will sometimes narrow the field of inquiry, and one can then appeal to local record offices and county and local histories.

Two examples from an important English Renaissance manuscript (probably compiled before 1613) will illustrate some of the editorial problems letters pose. Folger MS. V.a. 321, ff. 33ᵛ–34ʳ, contains a letter-copy addressed "To the most high and most mightie Prince, Sultan Mahumet Cham" from Queen Elizabeth. The queen writes that "our Neighbour and good brother, the kinge of Scotland" (James VI, and her successor) has sought her help in asking the Sultan's knowledge of two Scotsmen, "Lawrence Oliphant Master of Oliphant, and Robert Douglas, Master of Morton . . . Who havinge bene many yeeres since taken prysoners casuallie at Sea by Pirates, and by them solde in Barbarie for Bondmen, have ever since remayned in yt state of Captivitie . . . vntill yt of late it hath bene vnderstood (though not of certeintie) yt they are prysoners in Argier."[21] An appeal to *The Complete Peerage* will eventually inform the editor that these two individuals, Lawrence Oliphant and Robert Douglas, eldest son of the Earl of Morton, participated in an abortive rebellion against James in mid-1594. They fled Scotland and—the evidence is very strong—died during the escape.[22] So far, the editor has had to thread his way through the complexities of Scottish noble families, their titles, and royal politics in the 1580s. The copy of Elizabeth's letter ends: "Gyven vnder our Privie Seale at our Pallace of Westmynster, the 20. day of Ianuarij, in the year of our Lord God. 1600./ and of our Raigne the .43./"—that is, 20 January 1601 by modern reckoning and fully fifteen years after Oliphant and Douglas had almost certainly died. Is the letter a forgery? If so, why would any one bother? The best available answer, although not necessarily a satisfactory one, appears in another letter, this time from George Nicholson to Robert Cecil. On 15 September 1599 he writes from Scotland, "Here are letters come that" Oliphant and Douglas "should be living and prisoners in Turkey; but I see no appearance."[23] A probable answer, then, is that when a rumor of the two men's survival reached Scotland in 1599, James was still eager enough to pursue his enemies to ask Elizabeth's help in repatriating them. The letter is probably not a forgery, and the original may well have been sent.

The very next item (ff. 34ᵛ–35ʳ) is an Italian letter headed, ".1600. The Emperor of China his letter to the Queene of England./." The letter opens by reciting the sender's elaborate titles: "Il Potentissimo et Vittoriosissimo Principe Taicosama, Incomporabile gran Signor del Mondo, Figlio del Sole, al cui potente Nome tutte le Nationi Orientali prostrandosi l'adorano: Imperatore et gran Signor di tutti i Regni di China, et delle Territorij et Isole agiacenti;—Dayry ouer gran Re di Coray, Tambano, Bungo, Giamaco,—Xumoto, Ciazzure, Mino, Voari &c:'' The letter then proceeds to discuss future trade relations, based upon the representations of the ''famoso Nauarca Beniamino Vuod.'' Hakluyt does indeed report that Captain Benjamin Wood led a squadron of three ships bound from London for China, 11 July 1596.[24] Modern research has shown, however, that Wood and fellow unfortunates suffered a series of disasters and never reached China.[25] The letter is most probably a forgery, then, although its purposes are unclear. Further research yields two interesting facts. ''Taicosama'' was, in fact, the Europeans' mistaken name for Toyotami Hideyoshi, de facto ruler of Japan in the 1590s. Japan, not China. Even more curious than this error is the fact that the titles attributed to him precisely duplicate those on a scrap of paper in the archives of the East India Company: '''Title of the K[ing] of China.' Emperor and Great Lord over all the famous kingdoms of China and the territories and islands adjoining unto the same; Dayri or Great King of Coray, Tambano, Bungo, Giamaco, Xumoto, Ciazzura, Mino, Voari, &c.''[26] Into this list, which dates from 1596, another hand has inserted the ''name'' Taicosama. Why the same error (Taicosama) and the same list of titles should appear in the Folger MS and the company's archives is unclear. Perhaps the archival item was used in preparing the letter Elizabeth sent the Emperor when she dispatched the fleet; copies of that letter do survive.[27] In any event, the coincidences tease the mind and ask for some hypothesis.

The editorial activities exemplified here and the others described earlier all aim to identify the letter and its context, but the editor will also be forming an hypothesis concerning the provenance of the letter-book as an entity. That is, who collected the letters, when, and why? Judgments concerning the physical form and history of the manuscript will serve as a foundation, but the goal is to work reciprocally, back and forth between general conclusions about the document as a whole and specific observations about individual letters and other contents. Again, landmark and path are mutually defining, and a successful editorial enterprise will usually depend upon a great deal of circular reasoning, or at least on making that circular reasoning appear a persuasive interpretation of irrefutable facts and likely surmises.

The heterogeneous nature of most Elizabethan letter-books makes even these general observations rather too precise, and editing a letter-book (or, again, a commonplace book or miscellany) has numerous pitfalls. One is the Fallacy of Certitude: the editor will rarely be sure of every fact, every inference, every conclusion; he is very unlikely to account for every copy of a letter written by anyone who was at all well-known or for every reference made in a letter by anyone whomsoever. Another pitfall is the Crux of Copies: in principle, the editor is not likely to be examining the sole copy of a text written in the hand of its author. It may be a copy from dictation; it may be a copy of another original; it may be a copy of an original written for an individual who is neither a scribe nor the original owner of the manuscript. A final pitfall is the Sorrow of Sources: the editor is most unlikely to avoid the Fallacy of Certitude, escape the Crux of Copies, and arrive at full and convincing knowledge about the source of every letter and of the letter-book in which it occurs. With literacy and paper in short supply and given the Elizabethan ideas of order, most complex letter-books of the sort I have been describing here will never finally reveal their origins and the purpose of their compilation.

But do not despair. The joy is in the patient detection of quirks and habits malignly bound to make the editor's job harder. Along the way, the editor will meet old Elizabethan soldiers tired of unemployment and beggary, eager suitors courting rich widows, disgruntled authors demanding (or imploring) payment for a book's dedication, anxious politicians urging the Oath of Association, the narrative of a duel which did not take place between the Earl of Northumberland and Sir Francis Vere, and the queen rebuking the Polish ambassador in furious Latin. All these examples and many more—like Master N. Coote locked up for debt and asking his Inns of Court friends for help—appear in Folger MS. V.a. 321, a letter-book which also contains some precious copies (that dreaded word) of letters by Ben Jonson and George Chapman and Anthony Holborne and many others. Having spent more than five years working on this fascinating collection, I hope the general results of my labors will prove helpful and even encouraging to others.

An earlier version of this essay was presented to the Renaissance English Text Society at the Modern Language Association meetings, Houston, Texas, 1980.

NOTES

1. Francis Beaumont and John Fletcher, *Philaster*, ed. Andrew Gurr (London: Methuen, 1969), 2.1.22-27.

2. Historical Manuscripts Commission, *Calendar of the Manuscripts of . . . the Marquess of Salisbury*, VI (1895), 68.

3. There are many examples, for instance: Matthew Parker, *Correspondence . . . 1535-1575*, eds., J. Bruce and T. T. Perowne, Parker Society Publications, 49 (1853) and H. R. Plomer and T. P. Cross, eds., *The Life and Correspondence of Lodowick Bryskett* (Chicago: Univ. of Chicago Press, 1927).

4. Coverdale's *Certain most godly . . . letters of . . . true Saintes and holy Martyrs* (1564; STC 5886) has a marginal note suggesting the collector's methods: "they [the Protestant martyrs] wrote verye manye worthy and fruitfull letters moe: wherof sundry are mentioned in this boke which shall God willing, be published hereafter, if they in whose hands they remaine, wil bring them to light" (A4ʳ). Compare John Donne the younger's dedicatory epistle to *Letters to Severall Persons of Honour* (1651; Wing D1884), A3ʳ⁻ᵛ.

5. See, for example, Bertram Schofield, ed., *The Knyvett Letters 1620-1644*, Norfolk Record Society Publications, 20 (1949) and T. T. Lewis, ed., *Letters of Lady Brilliana Harley*, Camden Society Publications, 58 (1854; repr. New York: AMS Press, 1968).

6. See A. G. Rigg, ed., *A Glastonbury Miscellany of the Fifteenth Century* (Oxford: Oxford Univ. Press, 1968), p. 24; commonplace books are "collections of miscellaneous material assembled simply for the interest and amusement of the compiler." Cf. David M. Vieth, *Attribution in Restoration Poetry* (New Haven: Yale Univ. Press, 1963), pp. 23-24.

7. See F. C. Conybeare, ed., *Letters and Exercises of the Elizabethan Schoolmaster John Conybeare* (London: Frowde, 1905). In her edition of *The Oxinden Letters, 1607-1642* (London: Constable, 1933), Dorothy Gardiner notes that Henry Oxinden "kept letters received" and "drafts of letters dispatched . . . cramped, difficult, much corrected. . . ." "Henry also preserved," she continues, "letters neither addressed to nor penned by himself, letters written in his early boyhood and by people he had never met" (all quotations from p. xxii).

8. In *The History of Great Britaine* (1611; STC 23945), pp. 877-878, John Speed printed Egerton's letter (beginning "It is often seene, that a stander by seeth more than he that plays the game . . .") and Essex's reply (beginning "Though there is not the man this day living . . ."). The letters reappear in *Scrinia Sacra . . . A Supplement of the Cabala* (1654; Wing C184), pp. 27-31. This latter volume contains many letters which appear earlier in manuscript collections; Folger MS. V.a. 321 (*ca*. 1613), ff. 1-4ᵛ and Huntington MS. HM 36836 (*ca*. 1630), pp. 1-12 also include the letters for example.

9. Louis B. Wright, ed., *Advice to a Son* (Ithaca, N. Y.: Cornell Univ. Press for the Folger Library, 1962), pp. vii, xvii-xviii.

10. My quotation comes from Folger MS. V.a.321, f. 59ʳ. Folger MS. X.d. 212, an eighteenth-century text, expands the initials to "Essex" and "Ralegh," respec-

tively. When Burghley's "Advice" finally reaches print in *Certaine Precepts . . . for the well ordering . . . of a mans life* (1617; STC 4897), the title-page claims to be "Published from a more perfect Copy" than the "pocket Manuscripts" in wide circulation, and it omits the reference to "E." and "R."

11. Norman K. Farmer, Jr., "Fulke Greville's Letter to a Cousin in France and the Problem of Authorship in Cases of Formula Writing," *Renaissance Quarterly*, 22 (1969), 140–147.

12. In *The Art of Letter Writing: An Essay on the Handbooks Published in England During the Sixteenth and Seventeenth Centuries* (London: Univ. Press of Liverpool, 1942), Jean Robertson surveys this vast field, which touches my subject only insofar as private individuals created *ad hoc* manuscript formularies.

13. There are numerous anecdotes concerning individuals who presented counterfeit legal documents (for example, a royal warrant or commission) to achieve their purposes. Among the most extraordinary is a series of criminal attempts to "spirit" (or kidnap) unsuspecting citizens for shipment to the colonies. See *Calendar of State Papers Domestic, 1611–1618*, pp. 586 and 594.

14. Folger MS. V.a. 321, for example, contains a "privilege" for one John Rogers, an individual who has no discernible connection with any one else in the manuscript. It is most likely that the compiler copied a real document in order to have its form.

15. See J. Bruce, ed., *Correspondence of Robert Dudley, Earl of Leycester . . . 1585 and 1586*, Camden Society Publications, 27 (1844; repr. New York: AMS Press, 1968), p. iii.

16. See Octavius Ogle, ed., *Copy-Book of Sir Amias Poulet's Letters . . . 1577 London: Roxburghe Club, 1866), p. xii.*

17. See Josephine Waters Bennett, "Spenser and Gabriel Harvey's *Letter-Book*," *Modern Philology*, 29 (1931), 186.

18. Jonathan Marwil, *The Trials of Counsel: Francis Bacon in 1621* (Detroit: Wayne State Univ. Press, 1976), p. 209 n18; I owe this reference to F. J. Levy.

19. For the general argument, see M. B. Hansche, "The Formative Period of English Familiar Letter-Writers and their Contribution to the English Essay," diss. Univ. of Pennsylvania, 1902. Huntington MS. HM 1338, mentioned above, illustrates Hansche's point: it includes excerpts from Bacon's *Essays* (ff. 49^r–52^v) and from Overbury's *Characters* (ff. 58^r–60^r); it also contains a number of fairly lengthy texts on various subjects with such formulaic headings as "An Epistle: Discoursing of . . ." or "An Epistle of . . . ."

20. See, for example, James Whitelocke, *Liber Familicus*, ed. J. Bruce, Camden Society Publications, 70 (1858; repr. New York: AMS Press, 1968) or G. R. Batho's *Household Papers of Henry Percy . . . , ibid.*, 3rd ser., 93 (1962).

21. Quoted from my transcript of the MS., forthcoming as *A Seventeenth-Century Letter-Book* from the University of Delaware Press.

22. See G[eorge] E[dward] C[okayne], *The Complete Peerage*, rev. ed., V. Gibbs, *et al.*, 14 vols. (London: St. Catherine Press, 1910–59), IX, 294 and X, 54, respectively.

23. *Calendar of Scottish Papers, 1597–1603*, Part I (1969), p. 555.

24. Richard Hakluyt, *The Principal Navigations* . . . 12 vols. (Glasgow: MacLehose, 1903–05; repr. New York: AMS Press, 1965), XI, 407.

25. See Donald Ferguson, ed., *The Travels of Pedro Teixeira*, Hakluyt Society Publications, ser. 2, vol. 9 (1902), xliii–lviii and Ferguson's letter in *The Geographical Journal*, 21 (1903), 330–334. Hakluyt himself had expressed doubt about Wood's survival (*Principal Navigations*, XI, 417).

26. *Calendar of State Papers, Colonial: East Indies, China and Japan, 1513–1616* (1862), p. 98.

27. Hakluyt's version of the letter (*Principal Navigations*, XI, 417–421) does not give the emperor a proper name nor does it list his titles so elaborately.

Critical Editing
in the
Modern Languages

John McClelland

For the past ten years or so the theories which Anglo-American bib-liographers and editors derived from a specific set of problems in tex-tual transmission have spread beyond the English-speaking world. German scholars have attempted to apply these theories to their own problems—particularly to Goethe—and have found that they did not always work; as a result they too have produced a body of practical and theoretical writings which reveal a sure knowledge of thought in other disciplines, linguistics and semiotics especially, but which tend to be excessively dogmatic and so abstract as to be inapplicable.[1]

In France, on the other hand, and in spite of the proselytizing work of Laufer and Kirsop—in spite also of some critically fine editions go-ing back to 1914—Greg-Bowers's principles have been little known and produced little result.[2] Bemused as they are by the example of Montaigne, the great man constantly polishing and repolishing both his self and his thought so as to bequeath to posterity a "monumentum aere perennius," French editors have consistently chosen as copy-text the last authorized edition to appear in the writer's lifetime. They pay little, if any, attention to the earlier states of the work, except perfunc-torily to record such variants as they deem worthy of note.

Isolating what appear to be the dominant features of the Anglo-American, German and French schools, we can in fact identify three quite distinct attitudes toward the text which is to be the object of the editor's solicitations. For the English the literary work is a single ideal object; it physically exists, however, only in a set of corrupted forms. The editor's task generally is to reconstruct the lost original which was the exact mirror of the author's intentions. Hence there has to be devised a method which will be assumed to be an accurate gauge of those intentions. This attitude, though it stems immediately from the

Shakespeare editorial problem, derives ultimately from the principles of classical and medieval MS. editing, where it was assumed that the original was never revised and that the various extant non-concordant witnesses were all corrupted; their relative merits and proximity to the authorial original had first to be determined.

The French assume that a work of literature undergoes constant and repeated revision at the hand of the author (not only did Montaigne do this, but so did Ronsard and Balzac). Various intentions corresponding to different contingencies, developing beliefs, or a changing aesthetic sense are thus embodied in the various published versions. Only the last of these intentions really counts, however, because, as Pierre Barbéris describes the French view, "The value of a text is a function of its having become part of eternity, of its having entered into that state of definitive perfection which can only be reached by lengthy and arduous revision."[3] The German ideal is that of the "historisch-kritische Ausgabe," i.e., the Germans conceive of the text as being the sum of all its versions, hence of all the successive intentions which presided over its various states of revision. A text is not a static, synchronous phenomenon; once published it becomes autonomous, foreign to its own author, and the changes that the author may make in subsequent editions are dictated more by the text itself than by the intentions of its originator (examples are indeed legion of writers who at some years' distance no longer understand or recall what they first intended and so introduce "corrections" which are in fact errors). A text is thus a diachronous, dynamic system constituted by the total set of all the surviving versions of the work. Each of these is possessed of a greater or lesser degree of authority and is a self-contained, semiotically discrete, structure. In this view there is, strictly speaking, no text of a work, but texts, and it is the obligation of a critical edition fully to represent this fact: "In all parts of the edition the history of the work must be clearly visible."[4] The apparatus is thus all-important and Gunter Martens calls it the "core element" (Kernstück) of the critical edition.[5]

Whatever a textual editor's motivations, his starting-point is a set of MS. and/or printed documents, each of which contains all or part of what appears to be one or more versions of a single work. He may take it as given that the author intended to write something fairly closely resembling at least one of the versions contained in the documents, but in the absence of other evidence—letters or prefaces—the editor cannot know more of the author's intentions than what is embodied in the documents. These, of course, only came into being because there was a meaning to be communicated; but as events, the author's intentions and thought and language no longer exist except in the set of MSS. or printed signs which attempt to represent them. It is thus not possible to regress beyond the material object of the text for in fact nothing lies beyond it.[6] If bibliography and textual criticism have any philosophical basis, then it is materialism and not metaphysics. It also follows that they are not sciences, as some, mostly in the past, have held they were or ought to be.[7] At best they are practical, pragmatic technologies which rely perhaps now on some of the findings and techniques of hard science, but their fundamental methods are derived from the traditional "sciences" of history and philology.

In the absence of any MS. he knows to be holograph, the textual critic has before him documents which he surmises to be at least one remove from the author. When he has only printed sources at his disposal—and for simplicity's sake I shall assume this to be the case for the rest of the paper—the modern editor is certain that several hands have intervened: the scribe who made the printer's fair copy; the corrector or copy-editor who determined house style; the compositor who attempted to apply that style. Opportunities for noise to be introduced into the transmission are thus numerous, especially in view of the still unstandardized character of Renaissance spelling and grammar or eighteenth-century typographical practice. But even if we were to imagine a case where no noise existed, where the spelling and words and syntax and punctuation of the first printed edition conformed in every way to those of the holograph, the mere fact of translating a MS. into a printed book, with everything that entails with respect to the formal, measurable, regularity of the visual presentation, the choice of font, the use of varying type sizes and faces, etc., means that the printed edition is a very different document from the original MS., if not semantically in the strict sense of the term, then at least rhetorically. To then do a modern edition even of this ideal noiseless text will involve further changes of typography and textual density. These changes will moreover be accompanied by a certain degree of "normalization": *i* and *j, u* and *v* will be differentiated, accents and hyphens will be added, as will apostrophes, capitals and lower case may in some places be interchanged. Thus from a holograph MS. written some years or centuries ago through to a modern critical edition, there will have been at least several forms of intervention. These will, I think, always have taken the form of substitutions: one handwriting for another, one spelling for another, type in the place of handwriting, a new typography in place of the old, a different kind of layout. The uniform purpose of these interventions is to enhance certain details of the text's formal presentation so as ultimately to facilitate its transmission to a particular audience. But whatever the purpose, and however much these substitutions may have been guided by general criteria or sets of objective rules, there has always remained room for the exercise of subjective judgment on the part of the person intervening. Copying, printing, or editing a text are not simply matters of reproduction. We would do better to think of them as interpretations or rather as performances of the text (see Appendix 1).

It does not happen, of course, that a work is transmitted in a single unflawed printed version. A novel of Balzac may survive as a MS., as corrected proofs (sometimes several sets thereof), in serial form, as a frequently reprinted book, as one volume in a series (e.g., *Scènes de la vie privée*), and finally in the collected edition known as the *Comédie humaine* (1842). Obvious errors figure in all versions and each one is revised, sometimes drastically, with respect to its predecessors. There is hence no such thing as *the* text of, e.g., *Le père Goriot*, even in an ideal sense, but rather four or five texts which resemble each other to a greater or lesser degree. We cannot even say that the final version which appears in the *Comédie humaine* and which is the text most readers know was what Balzac had intended to write from the start. There can be no question of creating an eclectic text à la Greg-Bowers, because each printed edition corresponded to a specific set of circumstances. For example, Balzac introduced certain variants in order to outwit Belgian publishers of pirated editions. The "substantives" of the second edition are thus not simply an improved set of those of the first edition. And yet, if a critical edition of a Balzac novel is to be readable as well as usable, some one of the MS. or printed versions must be presented as the text to which the earlier and later variants are subjacent.

It is the text that will actually be read (subject of course to corrections) that I would call the "copy-text." By that term I mean therefore neither a text chosen "only on grounds of expediency" and which will be followed only in the matter of accidentals;[8] nor "an arrangement of words abstracted from their physical embodiment'';[9] nor a mere "working hypothesis."[10] It is what I have decided, for better or worse, to be the work as it should be read for the purposes which I as editor have in mind. It is to be reproduced with the utmost possible fidelity consistent with what I have said above and with what I shall say below, and it will be selected from among other possible copy-texts according to a set of pragmatic criteria.

First, by what one knows of the author's biography. What relation does a particular authorized edition of the work bear to his other activities at that time? To what particular phase of his development does it belong?[11] Second, the choice will be determined by history. What importance did the work have at each of the dates at which it was published and republished? Physical bibliography ought, of course, to tell us which of the documents are reliable and which are not, but an equally determining factor is the kind of edition one wants to do when confronted with the possibilities the documents allow. The copy-text of Montaigne's *Essais* must necessarily be the second (1588) edition as annotated by Montaigne himself. The first (1580) edition and its reprints are incomplete; the third (1595) posthumous edition, even though it was "authorized" to the extent that it was prepared by Montaigne's devoted protégée, does not record all the post-1588 variants. An edition of an author's complete work may have to use the first edition of each of the works as it appeared, since some writers in middle or old age prefer to eliminate from collected editions pieces that they rightly or wrongly consider to be *péchés de jeunesse*. That, for example, was Ronsard's practice.

There is a final factor which in my view and for most editions of single works—or even complete works—ought to be decisive in selecting a copy-text. G. Thomas Tanselle has distinguished between "horizontal" and "vertical" revisions which an author may make. The former kind of alteration is aimed at "intensifying, refining, or improving the work" and results from the same intention as that which initially produced it. Vertical revisions so modify a work as to move it onto another plane.[12]

This distinction seems difficult to define quantitatively, and I think it more useful to classify authorial modifications in later editions as being either corrections or variants. The purpose of the former is to bring the printer's imperfect text closer to the ideal one the author had imagined and intended. The latter carry the text forward to a new point in its history and, however few in number, enable us to identify a subsequent edition of a work as being something genuinely different from its predecessor.[13] Revisions of this sort can be measured quite accurately and it thus becomes possible to map out the diachronic axis of a literary work in the form of a graph with its highs and lows corresponding to the quantity and the importance of variants at the several dates of publication. The collation of the editions of any given work will, I believe, bear out in fact my hypothesis that this measurement will identify the point on the graph where the work has acquired its definitive structure, either as the result of the accumulation of variants or by a dramatic revision. Variants introduced after that point will either be trivial or simply complete the orientation of the definitive structure.

Miroslav Červenka holds that the first publication of a text marks its "break-through" from causality to intentionality (*Durchbruchsmoment*).[14] My view, however, is that the break-through is reached only when the work's structure becomes fixed, in the sense we have just defined. In most works that point will occur in the first edition, i.e., at the initial point on the graph or diachronic axis. But we cannot apply that theory *a priori*; only a close study of the internal history of the text will permit the editor to discover its real *Durchbruchsmoment*. To illustrate. The sixteenth-century French writer, Pontus de Tyard, composed a dialogue on "natural philosophy," entitled *L'univers*, in 1557. In 1578, the year he was elevated to the bishopric of Chalon-sur-Saône, Tyard published a second edition of the dialogue, now divided into two parts, entitled *Deux discours de la nature du monde*. This version is about fifty percent longer than the original. Nine years later a third edition appeared, augmented by a further fifteen percent and under still another title, *Premier Curieux* and *Second Curieux*.[15] In the history of this dialogue it is clearly the second edition that constitutes the break-through or, if I may propose a more suitable word borrowed from philology, the "stratum" of the text or work. In historical phonology the stratum of any language under study is the earlier language which contributed the bulk of its vocabulary and morphology. In the case of French the stratum is Latin, whereas earlier Gaulish and later Frankish constitute the substratum and the superstratum respectively. In English the Anglo-Saxon stratum rested on a Celtic substratum and was itself overlaid by a Norman French superstratum. In textual terms the word stratum is, I think, appropriate to designate the text at the point where it assumes its definitive shape and size, whereas substrata and superstrata will designate the apparatus (see Appendix 2).

There are persuasive arguments for choosing the stratum as copy-text. In a practical sense it is probably easier to handle the variants when we treat them as preparatory steps leading to the completion of the text, and as cosmetic operations designed to clear up some of the blemishes left by the major surgery. In an abstract sense we are probably being more faithful to the text itself by presenting it in the state at which it was receiving the author's closest attention; extensive revision requires as much concentration as does composition.

However much weight the notion of a textual stratum may have in determining the edition one is preparing, the other factors I have outlined may in fact be more decisive; hence I must stress again that the choice of a copy-text is ultimately a pragmatic and not a theoretical decision. The identification and correction of errors in that text cannot however be dealt with pragmatically. It may indeed be true, as Laufer would have it, that in the period 1500–1800 "the second edition really constitutes a corrected state of the original," but as he also adds, this is only true if the second edition appears within a few weeks or months of the first.[16] Otherwise the correction which the author himself proposes may be, as has often been shown, a misapprehension with respect to his original unfulfilled intention. It thus will not do to emend apparent error simply by borrowing a convenient reading from an earlier or later edition. On the other hand, I do not believe Zeller's rule to be any more acceptable, whereby an error which persists through two authorized editions thereby acquires authority and must not be emended.[17] In the sixteenth century as in the twentieth it was a mistake to spell the French number four, "quatre," with a final *s*. Tyard knew it was a mistake and so did the printer; the fact that neither corrected it in a second edition which appeared twenty-three years after the first does not mean that the error was granted "passive authorization" (Zeller's term), it simply means that neither noticed it.

A text from an earlier era is a thesaurus of structures, words, spellings, and meanings, some of which may now have disappeared. It is incumbent upon an editor to preserve all these traces of the earlier states of the language, as Zeller has been right to stress.[18] But it is equally incumbent on him not to confer official existence on forms which were simply typographical errors of spelling, omission, repetition, etc. There can, I think, be no such animal as a textual critic who is not also an historian of the language, though I have met some who thought they were both and were neither. Just as important as being a philologist, however, is possessing the patience and willingness thoroughly to analyze the spelling, punctuation, and syntax of the edition chosen to be copy-text. When an unusual word appears which might be explained as a typographical error and which has been altered in a later edition, the temptation to emend must be resisted at almost all costs. By the same token, one must not rashly assume that sixteenth-century punctuation was all chaos. The statistical analysis of a few pages will generally reveal that there is indeed a system that is being followed, however different from current practice. Once the system has been discovered, one can emend the pointing with confidence and with fidelity to the text (see Appendix 3). Charles Rosen has stated very nicely the proposition that it does a disservice to the text to replace its contemporary punctuation with our own modern signs.

> The real controversy lies deeper, however: it is whether these texts come closer to us cleaned up and in modern dress or in their original form. In modern dress, it seems to me, they direct our attention to their distance from us: they appear to be familiar only at first sight. In their strange, original form they force us to penetrate to their essential kinship with our own world. Above all for these autobiographical documents, only when they have been fully thrust back into the alien life from which they came, plunged back into history, can they commence to take on a significance that is not purely historical, and speak directly to us today.[19]

Rosen is speaking specifically about editing correspondence—Flaubert's and Byron's—but his remarks have an obvious general validity.

The actual manner of presentation of the apparatus will vary more or less significantly in direct proportion to its size and complexity. In the case of Montaigne it has proved relatively easy to incorporate the variants right into the copy-text. Poetry usually allows the variants to be presented on the same page. In some novels, however—here Balzac is once again the paradigm—they may have to be printed separately, after the main body of the text. No rules can be set, except first that the text should not be disfigured by asterisks or superscript numbers. Wherever the variant is reproduced, it should simply be preceded by page and line numbers and by the lemma. The curious and those who need to know will find their way and the others will not have their reading disturbed. Second, the variants should not be typographically downgraded by being set in a smaller size. The portions of the text they represent are not semantically inferior to the copy-text, but merely of earlier or later provenience.

Critical editions which aim at a readership beyond a few highly erudite specialists will generally be accompanied by an introduction, notes, glossary, and index. These are all forms of meta-text and unless suitably handled, they will be actually subversive of the text instead of supportive.

The first part of the introduction is, or ought to be, a chapter of bibliography, describing the documents the editor is working with (this is what the Germans call the *Befund*, or the "findings"), followed by an analysis of the variants and statements concerning the establishment of the text. In short, an account of the editor's work and an indication of just what it is that the reader is about to read. In most editions of French works this first meta-text is horribly scanted, often being nothing more than a page of inaccurate transcriptions of the titles of the original editions.

In its most frequently encountered form, the second part of the introduction is a meta-text which by its division into chapters subverts the text by decomposing it into its various causes (history, biography, sources) and its various components (language, ideas, imagery, versification). Only seldom does this meta-text attempt to resynthesize these disparate elements into a structure, and the reader is usually left with the impression that the text is somehow less than the sum of its parts. Further, by placing these commentaries before the text, the editor seems to assume that they are more important than the text, and that it will only be read as an illustration of what the commentator has been saying.

The notes are equally subversive because they scar the text with their tiny numbers and because they interrupt the continuous reading which the original edition permitted to the original reader. Notes to a meta-text, such as the present paper, are by way of parentheses or digressions, and no valid distinction can be made between the meta-text I write on the top and middle of the page and the meta-text that is numbered and typographically set off at the bottom; they both originate with me. The editor's foot-notes to a critical edition are sporadic projections of his insights and knowledge onto the specific parts of another person's text which the editor has singled out for clarification. The notes are often necessary and welcome, but they are, in the status generally accorded them, infringements on the text and not parentheses. If the notes are read the way their presentation seems to portend, then the reader's eye is forced to make a series of vertical moves along with the normal horizontal ones, and his mind is forced to assimilate two kinds of information simultaneously, the second kind usually being factual while the first is imaginative.

The introductory and annotational meta-texts are really re-creations of the text in a different form, some parts of it being expanded to demonstrate the text's causality or intentionality, other parts, judged less interesting or less difficult, being simply omitted. The function of the meta-text is to supply the text with the support it once had in its ambient culture. Its secondary purpose is to furnish the reader with some solid evidence on which to base his understanding of how the message came to acquire its shape and meaning.

Both of these purposes will be better served and the text's integrity better respected if the introductory and annotational meta-texts— excepting the chapter on bibliography—are grouped in a discursive, almost interlinear, commentary printed after the text but following its outline. Each modern reader brings his own individual baggage of knowledge and interests to an older text; he cannot know what his questions are until after he has read it. If the interlinear I propose is properly written, it will duplicate or replicate the text, but at the same time it will, by virtue of being a paraphrase of what the reader has just finished reading, allow him to skim those places he has already found less interesting. By indicating in the margin of the interlinear the page references in the text itself, the editor permits the reader who does not need the entire paraphrase—or who needs some element of it while still reading the text—to go directly to those parts of the commentary that involve his curiosity. By refusing to decompose the text or to impinge on it, the editor restores to the text its pristine unity and restores to the reader his right to read the text in his own fashion.

We have earlier characterized the activity of editing as philosophically materialist and as practically technological. Academically it derives from philology and history. Intellectually, however, it is both arithmetical and rhetorical. Arithmetical in an obvious sense, because it must quantify the documents which represent the text and bear witness to the work. Arithmetical also, because establishing the hierarchy of the authorized editions really means that one is establishing a system of proportions based on the calculus of the variants. Arithmetical, finally, because although the determination of what the text ought to be depends on what it seems to mean, the elucidation of meaning is a subjective, contingential act. The more an editor can conceive of the printed signs as objective ciphers, the closer he will come to generating a critical text whose internal system is a reasonable facsimile of what the author perhaps did intend.

Editing is rhetorical, obviously, because the editor must persuade his public of the critical validity of this text. He must therefore multiply the signs of his competence and knowledge. In short, he must make an Aristotelian ethical appeal. It is rhetorical because it is communicative: the purpose of editing is to reduce the noise which has prevented the transmission of a message from the past, and to introduce the redundancy necessary to ensure its reception and decoding. It is rhetorical in a formal sense, because the editor imposes an arrangement on his discovery, then arrays it in a diction—format, layout, typography—which will be pleasing. But editing is rhetorical in a final sense because it is probabilistic. The evidence is not hard, it is at best likely.[20]

NOTES

1. *Texte und Varianten. Probleme ihrer Edition und Interpretation*, ed. G. Martens and H. Zeller (Munich: C. H. Beck, 1971); *Edition und Wirkung*, nos. 19 and 20 (1975) of *Lili: Zeitschrift für Literaturwissenschaft und Linguistik*, ed. W. Haubrichs; H. Zeller, "A New Approach to the Critical Constitution of Literary Texts," *Studies in Bibliography*, XXVIII (1975), 231–264.

2. Wallace Kirsop, *Bibliographie matérielle et critique textuelle, vers une collaboration*, Biblio notes, 1 (Paris: Minard, 1970); Roger Laufer, *Introduction à la textologie: Vérification, établissement, édition des textes*, Collection L (Paris: Larousse, 1972); R. Laufer, "From Publishing to Editing *Gil Blas de Santillane*: An Evaluation of the Rival Claims of Practical and Ideal Editing" in *Editing Eighteenth Century Novels*, ed. G. E. Bentley, Jr. (Toronto: A. M. Hakkert, 1975), pp. 31–48; see also the "Etude de bibliographie matérielle" in Laufer's edition of Lesage's *Le diable boiteux* (Paris: Mouton, 1970).

3. "Le texte ne vaut que par son insertion dans une éternité, dans une perfection, dans un définitif auquel on ne parvient que par un long travail de révision" (P. Barbéris, "L'autobiographie: pourquoi? comment?" in *Balzac et la "Peau de chagrin,"* ed. Claude Duchet, Paris: SEDES, 1979, pp. 25–42). Many English-speaking editors of French texts seem to have remained ignorant of current bibliographical thought and practice, or at least have shown no sign of believing that

an "édition critique" ought to be something more than a pedagogically annotated reprinting of an old book.

4. Siegfried Scheibe, *Texte und Varianten*, p. 5. The late Bernard Weinberg once advocated such an edition for Balzac (B. Weinberg, "Editing Balzac: A Problem in Infinite Variation" in *Editing Nineteenth-Century Texts*, ed. John M. Robson, Toronto: Univ. of Toronto Press, 1967, pp. 60–76).

5. *Texte und Varianten*, pp. 171–172.

6. In "The Editorial Problem of Final Authorial Intention," *Studies in Bibliography* [hereafter *SB*], XXIX (1976), 179 and 183, G. Thomas Tanselle seems to be moving toward this position.

7. See G. Thomas Tanselle, "Bibliography and Science," *SB*, XXVII (1974), 55–89, for a review of the literature on the subject.

8. Sir Walter Greg, "The Rationale of Copy-Text," *Collected Papers*, ed. J. C. Maxwell (Oxford: Clarendon Press, 1966), p. 377.

9. G. Thomas Tanselle, "The Meaning of Copy-Text: A Further Note," *SB*, XXIII (1970), 192.

10. Fredson Bowers, "Greg's 'Rationale of Copy-Text' Revisited," *SB*, XXXI (1978), 153.

11. See S. Scheibe, *Texte und Varianten*, p. 32, for the relationship which he emphasizes ought to exist between the choice of copy-text and the particular "Entwicklungsphase" the editor would like to represent.

12. Tanselle, *SB*, XXIX, 193–197.

13. For the distinction "correction/variant," see my article, "Un exemplaire annoté des *Discours philosophiques* de Pontus de Tyard," *Bibliothèque d'humanisme et Renaissance*, XLI (1979), 317–338. Zeller has maintained that because a text is the sum of the relations existing among its signs, if a single one of these is changed, a new text is produced ("Struktur und Genese in der Editorik," *Lili*, 19–20, 1975, 115). Tanselle is right when he says it is a practical impossibility to take this proposition into editorial account, but his own effort to distinguish between authorial intention and authorial acquiescence seems equally impossible to apply (*SB*, XXIX, 196–197, n. 52, and 191).

14. M. Červenka, "Textologie und Semiotik," *Texte und Varianten*, pp. 143–163.

15. The late J. C. Lapp's edition of the third version of this dialogue—or rather these dialogues—misleadingly bears the title of the first version (*The Universe of Pontus de Tyard*, ed. John C. Lapp, Ithaca, N.Y.: Cornell Univ. Press, 1950).

16. R. Laufer, *Textologie*, pp. 25–26.

17. H. Zeller, *Lili*, 19–20, 121–122.

18. *Texte und Varianten*, p. 66.

19. Charles Rosen, "Romantic Documents," *New York Review of Books*, 15 May 1975, p. 20.

20. In addition to the titles quoted in the notes, to conversations with Professor John M. Robson, and to the writings of Fredson Bowers and G. Thomas Tanselle generally, I have derived particular profit from the following: Paul Baender, "The

Meaning of Copy-Text," *SB*, XXII (1969), 311–318; Anne-Marie Christin, "Rhétorique et typographie: la lettre et le sens" in "Rhétoriques, sémiotiques," *Revue d'esthétique*, I–II (1979), 297–323; Vinton A. Dearing, *Principles and Practice of Textual Analysis* (Berkeley: Univ. of California Press, 1974); Philip Gaskell, *A New Introduction to Bibliography* (Oxford: Oxford Univ. Press, 1972, 1974); Morse Peckham, "Reflections on the Foundations of Modern Textual Editing," *Proof*, I (1971), 122–155.

The original research for this paper was subsidized by a grant from the Social Science and Humanities Research Council of Canada.

APPENDICES

The following paragraphs attempt to expand or substantiate certain of the ideas and claims advanced in the foregoing paper. As they constitute either significant digressions from the main argument or the detailed exposition of the minutiae which are the textual editor's stock-in-trade, they seemed rather too extensive to consign to the footnotes.

(1) I prefer to designate the successive non-photographic reproductions of a text as "performances" rather than as simple "transcriptions," because factors of both technical competence and subjective attitude can be observed in the translation of the text from one medium to another. The resulting variants involve, in the first instance, sins of omission and commission, but conforming spelling and punctuation to house style, deciding on paragraph division and page layout, and, for modern books, "designing" the volume, are also involved. None of these modifications in shape and appearance is implicit in the text itself or is determined by it or the author. They will thus vary in direct proportion to the competence and desires of the "performers" who execute these changes.

Analogously, two singers performing, say, a Schubert song from the same Peters edition will produce different versions of that song as they translate it from the medium of print into that of sound. Leaving aside the autonomous matter of the inherent quality of the sound produced by the specific individual nature of the instruments, the most obvious differences derive simply from the fact that one singer-accompanist team will be more adept than the other at executing pianissimo or staccato passages or what have you. Another level of difference, considered more significant, is usually ascribed to the performers' capacity to "interpret" the song. Unlike a critic's interpretation of a work of art or literature, which mentions only certain features of the work because it cannot mention them all, a musician's performance of a piece cannot purposely omit any of the notes or sections of that piece; the performance of the piece is the text itself (re-)presented in another medium.

It is also the case that a musician's "interpretation" is doubly or even triply determined *a priori*: by the notes (pitches and time values), by the dynamic markings (volumes and speeds), and by the words. It follows, I think, that like the work of the copyist, the copy-editor, the compositor, and the textual editor, a performance of a piece of music is closer in nature to being a reproduction or a transcription than to being an interpretation. It is thus not a metatext, just as the transcriptions made by copyists, *et al.*, are not metatexts (see Anton Popovič, "Aspects of Metatext," *Canadian Review of Comparative Literature*, III [1976], 225-235). In that the labours of copyists, *et al.*, modify the text in ways that are personal and subjective, they are performances of that text.

To the extent that certain singers' performances have been typographically or electronically preserved (Malibran's and Adelina Patti's Rossini cadenzas, for example, or Schwarzkopf's renditions of Schubert), they have, positively or negatively, established standards for the aesthetic evaluation of subsequent performances by other singers. In the textual field two further illustrative examples may be useful, even though the subject has been thoroughly treated in Gaskell's matchless account of textual transmission (*A New Introduction to Bibliography*, pp. 343-357).

In 1553 or 1554 the famous humanist Jacques Peletier du Mans was appointed *correcteur* at the Lyonnese publishing house of Jean de Tournes to succeed the late Antoine du Moulin. Peletier was an innovator in the matter of spelling and had published a *Dialogue de l'ortografe* in 1550 (2nd edn. 1555). Nonetheless, his attempts to persuade the compositors to replace Du Moulin's system by his own were not wholly successful, and in a work such as Tyard's *Solitaire second* (1555) it is easy to discover the two systems co-existing, a fact which may reflect the hands of several compositors, or the inability of one compositor or copy-editor working under Peletier's supervision fully to assimilate the new system. Tyard's surviving autographs reveal that in spelling and punctuation his preferences were archaic. When we come to read the *Solitaire second* in the original edition, what we have before us is not materially what Tyard had in mind, nor his copyist, nor even Peletier himself, but the compositorial team's performance of that text.

Flaubert's copyist for *Madame Bovary* appears to have been so little inspired by his task that his MS. varies from the holograph in 737 places. Of these, some 110 still survived sixteen years later in the so called "édition définitive," and so found their way into modern editions, determining in turn our reading and interpretation of that text (see C. Gothot-Mersch's edition of *Madame Bovary*, Paris: Garnier, 1971, pp. 359-364).

(2) Three further examples may help to make the point. Erasmus' *Colloquies* first appeared in 1518, but by 1522–23 Erasmus seems to have conceived a more important role for these dialogues than he had earlier imagined. Greatly expanded editions of the *Colloquies* were published in those years, to the extent that one scholar has described the new editions of 1522–23 as a "different book" from the earlier versions. Though there would be further additions to the *Colloquies* between 1523 and Erasmus' death in 1536, it seems obvious that the 1522–23 editions, the true "second" editions of the *Colloquies*, constitute their virtually definitive structure and hence the stratum of the work (see Erasmus, *Ten Colloquies*, trans. Craig R. Thompson, New York, 1957, pp. xviii–xxi).

Rabelais's *Pantagruel* and *Gargantua* appeared in 1532 and 1534 respectively. In later editions Rabelais made a number of changes, many of which were dictated by the prudent necessity of avoiding the censors' wrath or conforming to their edicts. The "éditions définitives" of *Pantagruel* and *Gargantua*, incorporating these changes, were published in 1542, and modern French editors, following their usual practice, have customarily used these editions as copy-text. Apart from some minor additions and emendations, no structural or quantitatively significant modifications were introduced into *Pantagruel* and *Gargantua* after the first editions, which are, therefore, in my view the stratum of the two books and the logical copy-text. It has also been pointed out that Rabelais's satire had a more specific contextual relevance in the 1530s (e.g., the equation of Charles V with Picrochole) and that the earliest versions of the novels are therefore more interesting (see V. L. Saulnier's edition of *Pantagruel*, Geneva: Droz, 1946, pp. xlv–xlviii, and Calder and Screech's edition of *Gargantua*, Geneva: Droz, 1970, pp. xl–l and 1–2).

Finally, Proust's *A la recherche du temps perdu* exists in three versions, of which the first two, entitled respectively *Jean Santeuil* and *Contre Sainte-Beuve*, remained in MS. until the 1950s. Though many sections of these works are to be found more or less verbatim in *A la recherche*, the stratum of Proust's novel must be the third and final version because it is the only one that is complete and because structurally it is vastly different from its predecessors.

(3) With respect to the emendation of words and punctuation, the following illustration may in the first instance be useful.

In Tyard's *Solitaire premier* (Lyon, 1552) there occurs the word "'surnee' (past participle of *surnaistre*, with a feminine agreement). The meaning is figurative and this is the only such use recorded by the dictionaries. In the second, 1575, edition Tyard—or his Parisian publisher?—emended the word to "survenue" (spelt "suruenue"). Given the frequency of MS. confusion of *n* and *u*, and given too that "surnee" is divided at the end of a line, where errors frequently occur, it is easy to surmise how "suruenue" could become "surnee." "Surnee" does, however, have a recognizable meaning in the context and emendation would, I think, be out of place.

Second, it is undoubtedly worth recalling that spelling and punctuation are exclusively written codes which may convey information concerning a possible oral performance of a text, but which do not limit themselves to the phonetic and mimetic functions of representing sound, breathing, emphasis, and silence. Punctuation has a number of grammatical and semantic functions which, by the time of the Renaissance, humanists were beginning to codify. The proposition that spelling and punctuation are only "accidental" and ought therefore to be standardized or replaced wholesale, especially in earlier texts, seems to me wrong-headed. The triumph of typography over the MS. was coincidental with the transformation of the vernaculars from old and middle to modern and new. Contemporaries were not unaware of these transformations and sought, first, to preserve in print those elements which the spoken tongue quite properly neglected, i.e., the diachronous evolution of the lexicon, henceforth visible in the unpronounced "etymological" letters which humanists were fond of restoring from the supposed Latin or Greek originals.

Insofar as linguistic transformation was a factor of expanded syntactic possibilities created by the willful imitation of Ciceronian rhetoric and by the multiplication of the number of available conjunctions, punctuation served to mediate the often complex relations among clauses and syntagmas. Such mediation was not required in the spoken language, either because such complex sentences would not be uttered or because elements of the material context of the utterance would provide the clarification (see my article, "Une théorie de la ponctuation à la Renaissance d'après deux dialogues de Pontus de Tyard," in *La ponctuation, recherches historiques et actuelles*, fasc. 2, Paris, CNRS, 1979, pp. 102–122).

Burns and the Argument
for Standardisation

DAVID S. HEWITT

The textual introduction to James Kinsley's edition of the poems and songs of Robert Burns[1] (the standard critical edition of Burns) is not a lucid exposition of the textual problems or of the procedures he adopted to solve them. Fortunately, his practice is more revealing than his introduction.

Kinsley's aim was to produce a text as close as possible to that Burns submitted to his printers. Such a text must represent Burns's final known intentions; the first edition of his poems, and all subsequent editions, incorporate "improvements" to the spelling and punctuation, which might have been sanctioned by Burns but which are more probably the responsibility of others. So Kinsley bases his text upon manuscripts whenever possible.

There is a large and varied body of holograph manuscripts. There are several drafts of many poems; frequently there is more than one version—Burns provided copies from memory for friends and sometimes altered poems deliberately to compliment his correspondents. Professor Kinsley is scrupulous in working out the chronology and relationships of different manuscripts in order to establish the most authoritative text for each poem.

Where there is no manuscript or only an early draft, the text is based on an early version. Burns prepared his poems very carefully for the first edition of his work, the Kilmarnock edition of 1786; part of his holograph copy is extant and is now known as the Irvine Burns Club Manuscript. Although the printer was reasonably faithful to what Burns wrote, there are alterations in punctuation, in the provision of apostrophes, in hyphenation, in capitalisation, and some regularisation of spelling. It is thought that Burns read the proofs, but he cannot have been too attentive for there are a number of obvious errors.

The Edinburgh edition of 1787 adds twenty-two new pieces and includes all the poems of the Kilmarnock edition, but with some revision and some anglicisation of accidentals and substantives. There are two impressions, known as "skinking" and "stinking." In the earlier, we are told in *To a Haggis* that "Auld Scotland wants nae skinking ware / That jaups in luggies";[2] whereas, in the second impression, "Auld Scotland wants nae stinking ware"; (skinking means watery). Burns supervised the first impression; for instance, in a letter to John Ballantine of Ayr on 14 January 1787 he says "I have this day corrected my 152d page."[3] The supervision of the second impression, which involved some resetting, was not undertaken by Burns, and there are more than 300 differences in the accidentals of the two impressions.

A new edition was produced in Edinburgh in 1793 and reprinted in 1794. Burns provided new material and he asked Alexander Fraser Tytler to see the edition through the press. On 6 December 1792 he writes to Tytler from Dumfries:

> I again trouble with another, & my last, parcel of Manuscript. —I am not interested in any of these; blot them at your pleasure. —I am much indebted to you for taking the trouble of correcting the Press-work.[4]

As might be expected, the text of the poems reprinted in the edition of 1793 moves yet further away from spelling and the punctuation actually used by Burns himself in the Irvine Manuscript.

This brief bibliographical and textual history simplifies the situation; it does not discuss a poem like *Love and Liberty* which was not published in Burns's lifetime and which is not complete in any single manuscript; it omits consideration of the songs that were published in Johnson's and Thomson's anthologies; it does not deal with poems that were first published in magazines. Its purpose is to show that Professor Kinsley's procedures are justified. It provides further evidence, from another poet, in support of McKerrow and Greg's observation that reprints degenerate in accidentals, even when revised by the author; and thus it supports Kinsley's use of the Greg-Bowers principles for establishing the copy-text of a critical edition.

Even so, there are issues on which one might wish to challenge Professor Kinsley. The quality of his textual editing is not always what it should be; for instance, his text of *The Holy Fair* is derived from the Kilmarnock edition when he says it comes from the Irvine Manuscript. He even reproduces a printer's error—"Anither sighs and pray's."[5] (The intrusive apostrophe is not to be found in the MS.) And there are textual principles that should have been debated but never are. Many of Burns's songs, to choose one issue, were not written by Burns, but collected (some self-collected from the oral tradition he himself inherited). "Oh my Luve's like a red, red rose" is the best-known example. Some of these collected songs were defective; Burns repaired them. Others were crude; Burns refined them. In this Burns's practice is not significantly different from the editing procedures of other eighteenth-century song collectors. He also wrote songs to traditional tunes. But given that all his songs have tunes and belong to an oral tradition in one way or another, the quest for a definitive text may have been inappropriate.

Professor Kinsley should also have considered the literary and critical consequences of his eclecticism. The "improvements" made to the Edinburgh edition were not just the result of a printer's whim. Burns was under considerable pressure from friends and acquaintances, as well as printers, to produce a socially-approved text, that is, a text which involves some anglicisation as well as bowdlerisation. Professor Kinsley rejects the consequences of such pressure when he reproduces the accidentals of the manuscripts, but he accepts Burns's substantive revision, which is equally the result of social pressure. In the manuscripts and Kilmarnock version of *The Twa Dogs*, Caesar's straightforward crudity about the activities of men on the grand tour condemns by its bluntness:

> Then bowses drumlie German-water,
> To make himsel look fair an' fatter,
> An' purge the bitter ga's an' cankers,
> O' curst *Venetian* b–res an' ch–cres.[6]

The replacement lines are more polite; they are an elegantly ironic way of putting an unpleasant subject. But they do not reveal Caesar's contempt for the upper classes, and they make the anger of the last two lines appear abrupt:

> Then bowses drumlie German-water,
> To make himsel look fair an' fatter,
> An' clear the consequential sorrows,
> Love-gifts of Carnival Signioras.
> *For Britain's guid*! for her destruction!
> Wi' dissipation, feud an' faction![7]

I am criticising Professor Kinsley not because of the way he has established his copy-text, but because he never considers the issues raised by the application of his textual methodology. In spite of this, *The Poems and Songs of Robert Burns* is an important critical edition that furnishes the best scholarly text of Burns that we are likely to see published for a long time. Professor Kinsley has determined, more or less, what Burns wrote.

That, of course, *is* the business of the textual critic. But this description of the aims of textual criticism assumes the written text realises the author's intentions. I am not making any kind of metaphysical or epistemological point, but a practical one. I would like to argue that the means and conventions of writing the language used by Burns were defective, that the orthographic system available to him was deficient. The critical text undoubtedly establishes what Burns wrote, but it does not tell us what he was trying to write.

In the late eighteenth century, all the social classes of lowland Scotland spoke Scots, and only a few individuals, members of the aristocracy educated at Eton and other southern educational establishments, did not. There is abundant evidence about how people spoke; because speech was a topic of great concern, speech habits were frequently described.[8] And it is apparent from these descriptions that spoken Scots was still a functioning system. Of Lord Kames, a Scottish judge, John Ramsay of Ochtertyre wrote: "It must not be omitted that the language of his social hour was pure Scots, nowise like that which he spoke on the bench, which approached to English."[9] The evident desire of the upper classes of Scotland to speak English is not evidence that they spoke it. We cannot look at, say, the language of a Waverley novel to see how people spoke. Scott's representation of speech is a convention. He wishes to distinguish speech by social class; so in the "Scotch novels" the upper classes speak English, apparently, the middle ranks a light Scots, and the low a fully dialectal Scots. This is a convention because, while speech does vary according to social class, the variation is part of a linguistic continuum; Scott's distinct divisions are schematic. The nature of the representation is also conventional. In the most perceptive of the contemporary comments on Scots, John Galt says:

> It does not seem to be, as yet, very generally understood by the critics in the South, that, independently of phraseology, there is such an idiomatic difference in the structure of the national dialects of England and Scotland, that very good Scotch might be couched in the purest English terms, and without the employment of a single Scottish word.[10]

Scott's English does not represent English speech, but rather the speech of the Scottish upper classes.

Of course there was much linguistic innovation. Because of the political and economic structure of Great Britain, linguistic innovation consisted largely of importations from England. Many upper-class Scots tried to ape English accents, without success, for they spoke "English" as they thought it was uttered, not as it really was. (Ramsay is wise to say of Kames's speech on the bench that it "approached to English.") Many English words were adopted; some of these were new words to Scots and thus a clear lexical enhancement of it; others were just English equivalents to Scots words. English grammatical forms were infecting the Scottish grammatical system. In fact, such was the scale of linguistic innovation that James Boswell lamented in one of his "French themes":

> The Scottish language is being lost every day, and in a short time will become quite unintelligible. Some words perhaps will be retained in our statutes and in our popular songs. To me, who have the true patriotic soul of an old Scotsman, that would seem a pity. It is for that reason that I have undertaken to make a dictionary of our tongue, through which one will always have the means of learning it like any other dead language.[11]

The quotation is famous, and has been used frequently to illustrate the condition of Scots in the late eighteenth century. But few of those who have used it as evidence have made allowance for Boswell the poseur. Boswell predicts the termination of Scots so as to give himself the role of scholar–hero—he was much under Dr. Johnson's influence. And few have seemed to notice that earlier in his discussion of Scots, Boswell comments on the unintelligibility of Scots to most Englishmen and thus witnesses to the real separation of the spoken languages.

The written language, on the other hand, was far more anglicised. Cultural and political pressures in the seventeenth century spread written English; King James's Authorised Version of the Bible was used throughout the churches and homes of lowland Scotland, and the language of national politics, after the Union of the Crowns in 1603, was English. In the eighteenth century, following the Union of the Parliaments in 1707, commercial pressure was added to the cultural and political. Scotsmen wished to do business in England. Hume, Robertson, and Smith wished to address an international audience. They therefore wrote in English just as predecessors like George Buchanan wrote in Latin. Those like Allan Ramsay, or Robert Fergusson, or Robert Burns who wished to write in Scots had no standard of written Scots to employ and therefore created a mixed language, partly dependent upon the conventions of written English and partly upon a roughly-phonetic representation of speech. Their knowledge of the great literary achievements and fifteenth and sixteenth century Scotland, of James I, Henryson, Dunbar, Douglas, Lindsay, Scott, Montgomery, and others was severely limited, and therefore their models were limited. There was no means of resisting the take-over of written Scots by written English, other than the sentiment of individual writers. James Beattie, the professor of moral philosophy in Marischal College, Aberdeen, wrote to John Pinkerton in 1778: "Those who now write Scotch, use an affected, mixed, barbarous dialect, which is neither Scotch nor English, but a strange jumble of both."[12] Beattie was right. When we examine the work of those writing in Scots in the period, it does seem to be neither Scots nor English, but a strange jumble of both.

The appearance of Burns's language is not, however, coincidental with the reality, and I submit that very many of Burns's poems are written in a bad representation of Scots. For some years, critics have been pointing out that Burns's poems assume a Scottish voice and a Scottish accent.[13] I should go further and argue that when these poems are recited by a person of Scottish voice and Scottish accent, we may discern not just the Scottishness of the apparently English words, but a residual Scottish grammar. In phonology, lexis, and grammar, Burns's poems are distinctly more Scottish than they appear on the page.

This may be illustrated from *The Holy Fair*, from which, for ease of reference, I propose to draw the majority of my examples. An examination of the rhymes reveals something of its Scottish phonology. Burns uses many slant rhymes and perpetuates a number of comic rhymes—he rhymes "do't" with "spot" (48)—and therefore evidence from rhymes must be handled with care. But he links "lambie" (24) and "saw me" (26), which suggests that the "a" in "lambie" is a back vowel, rather than the front vowel that might be expected in English. "Hands" (33) was rhymed with "comman's" (35) in the Irvine manuscript and the edition of 1786, and with "commauns" in the editions of 1787 and 1793; in 1794 he substituted the eye rhyme "commands" for an ear-rhyme in which the "a" is a back vowel and in which the terminal "d" is mute. In line 160, where Burns uses an internal rhyme as he does at various points in the poem, "din" is linked with "end"; once more the terminal "d" is silent. "Show'rs" (73) rhymes with "wh-res" (75); the vowel in both sounds "oo." These are but a few examples. It is not possible to determine how Burns actually pronounced the words, of course, but the pairings may be sufficient to indicate that what Burns writes assumes the Southwest Scotland system of pronunciation.

The very inconsistencies of Burns's spelling are evidence of the Scottish basis of his writing, for he vacillates between English written forms and a roughly phonetic rendering of speech. There is a nice example in line 185, where Burns has a double internal rhyme—"piercin words" and "highlan swords." He drops the final "d" of highland in accordance with Scottish speech usage but leaves "high" in its English form, although he would have said "hielan." The liberal use of apostrophes is further evidence of the conflict between standard English spelling, of "and" or "with" or "of," and the words as said in Scots—"an'," "wi'," and "o'." I would submit that in Burns's mind there is no confusion between Scots and English; he is thinking in Scots but is without a consistent orthographic system to represent his intentions.

His vocabulary too has been thought to show a confused mixture of Scots and English. In *The Holy Fair* there are many peculiarly Scots words; in the first two stanzas there are "callor," "hirplan," "furrs," "*hizzies*," and "*lyart*." There are also Scottish idioms—"early at the road" and "a wee aback." But everything that is not clearly Scots is not English. The two languages have many words in common; after all, both have a common parent language, Anglo-Saxon, and both borrowed independently, but in parallel, from French and Latin. Burns renders some of these common words in a way that reflects a Scots pronunciation—"simmer" (1), "countra" (74) or "furms" (204) for example—but others are spelt in a way that does not differentiate them from English. If my earlier argument about the sound system of *The Holy Fair* is accepted, these must undoubtedly have had a Scottish pronunciation; "fright" (108) has a frontal "i" followed by a velar fricative, and "pow'rs" (128) would be said as though it were "poors."

Other words are borrowed from English. But there is no need to argue that lexical borrowings create a strange phonetic jumble. They were assimilated to Scots speech; "blackguarding" (80) would have become "blagayrdin" when said by Burns, although it retains an English appearance. Nor should one argue that imported words somehow dilute pure Scots. They offer Burns yet more synonyms (the number of synonyms is one of the features of the English languages in general) and a further range of expression. He uses the opportunities creatively. According to the *Oxford English Dictionary*, the word "blackguard" in the sense of "a low worthless character addicted to or ready for crime; an open scoundrel" comes into English in the mideighteenth century. Its first recorded use as a verb is by Burns in this poem. So Burns is not the victim of an English take-over of his Scots; he is linguistically inventive, borrowing words that he then turns to his own purposes.

There is also much evidence of a specifically Scots morphology in *The Holy Fair*. There are the Scottish forms of strong verbs: "cam" (13), "gaed" (16), "gien" (34), "hae" (38), "gaun" (41), "maun" (67). The verb "do" is used as an auxiliary, as it is in medieval Scots, without any implication of emphasis: "low did stoop" (25) and "does define" (133). He uses the Scottish form of the contracted negative— "canna" (121)—and also the contracted form of the future of the verb "to be"—"we'se" (49). He employs the Scottish grammatical suffix for the present participle—"an." Raymond Bentman in his article, "Robert Burns's Use of Scottish Diction," has claimed that throughout the vernacular poems "Burns interchanges, arbitrarily, the grammatical suffixes "an," "in," "in'," and "ing.""[14] In *The Holy Fair*, this is not so; all the gerunds end in "in"—"laughin" (44), "remarkin" (49), "rattlin an' thumpin" (110), which would suggest that Burns has some awareness of the middle Scots distinction between the gerund in "in(g)" and the participle in "an(d)." Admittedly, he varies the participial ending; that he does so is actually evidence of his own pronunciation, which would sound the suffix in the same way in each case—an undifferentiated vowel followed by an "n," without a terminal "g." If this were not the case, the mixture of forms would be intolerable.

Much of the rest of the morphology may look English, but the spelling "dismist" (202), although adopted to maintain the appearance of the rhyme with "past" (200) reminds us that the preterite of weak verbs in medieval Scots ended in "t" or "it," and that this is still how the "ed" morpheme is pronounced in many instances, in spite of the spelling in standard English.

My thesis, then, is that Burns's language is much more Scots than the printed page appears to suggest, and that the "notation" that he used (and there was no other available) obfuscates his actual language. I am aware that there will be objections. Raymond Bentman voiced one in 1965 when he argued that although Burns said in the Preface to the Kilmarnock edition that he sang "the sentiments and manners, he felt and saw in himself and his rustic compeers around him, in his and their native language,"[15] the "sprinkling of Scotch" that he talks about in his letters to George Thomson[16] better describes his practice.[17] To such a critic I would reply that in the Kilmarnock edition of 1786, before he was affected by the social pressures of success, he states what he is aiming to do; in his letters to Thomson in the 1790s he is defending the use of Scots and resisting his editor's desire to anglicise popular song and make it polite. I maintain that the Anglo-Scots appearance of the majority of Burns's poems and songs obscures the more purely Scots ideal original.

My argument, that there is a discernible and better text behind the written one, has serious implications for the Greg-Bowers school of textual scholarship, which has done so much to establish principles and methodologies for working out what an author wrote. And my solution to the problem I have outlined will be even more controversial than the diagnosis, for I wish to propose that the text of Burns be "transposed" into a Scots orthography and grammar, standardised on a historical basis. However, I wish to emphasise that I believe the proper objective of any critical edition is to establish, as far as is possible, what the author wrote. The only evidence of the ideal text is in the written one, which is therefore indispensible. I am not arguing then that a critical edition can be superseded by a standardised one. But in arguing that there are strong linguistic reasons for producing a text of Burns that is standardised in its orthography and grammar, and in claiming that such a text would provide a better representation of what the author intended than does Professor Kinsley's edition, I am providing both practical and theoretic justification for the standardised text.

Standardising need not involve the irresponsible practices of nineteenth-century editors, who frequently seemed to alter their text of Burns according to their own idea of what was proper in grammar, morals, or punctuation, and whose text was further altered by the printer's application of whatever printer's grammar he used. Standardising, if it has to be done at all, must be conducted in controlled and agreed circumstances. It must involve the historians of printing, bibliographers, textual critics, linguists, and literary critics. The principles and practices to be adopted must eschew modernisation and be directed towards producing a language and a text that has a historical basis in the period in question. And these principles and practices must be applicable to all the appropriate writers of the period. It would be futile to have one set of rules for Burns and another for his contemporary Robert Fergusson.

The creation of a standardised language on historical principles will begin with the choice of the poets and poetic manuscripts to be examined. Ideally, one should deal with them all. This might not be impossible if one confined oneself to Scottish poets of the eighteenth century, for they are few and did not write much, but if the scope of the enquiry included the novels of Scott in the early nineteenth century, there would be an immense volume of material to process. Selection would be essential. Where manuscripts are not extant, it will be necessary to establish a critical text. Bibliographical study will then be required to identify compositors, and to estimate their reliability in dealing with a poetic manuscript.

Linguists will next study each of the different ways in which a word was written; they will also examine rhyming words, and from this evidence and from their knowledge of the history of Scots they will work out an orthography that has a phonemic basis. We cannot be sure of what Burns sounded like, but we get a fair idea of his phonemic system from the way he represented sounds, from his rhymes, and from the differentiations he observed. The linguists must also examine every text for morphological evidence that is concealed, or partly concealed, by the present confused orthography and work out a Scots grammar that is appropriate to the late eighteenth and early nineteenth centuries. While doing this, they may even find elements of a distinctive Scottish syntax, which is the aspect of Scots that is least distinguished from English.

In other words, nothing less is involved than recreating the language Burns used but could not render. It may sound an impossible programme. I do not think it is. Firstly, the quantity of materials to be handled need not be excessive. Secondly, the team of scholars need not be large, and will not require decades to complete their task. Most of us are not just textual critics, or literary critics, or linguists but manage to be several at once. The team even has an embryo existence already; those of us in the Scottish universities who are concerned with Scottish language and literature have been co-operating closely over the last decade, and our co-operation has greatly developed the study of the subject and our understanding of it. And thirdly, language planning, "the activity of preparing a normative orthography, grammar and dictionary for the guidance of writers and speakers in a non-homogeneous speech-community"[18] to use Einar Haugen's definition, has already begun. We have the dictionary, *The Scottish National Dictionary*. Much work is now being done on the spelling and grammar of Scots,[19] and it would not be difficult to apply this knowledge and experience to a particular period of our literary history.

The application of the recreated language to Burns will not be easy. Burns is a dramatic poet who used language to represent the different voices of different people, from different classes, with different points of view. But he is not always successful in doing this clearly. Critics talk of his turning to English in the latter part of *The Cotter's Saturday Night*. It certainly looks like English, but, I believe, it would be better described as the language of the Authorised Version as understood by a Scotsman. In *Tam o'Shanter*, he is said to turn to English when he writes:

> But pleasures are like poppies spread,
> You seize the flower, its bloom is shed;
> Or like the snow falls in the river,
> A moment white—then melts for ever;
> Or like the borealis race,
> That flits ere you can point their place;
> Or like the rainbow's lovely form
> Evanishing amid the storm.—
> Nae man can tether time or tide;
> The hour approaches *Tam* maun ride.[20]

The abrupt return to Scots in the last two lines emphasises the Englishness of the previous lines. But the speaker is another of the warning voices of which Tam has experience; he is the minister or the fireside philosopher, whose educated Scots is written as though it were English. If Burns had trouble in putting this over, we should not be too inhibited when we try to make the new standardised language fit the needs of his poetry.

Nowadays, there is considerable scholarly opposition to the standardised text. But I believe that standardised texts are useful; scholars and experts greatly underestimate the reading difficulties posed by medieval literature that is not written in the London dialect, or later dialectal literature that does not employ a standard orthography. There are few scholars and experts; there are many students and general readers who are prepared to read *Sir Gawain and the Green Knight*, the poems of Robert Henryson and Dunbar, Douglas's *Ænid*, Burns and Scott, or Hugh MacDiarmid, a neglected writer who is unquestionably one of the greatest poets of this century; but these students and general readers are daunted by the peculiar language and fatigued by repeated reference to a glossary that tells them the word they have just looked up is yet another variant of one they have looked up five times already. I submit that it is a mistake for textual critics to limit themselves to the production of critical texts; we must recognise the demand and the need for standardised texts and be involved in the evolution of the rules and principles to be applied in the business of creating them.

In this essay I have tried to demonstrate that, when Robert Burns is considered, the case for standardisation has a theoretical as well as a practical justification. I hope that my arguments might be applicable to other periods of Scottish literature—to the late middle ages and to the twentieth century. I am confident that the methodology I have outlined is broadly applicable. And if this case can win a fair measure of support, I believe we could standardise with a clear conscience.[21]

NOTES

1. *The Poems and Songs of Robert Burns*, ed. James Kinsley, 3 vols. (Oxford, 1968), III, 963–994.
2. *Poems and Songs*, I, no. 136, 45–46.
3. *The Letters of Robert Burns*, ed. J. De Lancey Ferguson (Oxford, 1931), I, no. 77, p. 68.
4. *Letters,* II, no. 526, p. 138.
5. *Poems and Songs,* I, no. 70, 85.
6. *Poems and Songs,* I, no. 71, 165–168, and footnote.
7. *Poems and Songs*, I, no. 71, 165–170.

8. In, for instance, John Ramsey of Ochtertyre, *Scotland and Scotsmen in the Eighteenth Century*, ed. Alexander Allardyce, 2 vols. (Edinburgh, 1888); Alexander Carlyle, *Autobiography* (Edinburgh, 1860); Henry Cockburn, *Memorials of his Time* (Edinburgh, 1856).

9. Ramsay, *op.cit.*, I, pp. 211-212.

10. John Galt, *Ringan Gilhaize*, ed. D. S. Meldrum and W. Roughead (Edinburgh, 1936), vol. 2, note A.

11. *Boswell in Holland 1763-1764*, ed. F. A. Pottle (London, 1952), p. 161.

12. *The Literary Correspondence of John Pinkerton, Esq.*, 2 vols. (London, 1830), I, p. 7.

13. See, for instance, Thomas Crawford, *Burns: a Study of the Poems and Songs*, second edition (Edinburgh, 1965), p. xiii.

14. In *From Sensibility to Romanticism*, ed. Frederick W. Hilles and Harold Bloom (New York, 1965), p. 239.

15. *Poems and Songs*, III, p. 971.

16. *Letters*, II, pp. 122, 204, 205, 273.

17. In *From Sensibility to Romanticism*, pp. 240-241.

18. Einar Haugen, "Language Planning in Modern Norway," *Scandinavian Studies*, 33 (1961), 68-81.

19. For a summary and analysis of current language research in Scotland, see A. J. Aitken, "Studies on Scots and Scottish Standard English Today," in *Languages of Scotland*, ed. A. J. Aitken and Tom McArthur (Edinburgh, 1979), pp. 137-160.

20. *Poems and Songs*, II, 321, 59-68.

I wish to acknowledge with gratitude the advice of my colleagues Mr. Thomas Crawford and Mr. J. D. McClure.

The Four Ages of Editing and the English Romantics

Donald H. Reiman

I

As Shelley's friend Thomas Love Peacock discussed the evolution of literature from Homer into his own time under the rubric "The Four Ages of Poetry," so we can divide the texts of the English Romantics into products of Four Ages of Editing. In the first, or Golden Age of Innocence, the widow, son, daughter, son-in-law, nephew, friend, publisher, or enthusiastic disciple of the poet simply gathered whatever letters and unpublished literary manuscripts he or she could collect from other relatives and friends of the dead writer, added fugitive periodical publications, and either issued these as a supplement to the works already published during the poet's lifetime or (perhaps later) combined these with republication of those writings issued earlier. Such editions include Mary Shelley's editing of Shelley's poems and essays (1824, 1839, 1840); Cadell's "Magnum Opus" edition of Scott, with Lockhart's *Life* (1829–1840); the John Murray edition of Byron's *Works* (1832–33); editions of Coleridge by Henry Nelson Coleridge and Sara Coleridge (1835, 1836, 1840, 1849, 1850); Richard Monckton Milnes's *Life, Letters, and Literary Remains of John Keats* (1848); the Gilchrist-Rossetti *William Blake* (1863); and Moxon's and Macmillan's editions of Wordsworth's *The Prelude* and *Poetical Works* published under the supervision of Edward Quillinan and Christopher Wordsworth in the 1850s and 1860s. The prefaces and "texts" of these editions often contain apologetic biographical materials and notes, the main aim of the editors being to win for the writer the wide readership that the writer's publisher, heirs, and admirers thought he deserved. Though these editions also constituted serious attempts to expand and authenticate the canon, less effort was made to identify and follow the best textual authorities, and where the author's own publications and manuscripts seemed obscure, the editor or publisher often "clarified" the text by repunctuating it, filling in blanks, or omitting fragments of uncompleted poems. All these "improvements" were made in a spirit of affection or reverence for the author, rather than in the condescending search for superficial polish and decorum that so often characterized the subsequent Silver Age.

From the later Victorian period and into the twentieth century, there appeared a great many texts of the Romantics edited by those who thought, with Matthew Arnold, that the Romantics did not *know* enough—that (as Milton, Dryden, and their contemporaries too often thought of Shakespeare and his age) the poets of the early part of the century were untrained geniuses, warbling woodnotes wild in a rude and barbarous age. The more dedicated among these editors set about "improving" the texts of the Romantics right and left, patching and tinkering as they went.

William Michael Rossetti exemplifies the best editors of the Silver Age. On 28 March 1868 Rossetti entered a controversy in *Notes and Queries* on the text and meaning of Shelley's poems that showed him to be very knowledgeable about them. While declaring himself opposed to the "'cobbling and tinkering' of the verses of deceased poets," he argued that Shelley's poetry had suffered from numerous printers' errors in need of correction, and he followed with a series in *Notes and Queries* of proposed "Notes and Emendations on Shelley" (11, 18, and 25 April 1868) that won him the favorable attention of Moxon & Company (whom Rossetti had only two years before caught in unethical behavior connected with the suppression of Swinburne's *Poems and Ballads*.[1] By 5 November 1868, Rossetti and J. Bertrand Payne of Moxon's had agreed that Rossetti would make what he terms "editorial revisions of the text [of Shelley's poetry] to be, if practicable, such as will not render the stereotype-plates useless, but only entail alterations here and there." Payne, Rossetti continued, "concurs in my proposal of occasional notes, accompanying the actual revision of the text. For this work I proposed to charge £30, to which he at once acceded: indeed, I suspect it was sensibly less than he had expected to be asked."[2] In the same conversation, Rossetti notes, "Payne seems to have also some undefined notions as to a re-edition and Life of Coleridge; and I think it possible that he might eventually make some proposal to me on this subject also."

In carrying out his "editorial work," Rossetti relied chiefly on "editions of Shelley" sent to him by Payne on 17 November 1868. Naturally, these editions consisted primarily of texts Moxon's had published, especially multiple copies of the one-volume stereotyped edition (1866), which Rossetti cut up, marked with his insertions and changes, and eventually sent back to Moxon's as printer's copy.[3] By 4 January 1869 Rossetti had begun "a tabular compendium of the facts etc. of Shelley's life" in order to begin his introductory "Memoir" of Shelley, and thereafter he devoted most of his time to gathering material for that memoir. Much of his "editing" had been completed by this date, as emerges from his diary entry for 12 January 1869:

> Swinburne came for a Shelley discussion. . . . He is strenuous for sticking to the texts revised, or which might have been revised, by Shelley himself: urges the restoration of *Laon and Cythna* bodily—but this I shan't do. On various points he convinced me that alterations which I had introduced—however plausible—had better be excluded; and this I *shall* do. Got no further than the Prometheus in reading him the principal of my notes.[4]

Swinburne's advice to let the poet have his say was, however, counteracted by other friends and correspondents of Rossetti, including Frederick Gard Fleay (1831-1904), at that time headmaster of a grammar school, with whom Rossetti exchanged a series of letters on proposed conjectural emendations of Shelley's texts in 1869-70, and to whom Rossetti pays tribute as "the earliest & most systematic of Shelley's emendators."[5] Though Rossetti resisted many of Fleay's more elaborate plans to emend the text to improve Shelley's rhythm and rhymes, he doubtless was encouraged by Fleay's attitude to introduce a number of his own favorite conjectures into the text. In the end, Rossetti's two-volume edition of 1870 contains more such speculative changes than any other edition of Shelley's poetry. Moreover, as can be clearly seen from Rossetti's press-copy in The Pforzheimer Library, he made no systematic attempt—how could he, in the short time he devoted to the text?—to collate the Moxon editions with Shelley's original editions or with Mary Shelley's edition of Shelley's *Posthumous Poems*.

The nature of Rossetti's corruptions of Shelley's texts may be seen from the notes to Harry Buxton Forman's edition of Shelley's *Poetical Works*[6] and in the work of modern editors who have worked with the primary published and manuscript authorities.[7] Rossetti was devoted to Shelley and to the other Romantic and Victorian poets and was an industrious biographer and (in some ways) bibliographer of them. His emendations exhibit both common sense and attention to the poet's meaning. Nevertheless, he too often simply revised the poems to rep-

resent what *he* judged to be the best poetry or the most coherent meaning, rather than following the evidence of the author's intention. And
he soon became too busy to concentrate on detailed collation of any
poet, for he records in his Diary for 3 February 1869 a discussion with
J. B. Payne about what became the Moxon's Popular Poets series:

> He [Payne] has an idea of bringing-out a series of English Poets, non-copyright
> works, very cheap; a publication similar to one by Nimmo, but in better taste.
> Longfellow would be first: followed by Scott, Byron, Shelley, Thomson,
> Keats, Selections, etc. etc. . . . For these books he wishes to obtain brief prefa-
> tory memoirs, with some critical estimate (say 18 to 20 pp. apiece); and wishes
> besides to have a paper selection made of the editions to be printed from. This,
> without any following of the text through the press, would constitute the edito-
> rial work. . . . I proposed to do it for £25 per book, excluding selections, for
> which I would charge higher: he replied that his calculations admitted of only
> £21 per book (allowing the same exception): . . . I assented to this.[8]

The references in Rossetti's diary and letters make clear that though
he was assiduous in gathering new biographical material and some unpublished fragments for *The Complete Poetical Works of Percy
Bysshe Shelley* (2 vols., 1870), he made no serious efforts to establish
the authority of the texts; most of his concern in the other volumes
devolved on what selections he could or could not publish without
paying a copyright fee.

Even such questions as copyright seem not to have concerned
American editors of the period. A letter from James Russell Lowell to
"Mr. Bolles," perhaps a printer with H. O. Houghton and Company,
the printers of the 1854 edition of Keats published by Little, Brown &
Co., reads simply:

> 20th April.
>
> Mr. Bolles
>   Dear Sir,
>   You can begin
> printing from any edition of Keats's
> poems – putting the "Endymion" first
> as it now stands. There is nothing
> to be done to it in the way of editing.
> Before you get through that, I will
> have the other poems (of Keats) arranged
> & prefix a sketch of his life.
>   Very truly Yours
>   J.R. Lowell[9]

Landmarks of the latter end of this Silver Age include Thomas Hutchinson's texts of Shelley and Wordsworth and the other Oxford Standard Authors Editions, Macmillan's Globe Editions, and Houghton Mifflin's Cambridge Editions done around the turn of the century. Again, the aim of these editors was to gain as wide a public as possible, but, given the nature of their professional concerns and their opinions of the poets, some of them seemed to work not so much to enhance the reputation and influence of the writers as to increase the earnings of the publishers and themselves. The editors, who decided (after consulting the publishers) that their highest obligation was to the reading public that they hoped would buy their books, modernized and smoothed out the texts still further and in several cases observed the prudential standards of the day by softening anything overly radical or indecorous in the poetry and especially in the letters of the Romantics.[10] For example, in the Oxford Standard Authors edition of Shelley, Hutchinson (or the printer) added capital letters wherever Shelley alluded to the Supreme Being. In Canto VII of *Queen Mab*, in the midst of Shelley's most strident attack on Christianity, Hutchinson's text capitalizes such words referring to God as "Fiend" (VII, 97), "Tyrant" (VII, 199), and "Foe" (VII, 248), thus providing an ironic spectacle in which Shelley pays court through his reverent orthography to a god whose objective existence he denies and the morality of whose myth he denounces. By the same token, in 1898 Rowland E. Prothero and the firm of John Murray produced the Bowdlerized texts of Byron's *Letters and Journals* that have been corrected only now by Leslie A. Marchand and a more enlightened John Murray.

II

Developing concurrently with this Victorian compromise was another tradition of editing. When Harry Buxton Forman, whom John Carter hailed as a pioneer in descriptive bibliography,[11] undertook his editions of Shelley and Keats, we enter what may be termed the Brazen Age, or the age of "scientific" editors of the Romantics. Forman respected the poets far more than he did the reading public, but he had even greater respect for his own capacity to deduce the forms that the poet intended to use. From careful collations and analysis of the works of Shelley, Forman evolved what he took to be Shelley's rules of spelling, punctuation, and usage.

Forman, who never went to college and made his career in the Post Office while developing as an amateur scholar, nevertheless managed to establish his authority as a bibliographer and editor of the Romantics essentially both because he took more time to be meticulously accurate than his rivals did and because, as a collector of books and manuscripts and a haunter of auction rooms, he eventually owned or examined many more of the original authorities than did Rossetti or any other competitor.[12] Forman was constantly correcting his own published editions in later reprintings, and if he fell short of modern standards in his work on Keats, his Shelley editions remain the most carefully proofread and accurate (according to the evidence available to him) that have ever been produced.[13] Forman's striking superiority to his contemporaries in bibliographical knowledge not only led him into the temptation of initiating and/or abetting the printing forgeries circulated by T. J. Wise,[14] but also gave him an exalted sense of his own knowledge that may have led him to trust too securely in his pet ideas: "The sense that he was greater than his kind / Had struck, methinks, his eagle spirit blind."

In his playful notes to Wise and, by the end of his career, his equally flippant remarks in his transcription of three Shelley rough-draft *Note Books of Percy Bysshe Shelley* owned by W. K. Bixby (Privately Printed, 1911), Forman demonstrated that even one who began as a humble student and servant of the work of a great poet is not immune to a *hubris* that can transform the poet's writings into a mere occasion for the editor to display his own ingenuity and taste. I choose one example at random: the page on which Shelley drafted *Prometheus Unbound* IV. 495–502. There Forman quotes one rejected version of IV. 500 ("The caverns of my Pride's deep Universe") which reads "The solid heart of my glad Universe," and comments that this is "a line which no poet less opulent than Shelley could have afforded to reject. Indeed it is by no means clear that he could, for it is a nobler line than that to which it gave place, though presumably not satisfying the poet as an expression of his meaning" (Shelley, *Note Books*, I, 93). Luckily, by this date Forman's days of editing final versions of Shelley's poems were past, and he thus was not tempted to substitute rejected "nobler" lines for the ones Shelley had finally decided upon, as his successors (such as C. D. Locock) sometimes did.

The practice of editors emending according to their conception of "nobler" lines rather than evidences of the author's intention derives, of course, from the practice of editors of classical Greek and Latin and Biblical Hebrew and Greek texts. Given a transcription based on earlier manuscripts of uncertain origin or authority but in the hand of a scribe who lived many centuries after the composition of the text (in which all punctuation is known to have been later and non-authorial), there are ample grounds for the modern editor (who has often had the advantage of comparing several manuscripts of differing backgrounds) to try to reason back to the original text that had, through a series of scribal errors or attempted emendations, produced what seems to be nonsense. It is so much fun to display ingenuity in such conjectural arguments that many editors of nineteenth-century writers continued to play the same game, even though the survival of the author's own drafts, fair-copy manuscripts, and marked proof-sheets, as well as editions that the author had seen through the press, might have weighed against such freedom. Those such as Fleay who had been trained at Oxford, Cambridge, and other strongholds of the classical tradition were especially vulnerable to this temptation.

Luckily, A. E. Housman, one of the greatest of classical editors and textual critics, was also a significant poet and felt an author's outrage when such tinkering affected the texts of *his* poems. Housman's letters, laconic as they are, express his feelings on this topic better than do his formal lectures or publications on editorial theory and practice. His letters to Grant Richards, publisher of his poems, are filled with very specific instructions regarding the printing and presentation that are clearly designed to forestall textual changes due either to inadvertance or to editorial tinkering. On 11 December 1898, for example, he wrote to Richards: "I rather like the notion of a pocket edition. Large paper and illustrations are things I have not much affection for. In any case I should like to correct the proofs and to have them printed as I correct them. Last time someone played games with the punctuation."[15] And on 12 October 1902 he wrote: "When the next edition of the *Shropshire Lad* is being prepared, it would save trouble to the compositor as well as me if he were told that the third edition is almost exactly correct, and that he had better not put in commas and notes of exclamation for me to strike out of the proof, as was the case last time" (Housman, *Letters*, p. 61). In his classical studies, Housman conjectured corrections for Manilius, Juvenal, Lucan, and other

Latin poets in his area of specialization, and he also supplied Gilbert
Murray with conjectures on the plays of Euripides to aid Murray with
his translations. But he used much greater care in his treatment of
modern poets. His respect for the texts of the Romantics appears in his
refusal to publish his Cambridge Inaugural Lecture of 1911 because he
"was unable to verify a statement which it contained as to the text of
Shelley's *Lament* of 1821." Later research has confirmed his point.[16]
It appears also in his single application of the methods of conjectural
emendation (as practiced with classical authors) to Keats. In the *Times
Literary Supplement* for 8 May 1924, he published a letter on "Keats,
The Fall of Hyperion, I. 97," in which he argues that a reading in one
of the Woodhouse transcript books, "When in mid-way" and emended
by Milnes to "When in midday" should be "When in mid-May,"
arguing from the sense of the passage (including botanical accuracy)
as well as from Keats's use of the phrase "in mid-May" in "Ode to a
Nightingale."[17] Housman's crowning argument came from I. 103 of
the poem itself: "Sending from *Maian* incense." Housman's reading
is accepted by Stillinger and other modern editors, but the more significant fact is that Housman begins his discussion of the crux with a
clear understanding of the textual evidence available on the point:
"This poem was not printed in Keats's lifetime, and his manuscript
has been lost; but in the copy made under the direction of Woodhouse
lines 97-101 of the first canto run as follows. . . . " And he goes on to
show that Lord Houghton had already emended the text to "in midday." In short, Housman acted only within the province of his competence: there was no extant authorial version and the two chief
authorities, the Woodhouse transcript book and the first printing by
Lord Houghton, were in conflict. In such a case, he permitted himself
to examine the internal evidence and propose an emendation.

Though Housman's judicious distinction between the canons of
editing classical texts and those of editing modern texts was not shared
or emulated by all of his colleagues in British and American universities, the next advances in editing the British Romantics came out of
Oxford, in the work of Ernest de Sélincourt (1870–1943), who began
his editorial work with an edition of Keats's *Poems* (1905) and whose
1926 edition of *The Prelude*, presenting versions of 1805 and 1850 on
facing pages with accompanying notes and variants drawn from other
manuscripts, set new standards for the presentation of heavily revised
texts of modern literature. A decade later, H(eathcote) W(illiam) Gar-

rod (1878–1960), who had begun à la Housman as a poet and as editor, commentator, and translator of Statius, Manilius, and other Latin poets,[18] reached the zenith of his career as a serious scholar in his Oxford English Texts edition of *The Poetical Works of John Keats* (1939; second edition, 1958). Most students of Romantic texts consider Garrod's edition a milestone in the thoroughness of its editing, and Garrod himself felt the need to defend himself in the Introduction for the thoroughness of his work from those who were affected by an "ethical scruple . . . when it is proposed to go behind the printed text and to scrutinize its sometimes inglorious origins by recording variants from the drafts as well as from printed authorities and fair-copy manuscripts" (p. xxiii). Yet Garrod himself in his 1939 Preface credited Forman with having set *his* standards:

> A principal part of my work has consisted in collating MSS., or the facsimiles of MSS., collated before me by the late Harry Buxton Forman. In one of his prefaces, he professes to be, in respect of accuracy, only mortal. But of mortal frailty I have found, scrutinizing his work as rigorously as I was able, singularly few traces. . . . I have had the advantage of using a good many MSS. not known to him; and I should account myself fortunate if some one using them after me found my record of them comparable to his in accuracy.[19]

Garrod's hope was to be fulfilled in not quite the manner he would have intended, for Jack Stillinger criticizes him for his undue reliance on Forman's texts, especially in lending his name to an imperfectly revised reissue of Forman's error-ridden Oxford Standard Authors edition of 1906. Stillinger finds in the OET Keats that, treating only substantive matters, "Garrod has what I consider clear mistakes and inconsistencies—the latter most often the mixing of two or more discrete states of texts—in . . . fifty-seven poems" and after specifying his disagreements, he concludes: "Texts aside, Garrod's arrangement of the poems makes no sense, his introduction and headnotes are considerably out of date, and his cumbersome and error-filled apparatus does as much harm as good."[20] He goes on to analyze as "a large fault of Garrod's apparatus," his "treatment of all MS and printed texts as having equal authority" (p. 285). Stillinger in *The Texts of Keats's Poems* for the first time analyzes the transmission of the manuscripts and printed texts of a modern poet with the same care that paleographers, dialecticians, and textual critics of Biblical, classical, and medieval texts had applied to the surviving authorities in their fields, with the added advantage that surviving letters and journals by

Keats and his associates often supplement the evidence of the manuscripts and printings themselves. Garrod and, to a certain extent, de Sélincourt and Helen Darbishire in their editions of Wordsworth were both victims and perpetuators of the condescension toward the study of nineteenth- and twentieth-century English literature at such institutions as Oxford. They felt a greater need to defend expending efforts on "modern" authors than to convince their publishers of the need to do all that their textual training had prepared them to undertake. Their editions, however much they surpassed those of the casual Silver Age by returning to primary authorities, did not always choose the correct copy-texts or present substantive variants fully and clearly. These editors almost inevitably revised such features as orthography and punctuation on the grounds either of consistency or the need for easier comprehension by their readers. And, as Stillinger's criticism of Garrod's eclecticism indicates, they too often selected their base texts without expending the biographical and bibliographical research and collation that, once a larger number of MSS. were available for study, could (as Stillinger demonstrates) have established which ones are more, which less, authoritative.

III

If such classically trained editors as de Sélincourt and Garrod were in danger of applying "scientific" principles too sparingly to Romantic texts, a far more rigorous school was developing concurrently in the textual criticism of Renaissance drama that brought the Brazen Age to full flower. Its milestones began, perhaps, with Ronald B. McKerrow's edition of *The Works of Thomas Nashe* (1904–1910) and include such diverse recent and continuing works as Charlton Hinman's Norton Facsimile of *The First Folio of Shakespeare* (1968) and *The Writings of Herman Melville* now emanating from the Newberry Library and Northwestern University Press. Equally impressive is the theoretical tradition that grew up in connection with these editorial labors. Contemporary with "Note on the Treatment of the Text . . ." (I, xi–xvi) and "Preface" (V, v–ix) to the Nashe edition, in which McKerrow (1872–1940) briefly discussed his editorial procedures both before and after the fact, was the bibliographical study of *Shakespeare Folios and Quartos* (1909) by his senior, Alfred W. Pollard (1859–1944) of the British Museum. Pollard and McKerrow exerted great influence through their work in the Bibliographical Society, as editors of scholarly journals, within university circles, and, especially, through McKerrow's *An Introduction to Bibliography for Literary Students* (based on "Notes" first published by the Bibliographical Society in 1913).[21] Their efforts were actively aided and supplemented by their close friend Walter Wilson Greg (1875-1959) who, as heir to *The Economist* of London, was able to devote his entire life to bibliographical research, reviewing more than 200 scholarly studies and superintending the publications of the Malone Society, of which he served as General Editor (1906-39) and President (1939-59). Later landmark publications on the theory of editing by this circle include McKerrow's *Prolegomena for the Oxford Shakespeare* (1939) and, especially, Greg's "The Rationale of Copy-Text."[22] Other names associated with this British bibliographical tradition that have more direct relevance to nineteenth-century studies are R. W. Chapman (1881-1960), editor of Jane Austen's novels (1923) and other writings of Austen and Samuel Johnson, as well as Secretary to the Delegates of the Clarendon Press, 1920-42; and Michael T. H. Sadleir (1888-1957), the most noted collector and bibliographer of nineteenth-century fiction, as well as an active and influential member of the publishing firm of Constable from 1920 onwards.

By the 1940s, the spark of enthusiasm for this rigorous tradition of bibliography and editing had jumped across the Atlantic and was marked by the founding of *Studies in Bibliography* in 1948 and the publication of Fredson Bowers' *Principles of Bibliographical Description* (1949), which is dedicated to Greg. Both events reflected and stimulated new interest in North America in the broader discipline that Bowers usually refers to simply as "textual criticism." Bowers viewed literary criticism "as directly dependent upon expert textual criticism"; that expertise he applied to four basic situations: (1) analysis of an extant manuscript; (2) hypothetical "recovery of the lost manuscript" that served as press copy for a printed text; (3) study of the transmission of a printed text; and (4) "the presentation of the established and edited text."[23] Having by the late 1950s convinced or coerced students of Renaissance drama into paying serious attention to textual problems, the school emanating from Pollard, McKerrow, Greg, and Bowers—and now spearheaded by the energy and enthusiasm of Bowers himself—attempted to apply the principles derived primarily from the study of Renaissance plays to all areas of textual criticism and editing.

I denominate this school of textual scholars the Brazen Age of editing because of the too-sanguine hopes they, at least for a time, entertained about the results obtainable through systematic application of
fixed principles to a wide variety of literary texts. The keynote of
Bowers' *Principles of Bibliographical Description* is "system." His
Foreword makes clear that he has begun by considering "the whole
subject in the round" and has ended by "codifying the results of this
analysis" (p. vii). It is, he continues, "my purpose to present an
organized bibliographical system which is based on what I consider to
be the best current practices in scholarly works."[24] In the interest of
arriving at such a system, Bowers argued, "since this volume does not
purport to be an account of specific books . . ., the principles themselves are not affected if stray illustrations prove incomplete or
faulty" (p. x). He thus begins his first chapter by characterizing
"descriptive bibliography" as "one of the kinds of scholarship that
may be defined as 'pure' scholarship, and consequently very exacting
standards are applied to it" (p. 1), and he goes on to differentiate it
from the mere making of library catalogues, author or subject check-
lists, bibliographical descriptions of a few copies of a title in a single
collection, and other limited, unscientific enterprises.

Had Bowers been content to remain at this level of abstraction and
to work out ideal principles, based on a truly philosophical comprehension of the various theoretical possibilities that present themselves
(as has G. Thomas Tanselle, his more cogent successor in theoretical
bibliographical analysis and description), Bowers would be worthy of
even greater honor than he has deservedly received. But he (and some
of his less circumspect disciples) soon began to use such words as
"scientific" to describe the principles and practices of the McKerrow-
Greg-Bowers tradition or school. In 1969, James Thorpe called attention to this tendency, its concomitant limitations, and its accompanying abuses in a paper entitled "The Ideal of Textual Criticism."[25]
Bowers, by temperament a proselytizer, also chose to move beyond
work in Renaissance drama and sought wider influence primarily in
editions of American authors. After working on Whitman's manuscripts and serving as Textual Editor for the Centenary Edition of
Hawthorne's works undertaken at Ohio State in the 1960s, Bowers
and those in agreement with his principles, aided by grants from the
National Endownment for the Humanities to the Center for Editions
of American Authors (CEAA), set out both to produce texts of classic

American authors edited according to the best theoretical principles and to inculcate and enforce in other areas of literary studies the (undoubtedly higher) standards of textual criticism and editorial procedures that had evolved from the great tradition studying English Renaissance drama—the principles of Pollard, McKerrow, Greg, and Bowers.[26]

Here I shall mention only a couple of the inevitable excesses of this militant program and a few of the equally inevitable reactions. Bowers, who had naturally enough drawn his examples of textual problems in authors and periods with which he was not personally familiar from scholars whose work sounded plausible to him, began to systematize his theories in areas where not only was there too little evidence available, but where some of the evidence upon which he generalized was simply wrong. For example, impressed by Charles H. Taylor's solid work on the transmission of Shelley's texts in *The Early Collected Editions of Shelley's Poetry*, Bowers argued that "modern editors have contented themselves with reprinting the presumed authoritative text of 1839 . . . and in so doing they have perpetuated a number of errors by their negligence."[27] In fact, as specialists in Shelley's texts soon noted, though Rossetti and a few others had followed Mary Shelley's edition of 1839, Forman's reliance on the first editions and manuscripts had eliminated from modern texts most of the variants that (as Taylor demonstrated) had entered Mary Shelley's later editions through her use of error-filled piracies as press-copy. By making unsubstantiated claims for the importance of Taylor's work to the modern editor, Bowers opened the way for Neville Rogers and others unfamiliar with recent bibliographical and editorial methods to ignore the relevance of the entire discipline to their work.

Again, Bowers in his own editorial practice—especially in the Virginia Edition of *The Works of Stephen Crane*—carried to an excess the imposition of his own "system" and uniformity on works Crane had written at various times, for different purposes, and surviving in a variety of "authorities." David J. Nordloh, in a detailed review article,[28] wrote of Bowers' edition of Crane:

> The new texts are not simply reprintings of documents already available; they are the result of analysis of the materials which were part of the original process of Crane's creation, and of examination of correspondence and historical information bearing on that process. But such detailed research—and the detailed results which face the reader of this new edition—have yielded not

> definitive forms of Stephen Crane's various writings but muddles of editorial
> synthesis and intervention. . . . The texts based on these materials combine
> an insensitivity to what Crane was doing with an unwillingness to leave Crane as
> he was. . . . All the texts are battered by the intrusion of editorial conformity.
> . . . they bear no identifiable relationship to the Stephen Crane documents
> which supposedly constitute their basis.   (pp. 103–104)

Nordloh himself began as a graduate student in the CEAA works at Indiana and rose to become general editor of *A Selected Edition of William Dean Howells*, as well as Chairman of the MLA's Committee on Scholarly Editions (CSE)—the successor to CEAA. As a student of Ronald Gottesman, he was insulated from Bowers and some of his more fanatic disciples; and, though he accepted the goals they espoused, his understanding of the means to be employed was tempered by his own experience in the nitty-gritty work of collating Howells' fiction, by Tanselle's careful discussions of theory and practice (and the distinctions between them), and by the reactions to CEAA-prototype publications on Emerson and Hawthorne by such gadfly critics as Lewis Mumford and Edmund Wilson, and—with much greater authority—by Morse Peckham.

In the first volume of *Proof: The Yearbook of American Bibliographical and Textual Studies* (1971), Peckham contributed important "Reflections on the Foundations of Modern Textual Editing" that may mark the beginning of the end of the conjuring power of the names Pollard, McKerrow, and Greg in fields outside Renaissance drama. Drawing upon his experience as an editor of Charles Darwin and Browning (as well as an author's experience with publishers), Peckham—while dismissing as trivial the criticisms of Bowers by Edmund Wilson and James D. Thorpe—found some basic problems in Bowers' presuppositions. Peckham's critique begins, characteristically, with a fear of ossification: "the principles developed over the past thirty years (since Greg's *The Editorial Problem in Shakespeare*) are proving to be less satisfactory than they seemed to be ten years ago. Part of the difficulty lies in rhetoric, but much of it is the general truth that a great innovator's followers inevitably simplify and rigidify and sanctify their master's ideas." Centering on what he regards as the arbitrary differences between "substantives" and "accidentals," Peckham first cites Greg's precise and sensible distinction and then goes on to show how Greg's narrow and practical application had been reified. After instancing a number of cases (including some in the

Centenary Hawthorne) in which the distinction has been overapplied, he concludes:

> the lesson of this is that what to do about punctuation is an empirical matter, not a theoretical matter, not a matter of editorial principles or rules, as Greg pretentiously called them in *The Editorial Problem in Shakespeare.*
>
> The textual editor should do away with this theological terminology of accidentals and substantives, and talk simply and clearly about words, punctuation, spelling, capitalization, and whatever else he needs to talk about. These things are there, before our eyes; accidence and substance are not.
>
> (pp. 125-126)

If Peckham's essay signals the first serious reaction to the Greg-Bowers tradition in those circles, Philip Gaskell's *A New Introduction to Bibliography* (1972), designed to replace McKerrow's *Introduction*, is based on a broader body of bibliographical evidence from later periods than had been available to McKerrow. Gaskell, therefore, is less inclined in that volume to generalize on the basis of problems peculiar to a single field than were earlier bibliographers. Again, reviews and essays by a variety of scholars and editors who had encountered in their studies exceptions to Bowers' theories led to a constant reexamination of the orthodoxies of that school. Gaskell followed this well-received volume with a more controversial one entitled *From Writer to Reader: Studies in Editorial Method.*[29] After a brief analysis of some areas and problems to be considered by the editor, Gaskell stresses "not only that every textual situation is unique and should be approached without editorial preconceptions, but also that there is seldom only one right way of editing a work of literature" (p. 10). He then proceeds to examine twelve texts, ranging from Harington's translation of *Orlando Furioso* (1591) to Tom Stoppard's *Travesties* (1974), discussing the available evidence and concluding in each case that the principles of Greg and Bowers are inadequate to the situation.

The most cogent recent defenses of what we may, for the sake of brevity, call simply the "Greg tradition," have come from G. Thomas Tanselle. He refutes Gaskell's criticisms and departures from the Greg tradition in a review of *From Writer to Reader.*[30] Earlier, in his magisterial essay entitled "Greg's Theory of Copy-Text and the Editing of American Literature,"[31] Tanselle had discussed historically, in far greater depth, the significance of Greg's "The Rationale of Copy-Text" (pp. 170-182) and important additions to the theory in Fredson

Bowers' "Multiple Authority: New Problems and Concepts of Copy-Texts" (pp. 182–184).[32] In "Greg's Theory of Copy-Text . . .," Tanselle enumerates Bowers' general contributions to the dissemination of the Greg tradition through both his "general discussions of editing" and his "actual editions based on Greg's rationale" (p. 184), leading therefrom into an analysis of the principles employed by CEAA and promulgated in its *Statement of Editorial Principles: A Working Manual for Editing Nineteenth-Century American Texts* (1967). He also answers in detail a series of criticisms of the CEAA editions by Edmund Wilson, Paul Baender, Donald Pizer, John Freehafer, and Morse Peckham's essay in *Proof*, to which I have alluded.[33] While granting Peckham's essay higher status than the others as "a thoughtfully developed analysis of the nature of human communication" (p. 211), Tanselle is at pains to refute what he regards as Peckham's two principal arguments against Greg's theory: (1) Peckham's denial "that substantives and accidentals can be meaningfully segregated," and (2) "that the reconstruction of a text representing the author's intention is a meaningful (or attainable) goal" (p. 212).

Though Tanselle cogently refutes these objections or argues that their main points were implicit in Greg's theory, his summary of Peckham's argument does not fully reflect the message that Peckham's essay conveys to me. For I conceive Peckham's principal point as being that textual analysis is a branch of history, not a subdivision of philosophy. For all his own philosophical terminology, Peckham's thesis in this and other writings is that situational behavior—specific actions of human beings under very special (often unique) conditions—produces whatever we at any time choose to call works of art or literary texts. That Peckham's own theoretical propositions in the hands of the irresponsible *can* lead to an extreme relativism troubles me as much as it does Tanselle, but Peckham clearly does not think so himself, as should be clear from his praise of "analytical bibliography" and its "magnificent" "achievements in the past thirty years" and his further assertion: "Anyone who forces the noses of humanists onto the grindstone of hard, immutable fact has a genuinely redemptive function."[34] Peckham seems clearly to believe in the absoluteness of *facts*—"immutable" evidence resulting from behavior, past or present—but he has a relativistic position about *theories* developed to explain those facts. He wants the textual editor to present facts—to record variants accurately, for example—but to be very circumspect about developing theories on exactly how these variants came into existence, and even more so about what went on in the author's mind at the time. Peckham writes:

> The "human factor" is not something that occasionally enters into the bibliographer's thinking when he finds himself in a spot; it is almost exclusively all that he is concerned with. The analytical bibliographer is a historian, and he should not forget it for a moment. The object of his inquiry is not printed artifacts as physical objects but human behavior in the past, human behavior that no longer exists and cannot now be examined. (p. 131)

Knowing Tanselle's opinions both from his writings and from numerous conversations with him on these matters, I judge that he would agree in principle that the function of the analytical bibliographer is historical rather than philosophical. But Tanselle argues that the exceptions noted by any number of reviewers of Bowers' editions—including those by Nordloh—do not invalidate Greg's *principles* but simply illustrate ineffective specific applications of them. That may be so, but if Bowers, the leading exponent of those principles for his generation, was unable to make effective use of them in his own editing of Hawthorne and Stephen Crane, the usefulness of the principles themselves inevitably comes into question.

Watson Branch's recent review of the editorial practice of David Nordloh in the Howells edition suggests that for certain adherents to the Greg tradition, rules, laws, and principles have become a trap rather than a path toward greater knowledge.[35] Whether an editor is being true to the "principles" of Greg, Bowers, or Tanselle seems to have greater significance for Branch than whether or not the editor has accurately presented the surviving evidence from which all theories must derive. Doctrinal purity takes precedence over accuracy of transcription or collation. While acknowledging that Nordloh and his colleagues have described clearly and accurately the relevant textual materials and their editorial procedures, Branch writes, for example: "the editors are applying W. W. Greg's theory of copy-text. Unfortunately they have not applied it very well . . ." (p. 60). "The choices [of copy-text] are quite right, but a statement immediately following indicates a basic misconception regarding Greg's theory . . ." (p. 61). Branch glosses his statement of Gregian orthodoxy with citations to Greg's "The Rationale of Copy-Text" and to Bowers' "Remarks on Eclectic Texts" (*Proof*, 4 [1975]). He then asserts that, though his own collations uncovered no "nonauthorial *Century* readings" in the portions of *A Modern Instance* where the manuscript was the copy-text but corrected photocopies of the *Century* installments served as press-copy (i.e., was the version from which compositors set the text), he regrets Nordloh's use of this technical expedient because of its potentiality for error; he admits that by "careful proofreading" the Howells editors succeeded in frustrating Branch in his search for errors in the text, if not in the apparatus (pp. 62, 71). Branch, who studied under Hershel Parker, one of the editors of Melville, charges the Howells editors with heresy on a number of points where they deviate from Greg (p. 67), and on their practice of regularizing he quotes against them "the editors of the Melville edition" (p. 70).

This kind of petulant attack upon the CEAA-originated editions from within and without has finally led G. Thomas Tanselle to question the wisdom of invoking W. W. Greg's "Rationale" and Bowers' revisions and extensions of it as privileged texts. He believes that the *central principles* evolving from their writings (and his) will stand on their own feet, without the need to invoke authorities. In "Recent Editorial Discussion and the Central Questions of Editing,"[36] Tanselle first reviews the chief "editorial literature" discussing the CEAA since he wrote "Greg's Theory of Copy-Text and the Editing of American Literature" (1975) and, though he argues that many of the charges against CEAA editorial theory and practice are either uninformed or simplistic, he grants that reliance on certain terms has sometimes confused rather than clarified the issues. When in a succinct concluding section Tanselle delineates the three groups of "central questions of editing," he accepts the strictures of Peckham and Tom Davis by eschewing the use of "substantive," "accidental," and "definitive" and by carefully defining each term he introduces. In the "first set of questions," Tanselle distinguishes between "historical" editions—those that either reproduce "a particular text from the past" or attempt to reconstruct "what the author intended"—from "those in which the editor's own personal preferences" (rather than his judgment of what the *author* preferred) provide the basis of choice. "Historical" editions are the only "scholarly editions"; those in which the editor reproduces a single historical version of the text, from a manuscript or printing, without emendation are "noncritical" editions;[37] those in which "editorial judgment" determines "when, and whether, emendations are to be made in the text" are "critical" editions. Both regularizing and modernizing, writes Tanselle, "are ahistorical in orientation and therefore, have no place in . . . scholarly editions" (pp. 60–61). He underlines and supports this judgment by declaring that the author's "punctuation and spelling are integral parts of a text, affecting its meaning and impact" and thus must not be revised in a scholarly edition, "except possibly for some of the earliest works in a language, which might be said to require 'translation,' rather than simply 'modernization,' for the general reader" (p. 61 and fn. 73).

Secondly, Tanselle faces the question of authorial intention. He writes: "the aim is to emend the selected text [i.e., the copy-text] so that it conforms to the author's intention; one can never fully attain such a goal (or know that one has attained it)," but the editor moves "toward it by applying informed judgment to the available evidence" (p. 62). On the question of when an author's revisions "indicate a new conception of a work" rather than "the process of perfecting the expression of the same conception," Tanselle argues that this "difficult decision . . . is central to critical editing." (Here he upholds the central thesis in Greg's "Rationale.") Moreover, the critical editor must attempt to unravel the author's positive "intention"—what he or she preferred—from textual changes imposed on or acquiesced to by the author because of the physical, legal, or practical considerations of publishing at that time. In evaluating each individual situation, however, "one must be extremely cautious about attributing authorial intention or preference to alternatives simply because they were passed, in one fashion or another, by the author" (pp. 62–63).

Finally, Tanselle confronts the sticky question of the "copy-text," which the editor follows in cases of "indifferent variants" (i.e., those variants about which the application of the critical editor's knowledge and judgment to the extant evidence cannot determine which is more likely authorial). Tanselle point out that, if there are no "indifferent variants," "[i]t is not necessary to have a copy-text at all," but since, as a matter of fact, such variants "seem to occur, one needs a principle for favoring one text over another": "a copy-text is simply the text most likely to provide an authorial reading . . . where one cannot otherwise reach a decision" (p. 64).

Tanselle's answers to these three central issues of editing—his definition of a critical scholarly edition as an (always imperfect) *attempt* to present the author's intention; his defense of the need, toward that end, to construct an eclectic text on the basis of whatever surviving evidence can be assembled; and his reminder of the practical need to choose a basic text to follow when critical examination of all the evidence fails to reveal the authorial preference—all seem to me to be beyond reproach and to vindicate the central validity of Greg's "Rationale" against its critics. But they do more. By admitting the historical nature of the problems with individual texts, they also reiterate Peckham's main point that "system" and "principles" must always give way to the facts of the case, and they therefore take us from the Brazen Age, when all problems were to be solved by the systematic application of invariable principles (as many lesser followers of Bowers thought) to the Age of Iron, in which the rugged individuality of each text takes precedence over the theoretically "normal" or "accepted" patterns of punctuation and orthography that the "scientific" or, rather, doctrinaire editor once tried to impose on the recalcitrant vagaries of human behavior in authors and other editors alike.

IV

Karl Kroeber writes in his important essay "Experience as History: Shelley's Venice, Turner's Carthage,"[38] "'Romantic' sensibility . . . is alien to 'modern' sensibility, because the Romantic identifies individual experience with historical process, whereas to the modern, 'experience' and history are antithetical" (p. 321). Kroeber sees that for the Modernist poet, as for the Classic writer, history is a repetitive winding and unwinding of spools or gyres, expanding and contracting like a pulsating universe. Therefore, for the Modernist, the meaningful patterns of life are supplied by myths and archetypes. Taking Kroeber's distinction farther, we may say: for the Romantic (and many students of Romantic writers), history is linear and, at least sporadically, progressive. For the Classic or Modernist critic, the fitting analogies for human experience are the cycles of day and night and the four seasons. For the Romantic, who inherits the Judeo-Christian conception of man, the appropriate image is that of a journey toward a distant earthly (no longer a heavenly) destination. For the editor following a Classic or Modernist philosophy, the pattern or principle stands at the center of editing. For the Romantic or historical editor—Peckham, or (at this point) Tanselle—the individual case is unique and ought not to be subsumed or erased to fit a generalized archetypal pattern.

To ignore the historicist milieu of Romantic poetry in order to make it more "modern" and "relevant" is akin to trying to read Dante without reference to Thomist theology, or to read Milton in ignorance of both the new science and the theological disputes of the seventeenth century. If textual theorists wish to argue that all Elizabethan texts should be edited on a single set of principles appropriate to the hierarchical ideal invoked by church and state in the latter half of the sixteenth century, I am not in a position to challenge them. If they wish to regularize the texts of Pope, Swift, and Addison on the theory that these Augustan authors intended to follow Right Reason and the Common Sense of mankind, who am I to argue? But I know that I am on solid ground in saying that subtle peculiarities in orthography and punctuation are not only *characteristic* of the writings, but even *vital* to the meaning of Blake, Lamb, Shelley, and Keats—all authors who struggled hard to maintain their individuality amid an age of ever-encroaching uniformity. Though I am, therefore, willing to be convinced that a uniform application of principles evolved during the Brazen Age *may* be appropriate for the authors of other times and places, I am quite convinced that the Romantics should be edited according to the historicist conceptions of the Age of Iron.

To call the fourth age of editing the Iron Age is to suggest, first, a period of relatively rough and unpolished texts, allowed to reflect the vagaries of authorial behavior, rather than a regularized, polished redaction to fit an idealized conception of an author's intention. Beyond these qualities, the serviceable (rather than beautiful) texts of the Iron Age are expected to rust in time, as later generations of scholars discover flaws in the knowledge or understanding of the merely mortal historian-editors, or as newly discovered authoritative documents or analytical techniques corrode the cutting edge of these scholarly tools. For the editor of the Iron Age, editing is more nearly a practical craft than a science, and an edition is recognized as an attempt to serve the needs of a specified audience for a particular time, rather than to reach an immutable standard of perfection. The Romantic editor looks upon the turning cycle of sublunar mutability and (at least in moments of equanimity) accepts, as Shelley, Keats, and Yeats did, that the works of his mind and hands, like all products of creativity, are subject to the ravishment of "Fate, Time, Occasion, Chance, and

Change.'' He also believes that, if his work has been done with proper care and attention, though it may ultimately decay as a standard (never a "definitive") edition, it will provide a *more accurate* representation of the creations of great writers for the readers of its time. It will, moreover, transmit to future generations of scholars an example of diligent and responsible devotion to the great writers of the past, to their literary creations, and to new readers whose lives may be changed by encountering these records "of the best and happiest moments of the happiest and best minds.''

NOTES

1. See *Rossetti Papers, 1862–1870*, ed. William Michael Rossetti (New York: Charles Scribner's Sons, 1903), pp. 197, 199–200, 206, 224, 306, 352–353.

2. *Rossetti Papers, 1862–1870*, pp. 331–333; ultimately Rossetti persuaded Payne to abandon the stereotyped plates (see pp. 381–382).

3. These sheets, bound in three volumes, are now in The Carl H. Pforzheimer Library and are cited by permission of The Carl and Lily Pforzheimer Foundation, Inc.

4. *Rossetti Papers, 1862–1870*, p. 379 (ellipsis in original). Swinburne's ideas on the subject appear in his "Notes on the Text of Shelley," *Fortnightly Review*, n.s. 5 (May 1, 1869), 539–561; rpt. in *Essays and Studies* (London: Chatto and Windus, 1875), pp. 184–237.

5. Six letters from Rossetti to Fleay, 17 October [1869]–27 February [1870], are in The Carl H. Pforzheimer Library (Rossetti, 6–11). The phrase is quoted from the letter 14 November [1869]. The Pforzheimer Library also owns the manuscript of an unpublished study by Fleay, entitled "On the received text of Shelley's poems," that occupies 52 numbered, lined half-sheets and is at the end dated "12 Sep 1894." In it, Fleay systematically proposes emendations for all of Shelley's published poetry and (on page 8) calls attention to an earlier paper by him published in *The Provincial Magazine* for February 1859, in which he had first proposed a number of the same emendations that were later adopted by Rossetti and others. In the unpublished manuscript, Fleay proposes, among other emendations, changing several words in "Mont Blanc" to make sure that no lines in that poem remain rhymeless and canceling lines 95–96 of *Rosalind and Helen* because, he notes, the substance of their meaning appears in subsequent lines (p. 11).

6. Four volumes. London: Reeves and Turner. 1876–77.

7. My own detailed analysis of Rossetti's practice comes from work on the text of "The Triumph of Life" for *Shelley's "The Triumph of Life": A Critical Study* (Urbana: University of Illinois Press, 1965; rpt. New York: Octagon, 1979) and "Athanase: A Fragment" in *Shelley and His Circle*, VII (Cambridge, Mass.: Harvard University Press, 1984).

8. *Rossetti Papers, 1862–1870*, p. 381. W. M. Rossetti's editorial labors can be followed by means of the indexes to this volume and *The Diary of W. M. Rossetti, 1870–1873*, ed. Odette Bornand (Oxford: Clarendon Press, 1977); *Letters about Shelley Interchanged by . . . Edward Dowden, Richard Garnett and Wm. Michael Rossetti*, ed. R. S. Garnett (London: Hodder and Stoughton, 1917); and *Letters of William Michael Rossetti concerning Whitman, Blake and Shelley to Anne Gilchrist and . . . Herbert Gilchrist*, ed. Clarence Gohdes and Paull Franklin Baum (Durham: Duke University Press, 1934).

9. Manuscript in The Carl H. Pforzheimer Library; published by permission of The Carl and Lily Pforzheimer Foundation, Inc.

10. For the Bowdlerizing by W. M. Rossetti and John Camden Hotten of the first British edition of Whitman's poems, see Morton D. Paley, "John Camden Hotten and the First British Editions of Walt Whitman—'A Nice Milky Cocoa-Nut'," *Publishing History*, 6 (1979), 5–35.

11. Carter wrote: "Buxton Forman's *A Shelley Library* . . . was . . . no mere hand-list but a fully annotated and richly informative study of Shelley's original editions. Published by the Shelley Society in 1886 . . . , Forman's book marked a radical advance. . . . Forman set a wholly new standard both for his readers and for subsequent bibliographers. His *Shelley Library* was a prototype as well as a portent" (*Taste and Technique in Book-Collecting* [New York: R. R. Bowker, 1948], p. 15).

12. The bulk of "The Library of the Late H. Buxton Forman (1842–1917)," strongly centered upon manuscripts and rare editions of nineteenth-century poetry and biographical materials relating to those poets, was auctioned at the Anderson Galleries, New York, in three parts. A total of 3,572 lots were sold in fourteen sessions on 15–17 March, 26–28 April, and 4–7 October 1920.

13. The Carl H. Pforzheimer Library has one set of Forman's eight-volume Library Edition, corrected and interleaved by Forman with new information garnered from various sources, as well as piles of clippings, once belonging to H. B. Forman, taken from book catalogues, newspapers, magazines, and journals that contain mentions of Shelley, his family, or his writings. Forman obviously subscribed to a clipping service and followed up all leads. Within this collection, for example, is a copy of W. M. Rossetti's "Shelley in 1812–13" from the *Fortnightly Review* for 1 January 1871, upon which Forman has collated Rossetti's printing of "The Devil's Walk," recording over a hundred "variations of this reprint from the orginal broadsheet" in the Public Record Office.

14. On this question, see *Between the Lines: Letters and Memoranda Interchanged by H. Buxton Forman and Thomas J. Wise*, ed. Fannie E. Ratchford, with a Foreword by Carl H. Pforzheimer (Austin: University of Texas Press, 1945) and *Thomas J. Wise Centenary Studies*, ed. William B. Todd (Austin: University of Texas Press, 1959).

15. *The Letters of A. E. Housman*, ed. Henry Maas (Cambridge, Mass.: Harvard University Press, 1971), p. 49.

16. See A. E. Housman, *The Confines of Criticism*, with notes by John Carter (Cambridge: Cambridge University Press, 1969), pp. 9–12, and John Carter and John

Sparrow, "Shelley, Swinburne and Housman," *TLS*, 21 November 1968, pp. 1318-19.

17. See Housman, *Letters*, pp. 219-220.

18. Housman thought little of Garrod's work on Manilius II, as he made clear in his preface to Manilius V (1930); see Housman, *Letters*, p. 121, fn. 1.

19. *The Poems of John Keats*, ed. H. W. Garrod, 2nd ed. (Oxford: Clarendon Press, 1958), p. [ix].

20. *The Texts of Keats's Poems* (Cambridge, Mass.: Harvard University Press, 1974), pp. 277, 283.

21. Oxford: Clarendon Press, 1927. Pollard was Honorary Secretary of the Bibliographical Society, 1893-1934; co-editor of *The Library*, 1904-20, and sole editor, 1920-34; and Honorary Professor of Bibliography at London University, 1919-1932. McKerrow was joint Honorary Secretary of the Bibliographical Society, 1912-40 and founder and editor of *Review of English Studies*. In the *DNB, 1931-1940*, W. W. Greg writes of McKerrow: "he probably did more than any man to place the editing of English literature upon a scientific basis" (p. 580).

22. *Studies in Bibliography* [*SB*], 3 (1950-51), 19-36; reprinted in *Collected Papers of W. W. Greg*, ed. J. C. Maxwell (Oxford: Clarendon Press, 1966), pp. 374-391.

23. Bowers, *Textual & Literary Criticism* (Cambridge: Cambridge University Press, 1959), pp. vii-viii.

24. *Principles of Bibliographical Description* (Princeton: Princeton University Press, 1949), p. ix.

25. First printed in *The Task of the Editor: Papers Read at a Clark Library Seminar, February 8, 1969* by James Thorpe and Claude M. Simpson, Jr. (Los Angeles: William Andrews Clark Memorial Library, 1969). Thorpe included a revised version of his lecture as the second chapter of his *Principles of Textual Criticism* (San Marino, Cal.: Huntington Library, 1972), pp. 50-79.

26. In Thorpe's words, "Bowers has been eager, it would seem, to insure that abuses are stripped and whipped" (*Principles of Textual Criticism*, p. 64).

27. Bowers, *Textual & Literary Criticism*, p. 25. See also Bowers' review of Taylor's book in *Keats-Shelley Journal*, 9 (1960), 35-38.

28. "On Crane Now Edited: The University of Virginia Edition of *The Works of Stephen Crane*," *Studies in the Novel*, 10 (1978), 103-119.

29. Oxford: Clarendon Press, 1978: *A New Introduction to Bibliography* was also published by the Clarendon Press.

30. *The Library*, 6th ser., 2 (1980), 337-350; contrast with this the favorable review by Jack Stillinger, *JEGP*, 78 (1979), 422-424.

31. *SB*, 28 (1975), 167-229.

32. Bowers' essay appeared in *The Library*, 5th ser., 27 (1972), 81-115.

33. The essays by Pizer and Freehafer, and critical responses to them, appeared in *Bulletin of the New York Public Library* under the editorship of David V. Erdman. I treat Erdman's editorial work and principles, along with those of other

major editors of the British Romantics, in a companion essay to this entitled "Romantic Bards and Historical Editors," *Studies in Romanticism*, 21 (1982), 477–496.

34. Peckham, "Reflections on the Foundations of Modern Textual Editing," *Proof*, I (1971), 129–130.

35. "Two Recent Volumes of *A Selected Edition of W. D. Howells*," *MP*, 78 (1980), 59–72.

36. *SB*, 34 (1981), 23–65.

37. The term "noncritical" seems to me to carry pejorative connotations. In Tanselle's essay "Textual Scholarship" in *Introduction to Scholarship in Modern Languages and Literatures*, ed. Joseph Gibaldi (New York: Modern Language Association, 1981), he uses as a synonym the good paleographic term "diplomatic" for a text which the editor does not feel free to alter in any way (p. 34).

38. *ELH*, 41 (1974), 321–339.

Challenges in Editing
Modern Literary Correspondence:
Transcription

ROBERT STEPHEN BECKER

Since 1975, when I began to prepare a collected edition of the letters of George Moore, it has seemed to me that few if any rules have been established by our profession to govern the scholarly treatment of modern literary correspondence. We editors are like a party of weekend hunters, stalking and shooting our prey according to whim and habit. It may be argued that our diversity of style produces a more interesting, if unpredictable, bag. I should like, however, to advocate a method to our sport, for I believe that as we learn to observe certain standards of methodology we will become more efficient scholars, more useful to our public.

I shall limit the present inquiry to the subject of transcription. At a future date the range can be extended to methods of annotation and composition of prefatory matter, since decisions about transcription affect these subjects and ought to precede them. Some editors, including Leon Edel and Nigel Nicolson, recommend that we discover a more rational purpose than we have now for the publication of innumerable private letters. Most textual scholars agree, however, that all the writing of an important author is worthy of print. The question is not if, but how it should be published.

My concern is only with larger or comprehensive editions of letters, and therefore I want to settle the definitions of three bandied words. To allow readers to identify immediately the kind of work they have opened, one of these designations—"complete," "collected," or "selected"—ought to appear on the title page of all future editions. "Complete" should mean that all letters known to survive have been included. "Collected" should mean that a large and diversified selection has been made to imitate a complete edition. "Selected" should warn the reader that a particular selection has been made for a purpose extrinsic to the correspondence as a whole. Thus the Sanders and Fielding edition of Carlyle is complete, though the editors chose to call it collected. Joseph Blotner's edition of Faulkner is probably collected, though he called it selected. Henry Nash Smith's edition of the correspondence of Mark Twain and William Dean Howells is selected, since its purpose is to study the relationship between those two authors.

My reflections on editorial practice derive from three separate sources of information. First is my own survey of editions of nineteenth- and twentieth-century letters. I examined forty-seven editions published after 1900, sensing general agreement with Bradford Booth, editor of Trollope's letters, that "uncritical and dishonest tampering with texts on the part of nineteenth-century editors has made it necessary to repeat much of their work and to reevaluate the character of many prominent men of letters."[1] Second is my personal correspondence during 1980 and 1981 with thirty-two scholarly editors. Third is my own experience of George Moore's six thousand surviving letters, which seem to cry out painfully for editorial sympathy.

Bearing finally on this inquiry is the matter of readership. It may now be necessary to contradict Walter Harding, editor of Thoreau, who warned that "any editor of manuscript materials is immediately faced with the problem whether he is to aim his text at the general reader or the scholar."[2] Dan Laurence, editor of Shaw, writes, "there no longer *is* a general reader. With rare exceptions, editions of letters just don't sell." Our rules of editorial practice shall be devised for the benefit of scholarly readers, for these are our only readers.

For editors of correspondence, manuscripts take the highest seat in the hierarchy of source materials. We search for them tirelessly, like knights in quest of the Holy Grail. We study them most intensively. It is our chief ambition to understand and disseminate them in printed form to our profession and students. It will be useful to think of manuscripts as a kind of divinity. Homage to this divinity has been practised in two distinct ways: I will call these The Sacred Text and The Sensible Text. Each practice has its own ritual and code of ethics, but their practitioners have been warring with each other since the religion was founded. Rules to govern editorial practice could bring the two sides together.

The editors of The Sacred Text are those who attempt to replicate the holograph in the medium of print. Their general motive is to preserve both the literal meaning of an author's words and a more subtle meaning suggested by the way those words are written. This subtle meaning is contained in errors of spelling and punctuation, and in other holographic eccentricities including capitalization, paragraphing, marks of emphasis, cross-outs, repetitions, and abbreviations. More intricate holographic features were carefully identified by Merrell R. Davis and William H. Gilman, Melville's editors, to include elision, fusion, and expansion. Many editors of The Sacred Text believe that their methods of transcription predominate in current textual scholarship. Ralph Aderman, Herbert Kleinfield, and Jenifer Banks thus assert that their diplomatic transcription of Washington Irving's letters conformed entirely with "modern textual principles," though Irving himself had requested that his holographs be corrected before publication.

My survey of modern editions indicates that Aderman, Kleinfield, and Banks were somewhat arbitrary in their identification of textual principles. Only twenty-seven percent of the editors claimed to offer diplomatic transcriptions. This figure would probably be lowered after closer examination than I had time to make. For example, Bradford Booth wrote, "I have in no instance altered the text" (p.xi) of Trollope's letters, but he did alter punctuation. Gordon Ray, a model editor of The Sacred Text, paragraphed Thackeray's letters.

Where spelling is concerned, only forty-three percent of the editors neither altered silently nor corrected in brackets. "Modern textual principles" do not require the exact transcription of every spelling error. When Allan Wade corrected William Butler Yeats's spelling, he explained that not to correct it would "in the long run appear merely tediously pedantic."[3] David Krause, editor of Sean O'Casey, believes that were Wade to have resorted to diplomatic transcription of Yeats, "the result would be chaos." Wade, Krause, and Sir Rupert Hart-Davis have all expressed the opinion that Yeats requires and deserves editorial help with his spelling. John Kelly, editor of the new complete letters of Yeats, writes: "In general, I am all in favour of tidying up texts as long as this does not interfere with the primary meaning. I think that something written in manuscript looks quite different when in print, not merely in the obvious sense, but that it gives out different signs and involves different expectations of accuracy etc." Rather than having observed "modern textual principles," Dr. Kelly "shilly-shallied over whether to correct Yeats's texts and in the end decided, despite what I have just said, not to." Both Wade and Kelly decided on an individual basis in regard to the particular problems created by Yeats's handwriting.

Regarding punctuation, sixty-one percent of the editors altered or supplied it for the sake of clarity. Leslie Marchand is perhaps the most articulate defender of faulty punctuation. He explained that Byron's errors of punctuation were caused by ignorance rather than intent, but to alter or supply it "detracts from the impression of Byronic spontaneity and the onrush of ideas in his letters, without a compensating gain in clarity."[4] I read this to mean that there would be a gain in clarity, but that it would not compensate for other losses. Marchand continued: "In fact, it may often impose a meaning or emphasis not intended by the writer. I feel that there is less danger of distortion if the reader may see exactly how he punctuated and then to determine whether a phrase between commas or dashes belongs to one sentence or another." It is reasonable to ask, as Sir Rupert Hart-Davis did in my presence, that since Byron did intend a specific meaning when he wrote (in spite of his ignorance of punctuation), is it not better that the highest scholarly authority on Byron identify that meaning, or should it be left to the imagination of the casual reader or one of a multitude of less erudite scholars? "Any half-wit can copy," writes Leon Edel. The great editor, such as Professor Marchand, can and should do more. Marchand himself recommended Gordon Haight's *George Eliot Letters* as a model for future editors. "Punctuation I treated rather more freely," Haight wrote to me, "regarding the reader's convenience as more important than the mechanical reproduction of text." Eliot's punctuation was altered or supplied for clarity.

Regarding other holographic eccentricities, it is difficult to gain an editorial consensus since most editors are reticent about them. Betty Bennett, editor of Mary Shelley, writes: "I believe that holographic eccentricities do reveal as much about an author as the words themselves." Davis and Gilman's sixty-four pages of dense textual notes tell me little more than that Herman Melville's handwriting was hurried and careless. These editors warned that diplomatic transcription would lead to "a typographical monstrosity."[5] Walter Harding, editor of Thoreau, has seen the monster and feels that aspects of diplomatic transcription recommended by the CEAA are work "carried to an idiotic extreme." For needed perspective, I am guided by James F. Beard, editor of Cooper, who writes: "I consider it absolutely essential to acknowledge a fundamental difference" between the media of holograph and print. "Failure to make and acknowledge the distinction can be absolutely disastrous and incredibly expensive." Through examination of conflicting differences between media, it should be possible to estimate the proper scope of the printed medium and to arrive at a sympathetic perception of The Sensible Text.

The problem of George Moore's handwriting illuminates many of the difficulties of printing holograph. Moore had been expelled from secondary school for his inability to grasp the basic skills of reading and writing. Most of what might be called his education took place in racing stables, artist's studios, and cafés. At first sight, his letters thrilled me. Disregard of orthography and punctuation, peculiar flourishes and messy blotches, all spelled character. Language unharnessed in the "onrush of ideas"! My earliest transcriptions retained Moore's original spacing and line divisions. The awful consumption of time this caused forced me to abandon some scruples, but I continued to transcribe the first one thousand letters paying heed to every elision, fusion, and expansion and every accidental capital. I write accidental because in my judgment Moore's decisions to write the capital A or C were often made entirely in his wrist.

Having made my diplomatic transcriptions, I suffered a shock. The robust and engaging George Moore was suddenly not in my typescript. Vividness had become sloppiness, music was noise. Michael Millgate writes that his goal in editing Thomas Hardy has been to render the "flavour" and the "bouquet" of the holograph letters. I was dismayed because I tasted peppercorns and smelled vinegar. Eventually the cause of my problem became clear: I had passed Moore's messages from one medium into another, where different textual values prevailed. Leon Edel gives this process its correct name: translation. He advises that "putting holograph into print is itself a sea-change." With consciousness of inevitable and crucial alteration in the character of a holograph when it is typeset, I became convinced that the desire to replicate manuscripts with print was futile and would produce a text that was no more truthful than it was absurd.

In order to put my ideas in the context of the widest possible experience, I sent a questionnaire to several eminent editors. My questions, in various wordings, were these: (1) Do you regard a particular edition of letters as a model for future editors? (2) Did you invent your own rules of transcription or follow already established rules? (3) Should autograph, typed, and printed source texts be governed by different rules of transcription? (4) What exactly might the retention of slips and careless errors of spelling and punctuation contribute to the printed version of a holograph? (5) Do you acknowledge a fundamental difference between the media of handwriting and print? How should a difference influence decisions concerning the transcription of holographic eccentricities?

Fifty percent of the canvassed editors would not recommend any edition of letters as a model. In general, they felt that individual problems created by an author's correspondence are too great to be solved or even managed with a formula. Only three editions received more than one vote from the remaining editors. James Hepburn, editor of Arnold Bennett, and David Krause, editor of Sean O'Casey, both named Sir Rupert Hart-Davis's *Letters of Oscar Wilde*. I too have used this edition as a model. Richard Ellmann, who is preparing a new biography of Oscar Wilde, writes that "Rupert's edition of Wilde is so magnificent that I feel tempted to endorse anything he has told you" in regard to editorial practice. Gordon Haight, editor of George Eliot, and Michael Millgate, editor of Hardy, recommended Kathleen Tillotson's *Letters of Charles Dickens*. C. Richard Sanders, editor of the Carlyles, and Leslie Marchand, editor of Byron, endorsed Gordon Haight's *George Eliot Letters*. None of these three exemplary editions supplies The Sacred Text. Furthermore, the editors who avoided formula by not recommending a model have avoided endorsing, among others, the diplomatic text imposed in the name of "modern textual principles" on Washington Irving. It seems clear from these replies that our profession supports no coherent body of "modern textual principles."

All of the canvassed editors have synthesized editorial practice from their ideas and from examination of other editions. Some editors, including Gordon Ray and Leon Edel, were clearly more original than others, but none has suggested that editorial practice resulted from imitation rather than imagination. Even editions emanating from the same press display considerable diversity of technique. In the view of at least one publisher's senior editor, Mrs. Arthur Sherwood of Princeton University Press, a body of ground rules for editing letters would save money, time, and grief spent in harnessing the average editor's imagination to the dogcart of practicality.

The replies to question three, as to whether handwritten, typed, and copied letters ought to be transcribed differently, produced no consensus. A "copied" letter is the most problematic, since it is usually written by someone other than the author or the author's employees. Many of George Moore's letters were inscribed by an amanuensis or copied by scholars, collectors, booksellers, or newspaper editors. It seems clear that these letters include holographic or typographical errors probably or certainly not attributable to Moore. Should the editor allow those foreign errors to remain in the text or should the text be corrected? Fifty percent of editors advocate the same methods of transcription regardless of the nature of the source text. David Krause asks: "What else can or should an editor do?" It could be recommended that the secondary source text be altered so that it conforms with the author's known holographic character. This seems a dangerous procedure, since most editors become less than fully articulate when describing holographic character. Thomas Lewis, editor of Hart Crane, advises that "misspellings in printed sources should not be transcribed." Robert Elias "rectified, as though they were typographic errors, all mistakes, inconsistencies, and carelessness attributable to Dreiser's secretaries." Though Professor Elias does not voice the majority viewpoint, his method recommends itself because of its good sense. Whether or not holographic eccentricities belong somehow in print, editors should be able to agree that the typographical eccentricities of a bored secretary or journalist and the careless markings of a bookseller or mundane scholar have only an accidental relation to an author and can be excluded.

The replies to question four support my view that slips of the pen and careless errors of spelling and punctuation provide a holograph with some of its vivifying powers. George Moore died almost twenty years before I was born, yet the lively look and feel of his manuscripts let me imagine that I hear his voice and see his hands in their often noted pantomime of consciousness. Just what are those qualities of handwriting that inspire what Richard Ellmann calls "pietism" among editors? Michael Millgate writes that Thomas Hardy's holographic eccentricities "may tell us something about his mood that day, or about his attitude towards a particular correspondent." Nigel Nicolson offers an example: "The wrong spelling of a name can be a clue to how well, or how little, the author knew about that person. For instance, Virginia Woolf, in her first letter to her future husband Leonard, spelled his name Wolf. A year later she married him. The correct, or incorrect, spelling of the names of casual acquaintances (and she was usually correct) does indicate, I think, the trouble she took to identify people, and hence her social attitude.'' Mr. Nicolson also suggests that common words could be significant ''as an indication of how even the most literate people can sometimes fail to observe what they have often seen correctly spelled. I don't think it has any psychological significance, as some would say.'' Karl Beckson, editor of the mentally unstable Arthur Symons, has decided that ''orthographic peculiarities should be preserved to reflect the writer's state of mind.'' Now comes to mind a particular letter in which George Moore tried four different spellings of eunuch before going to a dictionary, in a state of irritation, and carving the correct spelling of that word at the top of the letter, above the salutation. When editing the letters that passed between John Synge, W. B. Yeats and Lady Gregory, Anne Saddlemyer ''wished to convey through the edition the basic trust each had in the other's comprehension—even when they were all annoyed with each other.'' By preserving holographic eccentricities, Professor Saddlemyer revealed her own trust in the comprehension of her readers.

Aside from trust, eccentricities ''give a sense of 'flow''' in the letters of Synge. J. T. Boulton writes that holographic eccentricity ''gives us a more personal 'feel'—demonstrates that the writer is human like his reader!'' Professor Boulton believes that ambiguous punctuation and slips of the pen put the reader of his edition ''(so far as text goes) in the same position as the original recipient'' of D. H. Lawrence's letter. Norman Kelvin, editor of William Morris, similarly desires to recreate past moments of confusion ''in the belief that the reader will prefer to work things out or ponder the ambiguities as Morris's actual correspondents may have had to do.'' Betty Bennett finds that oddities of Mary Shelley's handwriting produce ''tone.'' Dan Laurence, on a more literal level, writes: ''If I were dealing with an author who was a chronic misspeller, I would retain all the errors, as I think it adds verisimilitude to the text, which should be a reasonable reflection of the personality and education and experience of the writer of the letter.'' On a less solemn note, Richard Garnett remembers that ''Lady Diana Cooper's manuscript of her memoirs spoke of someone who had a cold in which nose and throat reinfected one another in 'a viscous circle'—a brilliant joke, unintentionally brought about by dotty spelling.'' Slips of the pen and careless errors can make us laugh; they give flow, feel, tone; C. L. Cline removed them from

George Meredith's letters, where they seemed to signify nothing, but he writes that they "flavor" the letters of Thackeray; Professor Millgate writes that they achieve "bouquet"; when Richard Ellmann mentions "haste" he seems to echo J. T. Boulton's "dash." These terms describe the intangible spirit of the holograph. This spirit can have a pleasing, magical effect on the reader of a handwritten letter. But can that effect spring from the printed version?

The replies to question five help to clarify the differences between the media of holograph and print. Leon Edel, having deeply appreciated the superior quality of holograph and questioned whether it can be replicated in print, formulated editorial practices which he knew would worry his pietistic critics. Perhaps as a gesture of good faith he has asked scholars to note that we live in "the age of photoduplication," in which The Sacred Text can be disseminated on Kodak or Xerox paper. This is not entirely true. Experienced textual scholars know that some curators of important manuscripts forbid photoduplication. For example, I was unable to order photocopies at the Bibliothèque Littéraire Jacques Doucet in Paris and at the Tolstoy Museum, Moscow. Some literary correspondence is owned by individuals or autograph dealers who forbid photoduplication in anxious anticipation of a commercial transaction. Some curators who permit photoduplication do so only at prohibitive rates. Finally, the products of certain forms of photoduplication, microfilm and rapid copy in particular, frequently impair rather than clear the vision of the textual scholar. I spent several days agonizing over the Chadwyck-Healey microfilm publication of Swan Sonnenschein's correspondence files before going in desperation to the dusty basement of Messrs. Allen and Unwin, where the original documents were at last transcribed. The experience of working with photoduplicated holographs can convince the scholar that manuscripts guard their own spirit and compel us, as it were, back to the source.

Admitting our practical inability to replicate manuscripts photographically for scholarly purposes, but also desiring to capture the spirit of the holograph in our transcriptions, editors ought first to acknowledge that transcription is, in Leon Edel's phrase, *translation* from one medium into another. A few editors are not prepared to make this acknowledgment. C. L. Cline, who altered the text of George Meredith's letters to increase readability, writes: "I do not think it would have been difficult to replicate holograph in the medi-

um of print with the Meredith letters." J. T. Boulton denied a fundamental difference between the media, though he has made concessions
to a few differences, considered trifles, in the letters of Lawrence. Neither Anne Saddlemyer nor Michael Millgate has faced an insurmount-
able barrier to the printed replication of letters by Synge or Hardy. C.
Richard Sanders does "not acknowledge, psychologically, a fundamental difference between holograph and print. I think that the difference is superficial and could be ignored altogether." But these are
minority views. Most of the canvassed editors confirmed the conclusion of my survey of editions: that the regular form and spacing of
print, its size on the page and the bound page itself, are all intrinsic elements of the printed medium that are foreign, even contrary, to the
corresponding elements of the holograph. The difference between
them is fundamental because the spirit and, for some editors, part of
the literal meaning of the message are rooted in idiosyncrasies of character form, spacing, and the physical properties of the holograph as a
whole.

Transcription then is translation. To discover a practical mode of
translation, editors might be usefully guided by Professor Sanders's experience of the Carlyle letters. "We retain slips, misspellings, and
careless errors for the sake of fidelity to text," he writes, "but I now
believe they are more of a distraction than anything of positive value.
About all that we can come up with in studying them is that Jane was
more careless and a poorer speller than Thomas. If I were starting
again, I would normalize the text." The failure of Professor Sanders
to observe a revelation of Carlyle's personality in erratic wrist movement and orthography might be ascribed to lack of imagination. By
contrast, Edwin H. Miller confesses that he is "a psychological critic,
and most interested in the latent level." Professor Miller believes that
the difference between holograph and print is so great that "it is impossible to reproduce a letter exactly under any circumstances." He
transcribed a normalized text of Walt Whitman not out of insensitivi-
ty to the most subtle qualities to the holograph, but because these
qualities are not translatable. "People looking for hidden secrets will
have to go to the originals," he writes, echoing exactly the sentiments
of another psychological critic and editor, Karl Beckson. The word
Professor Miller summons to characterize diplomatic transcription is
not psychology but pedantry.

Kathleen Coburn has urged that literary correspondence radiates "some sort of warmth that ought not to be damped with the cold water of pedantry."[6] The pedantic capability of some editors has also disturbed Dan Laurence: "I would like the text to be as close to transcription in facsimile as I can make it without irritating the reader with extraneous signs of the pedant's presence, or trying to carry scholarship to the point of noting that there are inkblots in the margin, an uncrossed 't' on line 17, and a dropped letter in a typewritten word!" Shaw's editor thus objects to the paraphernalia of The Sacred Text—the brackets, squiggly lines and textual notes—and in so doing he objects, perhaps unwillingly, to The Sacred Text itself. Editors do not invent numerous symbols and assign valuable space to textual notes merely to make themselves visible. The symbols and notes, which make many printed texts downright unreadable, are necessary to diplomatic transcription. Herman Melville's editors found it impossible to "reproduce his orthography without typographical obtrusiveness and a resulting irritation to the reader. A text of the letters which Melville wrote rapidly and spontaneously would end up a typographical monstrosity" (p. xxv). Leon Edel adds: "To reproduce every henscratch in collections of letters running into thousands is not only pedantic, it is futile." Thus Professors Edel and Sanders, model editors of opposing traditions, seem to occupy common ground. Edel continues: "The correspondence needs to be characterized; and if it is sown with ampersands by the bushel the editor should decide whether he wants to have his page look like a series of potato mounds or whether he wants to bestow on the reader the legibility that *print* is bestowing." Gordon Haight, correctly regarded as a very different kind of editor, supplies a comment about George Eliot's letters which summarizes Professor Edel's viewpoint: "To reproduce in type all the vagaries of manuscript is neither feasible nor desirable; and though I tried to provide an accurate text, it was never an exact transcription."

To characterize a correspondence is the editorial alternative to excessive paraphernalia. From experience of editing Virginia Woolf, Nigel Nicolson may direct us to an agreeable and practical perception of the editor's responsibilities: "The principle, I believe, is to convey the raciness of a letter, as distinct from something intended for print (where she was very careful), but without putting unnecessary strain on the reader's understanding of the passage. One ought to hear the writer's voice in reading a printed letter, and this depends largely on retaining her original punctuation; but it is legitimate, I think, for the editor to supply very occasionally a punctuation mark to make the passage intelligible, without pedantic *sics* or square brackets. . . . A letter should be read, as it is written, as cursively as possible, to convey sense, mood and spirit, and the intrusiveness of an editor with niggling amendments can often prevent this.''

So to characterize a literary correspondence, to translate the holograph into print, the editor must make judgments on behalf of the author, for the benefit of the reader. It is admitted that editorial paraphernalia is far more harmful to the spirit of the correspondence than responsible, often silent normalization of text. Edwin Miller and Thomas Lewis have identified the Harvard University Press publication of Emerson's *Journals* as an unfortunate but logical outcome of diplomatic transcription. "It seems an outrage," writes Professor Miller, "to make it almost impossible to read perhaps the greatest autobiography in American literature." It is equally outrageous to maim and cripple the correspondence of great writers through transcription that vainly aspires to replicate every iota of holographic information. If the aspiration is excusable, the product is not.

In place of The Sacred Text, we can, as editors responsible mainly to authors and readers and not merely to scholastic critics, formulate better ground rules for the transcription of literary letters. Bound together by common interests and experience, we should do this together. To begin the process, I shall offer the following recommendations:

(1) Because the editor devotes years to the concentrated study of his author, achieving mature and comprehensive understanding of the author's life and work, he gains authority to identify what Nigel Nicolson has termed the author's "voice." The duty of the editor is to make that voice as audible as possible.

(2) What is possible is defined not by what Edwin Miller calls a "mindless and pedantic" replication of the holographic medium. It depends rather on a realistic appraisal of the medium of print. Instead of engaging in futile experiments to expand that medium beyond its inflexible limits, the editor resigns himself to translate the holograph into it.

(3) It is agreed that typical holographs include numerous eccentricities, not all of which are vitally important to an under-

standing of the holograph. The editor segregates those eccentricities which, in the words of Merrell Davis and William Gilman, are "characteristics within the author's intention that seem important to the reading and understanding of the letters."[7] These will be represented in the printed medium; the others may be ignored.

(4) Eccentricities to be ignored are erratic spelling and any punctuation and capitalization due, in the editor's opinion, to slips of the pen. For example, the fusion or elision of letter characters which result from hasty writing, a full stop lengthened by a heavy hand to form a dash, a lower case character written large so that it appears as a capital. The editor may also ignore eccentricities which the author committed consciously to the holographic page but not, in the editor's judgment, with any intended signification. For example, ampersands may be transcribed "and" and the abbreviated "wd" may be printed "would." Errors of spelling *due not to ignorance or intent* but simply to carelessness may be corrected. Thus the word "their" can replace "there," "for" can replace "four." Such careless errors, while interfering with the reader's attention, tell his mind and heart nothing important about the author.

(5) In deciding further which eccentricities to represent in print, the editor should not transcribe those which create typographical obtrusiveness. For example, crossed out words which do not contribute to final meaning, multiple underlinings, exotic word spacing, and line division. Here the editor may regularize the text and describe the omitted eccentricities in footnotes. Spelling errors caused by ignorance or intent and highly personal punctuation should be transcribed as written. Since these peculiarities are seldom abundant, the editor can utilize the word *sic* or employ brackets if the sense of the passage requires them without chilling the original "warmth" of the text.

(6) The editor may acknowledge the silliness of holding his author responsible for a typist's, bookseller's, or journalist's carelessness and therefore may normalize typed and printed source texts throughout.

(7) In the prefatory matter, the editor should provide a definitive explanation of his methods of transcription. Variations be-

tween holographic and printed texts, including omissions and alterations, should be described so that in summary the reader can understand how and why the correspondence has been characterized.

In appealing for the general implementation of more sensible editorial standards, I mentioned that two distinguished editors expressed outrage over the recent crippling of Ralph Waldo Emerson. It was Emerson who wrote: "Raphael paints wisdom, Handel sings it, Phidias carves it, Shakespeare writes it, Wren builds it, Columbus sails it, Luther preaches it, Washington arms it, Watt mechanizes it." We can act together so that, at some future date, the maimed spirit of Emerson will add to his survey: Editors practise it.

NOTES

[All unnumbered quotations are from personal letters.]

1. *The Letters of Anthony Trollope*, ed. Bradford Booth (Oxford: Oxford Univ. Press, 1951), p. xi.
2. *The Correspondence of Henry David Thoreau*, eds. Walter Harding and Carl Bode (New York: New York Univ. Press, 1958), p. xix.
3. *The Letters of W.B. Yeats*, ed. Allan Wade (London: Rupert Hart-Davis, 1954), p. 16.
4. *Byron's Letters and Journals*, I, ed. Leslie Marchand (Cambridge, Mass.: Harvard Univ. Press, 1973), p. 28.
5. *The Letters of Herman Melville*, eds. Merrell Davis and William Gilman (New Haven: Yale Univ. Press, 1960), p. xxv.
6. *The Letters of Sara Hutchinson from 1800 to 1835*, ed. Kathleen Coburn (London: Routledge and Kegan Paul, 1954), p. xii.
7. *The Letters of Herman Melville*, p. xxvi.

How To Read Gertrude Stein: The Manuscript of "Stanzas in Meditation"

Ulla E. Dydo

INTRODUCTION

When I began my study of "Stanzas in Meditation" (1932), Gertrude Stein's longest work of poetry, I did not expect to discover serious textual problems. And certainly I did not know how central textual considerations are for understanding Stein's work, her rhetoric, and her mind. I did know that the manuscript notebooks sometimes yield insights printed texts do not permit. Stein wrote most of her pieces in copybooks or *cahiers* used by French school children. Many have educational covers with pictures and short texts about topics such as French regions, French history, scientific discoveries or famous men. The pictures, texts, or titles of these *cahiers* are often reflected in Stein's compositions. For example, Richard Bridgman notes that the pieces "Dahomey or As Soft a Noise" (1924) and "A Bouquet" (1927) were inspired by the covers of the notebooks. "Dahomey" refers to the title of one *cahier* in a series on the French colonies, and "A Bouquet" is named for the illustration on another.[1] Wendy Steiner also considers the notebooks, showing in detail how Stein's 1923 portrait, "He and They, Hemingway," among others, becomes meaningful by reference to a series of ideas in the pictures and words of the notebook.[2] As these examples suggest, sections of many Stein pieces derive from elements of the French *cahiers*, which are not only containers of Stein's writing but also source materials for her writing. The relationship of the notebooks to the texts, however, is far more complicated and important than had been thought: a full study of the Stein autograph notebooks can make works accessible that have been considered hermetic or incomprehensible.

Not all Stein's works present great difficulties. Her well-known autobiographical books can be discussed in traditional critical language without recourse to the manuscript notebooks. Among these books are *The Autobiography of Alice B. Toklas* (1933), *Everybody's Auto-*

biography (1937), *Paris, France* (1940), and *Wars I Have Seen* (1945).
Likewise, Stein's critical works such as *Lectures in America* (1935)
and *Narration* (1935) present no special textual problems. Stein characterized these autobiographical and critical works as her "open" and
"public" works, terms originally used by Alfred Harcourt during ne-
gotiations for Stein publications after the "public" *Autobiography*:
Harcourt hoped for more "open" books that would sell. And she
contrasted these books with her "real kind of books." Although some
of these have become famous and familiar—*Three Lives* is an example, as is Stein's much quoted portrait of Picasso—others remain
known only to a small group of poets and painters, playwrights, actors, and film makers who insist that Stein liberates them from the
stifling constraints of dead tradition and validates their own artistic
perception.[3]

Many readers continue to reject Stein's experimental work because
it resists paraphrase, defies classification, and refuses to submit to logical analysis. Impatient with her writing, they become impatient with
Stein as a person and shift from discussing her work to talking about
her personality and her life. And since her life has elements of notorie-
ty, it becomes easy to substitute gossip about her life for an examination of her work. Yet Stein always insisted that her personal history
explained nothing about her work and that all the clues to her art were
in her writing and not in her life. The autograph manuscripts, however, not only contain the texts that are Stein's works but also yield a
special kind of biographical information that is not found in the
printed books or in the existing Stein biographies but that is of central
importance for determining how and why she composed what she
composed.

Most of the Stein papers were available at the Yale University Library (now the Beinecke Rare Book and Manuscript Library) by 1947,
some having been deposited as early as 1937, 1939, and 1940.[4] The papers given to Yale included manuscripts and typescripts of a large
number of works which had not been published in Stein's lifetime.
These make up the eight-volume *Yale Edition of the Unpublished
Writings of Gertrude Stein*, which appeared between 1951 and 1958.
Until these volumes were printed, the extent of Stein's literary production was known only to some of her friends and fellow writers. Detailed
scholarly investigation did not begin until well after the posthumous
work had become available in print.[5] The printed works, however, tell

only a part of the story of Stein's writing. For what appears on the handwritten pages raises questions that would never occur to the reader of the printed pieces.

"Stanzas in Meditation" is an example of such a manuscript text, for the way in which it differs from the printed text necessitates a new reading of "Stanzas" and demands a reconsideration of all Stein's writing of 1932.

I

"Stanzas" is Stein's most substantial work of poetry. It consists of 164 numbered stanzas of irregular length, arranged in five parts. Except for a small number of stanzas printed in a few magazines and in one anthology, the work was not published in Stein's lifetime.[6] It takes up the first one hundred fifty pages of *Stanzas in Meditation and Other Poems* (1956), the sixth volume of the posthumous Yale edition, and is reprinted in the *Yale Gertrude Stein*, a one-volume selection from the posthumous edition which appeared in 1980. Alice Toklas mentions that Gertrude Stein asked her to prepare an announcement of the publication in Stein's own Plain Edition of a volume of poetry which was to include "Stanzas" as its main piece.[7] However, no such announcement was printed nor was the volume of poetry published. By early 1933, when this volume could have been prepared, *The Autobiography of Alice B. Toklas* was about to be published and Stein was about to become a best-selling author, which eliminated the need for publishing herself. In 1937, Stein's friend, Sir Robert Abdy, made preparations to print "Stanzas" in a fine edition on hand-made paper. A connoisseur and a perfectionist, Sir Robert planned the volume with great care. However, although proofsheets were apparently printed, the volume was not published. According to the Haas-Gallup *Catalogue of the Writings of Gertrude Stein*,[8] the work was written in 1932, just prior to *The Autobiography of Alice B. Toklas*, which was composed in October and November 1932. Internal evidence indicates that "Stanzas" was begun at Stein's country house in Bilignin immediately after her arrival from Paris in May 1932 and that composition continued throughout the summer and autumn; exactly when the work was completed is not certain, but presumably it was finished in November of 1932, as Stein suggests in the *Autobiography*, where she describes "Stanzas" as "the last thing that she has finished'' (p. 276). During the summer and fall of 1932 in the country, Stein also wrote numerous other pieces, often working on several concurrently.

Stein said almost nothing about this work in any of her letters. To a few friends she spoke of writing stanzas or meditations but, not surprisingly, she made no further comments. Stein rarely ''explained'' anything about her work in correspondence.

What is ''Stanzas in Meditation''? Stein would consider it inappropriate to ask what it is about. The subject of this work is not the process of meditation, but the work itself *is* a meditation or rather a long series of meditations, as Stein's alternative title, ''Meditations in Stanzas,'' makes clear. Stanza after stanza, Stein follows the verbal movement of her mind in the act of concentrated, conscious meditation. All sorts of ''subjects'' here and there do enter the meditating in ''Stanzas''—dog fights, parties, cutting roses, proofreading the Plain Edition text of ''A Long Gay Book,'' an eclipse of the moon, a fire on a cold summer night, birds, and always writing problems. But such topics are present not as subject matter to be developed in the stanzas but as words or as elements of writing in the process of being composed. The act of composing words—not subject matter—is the act of meditating. The voice of the meditations is the voice of Stein composing her words. ''Stanzas'' is a difficult work, unlikely ever to become popular, but it generously rewards the patient reader who is willing to follow the rhetoric of the verbal meditations as he or she would follow the choreography of dancers in a dance.

A few short passages may suggest the range of Stein's meditations.[9] Here she wonders why anyone writes at all and why writing is such a struggle. (Contrary to what Stein suggests in the *Autobiography*, writing was not at all easy for her.)

> Believe me it is not for pleasure that I do it.
> Not only for pleasure for pleasure in it that I do it.
> I feel the necessity to do it
> Partly from need
> Partly from pride
> And partly from ambition.
> And all of it which is why
> I literally try not only not why
> But why I try to do it and not to do it
> But if it is well-known it is well-known

(IV, iii)

Here she is humorously literal:

> I have lost the thread of my discourse.
> This is it it makes no difference if we find it
> If we found it
>
> (V, xvi)

And she considers how words connect to make meanings:

> Next to next to and does.
> Does it join.
> Does it mean does it join.
> Does it mean does it mean does it join.
> If after all they know
> That I say so
>
> (V, lx)

In her focus on words as words rather than words as signs for things, Stein attempts to divest her writing of all references to things outside the poems themselves. She tries to "unhook" the words from events, persons, and objects. That is why there are so few concrete words in the stanzas and why the language appears so abstract. She succeeds to an astounding degree in removing her words from object reference and narrative content, but she does not totally succeed. It is possible to detect traces of the autobiographical references that are "abstracted" from "Stanzas." There are occasionally very personal and painful moods finely shaped in words.

> I wish to remember that there was a time
> When they saw shapes in clouds
> Also as much.
> And now why why will they if they will
> See shapes in clouds but do not
> Do not draw the attention of any other one to it
>
> (V, xliv)

In one sense, as Stein says, "Stanzas" is "her autobiography one of two/ But which it is no one which it is can know" (IV, xiv). But in another sense, this work composes pure words that have been emptied of object content and freed of grammatical prescriptions for how to behave.

Although Stein jotted down notes, sentences, and whole sections of pieces wherever she happened to be when they occurred to her, she apparently did most of her sustained writing at home, alone, often at night, when distractions for eye and ear were fewer than in daytime. Each night she left what she had written so that Alice Toklas could type it the next day. The manuscripts show Alice's page numbers for the typescript pages in red and purple pencil. Alice, familiar with Stein's difficult handwriting, typed with great care, often checking troublesome words with Stein before she began typing, but in spite of careful typing and proofreading, her typescripts contain errors. Anyone who has ever copied or memorized a Stein piece knows that it is difficult to transcribe Stein accurately. Stein's syntax, grammar, and punctuation do not allow the typist or reader to rely unthinkingly on language habits when preparing or proofreading a Stein text. Errors made in copying a Stein passage cannot be corrected by appeal to standard usage.[10] The result of these difficulties is that some typescripts contain errors which are transferred to the printed texts. Additional errors were made by typesetters and not caught by proofreaders. When the posthumous edition was prepared, the discrepancies between the manuscript and typescript texts were not known. Now, however, it is clear that an accurate Stein text cannot be obtained without the autograph manuscript.

In addition, Alice Toklas was not beyond occasional editorial interference, a very different matter from typing errors. It is not usually difficult to determine whether a textual discrepancy is the result of an error or of a conscious revision.[11] Alice's participation in Gertrude Stein's writing took many forms. For certain purposes she was the typist, for others the editor who checked and corrected facts and details (although these corrections sometimes also involved opinions), for others the translator into French of letters that Stein drafted in English. Alice also reviewed with Stein all business contracts before Stein signed them.

In some manuscripts Stein added editorial instructions or personal commentaries addressed to Alice Toklas that were not parts of her pieces and do not appear in the transcript or in print. On the title page of the manuscript notebook of "Selected Poems" (1918) are the following instructions: "Do these together under the title of Selected Poems beginning with end of book and making subtitles [sic]." The manuscript of "More Grammar for a Sentence" (1930) has a personal note, almost like a short letter, on a topic that must have been discussed: "I am delighted with it it is completely good, you are quite right about my relation to America." These words, of course, do not appear in the typescript. In other pieces, however, passages addressed to Alice are parts of the composition and appear in typescript and in print. "Natural Phenomena" (1925), for example, ends with a tiny dialogue that is undoubtedly an exchange between Stein and Toklas: "I choose you. I choose you too." Plainly Alice Toklas is crucial for Stein's writing, whether or not she appears in the printed text.

Alice Toklas's function was not confined to typing and editing, encouraging and house-keeping. It was Alice who was the central presence in Gertrude Stein's life, Alice who both inspired and antagonized her, Alice who was her primary audience. Alice protected her from uninvited visitors, from business that interfered with writing, and even from distractions that offered escape from work. By freeing Stein to write, Alice defined the limits of Stein's freedom. All along, whether by opposition or by agreement, Alice was involved in the process of living at whose center lay the process of writing. Explicitly and implicitly, she was a presence in the words of Stein's writing and in the pieces that were sent to her publishers. Many Stein pieces sound like talk between two people steadily exchanging words. The moods and ideas vary, but the talk goes on. In "Stanzas" Alice is frequently addressed or quoted as antagonist:

> I forgive you everything and there is nothing to forgive.
>
> (IV, i)
>
> Let me see let me go let me be not only determined . . .
>
> (II, xix)
>
> Who is winning why the answer of course is she is.
>
> (IV, xxiv)

In addition to the problems of accurate texts and the evidence of Alice Toklas's presence, several other features characterize Stein's manuscripts. Stein was a doodler. In many of her notebooks, she plays with initials, with calligraphic shapes or reversed letters (b, d), and she also does cartoon-like drawings. Occasionally she tries out various pens. Frequently she follows in ink the outlines of the pictures on the French *cahiers*, here and there adding lines of her own to the illustrations. It is a good idea to look at these doodles with care. Sometimes they suddenly speak.

Stein's notebooks also become incidental personal notepads. Phone numbers, names, addresses, and other personal reminders frequently appear in them. Sometimes these notes relate to the compositions, but more commonly they do not. They do, however, frequently date compositions by dating the notebooks.[12]

Stein was given to making lists of all kinds. The manuscripts show grocery lists, lists of guests to be invited, lists of numbers, lists of words, additions of projected dollar income, instructions from the veterinarian. The innumerable lists suggest Stein's fascination with visual arrangements of words in columns or on pages. They also sometimes offer valuable biographical information, and they perhaps suggest her awareness of her problems with organization.

Stein was often sloppy and careless. One piece simply stops in the middle of a sentence. Others appear unfinished in other ways. Some show a handwriting so erratic that it is no surprise to find the substance of the writing disorganized and ineffective. (This kind of handwriting must not be confused with the fast, sweeping hand that allowed her, in passages where she played with a series of modulated phrases, to maintain momentum and rhythm.) Changes in handwriting often mark the beginnings of new sections in a composition, whether they are a day's work or a part of a day's work. They sometimes give clues to the completion of one section of a piece and the beginning of another, suggesting units of thought that are easily overlooked. So much does the handwriting in the notebooks tell us about Stein's composing that serious scholarly analysis of a Stein text cannot be done without the context that the manuscripts reveal.

II

Many of Stein's stylistic peculiarities are familiar to anyone who knows even a little about her work. She writes in forms—words, phrases, idiomatic sequences, sentences, paragraphs—that often appear to go counter to standard English usage, syntax, and word order:

> It is not which they will not like or leave it as a wish which they compare
> All of most all for that did they if not as it is
> Should they dare or compare
> Could it have been found all round
> Or would they take pleasure in this
> Or can they not be often whichever
> As they told theirs in any day.
> Does it make any difference if they ask
> Or indeed does it make any difference
> If they ask.
>
> (III, xvi*b*)

While these lines (surely they echo Eliot's Prufrock) sound entirely English, the sequence of words and phrases is not predictable. Nor is Stein's punctuation predictable, for it is not syntactical. If the printed text of these lines is checked in the manuscript, errors show up. Line 2 contains a misprint: the word *of* should be *for*. The last but one line should end with a period. A different problem occurs in line 6, where *can* in the manuscript is inked in over the original *may*; one of the two typescripts reads *may* and the other *can*. Yet the printed text does not immediately make the reader feel that *of* is an error, that a period is necessary at the end of the last but one line, and that *can* is more desirable than *may*. Language habits offer no useful guides for reading this passage. If expectations about the habitual behavior or choice of words rather than attention to the actual words determine the reading, Stein is likely to be misread. The Stein reader, unless he is unusually attentive, is not in a position even to suspect inaccuracies in the printed text without recourse to the autograph manuscript. Rarely does the printed text give away its own faultiness.

In a very different but not less typical passage from a somewhat earlier poem, Stein writes in the fast, even, rhythmic hand described earlier. Sweeping across many pages, she maintains the momentum of the rushing words. Her lines are easy to speak and create the urgent mood of someone who begs, "Let me be!" "Let me try to be me!" "Let me be shy if I feel shy!"

> Let her be let her be let her be to be to be shy let her be to be
>   let her be to be let her try.
> Let her try.
> Let her be let her be let her be to be to be shy let her be to be
>   let her be let her try.
> To be shy.
> Let her be
> Let her try.
> Let her be let her let her let her be let her be let her be let her
>   be shy let her be let her be let her try.
> Let her try.
> Let her be.
> Let her be shy.
> Let her be.
> Let her be let her be let her let her try.
> Let her try to be let her try to be let her be shy let her try to be
>   let her try to be let her be let her be let her try.

> Let her be shy.
> Let her try.
> Let her try.
> Let her be
> Let her let her be shy.
> Let her try.
> Let her be.
> Let her let her be shy
>
> ("Patriarchal Poetry," 1927)

Typing and proofreading lines like these is far more difficult than speaking them and requires a form of concentrated attention that more conventional writing does not demand. As a result, variants easily appear in Stein books that do not become apparent until the manuscripts are consulted.

It is often said that Stein's writing is not concerned with people, events, or objects. This is why it is sometimes called *abstract* or non-referential. Yet throughout her life Stein focused on the here and now, on the actuality and immediacy of daily life among objects. She observed commonplace things around her, and these entered directly into her writing although she did not write *about* these things as subject matter. She composed her poems with the objects of her world, which were never invented. Her pieces can of course be read without knowledge of the references to her world, but a full analysis must take these references into account.

Here are the opening lines of "A Little Love of Life" (1932), a piece Stein wrote at the same time as the later stanzas:

> It is quite worthwhile to have a pen. And to look at all those
> that are for sale. Because each time there are different ones
> and it is actually always attractive. To possess them.
> A pen is a pencil and I never thought about it before.

The *cahier* of this piece shows that Stein wrote this passage in pencil but then re-traced *pen* in ink over the pencilled word *pen* in the first sentence. The manuscript lines literally represent the pen/pencil relationship, which the printed lines cannot show. A pen is indeed a pencil, as Stein says. (Stein also re-traced in ink the letters *or* of the word *for*. In what I look upon as a form of doodling she made the word *or* stand out within the word *for*. She commonly played such word games.)

On the back cover of the manuscript notebook of "A Little Love of Life," in the same pen and the same black ink as the one used in the quoted passage, the words *But which* are written three times in slightly different ways in careful calligraphic shapes. (The words *But which* also occur later in the text.) Stein was perhaps trying out a pen or a phrase. The back cover in addition has pencilled notes—a short list of names and a telephone number. The notebook tells more than the text, even though the printed text is complete and correct.

The question of pen and pencil is relevant in other ways. In some pieces, Stein alternated writing in pencil and writing in ink. For example, the long poem "Winning His Way" (1931) is written in sections that are fairly even in length—about two and a half printed pages in the Yale edition—and that are marked off in the manuscript by the switch from pen to pencil. The same procedure appears in a number of other manuscripts. What does the switch from pen to pencil mean? It is common enough in Stein's notebooks to require investigation.

In "A French Rooster" (1930) the following passage appears:

> He is not apt to be only careful he is apt to be cautious
> as well. He is apt to be as careful and then he is sure
> to be better. An erasure is our politeness.

The first two sentences are easy enough to understand. The third appears disconnected. A look at the manuscript shows the connection. The end of the second sentence is followed by a number of crossed out and erased words, which are correctly omitted in the typescript and the printed text. After these comes the last sentence. The section looks like this:

> He is not apt to be only careful he is apt to be cautious
> as well. He is apt to be as careful and then he is sure to
> be better ~~as if it~~   ~~should~~. An erasure is our politeness.

After writing the word *should*, Stein attempted to erase the last five words but completely erased only the one which had filled the open space. She then crossed out the four partially erased words to prevent their being typed. The erasure of the eliminated word (what was it before Stein abstracted it?) is a matter of politeness. The manuscript pages show Stein writing, thinking, erasing, and continuing writing. They make visible how her mind became conscious of its own movements and how she put her perceptions down on paper. This is what Stein's compositions are all about.

A "text event" similar to the erasure may be found in these lines:

> Should it be mine as pause it is mine
> That should be satisfying.
>
> (II, ix)

The manuscript and the printed text are the same. What is interesting is that Stein states in words exactly what happened—in this case, the word *pause* spells the act of pausing in her discourse. Rather than being excluded as extraneous, the pause becomes known to the consciousness in the form of the word which is a part of the meditation.

The erasure and the pause also illustrate a form of humor characteristic of Stein: it is the humor arising from a statement so simple and so literal that is puts learned brains to shame. Neither the erasure nor the pause require elaborate interpretation. Stein had simply erased and paused, and she said so. The reader almost overlooks these simple facts, especially if he looks for "important ideas." But to Stein these small events were important because they were literally true. She must be read literally.

"Stanzas in Meditation" is full of passages for which the manuscript notebooks establish contexts. Stein does not include these contexts in her texts because she considers them beyond the immediacy of her pieces. Contexts and explanation are matters of speculation and memory, and Stein does not speculate or reminisce in writing. She concentrates entirely on what is immediately present. This is part of what she means when she says that she is meditating. What she writes is what she means, and what she means refers to the actuality of her life, but the context visible in the autograph manuscripts is not a part of that actuality for her. Of course, it may be asked where context becomes text: the *pause* that is registered is quite clear, but can the *erasure* be understood by the reader without a context? Impatient Stein readers tend to cry for more context in the hope that it will help them understand what they read. Stein's most effective writing requires no context beyond her words, which are their own context. Yet some other pieces, which are less successful as "self-contained movement," are almost incomprehensible without context and explanation. In these pieces the text is no longer its own context.

Here is an excerpt from Stanza xxiv of Part IV:

> It is very difficult to plan to write four pages.
> Four pages depend upon how many more you use.
> You must be careful not to be wasteful.
> It uses up the pages two at a time for four
> And if they come to and fro and pass the door
> They do so.

The reference to four pages seems arbitrary or obscure although it is not incomprehensible. The manuscript notebook explains what happened. Beyond the page where Stein wrote this passage, four more blank leaves remained in the notebook. Stein had obviously looked ahead, realized that four leaves were left and immediately considered this fact in writing. The passage, once again, is literally true.

Beyond the literal, however, these lines become a brief meditation—here is Stein's art—on the problem of filling an assigned space or of writing in accordance with a plan. Any writer who has ever had to produce a piece of a given number of words or pages knows the agony of writing a set number of words or of condensing his substance to fit a prescribed space. Why should Stein, who had the freedom to create her own forms, worry about filling four pages? Again the notebooks suggest some answers. Stein very often, though not always, fits her words into the given space of a notebook as container, filling up the book to the very end. For example, a single notebook, filled to the end of the last page, contains all of Part IV of "Stanzas," from which the lines about the last four pages are quoted.

What is the reason for this unusual procedure? Both personal and artistic considerations provide clues. Gertrude Stein considered herself lazy and undisciplined. She apparently needed clear tasks if she was to write. Alice Toklas, the crucial figure who validated her writing, apparently helped her set daily tasks. The two women may somehow have worked out modes of discipline which helped Stein write though they obviously also contributed to tensions that appear in "Stanzas" and in other pieces. A few lines after the section on the four pages Stein says that "it is very important not to disturb him" (*he* refers to Stein, *she* to Toklas). And in "Narrative" (1930) Stein acknowledges that "when it is not with her he can make no verses." Without Toklas's affection and without the discipline that Toklas made possible, there was no writing. Filling assigned pages may have been a form of discipline.

Filling a whole notebook also means that the space in the book determines the shape of a piece. This is the same situation as that of painter who fills a canvas of a given size. The interdependence of form and content in those Stein compositions that completely fill manuscript notebooks is a matter of special interest. What is astounding about many of Stein's finest texts is precisely the art that allows her to complete poems or sections of poems within the given space. She exercises the rhetorical skill to complete a composition by the end of a notebook or even by the end of a page rather than simply to stop it. Sometimes she is highly successful; at other times impatience gets the better of her and her endings are forced or her pieces fall apart. Stein's forms must be examined with special care in the many pieces that are deliberately constructed within such frames.

In the section on the four pages, Stein was speaking literally. She realized that planning to write four pages was difficult and depended upon how many pages were used up. She had been raised not to be wasteful. Stein frequently wrote only on the *recto* of each leaf, which meant that she used the pages "two at a time for four." She did not follow this practice in the notebook for Part IV, but she did follow it in the book for Part V, which she began after completing the stanza that speaks of the four pages. The quoted passage is thus a literal description of how Stein wrote.

III

Even the title of "Stanzas in Meditation" suggests Stein's refusal to give concrete references. Reading for a short while in this book forces the attention away from objects, events, people, and ideas about life toward the rhetorical configurations of the words and their discontextuated movements in lines, sentences, and stanzas. The manuscript notebooks and the textual revisions of these poems, however, contain a wealth of information about the context of "Stanzas."

The text of the five parts of "Stanzas" is contained in six French notebooks. Part I begins in a thin brown *cahier* with a line drawing of a rooster but with no text on its cover. By the middle of the ninth stanza, this *cahier* is filled and Stein continues in a second notebook with the same picture but in a different color. This second notebook, also filled to the end, completes Part I of "Stanzas." Stein must have realized that the stanzas were developing into a larger work and therefore decided to switch to larger notebooks for the next four parts.

Parts II, III, and IV are each contained in a large notebook, and each of these is filled to the very end. Line drawings on the covers do not enter the text.

Part V is written in a hand-sewn dummy volume without covers. (Another dummy book, with different paper and different in size, contains the play *A Manoir*, written during the same summer as "Stanzas"; these were perhaps sample volumes for the Plain Edition, Stein's publishing venture for her own works.) This notebook, filled to the end like the others, is much fatter than the preceding three and contains more stanzas. In the printed volume, Part I of "Stanzas" (two thin notebooks) takes up 15 pages, Parts II, III, and IV (one large notebook each) take up 21 to 24 pages each, and Part V (one dummy book) takes up 60 pages. What appears as the excessive length of Part V is not surprising if the size of the dummy book and Stein's habit of filling notebooks to the end are taken into consideration.

The title given on the six notebooks is *81 Stanzas* or simply *Stanzas*. The number 81 is the number of the last stanza of Part V in Stein's notebook and does not represent the total number of stanzas. (Stein had also made errors in numbering. Part V contains 83 stanzas, not 81. The number 81 on all covers was crossed out when Stein apparently realized that she had made an error.)

Two typescripts of "Stanzas" are in the Stein archive. The first (#1) bears the typed title *LXXXIII Stanzas* (Alice Toklas corrected the errors in numbering.). The second (#2) shows a title written in Stein's hand, *Two Hundred Stanzas in Meditation*.

The fourth notebook (Part III) has on the outside cover a title like the others: "Vol. 4 / 81 Stanzas. / Part III." On the inside cover of the notebook, however, appear designs for titles in Stein's hand (see Fig. AA).

The volume *Matisse Picasso and Gertrude Stein* (known as *G.M.P.*) includes, in addition to the title piece, the two shorter stories "A Long Gay Book" and "Many Many Women" and is the fifth volume in Stein's Plain Edition. The cover design of this book is similar to the one with which Stein played here. The book was published in February of 1933. In Stanza xx of Part V, Stein writes, "In reading and reading a long gay book/ I look/ This is what I see with my eyes." These lines undoubtedly concern proofreading, which was done in August of 1932. The title design and the lines about proofreading the new volume offer biographical information which makes it possible to date this stanza. The stanzas are filled with references, rarely obvious to the casual reader, to Stein's daily life.

The design for the second title illustrates Stein's predilection for balanced graphic patterns, her interest in typography, and her concern with the visual appearance of her words. This title design was done in preparation for the publication of "Stanzas" in a volume that was to include "Winning His Way" (1931), the second long poem, and what Alice Toklas called an "abundance" of short poems. The content of the posthumous Yale volume, *Stanzas in Meditation and Other Poems*, approximates what Stein had in mind when she played with the design for the title of a volume of poetry.

The fifth notebook, containing Part IV, has a stiff, dark green cover without pictures. On the outside front cover is the same designation that is used for all the volumes, identifying Part IV. But on the inside front cover appears almost illegible writing in dark blue ink on the dark green background:

> of commonplace
> Stanzas ~~of my ordinary~~ reflections
> Stanzas of Poetry

These descriptive phrases are helpful commentaries upon what Stein thought she was writing in "Stanzas." She did not retain the descriptive titles with which she played in this notebook but chose the starker, less suggestive "Stanzas in Meditation." However, in the *Autobiography* the work is described as "her real achievement of the commonplace" (p. 276). The descriptive or referential suggestions attached to "ordinary" and "commonplace" are abstracted from the long poem and placed in the totally referential autobiography, where they belong.

Stein claimed that she did not revise her work. She said that she did not believe in revision, for if writing involved the perception of the here and now, revisions were bound to force a text into a different here and now, which required different verbal forms. Therefore revisions would falsify the original text. Given this view, it is not surprising to find very few revisions in many of Stein's works. Her practice varied, however. Some pieces show little or no revision while others show considerable revision. Her claim that she did not revise is not entirely true. It contributed to the myth that hers was "automatic" writing. The Stein Archive offers evidence that throughout her life she took notes, jotting down long and short passages which she later used in compositions, that she planned, drafted, and revised certain pieces extensively, and that writing was not, as the *Autobiography* suggests, the creation of genius which required little effort and no revision. Even pieces that show no evidence of revision were not tossed off without the hard work and concentrated effort that Stein called *meditation.*

"Stanzas" apparently did not go through a process of rewriting. The few and minor changes visible in the manuscript are not revisions made after Stein completed the first version of a stanza but small alterations entered as she went along. Occasionally she finished a stanza and entered the Roman numeral for the next stanza, then crossed out this title and continued the earlier stanza for a few lines before she definitely began the next stanza (endings are often problematic for Stein). Some other minor revisions are also visible: a word crossed out and replaced by another, a slip or false start immediately corrected, a word changed in form, as from the noun to the -ing verb form.

"Stanzas" also shows revisions quite unlike the minor adjustments just described and entirely different from those in any other Stein work. They are visible in the autograph notebooks and the two typescripts. Only a detailed comparison of these three forms of the text allowed me to decipher what Stein was doing.

Typescript #1 reproduces with almost no errors the original text of "Stanzas." (The few errors that do appear in #1 are simple misreadings by Alice Toklas of Stein's handwriting.) Inked into the manuscript in Stein's hand, however, are some changes that appear also in typescript #2 but not in #1. That typescript #1 is first is clear because it reproduces the text without the revisions which were added after #1 but before or while #2 was prepared. The text printed in the Yale edition is the text of #2, the revised text, an entirely logical and reasonable choice.

The revisions are very odd. Almost consistently, the auxiliary verb *may* is changed to *can.* This change is made in several ways, and all revisions are in Gertrude Stein's hand:

a) In the manuscript, *may* is most of the time, but not always, crossed out, and *can* is inked in above or over it.
b) In typescript #2, the change appears in several different forms:
  —*may* is crossed out by hand and *can* inked in;
  —a space is left open in the typed line and *can* is inked in;
  —*can* is typed in from the start, even in a few cases where *may* is not changed to *can* in the manuscript.

This change is made almost consistently throughout the long text of "Stanzas." In the few instances where *may* is retained unchanged, it appears to have been unintentional.

Sometimes *may* is changed to *can* without great effect upon the meaning. But at other times, as when *may be* (*maybe*?) becomes *can be*, the result is odd indeed. The difference in meaning between *may* and *can* does not explain the revision. In a few cases the revision destroys a rhyme (*may / to-day* becomes *can / to-day*). The reason for the substitution of *can* does not seem to be stylistic or rhetorical. Yet the changes are so consistent and so laborious that they cannot be considered word games. Even if they contained elements of play, these would require an explanation: like all Stein's writing, her play on words contains literal truth. The revisions show much effort but no fun.

In pondering the revisions I suddenly discovered that, in addition to the changes of the auxiliary verbs, a small number of further changes suggested a pattern that could be interpreted. The following pages reproduce in facsimile the second half of Stanza vi of Part I (the stanza is full of echoes of *As You Like It*). The two typed pages are from typescript #2; they are followed by the manuscript pages of the same lines (see figs. A and B).

May/can revisions are visible in several forms. In lines 6, 8 (first occurrence of *may*), 13, 33, and 38, the word *may* is not changed in the manuscript but is changed to *can* in the typescript. In the second half of line 8 and in line 14, the typescript leaves space open for words that are inked in by the author. In line 26, the revision is entered both in the manuscript and in the typescript. In line 35, however, an entirely different revision occurs. It is entered in both manuscript and typescript. Here are the original and revised phrases:

> This May in unison
> This day in unison

"Stanzas" shows a number of further revisions that do not concern the auxiliary verb. The following paired lines show the original and the revised wording of each:

> Knowing that there is a month of May
> Knowing that there is a month today
>
> (II, iii)

They call meadows may or all
They call meadows are or all

(II, iv)

They say August is not May
They say August is not April

(V, xvi)

Only righteous in a double may
Only righteous in a double day

(III, x)

Which in the midst of may and at bay
Which in the midst of can and at bay

(IV, xiii)

In all these lines, Stein eliminted not the *auxiliary verb* 'may' but the *word* 'may' or 'May' in all its possible forms. The revisions not only fail to improve the stanzas but destroy the sense of Stein's lines. What do they signify? What context explains the original and the revised text?

It is time to tell a story.

Late in April 1932, Stein and Toklas one day were looking for the manuscript of *The Making of Americans*. Louis Bromfield, the American novelist, was present, and perhaps also Bernard Faÿ, a professor of American History and a friend. In the course of their search, the women accidentally came across a different manuscript which, according to *The Autobiography of Alice B. Toklas* (p. 104), Gertrude Stein had completely forgotten and had therefore never mentioned to Alice Toklas. The *Autobiography* says that Stein was "very bashful and hesitant" about the discovery and that she handed the manuscript to Louis Bromfield, asking him to read it in view of the possibility of publication. Two days after this episode, the women went to their country house in Bilignin for the summer.

The discovery of this early manuscript is also described in another piece, entitled "Here. Actualities." and written in Bilignin very soon after their arrival. This piece records the discovery of the early novel as the culminating event in a "season of debuts" during the winter and spring of 1932. All these debuts were newsworthy, as the French word *actualités*, or news, which the title echoes, makes very clear. Among the debuts were the appointment of Bernard Faÿ to a coveted professorship at the Collège de France on 29 February, the first communion of Paolo Picasso, the painter's son and Stein's godson, in April,[13] and the first show of the painter Sir Francis Rose, a Stein protégé, in April. The discovery of Stein's early novel—her literary debut—had historic significance. The work was *Q.E.D* (*Quod Erat Demonstrandum*), Stein's 1903 novel about her love affair with May Bookstaver, a fellow student at Johns Hopkins.

The story of the relationship of Gertrude Stein and May Bookstaver is told by Leon Katz in his introduction to *Fernhurst, Q.E.D., and Other Early Writings.*[14] What matters for "Stanzas in Meditation" is the discovery of the manuscript of *Q.E.D.* and the effect of that discovery upon Stein's life and her writing.

Q.E.D. had indeed been withheld from readers, including Alice Toklas. The Stein bibliography, done in 1941 with Stein's cooperation, does not list the novel because Stein refused permission to include it. In "Here. Actualities." Stein asks teasingly whether the early work "was . . . hidden with intention." And she adds, "There is no blindness in memory." What Stein says here belies the incredible suggestion made in the *Autobiography* that Stein had forgotten her first work. The contradictions and the secretiveness surrounding the Bookstaver affair make it clear that this relationship was never a matter of indifference.

The elimination of the word *may* or *May* from the text of "Stanzas" purges the poems of anything suggestive of May Bookstaver. Though the revisions are entered in Gertrude Stein's hand, I believe that they were initiated by Alice Toklas, who was enraged by the discovery of *Q.E.D.* and of the continued presence of May Bookstaver, or May Mary, in Stein's writing. In the manuscript of "Here. Actualities." Stein plays with two capital letters *M M*. These are the initials of May Mary. A faint *G* is joined to the first *M*. And the whole set of initials is then crossed out though it remains legible. While doodling with initials is common in Stein's manuscripts, the initials chosen are never made up and never accidental. A casual survey of other manuscript notebooks suggests that the word *may* or indeed the name *May* is far more significant than had been thought, not only in "Stanzas" but in many other works of different periods. Here are a few examples:

May.   \   And Mary
Marilyn   /

Mabel ⎫
Maryas ⎬   We may marry.
and   ⎪
Mary   ⎭

("A List," 1923.
The names are characters
in a play.)
What is the difference between Mary and May
("Patriarchal Poetry," 1927)
It is in ingredients that mays are a measure,
("To Kitty or Kate Buss," 1930)
She made May be Mary.
("More Grammar for a Sentence," 1930)

The elaborate word games Stein played with *may*, *May*, and *Mary* concealed the fact that these words were not neutral for her. Until April of 1932, they remained neutral for Alice Toklas, who had typed many buried references to May Bookstaver that she did not even know could be identified. But with the discovery of *Q.E.D.* and its history, these words ceased to be mere words for Alice. They emerged from the text and became part of the context, returning from literature to life.

What was devastating to Alice Toklas about the Bookstaver affair of 1901–1903 (long past by 1907, when Alice arrived in Paris) was not the love affair itself but the discovery that, when Stein and Toklas, upon falling in love, exchanged "confessions" of all their earlier experiences, Stein had not told about the relationship with May May, as she was also called. Alice felt betrayed in her trust and was left in a state of rage that continued intermittently for years. One result was that she made Stein destroy the letters of May Bookstaver.

Although the affair was over early in 1903 (*Q.E.D.*, the book which Stein wrote to come to terms with the experience, was finished in October 1903) and May had in 1906 married a man by the name of Charles Knoblauch and settled in New York, the two women remained in touch by correspondence and perhaps met when Mary Knoblauch traveled abroad. An educated, enterprising woman, Mary Knoblauch worked for women's suffrage and birth control and was actively involved in the modern art movement and modern literature. Stein sent her typescripts of her works, partly to assure their safety and partly to make them available for potential publishers in America. It was Mary Knoblauch who in 1908 negotiated with the Grafton Press for the publication of *Three Lives* and who interested Alfred Stieglitz in the

Stein's portraits of Matisse and Picasso, which appeared in *Camera Work* in 1912.

The *commonplace reflections* that are the stanzas are Stein's word compositions of the difficult summer and fall of 1932. She attempted to go as far as she could in creating stanzas whose words would function only poetically, within the poem, and not referentially, as signs pointing to things in the world beyond her words. Stein meant to write pure texts that would not point to contexts beyond themselves. But it was not possible to strip words of all referential content. The words of her stanzas not only create poems but also speak of life. Again and again conflict is voiced, and the speaker worries about who is winning in a power struggle. "Which of two" is a key phrase in the poems which points to the central Stein question of identity. The painful separateness of "I wish no one were one and one and one" (V, xxviii) yields to the hymn of "I am I" (V, xx) and returns to say that "It is useless to introduce two words between one" (II, vii). The struggle for identity and wholeness is the struggle of composition.

Exactly when the purgation of "Stanzas" was undertaken is not clear. The textual changes are unlikely to have been made very long after the stanzas were composed although only the second typescript reflects them. This typescript, where Alice Toklas is a particularly strong presence, shows more consistent revisions than the manuscript. Typescript #1, on the other hand, which reproduces the original text as Stein presumably intended it before Alice Toklas entered as an editor, is the one that Stein sent to her old friend Carl Van Vechten in New York for safekeeping, who eventually turned it over to Yale. Stein apparently tried to make sure that the original text of "Stanzas" would be preserved with the papers she entrusted to Van Vechten, who became her literary executor. Van Vechten, however, could hardly have known that the text in his safekeeping was an uncorrupted text of "Stanzas" and that the "revisions" in Typescript #2 were in fact corruptions.

Evidence in support of the interpretation of the textual problems of "Stanzas in Meditation" offered in these pages may be found in the play *Short Sentences*, also written in the summer of 1932. In this play, innumerable characters and a chorus each speak in quick succession one short, simple, abstract phrase of sentence. The play creates the impression of a dance of names or identities (characters?) interwoven with a dance of sentences or phrases. The names of the characters, if that is what they are, are partly actual names of friends or acquaintances of Stein and partly names made up from the first name of one acquaintance and the last name of another. Familiar names like Mildred Aldrich (*A Hilltop on the Marne*) or Jane Heap (*The Little Review*) mingle with composite names like Sir Robert Albi (Abdy) and Edith Acton (Edith Sitwell and Harold Acton). Finally there are wonderful inventions like Grace Church and Belinda Court.

The autograph manuscript of *Short Sentences* shows startling features that are not in the printed text or the typescript. The first is familiar: throughout the manuscript pages the auxiliary verb *may* is systematically underlined in Alice Toklas's indelible purple pencil. More dramatic, however, is a pattern that emerges from the names, which create the visual impression of a list printed in a column on the left margin of the text of the play since the sentences assigned to each name are so short that almost every line begins with a new name. The list begins innocently and neutrally enough, but soon appear May Hatteras, May Welch, May Janes, Ivan May, May Glass, May Coleman, Mary Coburn, Mary Harriman, Ada May, and so on. Every time *May* or *Mary* appears, whether as a first or last name, it is underlined. In the case of Mary Knowlton, however, not only the first name but also the initial K of the last is underlined. What can the reference be but Knoblauch?

Even this is not all. In the printed text of the play,[15] two characters appear whose names differ from the names in the manuscript: the first is Henry Winthrop, the second Anne Nicholson. In the manuscript, the first is Alice Winthrop, with *Alice* crossed out; the second is Babette Nicholson, with *Babette* crossed out. In the typescript, the two last names are typed in, but the two first names *Henry* and *Anne*, which are in the printed text, are entered in ink in Alice Toklas's hand. As in the case of "Stanzas," the printed text relies on the typescript; it takes the manuscript to establish the context of the revisions.

In two final cases, footnotes in the printed play comment on problems. One note indicates that "first names are missing in the manuscript" for the two last names *May* and *William*. Another footnote, in a space with no name, claims that a name is altogether missing in the manuscript. The footnotes are in error. Names are missing in the typescript, not in the manuscript. In the manuscript, the two first names are again crossed out: the full original names are *Alice May* and *Babette William*. The first names, crossed out in the manuscript, are

omitted in the typescript. In the last case, where the footnote claims
that the whole name is missing, the manuscript shows the full name
Alice Babette, crossed out but entirely legible. Plainly Alice Toklas
systematically took herself out of the play.

The last two lines bring the play to a fitting conclusion. Before the
Chorus ends the piece, a last character appears whose composite name
is *May Helen*. Helen is the young woman modeled on May Bookstaver
in *Q.E.D.* Stein's choice of *May Helen* as the final name is deliberate
and consistent. Underlined in Alice Toklas's indelible pencil in the
manuscript, the name shows that Alice knew Helen of *Q.E.D.* to be
May Bookstaver. In her typescript, Alice perhaps hoped, by changing
or omitting the names she had accusingly underlined and crossed out
in the manuscript, to exorcise the ghosts—or to punish Gertrude.
However, at the end of the play stands May, the real person, coupled
with Helen, her literary image, context and text joined in one name.
Which of two? Which of three?

In "Stanzas in Meditation" Stein struggled to create self-contained
poems free of the associations and the history that words usually carry. But the context of the stanzas is revealed in part by Alice Toklas's
interference with Stein's text. The irony is that the editorial changes
meant to conceal the story behind "Stanzas" ended up by giving it
away.[16]

FIGURE A A.

FIGURE A.

It is just neither why they like it
Because it is by them in as they like
They do not see for which they refuse names
Articles which they like and once they hope
5 Hope and hop can be as neatly known
Theirs in delight or rather can they not
Ever if shone guessing in which they have
All can be glory can he can glory
For not as ladling marguerites out.
10 It is best to know their share.
Just why they joined for which they knelt
They can call that they were fortunate.
They may be after it is all given away.
They Can. Have it in mine.
15 And so it is a better chance to come
With which they know theirs to undo
Getting it better more than once alike
For which fortune favors me.
It is the day when we remember two.
20 We two remember two two who are thin
Who are fat with glory too with two
With it with which I have thought twenty fair
If I name names if I name names with them.
I have not hesitated to ask a likely block
25 Of which they are attributed in all security

FIGURE B.

As not only why but also where they may can
Not be unclouded just as yes to-day
They call peas beans and raspberries strawberries or two
They forget well and change it is a last
30 That they could like all that they ever get
As many fancies for which they have asked no one.
Might any one be what they liked before
Just do they come to be not only fastened
It should be should be just what they like
35 This day in unison
All out of cloud. Come hither. Neither
Aimless and with a pointedly rested displeasure
She can may be glad to be either in their resigning
That they have this plan I remember.
40 Well welcome in fancy.
Or just need to better that they call
All have been known in name as call
They will call this day one for all
I know it can be shared by Tuesday
45 Gathered and gathered yes.
All who come will will come or come to be
Come to be coming that is in and see
See elegantly not without enjoin
Soo there there where there is no share
50 Shall we be there I wonder now

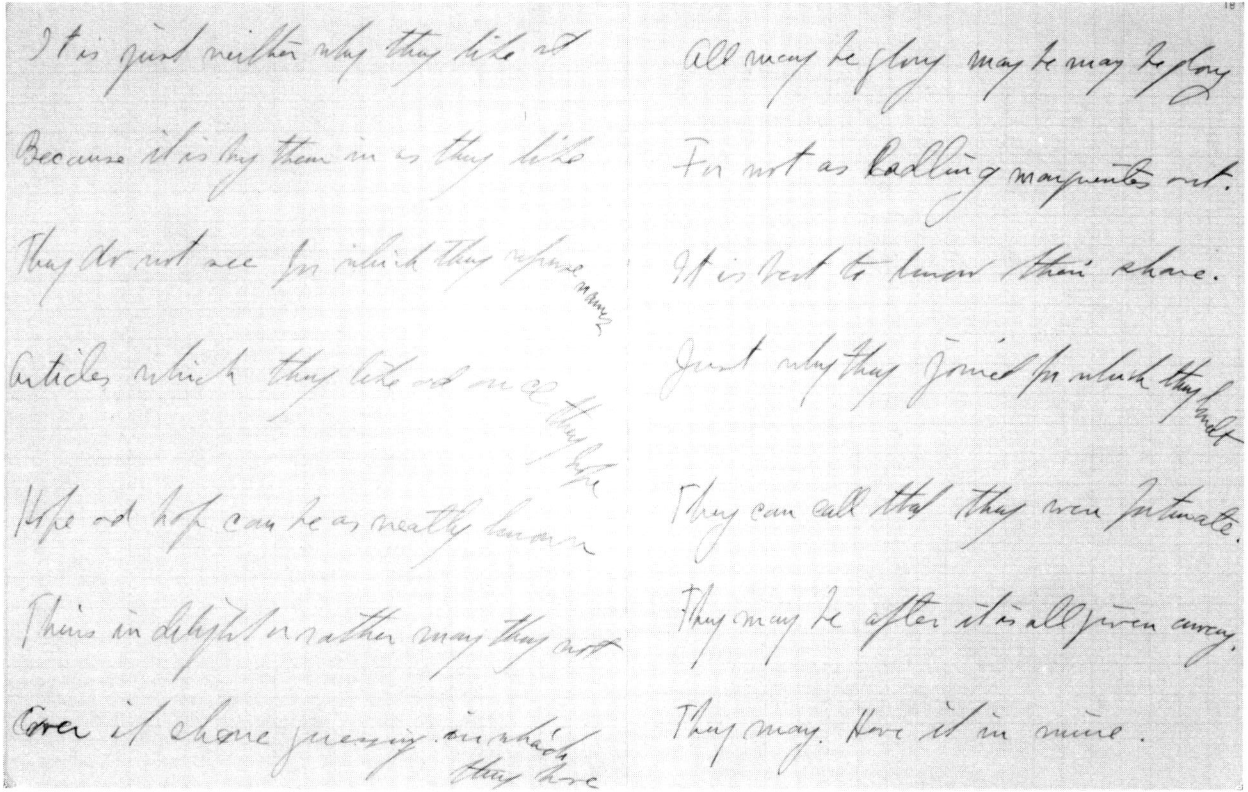

FIGURE C.

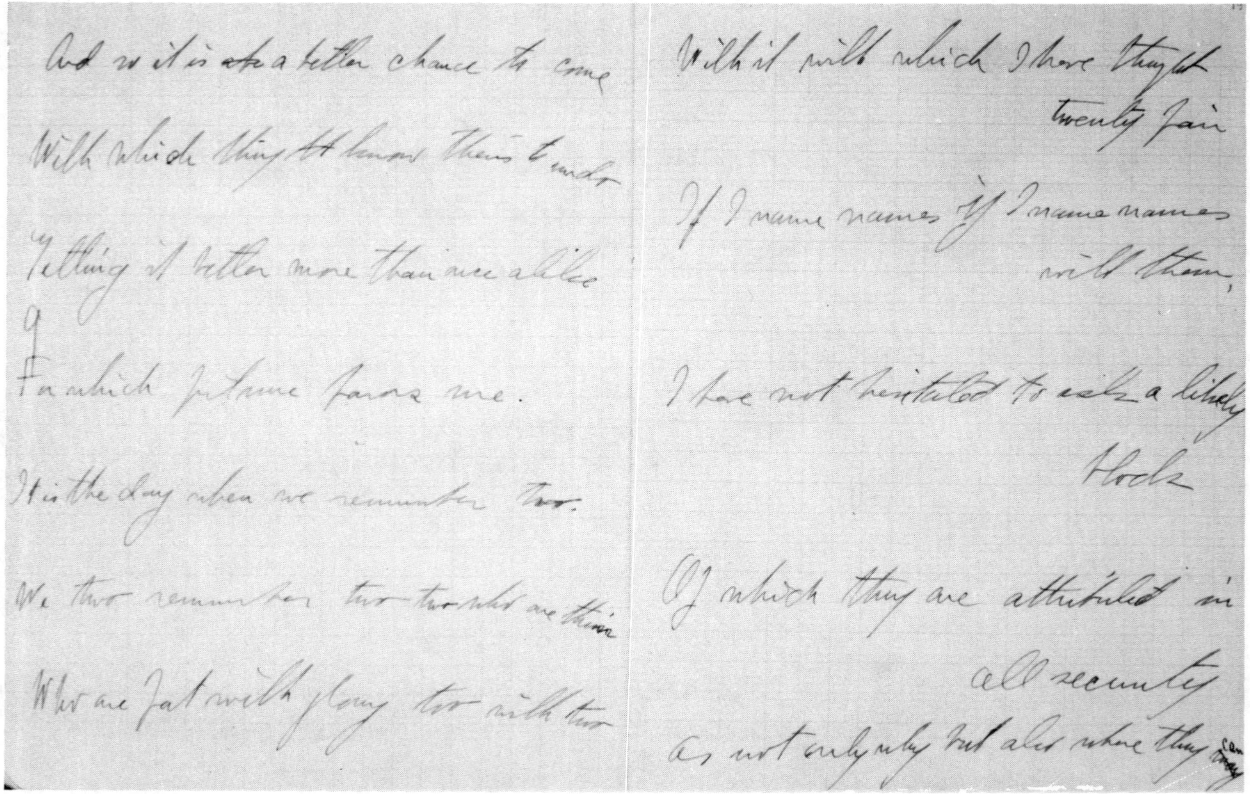

15

20

25

FIGURE D.

FIGURE E.

All here been human in name in
call

They will call this day me for all

I trust it may be shortly Tuesday

Father at fathead you.

All who come will will come in
come to be
10
come to be coming that is in at
all

Unless at with a partially realist
difference

She may be glad to be either sin
their respiring

That they live that fellow remember.

We'll welcome in fancy

On first need to tell that they
call

FIGURE F.

FIGURE G.

NOTES

1. *Gertrude Stein in Pieces* (New York: Oxford Univ. Press, 1970, p. 220n.

2. *Exact Resemblance to Exact Resemblance* (New Haven: Yale Univ. Press, 1978), pp. 111–116.

3. Julian Beck, "Storming the Barricades," in Kenneth H. Brown, *The Brig* (New York: Hill and Wang, 1963), pp. 7–8.

4. See Donald Gallup, "The Gertrude Stein Collection," *Yale University Library Gazette*, 22 (October 1947), pp. 21–32.

5. The finest study of Stein's work is also the earliest: Donald Sutherland's *Gertrude Stein: A Biography of her Work* (New Haven: Yale Univ. Press, 1951). As the title indicates, this book concerns not Stein's life but the development of her art. Written within three years after Stein's death, this volume does not include a detailed discussion of the unpublished works or of the circumstances of composition. When Sutherland wrote his book and even when he prepared the introduction for the volume *Stanzas in Meditation and Other Poems* in 1955–56, he had not seen the Stein manuscripts. (Information from Lynn Martin.)

6. *Orbes*, 4 (Winter, 1932–1933) 64, 66. Part V, Stanza lxxi, with French translation by Marcel Duchamp printed *en face*, 65, 67.
   Life and Letters Today, XV, 6 (Winter, 1936–1937), 77–80. Part I, Stanzas i, xii; Part IV, Stanza iv; Part III, Stanza xi.
   Poetry, LV, 5 (February 1940), 229–235. Part II, Stanza i; Part IV, Stanza iv; Part III, Stanza ii; Part V, Stanzas xxxi, xxxii, xxxiii.
   Muse: An Anthology of Modern Poetry, Poe Memorial Edition (New York: Carlyle Straub Publisher, 1938), p. 839. Part III, Stanza xii; Part II, Stanza xiii; Part III, Stanza xiv.

7. Letter to Robert Bartlett Haas, 2 March 1952, Yale Collection of American Literature (YCAL).

8. Robert Bartlett Haas and Donald Clifford Gallup, *A Catalogue of the Published and Unpublished Writings of Gertrude Stein* (New Haven: Yale Univ. Press, 1941), p. 54.

9. Quotations from "Stanzas in Meditation" will henceforth be indicated by capital Roman numerals for Parts I to V and lower-case Roman numerals for the stanza numbers within each part. The text quoted, unless otherwise indicated, is the autograph manuscript text, which sometimes differs from the printed text. In one case, an error in numbering the stanzas, not corrected in the Yale edition, produced two stanzas with the same number; I distinguish these by adding a lower-case letter a or b (III, xvia or xvib).

10. Of course this is exactly what Stein wanted. She composed and expected to be read with great and conscious care. It is not at all true, as some readers say, that one more repetition or one less modulation of a phrase does not matter. Stein was very clear about the effects she wanted to obtain. In her most carefully wrought pieces, the exact sequence of words mattered deeply to Stein, who saw and heard words in their movement more sensitively than most.

11. Richard Bridgman has discussed Alice Toklas's editing of the *Autobiography* and other works in *Gertrude Stein in Pieces*, pp. 210-213.

12. Letter from Donald Gallup to the author, 18 September 1980.

13. Information from Edward Burns, May 1980.

14. Gertrude Stein, *Fernhurst, Q.E.D. and Other Early Writings* (New York: Liveright, 1971). Additional information from Leon Katz, August 1980, September 1981.

15. Gertrude Stein, *Last Operas and Plays*, ed. Carl Van Vechten, (New York: Rinehart and Co., Inc., 1949), pp. 317-332.

16. Research for this paper, a part of a study of the poetry of Gertrude Stein, was supported by Grant number 13220 from the PSC-CUNY Research Award Program of the City University of New York and by a Fellowship for College Teachers from the National Endowment for the Humanities. For permission to reproduce manuscript and typescript pages of works by Gertrude Stein, grateful acknowledgement is extended to the Collection of American Literature, Beinecke Rare Book and Manuscript Library, Yale University.

Copyright © by Ulla E. Dydo.

The Synchrony and Diachrony of Texts: Practice and Theory of the Critical Edition of James Joyce's *Ulysses*

HANS WALTER GABLER

The address today on "The Synchrony and Diachrony of Texts" will put before you some reflections on the critical implications of a scholarly edition's apparatus of variants. It will open with some remarks on a short story by William Faulkner; proceed to observations on the manuscript development of John Milton's poem "At a Solemn Musick"; and thus approach James Joyce circuitously.

In *These 13*, his collection of tales published in September, 1931, William Faulkner included a story entitled "That Evening Sun." We find it anthologized in A. Walton Litz's *Major American Short Stories*, whence, for present purposes, I derive the text of segment VI.

> We left her sitting before the fire.
>
> "Come and put the bar up," Father said. But she didn't move. She didn't look at us again, sitting quietly there between the lamp and the fire. From some distance down the lane we could look back and see her through the open door.
>
> "What, Father?" Caddy said. "What's going to happen?"
>
> "Nothing," Father said. Jason was on Father's back, so Jason was the tallest of all of us. We went down into the ditch. I looked at it, quiet. I couldn't see much where the moonlight and the shadows tangled.
>
> "If Jesus *is* hid here, he can see us, can't he?" Caddy said.
>
> "He's not there," Father said. "He went away a long time ago."
>
> "You made me come," Jason said, high; against the sky it looked like Father had two heads, a little one and a big one. "I didn't want to."
>
> We went up out of the ditch. We could still see Nancy's house and the open door, but we couldn't see Nancy now, sitting before the fire with the door open, because she was tired. "I just done got tired," she said. "I just a nigger. It ain't no fault of mine."
>
> But we could hear her, because she began just after we came up out of the ditch, the sound that was not singing and not unsinging.
>
> "Who will do our washing now, Father?" I said.
>
> "I'm not a nigger," Jason said, high and close above Father's head.
>
> "You're worse," Caddy said, "you are a tattletale. If something was to jump

305

out, you'd be scairder than a nigger."
"I wouldn't," Jason said.
"You'd cry," Caddy said.
"Caddy," Father said.
"I wouldn't!" Jason said.
"Scairy cat," Caddy said.
"Candace!" Father said.

The elements of the narration in this conclusion to the story are likely to give main directions to critical exegesis and interpretation. The
ditch dividing and distancing the whites from the blacks, the contrast
of Nancy's immobility, despite the open door, and the onward-strid-
ing generations of the Compsons—in their turn emblematized in the
silhouette against the evening sky of Jason carried on Father's back—
or the utter mental and physical disintegration of the black woman under terror of a *deus absconditus*: "If Jesus *is* hid here, he can see us,
can't he?" Caddy said. "He is not there," Father said. "He went
away a long time ago."—these elements will represent, for the critic,
central articulations of the story's meaning. In the interpretation that
is his professional task he will link them back to the total narrative development of the text: the text before him in the book, the text he has
read and re-read, the text which was constituted in and by the act of
publication in *These 13* in September 1931.

From its constitution in the act and moment of publication derives
the concept, in current theory, of 'text' as a synchronous system of
signification. Common notions and consequent methods of the art of
interpretation of works of literature are essentially based on this concept of the text as a synchronous (and thereby, in a sense, static) structure, released, if not created, as such by its author in some discernible
act of publication—and constituted also, in a post-Gutenberg era, by
the book in which it had its first appearance, as if 'book' and 'text'
were synonymous. It is but a short step, then, for the synchronous
structure of the public text to become by conceptual extension
equated with the work—it *is* the work, according to the most widespread critical assumptions.

Consequently, textual instability and variation are felt to be extraneous irritants, if not embarrassments; in order to neutralise them we
are strongly conditioned to regard variation as deviation, and (as
textual critics, editors) to eradicate it. The conditioned impulse is defensible where the variation, as corruption of the author's text in
transmission, indeed *is* deviation. Here, textual criticism and the con-

comitant procedures of scholarly editing offer to literary criticism the work in an ideal purity of text. But a fundamental problem arises when the notion of deviation equally influences critical response to authorial variation, as it customarily does both in literary and textual criticism.

Consider the case of a literary critic (budding or otherwise) faced with William Faulkner's "That Evening Sun Go Down" as first published in *American Mercury* in March, 1931, which ends thus:

> Father carried Jason on his back. We went out Nancy's door; she was sitting before the fire. "Come and put the bar up," father said. Nancy didn't move. She didn't look at us again. We left her there, sitting before the fire with the door opened, so that it wouldn't happen in the dark.
>
> "What, father?" Caddy said. "Why is Nancy scared of Jubah? What is Jubah going to do to her?"
>
> "Jubah wasn't there," Jason said.
>
> "No," father said, "He's not there. He's gone away."
>
> "Who is it that's waiting in the ditch?" Caddy said. We looked at the ditch. We came to it, where the path went down into the thick vines and went up again.
>
> "Nobody," father said. There was just enough moon to see by. The ditch was vague, thick, quiet. "If he's there, he can see us, can't he?" Caddy said.
>
> "You made me come," Jason said on father's back. "I didn't want to."
>
> The ditch was quite still, quite empty, massed with honeysuckle. We couldn't see Jubah, any more than we could see Nancy sitting there in her house, with the door open and the lamp burning, because she didn't want it to happen in the dark. "I just done got tired," Nancy said. "I just a nigger. It ain't no fault of mine."
>
> But we could still hear her. She began as soon as we were out of the house, sitting there above the fire, her long brown hands between her knees. We could still hear her when we crossed the ditch, Jason high and close and little about father's head.
>
> Then we had crossed the ditch, walking out of Nancy's life. Then her life was sitting there with the door open and the lamp lit, waiting, and the ditch between us and us going on, the white people going on, dividing the impinged lives of us and Nancy.
>
> "Who will do our washing now, father?" I said.
>
> "I'm not a nigger," Jason said on father's shoulders.
>
> "You're worse," Caddy said, "you are a tattletale. If something was to jump out, you'd be scairder than a nigger."
>
> "I wouldn't," Jason said.
>
> "You'd cry," Caddy said.
>
> "Caddy!" father said.
>
> "I wouldn't," Jason said.
>
> "Scairy cat," Caddy said.
>
> "Candace!" father said.

Unforewarned, but with a few minutes for silent preparation, a student who had no training in textual criticism was given these two texts for an oral exam. Very interestingly she was thrown off balance for a moment when told that this, too, was Faulkner's text. She had been all set to explain the differences observed in terms of deviation, assuming that someone—not the author—must have done something to the text she knew from previous reading. By contrast, we will immediately assume from our own experience that this is a different authorial version of the text. Published separately, it possesses its own synchrony of structure; and if the (later) text we first encountered were not extant, or unknown, the *American Mercury* version would represent the work.

In face of both versions, however, there arises a critical problem of correlation. I believe the trained critic, too, will soon catch himself in the act of regarding the one somehow as a deviation from the other. He will take, say, the book text as ideally constituting the work. The textual difference will command his interest to the degree that it adumbrates that ideality, or indeed falls short of it, exemplifying as it often does the less-than-perfection inherent in artistic creation. The argument, having a premise in a critical value judgement, may of course be exactly reversed. One way or the other, the notion of deviation will tend to relegate revisional authorial variation to a category not sufficiently distinguished from that of corrupting transmissional variation. Critically, it will be used as mere material for illustration to enhance the quality discerned in the work's ideal state. Any persisting irritation would seem to be due to a residual—if not, indeed, seminal—uncertainty as to the proper relation of the critical discourse to textual revision. Editorially, the revisional variants will be taken note of in a lemmatised apparatus of the kind devised for the record of transmissional corruption, a procedure which commonly causes, or has caused, little if any embarrassment.

The problems of attitude in the critical discourse, on the one hand, and the format of the editorial apparatus presentation, on the other, are correlated. For there is an apparent dependence of editorial procedure on the broad assumptions—explicit or implicit—of literary criticism. The notion of the ideality of the work manifested in an ideal text purified of all variation is an implicit critical assumption that is much strengthened, circularly, by the editorial thinking which in a sense derives from it. Yet let there be no mistake: it is in no way a theoretical axiom of literary criticism. Indeed, one should recognise an *a priori* hindrance to its explicit formulation as such in the manifest existence of discrete authorial versions of a text. It is this recognition which, on close reflection, leads to a conception of what I will call a natural condition of the literary work.

No creation of the human mind springs to instant life and perfection without revision. Whether preserved or not, there must always have been discrete textual states, in temporal succession, of a literary composition. Thus the work may be said to comprise all its authorial textual states. By such definition, the work attains an axis and extension in time from earliest draft to final revision. Its total text presents itself as a diachronous structure correlating the discrete synchronous structures discernible, of which that conferred by publication is only one, and not necessarily a privileged one. It is thus a kinetic system of signification whose dynamics revolve on the variant. The variant, far from being an extraneous irritant, becomes an integral textual element of pivotal significance in the textual totality of the work.

It remains for both literary analysis and textual editing to draw conclusions and to derive an appropriate methodology from such theoretical assumptions. For critical discourse, they broaden decisively the textual basis of reference, and provide, in the conceptual status conferred upon revisional variants, an essential category of controlled stimuli to interpretation. We never come closer to an author's willed structuring of design and meaning than through his conscious choices of language, expression and style. Where revisional variants manifest themselves, they make evident crisis points of articulation through which the work passed in the writing. Correspondingly, the articulation of critical understanding—which may at will relate to the diachronous succession of textual states, or to a given synchronous textual structure such as that of the published text—will reach its highest degree of definitiveness from a critical interpretation of the work's revisional variation.

With these ideas in mind, we may conclude, as briefly as possible, the discussion of our Faulkner example. Where the two versions of the text, each a discrete synchronous structure, correlate on the work's axis of diachrony, they command attention no longer by the degrees of textual deviation in one version or the other (or, as the case may be, in both) from an assumed ideality of the work. Their interest lies in the alternatives of expression and meaning within the total structure of the text, as revealed in the choices made manifest by the variation which is an integral element of that structure. The variation forms patterns of opposition within the diachronous text which become central stimuli to interpretation. Such opposition patterns, in our example, are the non-segmentation as against the segmentation of the text; the telling, as it were, as against the showing of the symbolic significance of the ditch; the absence as against the presence of the emblematic silhouette before the night sky of Jason on Father's back; or the renaming of Jubah as Jesus. The critic, in his discourse, will of course have to account very carefully for absences as well as for new presences of elements of meaning in the text. Nevertheless, by referring to the evident revisional choices, he may assert his understanding of the work, as of each of its discrete textual states, from the textual authority itself of the work's diachronous totality.

So much for the critical side of the matter. On the editorial side, let me state directly my contention that, in the field at least of textual scholarship as practiced in the area of English and American Literature, we have currently no methodology or model for the constitution of critical texts, or of variance recording and presentation, that will answer sufficiently to the concepts of 'work' and 'text' as I have outlined them. The reason is not far to seek. Our paradigms have not been shaped by texts, or textual situations, where the manner of editorial treatment could possibly have been centrally determined, or defined, by authorial revisional variation. Textual scholarship within Anglo-American literary studies has developed, in the copytext-editing approach and its concomitant highly formalised system of lemmatised apparatus listings, perhaps the most sophisticated and versatile pragmatic methodology available today for the editing of literary texts transmitted predominantly in print. But with that focus, its methods and modes of presentation are basically designed to meet textual situations dominated by corrupting transmissional variation, and they have the ultimate goal of critically constituting ideal texts. Transmissional corruption, like the poor, being always richly with us, there can be no question of fundamentally doubting either the validity or the necessity of the approach, or its proven results, so far as they carry; and in the appropriate situations, they carry far. The ideal text itself, if by 'ideal text' may be meant the authoritative text free of corruption, is an eminently desirable achievement; though of course I am aware that the term means more: that, by accepted definition, the 'ideal text' is to be conceived of as the critically constituted text of final authorial intention established by bibliographically controlled editorial eclecticism. This, too, let me emphasize, must be considered the pragmatic optimum of editing where, besides being thoroughly intermingled with transmissional corruption, all discernible authorial revision recognisably strives towards the perfection of a text.

But the foreshortening of the diachronous textual dimension implicit in the pragmatic approach of eclectic copytext editing—a foreshortening in most cases quite simply necessitated by the material in hand—ceases to be defensible, or even possible, where the proportional relation of corrupting to revisional variation familiar from dominantly transmisional textual situations is reversed; where, as typically in the manuscript and proof development of texts, textual error and corruption are reduced, or reducible, to an almost negligible—that is, critically negligible—entity and where, instead, authorial revision, by quantity and quality, commands pervasive attention.

* * *

The extant manuscript materials of works so diverse as John Milton's hymn "At a Solemn Musick" and James Joyce's *Ulysses*—to name only these from which I shall illustrate my argument—display alike in their revisions a progressive structuring of meaning by which the discrete textual states in each case are correlated. Focussing on the rich revisional variation in the manuscripts, we naturally find it meaningful only in its contextual relations. It is not our task as editors to undertake its exegesis or interpretation. But our critical sense should make us aware that the authorial revision is inextricably embedded in invariant contexts. This should lead us to devise modes of apparatus presentation which leave the contextuality intact. Lemmatised fragmentation is categorically not suitable for the purpose.

The inadequacy of a lemmatised notation of revisional variance may be strikingly exemplified from Milton's "At a Solemn Musick." Footnotes keyed, say, to one possible copytext, in this case the first printed text in the 1645 edition of Milton's *Poems*, are apt totally to obscure all clues to the significance of the textual facts they record. To give just a few illustrations: quite properly in common editorial procedure, such notes would cite from the first draft the four lines of text following (final) line 4, or the two lines following (final) line 16. They would indicate that (final) lines 21–24 were missing in the first and second drafts; or that line in the first draft "Heavns henshmen in ten thousand quires" was revised in the second draft to read "touch thire immortall harps of golden wires." Lastly, they would record, in lemmatised isolation, that between the holograph fair copy and the printed text, the beginning of the final line was altered from "To live & sing wth him" to "To live with him, and sing."

From this last example may be demonstrated succinctly the all-important correlation of revision and invariant context. The authorial revision was from

To live & sing wth him in endless morne of light

to

To live with him, and sing in endlesse morne of light.

The change is connotational: it avoids the somewhat awkward notion, common to the manuscript states of the text, of God as cantor leading the congregation of the blessed. It is also prosodic: it repositions the alexandrine's caesura, thereby rhythmically enlivening the poem's closure. Moreover, it has a numerologic significance: it proportions the stresses in the line as 2:4, equalling the 1:2 proportion of the musical octave, the finishing touch to the entire process of revision which, as I have been able to show in an analysis of the poem's textual diachrony which cannot be unfolded in detail here, appears governed by numerological considerations.

Under the title "Song," the work was first drafted in an irregular line-length pattern as a madrigal– or *canzone*–type poem of 30 lines, grouped as 22 + 8 lines. These significant biblical numbers subsequently gave way to the Platonic-Pythagorean musical octave proportion as a module for the numerologic design. Entitled "At a Solemn Musick," the poem emerged from its sequence of drafts as a twenty-eight-line hymn celebrating the harmonic diapason, or octave, of *musica humana* and *musica mundana*, visionally restored in Christian salvation. In "At a Solemn Musick," the hymnist's vision is made visible and, as it were, calculable as the result of the revision of the individual line-lengths as well as of the re-proportioning of groups of lines: formally, octave extensions and octave proportions structure the poem throughout in its final revised state.

Its entire form is thus an essential significative aspect of a poem at each stage of its development—a thesis which should hold true beyond what may at first sight be regarded the special circumstances of numerological organisation in "At a Solemn Musick." As a comprehensive signifier, the poetic form is subject to semantic revision just as are individual words and phrases. To render interactive revision of form and words critically analysable from the edited total text in a scholarly edition, it would seem an absolute necessity to devise, in the parlance of German textual scholarship, some manner of "integral apparatus" for the visualisation of revisional variance in invariant contexts, which in this case should display the work's entire shape, or sequence of variant shapes, in apparatus form before the critic's eye.

An "integral apparatus" may range from multiple parallel printings of the textual states to their full superimposition in one continuous synopsis. Without losing sight of essential tenets, such as those of the situatedness in context of the revisional variant and its integrity to the work's total text, the actual form adopted for the apparatus presentation of textual diachrony will depend on the given situation—no amount of theoretical reflection, after all, is going to change the pragmatic nature of editing. For "At a Solemn Musick," I would opt for an apparatus design intermediary between parallel text display and synoptic superimposition of the textual states. The entire poem in apparatus display is presented diachronically and in discrete states of synchrony in Figure 1.

FIGURE 1.

Song

1   1 < >   Blest paire of Sirens pledges of heavens joy
2   2 < >   Spheare-borne harmonious sisters Voice, & Verse
                             [Mix yor choice chords, & happiest sounds]
3   3 < > vine power & joynt force employ   3 Wed yor divine sounds, & mixt power
                                                                           employ
4   4 < >   dead things wth inbreath'd sense able to peirce
    5 < > whilst yor ⁺equall⁺ raptures   5 and ⁺[whilst] as⁺ yor equall raptures
                     temper'd sweet   temper'd sweet
    6 < > happie spousal meet   6 in high misterious ⁺[holie] happie⁺
                                                                     spousall meet

    7 < >   snatch us from earth awhile
    8 < > home-bred ⁺ woes ⁺ beguile   8 us of our selves & ⁺[home-bred] native⁺
                                                                      woes beguile
5   9 <and to our high-rays'>d ⁺[fancies   9 and to our ⁺highraysd [highrays'd]
            then] fantasie ⁺ present   [uprays'd] Phantasie præsent
6   10 < >   that undisturbed song of pure concent
7   11 < > ay surrounds the ⁺[soveraigne]   11 ay sung before the saphire-colour'd
            saphire-colourd⁺ throne   Throne
8   12 < > irce< >e   12 ⁺[&] to ⁺ him that sits thereon
9   13 < > versa< > & sollemne crie   13 wth saintly shout, & sollemne jubilie
       wth saintlie shout & sollemne jubilie
10 14 <wher>e the ser<aphick> princely   14 where the bright Seraphim in ⁺[tripled]
                                      row   [triple] burning⁺ row

       [<th>ire loud ange<lick> trumpets   ⁺[high lifted loud archangell]
11 15   blow]   15
       loud symphonie of ⁺silver⁺   thire loud uplifted⁺ angell trumpets blow
                      trumpets blow.
       ⁺[and] [the]
12 16   the ⁺ youth <ful cheru>bim   16 and the Cherubick hoast in
                     sweet winged squires   thousand quires
13 17 ⁺Heavns henshmen⁺ in ten   17 touch thire immortall harps of golden
                  thous<and quir>es   wires
14 18 wth those just <spirits> that beare   18 wth those just spirits that weare the
                                    weare   blooming palmes
                                                                  victorious
            the ⁺[fresh greene]
            blooming
            victorious ⁺palmes
15 19 [in] hymnes d<evout> & sacred   19 hymnes devout & sacred psalmes
                            psalmes   holie
16 20   singing everlastingly
       ⁺[that] while⁺ all the f<ram>e of
                     heaven and arches blue
       21 whilst the whole frame of <heaven
                     and arches blue>
       ⁺[then] [whilst] while⁺ all the starrie   [while all the starrie rounds & arches blue]
              frame <and arches blue>
       22   resound & eccho Hallelu]
17 23 that we ⁺[below may learne wth]   21 that we ⁺on earth⁺ wth undiscording
            wth undiscording⁺ hart & voice   [⁺hart &] voice

At a solemn Musick

Blest paire of Sirens, pledges of heavens joy,	1
Spheare borne, harmonious sisters Voice, and Verse,	2
Wed your divine sounds, and mixt power employ	3
Dead things with inbreath'd sense able to peirce,	4

And to our high-rays'd phantasie præsent	5
That undisturbed song of pure concent	6
Ay sung before the sapphire-coulour'd throne	7
To him that sitts theron	8
With saintly shout, and sollemne jubilie,	9
Where the bright Seraphim in burning row	10
Thire loud up-lifted angell trumpetts blow,	11
And the Cherubick hoast in thousand quires	12
Touch thire immortal harps of golden wires,	13
With those just spirits that weare victorious palmes,	14
Hymns devout and holy psalmes	15
Singing everlastingly.	16

21 that wee on earth wᵗʰ undiscording voice	That wee on earth with undiscording voice 17

18	24	$^+$may$^+$ rightly [$^+$to] answere that melodious noise	22 may rightly answere that melodious noise
19	25	by leaving out those harsh chromatick jarres	23 by leaving out those harsh $^+$[chromatick] ill sounding$^+$ jarres
20	26	of sin that all our musick marres	24 of [ ] clamourous sin that all our musick marres
21			
22			
23			
24			
25	27	& in our lives & in our song	
26	28	may keepe in tune wth heaven, till God ere long	
27	29	to his celestiall consort us unite	
28	30	To live & sing wth him in	28 to live & sing wth him in endlesse morne of light

ever-endless
ever-glorious
uneclipsed light
where day dwells without night
in endlesse morne of light
   cloudlesse birth

in never parting light

The *vertical* parallel columns correspond to 1st draft, 2nd draft, partial 3rd draft, and fair copy. The fair copy, in this case, is well suited to function as an orientation text for the apparatus, and also as a reading text. For the reading text, editorial emendation is an optional procedural device. The last line of the fair-copy text, in this instance, has been emended from the printed text, a fact which needs to be properly noted in an appropriate section of an edition. A textual display in the *horizontal* parallel is used in columns 1–3 for progressive verbal revisions of individual lines. (In line-bound texts, such as poems or dramatic texts in verse, both the vertical and the horizontal can of course be employed for parallel text display.) The aspect of *synoptic superimposition* enters for columns 1 and 2 where lines are identical, or are critically inferred to be identical, to the drafts. (Pointed brackets indicate where text has been lost through mutilation of a manuscript leaf.)

Needless to say, the proposed apparatus endeavours to record all revisional variation and should thus provide a basis for all manner of

22 may rightly answere that melodious noise	May rightly answere that melodious noise 18
23 as once we ⁺ [could] did ⁺ till dis<pro>portion'd Sin	As once wee did, till disproportion'd sin 19
24 ⁺ [drown'd] jarred against ⁺ natures chime & wth ⁺ [tumultuous] harsh ⁺ din	Jarr'd against natures chime, and with 20 harsh din
25 broke the faire musick that all creatures made	Broke the fair musick that all creatures 21 made
26 to thire great Lord whose love thire motion swaid	To thire great Lord, whose love thire 22 motion sway'd
27 in perfect diapason whilst they stood	In perfect diapason, whilst they stood 23
28 in first obedience & thire state of good	In first obedience, and thire state of good. 24
29 Oh may wee soonc ⁺ againe⁺ renew that song	Oh may wee soone againe renew that song 25
30 & keepe in tune wth heaven, till God ere long	And keepe in tune with heav'n, till 26 God ere long
31 to his celestiall consort us unite	To his celestiall consort us unite, 27
32 To live & sing wth him in endlesse morne of light	To live with him, and sing in endlesse 28 morne of light.

analysis and interpretation, and not merely for the inquiry into the poem's formal structure which first induced me to construct it.

* * *

James Joyce's *Ulysses* is not a twenty-eight-line poem in verse; it is a 732–page novel in prose. To present its textual diachrony in the integral apparatus of a critical edition, the expansiveness of a parallel text display is not a practicable proposition. The nature of the work's development in extant documents may be briefly characterised. Early drafts, mostly fragments, exist for a minority of the eighteen chapters, or episodes. For every episode, we have a fair copy, or else a final authorial draft of equivalent developmental status. Beyond the fair copy/final draft stage, the text was first typed, then typeset. Concurrently, it was cumulatively augmented by some 30% in revisions and additions entered in autograph onto the typescripts and proofs (there being sometimes up to nine or ten successive proof stages for a given page, or gathering, of the book). There is, as a document, no one authorial manuscript corresponding to the text as published.

However, if over the entire extension of the pre-publication development and transmission we isolate the autograph inscription of the
text, as the extant documents allow us to do, from its transposition
into typescript and letterpress by the agency of typists and compositors, we may define a continuous manuscript of *Ulysses*. This extends
over a sequence of witnesses which, for the purposes of the critical edition, begin with each chapter's fair copy, or final draft. If the continuous manuscript were thought to be projected onto one imaginary
document, it would there be contained in a multi-layered inscription
as a synopsis of the textual diachrony of *Ulysses*. It is the continuous
manuscript which provides the basis text for the critical edition. The
synoptic form of presentation for the integral apparatus is, in a sense,
prefigured in the textual materials themselves.

At least three self-contained synchronous states of the text may be
distinguished along the diachronic axis of *Ulysses*. There are the fair
copy/final draft text; the first published text of 14 of the 18 chapters
as serialised in *The Little Review*, corresponding to the stage of first
revision of the respective chapter typescripts; and the text of the first
edition in book form, published in 1922. Though teeming with transmissional errors—2000? 4000? 6000? 8000? we shall know when the
edition is completed—the first edition text corresponds to the final
level of revision, free of transmissional corruption, of the continuous
manuscript text. It is this final level of revision of the continuous
manuscript text which the critical edition endeavours to establish as
the edition text, and to present as a clear reading text. In view of the
complex interaction of authorial and transmissional inscription during the pre-publication process, the critical constitution of the edition
text entails a considerable amount of emendation of the actual notation of the continuous manuscript text in the documents. The result of
the emendation is an ideal text in the more restricted sense of the term
used above, i.e., an authoritative text free of corruption. All emendations are duly recorded in the type of subsidiary apparatus best suited
to the purpose, i.e., an appended lemmatised emendation list; and,
where necessary, they are explained, or refusals to emend are de-
fended, in a set of discursive textual notes. Moreover, the edition
features an historical collation list recording the history of the text's
corruption in such editions during Joyce's lifetime as may lay any
hypothetical claim to authorial influence. Thus the traditional apparatus format has not been abandoned, though it has been firmly

restricted to the kind of use for which it was designed, namely the recording of transmissional variation.

It is the fully emended, 'ideal' text of the first edition, then—i.e., the critical edition's clear reading text—which is provided with an accompanying integral apparatus in the form of a synopsis of the text's diachrony from fair copy/final draft to book publication. The synoptic apparatus is designed as in the example in Figure 2. It does not use the dimension of the vertical parallel—except of course that to its right is printed out in parallel its final state of development in cleartext form; and, since it surveys the revisional progression of a prose text, it cannot utilise the dimension of the horizontal parallel. Prose progresses line by line endlessly; and so the synopsis is superimposed, by means of diacritics, onto the continuous prose line.

Raised halfbrackets in opening and closing pairs, indexed as to the document levels of the changes, delimit the extension of variation within the invariant continuum of the text. Where changes take place within the autograph notation of one document, rather than on a document subsequent to an earlier one, the marks of delimitation are raised pairs of carets, rotating clockwise/anticlockwise where there are two or more levels of change in the autograph text of the one document in question. Text simply enclosed in halfbrackets or carets is added text at the given level. Deletions effected on the document of entry itself of the text deleted are enclosed in pointed brackets, and, where possible, indexed inside the opening bracket as to the caret-level of the deletion. (*Currente calamo* deletions receive no caret index.) Deletions of earlier text on a later document are enclosed in square brackets and indexed inside the opening bracket correspondingly. Revisions are represented as replacements, or deletions-*cum*-additions, with the caret or halfbracket opening before the bracketed text and closing after the replacement text.

The functional correlation of the edition text and the synoptic apparatus is very important. The user of the edition should be in a position to read the textual development in reverse—i.e., he should be able to begin his analysis from the final synchronous state of the text which he finds printed out separately on the edition's right-hand pages and, subtracting from it level after level of revision, work his way backwards to the earliest such state included in the synopsis. Conversely, by following the indices to the textual development, letters of the alphabet first and then rising numerals, he should be able to build up

FIGURE 2.

Sardines on the shelves. [2]^Almost taste them by looking.^ Sandwich? Ham and his descendants musterred and bred there.[2] Potted meats. What is home without Plumtree's potted meat? Incomplete. What a stupid ad! ^[Right under] Under[2] the obituary notices [too:] they stuck it.[2] [2]All up a plumtree.[2] Dignam's potted meat.^ [Cannibals would with lemon and rice. White [5][men] missionary[5] too salty. Like pickled pork.[2] [5]Expect the chief consumes the parts of honour. Ought to be tough from exercise. His wives in a row to watch the effect.[5] [7]*There was a right royal old nigger. Who ate or something the somethings of the reverend Mr MacTrigger.*[7] With it [an] abode of bliss. Lord knows what concoction. [Cauls mouldy tripes windpipes faked [4]and minced[4] up. [2]Puzzle find the meat.[2] Kosher. [2]No meat and milk together.[2] Hygiene that was what they call now.[2] [7]^Yom Kippur fast spring cleaning of inside. Peace and war depend on some fellow's digestion. Religions. Christmas turkeys and geese. Slaughter of innocents. Eat drink and be merry. Then casual wards full after.^ [2]Heads bandaged.[2] Cheese digests all but itself. Mity cheese.[7]
– Have you a cheese sandwich?

the textual genesis from the apparatus presentation. The apparatus is thus consciously designed analytically, contrary to attempts at reproducing textual genesis elsewhere, which might be termed mimetic. These start, say, from the norm of an early manuscript and then indicate revisions, deletions and accretions as deviations, using a system of typeface variation and bracketings, whereby the final revisions tend to get hidden in close-to-impenetrable thickets of brackets. In such a manner, a progressive textual integration by successive revision towards intermediary or final stable textual states of the work becomes incongruously visualised by escalating typographical disintegration. By contrast, the synoptic apparatus for *Ulysses* should encourage a reader to move as freely along the type-line in print as forwards and backwards along the axis of diachrony of the work's total text.

* * *

Sardines on the shelves. Almost taste them by looking. Sandwich? Ham and his descendants musterred and bred there. Potted meats. What is home without Plumtree's potted meat? Incomplete. What a stupid ad! Under the obituary notices they stuck it. All up a plumtree. Dignam's potted meat. Cannibals would with lemon and rice. White missionary too salty. Like pickled pork. Expect the chief consumes the parts of honour. Ought to be tough from exercise. His wives in a row to watch the effect. *There was a right royal old nigger. Who ate or something the somethings of the reverend Mr MacTrigger.* With it an abode of bliss. Lord knows what concoction. Cauls mouldy tripes windpipes faked and minced up. Puzzle find the meat. Kosher. No meat and milk together. Hygiene that was what they call now. Yom Kippur fast spring cleaning of inside. Peace and war depend on some fellow's digestion. Religions. Christmas turkeys and geese. Slaughter of innocents. Eat drink and be merry. Then casual wards full after. Heads bandaged. Cheese digests all but itself. Mity cheese.
– Have you a cheese sandwich?

The practical results of a reflection on the theoretical problem of the synchrony and diachrony of texts are thus new forms of apparatus presentation in scholarly editions to do justice to revisional variation, a distinct and an essential textual category in both critical and editorial terms. By way of an analysis of a passage chosen at random from Leopold Bloom's lunchtime chapter "Lestrygonians" I should, in conclusion, like to demonstrate how, in the case of *Ulysses*, the integral apparatus of the work's diachronous synopsis may be used to direct the critical discourse.

Comfortable in the atmosphere of Davy Byrne's, Bloom decides to order his lunch. "Let me see. I'll take a glass of burgundy and . . . let me see." His mental wanderings as he hesitates are briefest in the earliest extant draft stage represented by the basic inscription in the Rosenbach Manuscript. "Sardines on the shelves. Potted meats. What is a home without Plumtree's potted meat? Incomplete. What a

stupid ad! With it an abode of bliss. Lord knows what concoction.
—Have you a cheese sandwich?''

The moment is quite unobtrusive within the flow of the narrative.
Its dialectics are perfunctory. Disliking the idea both of fish and flesh
suggested by the exposed sardines and potted meats (in contrast to his
matutinal relishing of "the inner organs of beasts and fowls"),
Bloom asks for a cheese sandwich. Fleetingly, his professional mind
recalls the Plumtree's advertisement and condemns both product and
promotion. Though the reader may recall earlier uses in the novel of
the motif of the Plumtree's ad, Bloom does not yet make the connection. The gruesome reference back to the "Hades" chapter seems to
have occurred to Joyce in the very act of faircopying the passage.
"Dignam's potted meat." is crammed in between the lines, and on
second thoughts additionally prefixed by "Right under the obituary
notices too:" Transferred back to the final working draft, the composite addition reappears in the typescript in a revised shape more
idiomatically conforming to the style of Bloom's stream of consciousness: "Under the obituary notices they stuck it. Dignam's potted
meat." Moreover, the typescript reveals how the passage, once defined in structural outline, begins to expand by its own law of dialectical opposition and to be exposed to variants of overarching thematic
import. On the plane of Bloom's realism, set against the doubtful
"concoction" (now specified as "Cauls mouldy tripes windpipes
faked up") is the idea of "Kosher," which in its turn is immediately
translated into the modern analogy of "Hygiene." Two of Bloom's
constant preoccupations, his Jewish heritage and his urge for cleanli-
ness, are thereby simultaneously brought to bear. Purportedly also on
the realistic level, but with overtones of the Homeric myth of the
Lestrygonians discernible to the reader's ear, "Dignam's potted
meat" leads to the association of "Cannibals."

FIGURE 3.

```
 Sardines on the shelves. Potted meats. What is home
without Plumtree's potted meat? Incomplete. What a stupid
ad!  ᶜ[Right under] Under ᵉ⁊ the obituary notices
ᶜ[too:] they stuck it.ᵉ⁊  Dignam's potted meat.
ᶜCannibals would with lemon and rice. White men too
salty. Like pickled pork.ᵉ⁊  With it  ᶜanᵉ⁊  abode of
bliss. Lord knows what concoction.  ᶠCauls mouldy tripes
windpipes faked up. Kosher. Hygiene that was what they
call now. ᵉ⁊
—Have you a cheese sandwich?
```

Thus, from the final working draft, the passage stood for the pre-publication in *The Little Review* in February 1919. The revisions made on the typescript submitted to the French printers in the summer of 1921 (stage 1 in the post-final-draft textual development) document the subsequent two-year evolution under the influence of the novel's entire growth. Importantly, the synthesis of the fish:meat opposition is drawn into the stream of consciousness itself with the proverbial adage of "Cheese digests all but itself," and a Bloomian pun is flourished in conclusion: "Mity cheese." The adjective's homophone (which all printed texts of *Ulysses* display: "Mighty cheese," thereby unauthoritatively suppressing the cheese-mite as the material cause for the cheese's self-digestion) is a common attribute of the Lord (who "knows what concoction"). "Kosher" is his command; so the line of association is open to "Yom Kippur" and "Religions," and thence to an attempted resolution in "Christmas" of the heathen:jew opposition as implied in cannibals:kosher. But 'kosher' combines the notions of religion and food. So the contrapuntal strand of eating and digestion, inducing the new opposition of peace and war, also radically subverts all positive valencies of Christianity by evoking only its worldly manifestations of injustice, belligerence, and gluttonous materialism. "Christmas turkeys and geese. Slaughter of innocents. Eat drink and be merry. Then casual wards full after." Bloom's original slight hesitation over his order for lunch has become transformed into a multidimensional acid sketch of a hungry man's world view.

FIGURE 4.

```
    Sardines on the shelves. Potted meats. What is home
without Plumtree's potted meat? Incomplete. What a stupid
ad! Under the obituary notices
they stuck it. Dignam's potted meat.
Cannibals would with lemon and rice. White men too
salty. Like pickled pork. With it an abode of
bliss. Lord knows what concoction. Cauls mouldy tripes
windpipes faked up. Kosher. Hygiene that was what they
call now. ⌐∧Yom Kippur fast spring cleaning of inside.
Peace and war depend on some fellow's digestion.
Religions. Christmas turkeys and geese. Slaughter of
innocents. Eat drink and be merry. Then casual wards full
after. ∧  Cheese digests all but itself. Mity cheese.⌐ı
━Have you a cheese sandwich?
```

The subsequent revisions to the first, the third, the fourth and the sixth proofs (stages 2, 4, 5 and 7 of the whole chapter's textual development) add enriching details and virtuoso touches to the narrative unfolding of Bloom's agile, albeit undisciplined, mind and witty perception, while at the same time tightening the net of correspondences among the book's motifs and incidents. Within the ambience of religions now established, the specification of the cannibals' victim as a "missionary" seems inevitable. It sparks off the crowning vision of the chief consuming the parts of honour (like Mr Bloom, he ate with relish the inner organs . . .), with his wives in Mollean expectancy watching the effect of their digestive transformation. The picture of the missionary's fate at the hands of the cannibals is an allusive counterpoint, surely, to the Alaki of Abeakuta's visit (in "Cyclops") to civilised Cottonopolis, his ethics sustained by the gift of Queen Victoria's bible. The savages' potential marital bliss inspires, as a final signature to the passage, Bloom's literary creativity to mirror Joyce's in the incipient composition of a limerick. "There was a right royal old nigger. Who ate or something the somethings of the reverend Mr MacTrigger." Bloom's hunger, however, proves stronger than his powers of concentration, so he fails to complete it until preparing to eat his cheese sandwich. Not only may the limerick by this delayed completion have eluded the skimming eyes of censors; the passage from which it springs has also escaped the danger of isolation as a set piece of brilliant writing by becoming firmly reintegrated into the flow of the narrative.

But this narrative, it should be seen, has been transmuted from the one of the final working draft/typescript/*Little Review* version of "Lestrygonians." Its focus was on the fictional character of Leopold Bloom, constructed with skill in a stream-of-consciousness technique to lend psychological verisimilitude to his actions and thoughts. As a fictional character, he does not become displaced by the text in revision. But, since his identity is a device of language, his centrality to the tale may now take on a new function. Once established, the structures of his mental behaviour no longer exclusively, or even predominantly, serve to unfold a personality. They become employed by the narrative to penetrate the world of everyday which Bloom, as a person entrapped in the nets of his idiosyncratic sensibilities, strives to evade. Bloom's momentary distraction as he hesitates over his sandwich order at the earliest stage of the text is plausible action. But by no stretch of critical good will can the multidirectional linguistic display of the final version be taken as an instance alone of verisimilitudinous character portrayal to fit the narrative situation. Autoreflexively, the text of *Ulysses* has turned in upon itself to expand in a constant playback of variation and alternatives, re-using as a style of language to encompass the world in the fiction what at first was a mere device of character construction.

* * *

Ulysses presents an amply documented case from which to work out the implications of the basic assumption that the object of scholarly and critical analysis and study—as opposed to an author's object of publication, and a general public's reading matter—is not the final product of the writer's art alone, but beyond this, the totality of the Work in Progress. It is an assumption that follows from the theoretical premise that the work of literature possesses in its material medium itself, in its text or texts, a diachronic as well as a synchronic dimension. The act of publication which confers upon it a synchronous structure does not at the same time have the power to obliterate the coexisting diachronous structure of the work, to which the discrete temporal states of its text coalesce by complex hierarchical interrelationships. The synchronous and diachronous structures combine to form the literary work in the totality of its real presence in the documents of its conception, transmission and publication. Joyce's textually manifest creation, in the case of *Ulysses*, is not the published text of 1922 alone, but this text in its relationships to the cumulating succession of notebooks, notesheets, drafts, fair copies, typescripts, *Little Review* serialisations, and author's augmentations and revisions in typescripts and proofs; and beyond, in its manifest links with the oeuvre of which it is a part. The relationships observed require stringent definition and classification. Suitable methods of approach, with their appropriate critical tools, need to be developed to master the analysis of a text of which the elements are not merely juxtaposed as it were spatially, but also succeed one another in time. This is as yet essentially virgin land for criticism. It should be explored from a firm base of editorial presentation controlling both the synchrony and the diachrony of the text. And to reevaluate our notions of the artistic nature of the literary work there may be no better paradigm that that of *Ulysses*.

NOTE

This paper was written for oral delivery, and no essential changes in the script have been made to the section read at the first STS conference in 1981. For reasons of time, the concluding extended analysis of an example of textual diachrony from the "Lestry-gonians" chapter of *Ulysses* was not given in New York. In the meantime, the *Critical and Synoptic Edition* of James Joyce's *Ulysses* has been published (3 vols., New York: Garland Publishing Inc., 1984). Its principles and format of apparatus presentation are as here detailed, minor modifications in the externals of the diacritical system notwith-standing. My analysis of the genesis of "At a Solemn Musick" has appeared as "Poetry in Numbers: A Development of Significative Form in Milton's Early Poetry" in *ARCHIV*, 220 (1983), 54–61.

The lack of specific footnoting in this article is the concomitant of its oral delivery. My debts to the Anglo-American school of bibliography and textual editing should be obvious. I equally draw on current German approaches to editing. They are reflected in Hans Zeller's "A New Approach to the Critical Constitution of Literary Texts," *Studies in Bibliography*, 28 (1975), 231–264. A much broader survey of the complexity of issues digested and developed in the present paper may be gained from Gunter Martens and Hans Zeller, eds., *Texte und Varianten. Probleme ihrer Edition und Inter-pretation.* München: C. H. Beck, 1971 (with a bibliography of exemplary editions), as well as from the special numbers *Edition und Wirkung* of *LiLi. Zeitschrift für Litera-turwissenschaft und Linguistik*, 5 (1975) (Heft 19/20), and *Probleme neugermanis-tischer Edition*, Band 101 (Sonderheft) of *Zeitschrift für Deutsche Philologie* (1982).

Finally, I wish to express my gratitude to the Deutsche Forschungsgemeinschaft who, with funds from the German Foreign Office, enabled me to attend the 1981 STS conference.

Some Problems in
Modern Enumerative Bibliography

A. S. G. Edwards

It would be unwise to read too much into my title. My expertise in modern enumerative bibliography cannot, by any standards, be described as extensive. I hope, however, that the thin gruel of my experience may prove adequate to sustain the position I wish to take. It seems to me that some aspects of enumerative bibliography raise questions about the practice of the craft which do not seem to have been generally as fully assessed as they might be. I wish to argue for a greater consideration of certain problems (as I see them to be) and at the same time to sound a note of muted pessimism.

Certain basic aims constitute the purposes of modern enumerative bibliography: the location, identification and recording of the significant forms of all a writer's utterances that have been disseminated through the printed word. The aims are quite clear-cut—or should be. Their execution is another matter. For I grow increasingly uncertain whether it is feasible in many cases to contemplate a bibliography of a modern author that can lay claim to definitiveness in the terms I have just enunciated. I am not simply suggesting that any bibliography is likely to be incomplete to a greater or lesser degree depending upon the capacities of the particular bibliographer. It may be that there are certain problems inherent in modern bibliography which in both degree and kind are not fully solved and may indeed be unsolvable.

Let me begin with an obvious problem: the establishment of the canon. The identification of anonymous or pseudonymous contributions is not, of course, peculiar to modern bibliography. But some kinds of modern literary activity pose the problem in distinctive forms.

It seems quite possible that for some modern authors at least any attempt to identify such unattributed works must fall short of definitiveness, even far short. We lack the key to unsigned contributions to many periodicals. The *Times Literary Supplement* is only the most obvious instance of such difficulties. How many authors lurk unidentified in its columns before 1974?[1] There appears no way of knowing. The only accessible source, the annual *Times* desk diary, identifies only some of the weekly contributors—the number varies from editor to editor but can be very few indeed. For some years (e.g. 1939–45) no record at all seems to exist. If a particular author had a meticulous agent (whose records have survived) or if the author was exact in his financial records then progress may be possible, given general good will and collaboration—not necessarily a small proviso. But even under ideal circumstances there can be little cause for unqualified optimism. B. J. Kirkpatrick had the active cooperation of Leonard Woolf in her splendid bibliography of Virginia Woolf. But he mislaid payment records that identified some *TLS* contributions. They were found for the second edition,[2] but Ms. Kirkpatrick records ruefully that "there are, undoubtably, further early unsigned contributions to the *Guardian*, the *Speaker*, and possibly the *Outlook* [that have gone unrecorded]."[3]

Similar situations obtain to a greater or lesser degree with other journals. There appears to be no marked file of the *New Statesman*. The various contributions of (for example) Louis MacNeice to the "London Diary" of that journal remain therefore unidentified.[4] How much of the "Talk of the Town" section of the *New Yorker* or other portions of this journal were contributed by such figures of literary importance as John Updike or Peter de Vries? Their bibliographers seem unable to tell us.[5]

These are obvious examples of a recurrent problem: the existence of a pool of unrecoverable attributions of undeterminable size and depth. There are, in addition, such related issues as unverifiable attributions[6] which suggest that there can often inevitably be a degree of indeterminacy about some bibliographical undertakings.

Other kinds of material may be irretrievably inaccessible for quite different reasons. Dustjackets and the blurbs they contain are one such problem. On occasions the copy may have been composed by the author or contain identifiable statements by him which should be recorded in the canon of his works. Or the blurb may include solicited comments by figures of distinction which need to be added to *their* bibliographies. Or the blurb may have been written by someone of literary importance in his own right.[7] The most famous example to fall into this final category is, I suppose, T. S. Eliot who was for many years a director of Faber and Faber and frequently wrote blurbs for the firm's books. Donald Gallup made a deliberate decision to exclude them from his Eliot bibliography,[8] a decision I find regrettable especially since he had access to material that would have identified many of them. Any attempt at a comprehensive listing of Eliot's writings ought to aim to include them.

For most authors there are often two aspects to the question: knowing, or suspecting that someone may have written a blurb and then locating it. Both can be very difficult. There are many possible avenues by which one can become aware of the possible existence of such blurbs: publisher's records, private correspondence and the like. But it is quite possible that an item of this kind could exist without any certain indication of the fact from external evidence. A diligent bibliographer may pursue hunches to examine possible words and their dustjackets. Here he is likely to run into the problem of availability. Scholarly libraries necessarily preserve dust jackets on a selective basis, if at all. For the generality of authors' dustjackets we must rely on chance, the private collector, or, in more recent times, the blessings of lamination which have enabled public and other libraries to preserve dust jackets on books. An example from my own experience: I was aware that the writer Selwyn Jepson was a close friend of Robert Graves, in whose bibliography I have a small interest. I naturally checked a number of Jepson's works to see if they included any comments by Graves. I discovered that Graves's words of praise for *The Angry Millionaire* appear on the first page of that novel. But the copy I examined was in a copyright library, hence bereft of jacket. It was largely fortuitous that I came upon a (laminated) dustjacketed copy in a public library and was able to discover that the comments in the book were extracted from a much longer blurb on the jacket.

I suspect my experience is not untypical. Some bibliographers make a point of ignoring contributions to dustjackets. For most others treatment must almost necessarily be unsystematic, given the circumstances I have indicated. Blurbs remain an unresolved and possibly unresolvable problem in modern enumerative bibliography.

The problems that I have outlined so far may provide a certain context of pessimism, even if they do not make anyone feel positively no longer at ease under the old dispensation. They constitute, however, the tip of an iceberg of unrecorded and, at times, unrecordable data that confronts the modern bibliographer.

A more serious problem is the treatment of published correspondence in newspapers or weekly journals. It is in one sense odd that this should be a problem since there are rarely any problems in establishing authorship and most newspapers or journals are at least theoretically accessible.

The issues involved here are problems of retrieval. Most journals do produce indexes; very few newspapers do. Yet almost all have in common a failure to index correspondence columns. The only major English newspapers or journals that regularly index correspondence are the *Times* and the *Times Literary Supplement*. (The *Spectator* did for a brief period in the 1940s.) Most of the others do, I repeat, have indexes that generally appear punctually for each volume. But it often seems that bibliographers have been content to rely on these without grasping a limitation that is of some importance.

Hence the treatment of correspondence in many bibliographies tends to be an aspect of their coverage that is often most incomplete. And yet for many writers correspondence columns provide a regular outlet for their views on a wide range of matters. Donald Gallup in his bibliography of T. S. Eliot includes a hundred and forty-seven letters among the six hundred and eighty-one periodical contributions he includes. The bibliographer of Robert Graves, F. H. Higginson, includes seventy-three among seven hundred and sixty odd items. And so on. The point does not need labouring that such items can constitute an important part of a writer's corpus.

Yet the difficulties posed by any attempt at a comprehensive listing of such items can be very great. Recently I had occasion to read through files of a number of British journals for periods of between fifteen and thirty years—specifically, the *New Statesman*, *Spectator*, *Listener* and *Sunday Times*. I began in pursuit of a single figure, but as time went on I found myself noting items by other writers in whom I had some interest, paying some attention to correspondence columns. My notes were therefore highly selective in scope and chronological range. But when I checked them against published bibliographies of various authors I did find some tendencies which may prove of some interest.

I found about twenty-five unrecorded items each for Graves and Graham Greene, some twenty by Evelyn Waugh, ten by Kingsley Amis, half a dozen by T. S. Eliot, four by Dorothy Sayers as well as individual items by such writers as Iris Murdoch (her first publication, I suspect), Ezra Pound, and Philip Larkin. This may not seem a particularly rich trawl. But I would stress that it was based on a limited survey of a limited number of journals for a limited period. And while my results are not dramatic, they are suggestive—and of something more than the epistolary habits of various authors or the relative fallibility of their bibliographers.

One accepts, I assume, that the aim of any enumerative bibliography is to achieve as close an approximation to definitiveness as is practicable. What then are the likely constraints on practicability that will operate here? They are likely to be threefold: time, money, and access. In practice the three are interconnected.

For a search through (say) forty years of a number of major journals scanning the correspondence columns may not daunt the ardor of a resolute bibliographer. But when you add to that the columns of a number of newspapers his resolution may begin to weaken. How much time is that likely to add to labours that may already be formidable? And how is that time likely to be justified in terms of its end result? Indeed, even if the flesh is willing is it likely to find sustenance? How many bibliographers are likely to have regular access to files of newspapers, for example? Let me give an example from my own experience which may focus the problem a little. My university library does not possess a file or microfilm of the *Sunday Times*. It informs that it is impossible to obtain through inter-library loan copies from anywhere in any form before 1950. If I wish (as I do) to examine files for the years 1930–1950 I must either betake myself elsewhere or buy a microfilm. Neither will prove cheap. As research funds of all kinds continue to shrink, it may grow steadily more difficult to justify such speculative expenditures in terms of money—or time. Both I or (ideally) my patron have to weigh investments against likely return.

Similar difficulties exist with reviews or articles in most newspapers. In most cases there is, once again, no alternative to a page by page search, with the attendant logistical problems. One may well, on occasions, be unable to establish where to begin and when to stop. To some extent the situation can be mitigated by the use of newspaper clipping files—in my experience a source insufficiently exploited by bibliographers. But even these tend to be unsystematic and incomplete even in the coverage of their own papers. And occasionally, even a complete file of a relevant newspaper may itself prove unobtainable.[9] I do not want to elaborate on these questions now. But I hope I have said enough to show that the avenues through which a modern author may be able to disseminate his work can be very difficult to retrace with any expectation of definitiveness.

Thus far my observations have been confined to difficulties of re-
trievability—to categories of material which ought to be included in
bibliographies but which by their nature resist discovery. I would now
like to turn, briefly, to some rather different, methodological problems, to some classes of material which seem not to be treated with any
degree of consistency or logic in some bibliographies.

The first such problem is the nature and status of offprints. Offprints have had an existence as distinct bibliographical entities since at
least the middle of the sixteenth century, although they became especially common during the nineteenth and twentieth centuries. Their
particular importance has been authoritatively argued: "To the author they often seem the real first edition. It is in that form that he
thinks of his work, for it is copies of offprints he presents to his
friends."[10] One may add that the textual importance of offprints cannot be ignored since they often contain corrections or revisions by the
author to the more generally published text. But considerable uncertainty seems to exist as to their bibliographical identity. Is an offprint
a distinct separate publication, in effect to be treated as a book?
Should it really be viewed as "the real first edition"? Or should it be
viewed as a piece of bibliophiliac irrelevance?

There are no clear precedents. At one extreme is Timothy D'Arch
Smith who in his excellent bibliography of Montague Summers consistently treats offprints as both books and contributions to
periodicals.[11] At the other extreme is perhaps the Bloomfield/Men-
delson bibliography of Auden which seems strangely inconsistent in
its treatment of this problem.[12] At one point they treat a single leaf
offprinted from the *Listener* as a book;[13] yet elsewhere, while they intermittently note the existence of offprints, they decline to accord
them any status.[14] Donald Gallup in his bibliographies of Eliot and
Pound occasionally records offprints, but very rarely describes them
and does not include them as separate publications. One could go on.

But instead it might be profitable to reflect that there seem to be no
generally held assumptions as to what constitutes an offprint. John
Carter gives a helpful definition: "a separate printing of a section of a
larger publication (generally of composite authorship) made from the
same setting of type."[15] He goes on to distinguish between offprints
and extracts made by disbinding a journal. There are some problems
with these formal definitions—although I am unaware of better. One
is familiar with the practice of some journals of sending contributors

what are termed tearsheets, that is, unbound or stapled sets of the relevant pages. I cannot immediately think of a technique that would differentiate them from extracts. Some journals complicate matters by offering both tearsheets *and* wrappered offprints. And some journals change policies from time to time. An extreme case of the difficulties involved is provided by Ezra Pound's "Translations from Cavalcanti" published in *The Quarterly Review of Literature* (1949). Or was it? Gallup describes this item thus: "Printed one on each side of a leaf of green paper, laid into the issue. Some copies were distributed separately. . . ."[16] The status of this item seems fraught with ambiguity. Do we regard this as a periodical publication—as Gallup does? With some offprints? Or as a wholly distinct item, a broadside, arbitrarily inserted into a periodical, yet bibliographically separate? I raise the point simply to suggest there can be a degree of imprecision in thought and hence in terminology that attends our attitude to offprints.

And there are larger problems involved than those of definition. One hardly needs to do more than invoke the names of T. J. Wise and H. Buxton Forman to recall that the identification and description of genuine offprints can be a crucial aspect of the bibliographer's responsibility, since they constitute the first separate publication of a work. Hence the treatment of offprints involves important questions of priority that are fundamental to the purposes of enumerative bibliography. Unless and until a satisfactory methodology for the treatment of offprints can be devised, an important issue in modern bibliography must appear in some disarray.

In the case of offprints questions of form and priority are crucially connected. My final problem is concerned solely with a question of form. It is posed in the form of a question: what constitutes, for the purposes of enumerative bibliography, an 'appearance' in print? I am particularly preoccupied with the bibliographical status of interviews. There seems to have been little attention given to any attempt to formulate general principles for the bibliographical treatment of interviews. The only attempt I am aware of is Donald Gallup's. "Most interviews," he suggests, should not be included "unless one has the evidence of manuscripts or recordings that the words attributed to the author were indeed his own (or unless the interviews are listed separately for the often important information they contain)."[17]

This position has its merits. But it may be insufficiently flexible to accommodate the variety of situations confronting a bibliographer in dealing with the various printed manifestations of the spoken word. To take an extreme case, where would one wish to put verses by Robert Graves composed extempore over the telephone to William Hickey of the *Daily Express* on the occasion of his election to the Oxford Professorship of Poetry?[18] I doubt whether anyone would oppose very strongly its categorization as a periodical contribution of an unrecorded poem. And there are indeed other categories of material which are preserved only through the undeterminable accuracy of reporters' shorthand. Gallup himself includes a number of items in his bibliography of T. S. Eliot on this basis.[19] Some of Oscar Wilde's lectures in America can only be reconstructed from newspaper reports.[20] Somerset Maugham's bibliographer notes an item, among his periodical publications, of which the sole form is a reported speech.[21] Robert Graves's bibliographer includes some interviews among Graves's publications but relegates others to his secondary bibliography on no stated principles.[22]

This list of examples could doubtless be extended. But I am more concerned with its implications. For the status of oral utterances in printed form can raise daunting problems for the bibliographer. Where and how does one draw the line? Logically any form of reported speech that achieves the status of print can therefore be an appropriate candidate for inclusion. The problem of any definition like Gallup's is that it can leave important items out. The problem of a policy of more generous inclusiveness is that it can leave the bibliographer contemplating a Sisyphean undertaking where the possibility of completeness perpetually slips beyond his grasp as he pursues stray quotations in obscure newspapers.

Most of the matters I have raised may appear relatively trivial when seen in the total context of a bibliography of a major writer. But to ignore them or to treat them unsystematically or incompletely is to suppress or misrepresent data that is a relevant part of a writer's corpus. There may be no clear or final solutions to the problems I have sought to raise. But it may at least be possible to consider them with greater clarity than is sometimes evident in the work of some modern bibliographers.

NOTES

1. I am grateful to Mr. Gordon Phillips, the *Times* Archivist, for information on these matters and for the opportunity to consult the desk diaries.

2. See B. J. Kirkpatrick, *A Bibliography of Virginia Woolf*, rev. ed. (London: Rupert Hart-Davis, 1967), p. ix.

3. Kirkpatrick, pp. ix–x.

4. See C. M. Armitage and N. Clark, *A Bibliography of the Works of Louis MacNeice* (London: Kay & Ward, 1973), p. 7.

5. See M. A. Olivas, *An Annotated Bibliography of John Updike Criticism 1967–73 and A Checklist of his Works* (New York: Garland, 1975) and E. T. Bowden, *Peter de Vries: A Bibliography, 1934–1977* (Austin: Humanities Research Center, 1978); de Vries has been cartoon caption editor of the *New Yorker*; I am indebted for this point to the very thoughtful review of Bowden's bibliography by D. Vander Meulen, *Analytical & Enumerative Bibliography*, 4 (1980), 156.

6. For example, both Robert Graves and Laura Riding have claimed for their canons various contributions signed "Madeleine Vara" in the periodical, *Epilogue*; see F. H. Higginson, *A Bibliography of the Works of Robert Graves* (Hamden, Conn.: Archon Books, 1966), nos. B 22 and B 25, and Laura (Riding) Jackson, "Some Autobiographical Corrections of Literary History," *Denver Quarterly*, 8 (1974), 5–6.

7. For a useful discussion of this matter see D. Gallup, *On Contemporary Bibliography* (Austin: Humanities Research Center, 1970), p. 13.

8. See D. Gallup, *T. S. Eliot: A Bibliography*, rev. ed. (New York: Harcourt, Brace & World, 1969), pp. 12–13.

9. For discussion of problems of this kind as they apply to the would-be bibliographer of Gissing, see P. Coustillas and R. L. Selig, "Unknown Gissing Stories from Chicago," *Times Literary Supplement*, 12 December (1980), 1417–1418.

10. The late W. A. Jackson, quoted in *Book Collector*, VI (1957), 119.

11. See *A Bibliography of the Works of Montague Summers* (London: Nicholas Vane, 1964).

12. B. C. Bloomfield and E. Mendelson, *W. H. Auden: A Bibliography, 1924–1969*, 2nd ed. (Charlottesville: University Press of Virginia, 1972).

13. Cf. Bloomfield and Mendelson, A5.

14. Cf., e.g., items C418 and C534.

15. J. Carter, *ABC for Book Collectors*, 4th ed. (London: Rupert Hart-Davis, 1966), p. 138.

16. D. Gallup, *A Bibliography of Ezra Pound* (London: Rupert Hart-Davis, 1963), item C1715.

17. Gallup, *On Contemporary Bibliography*, p. 20.

18. The item appeared in the *Daily Express* for 17 February, 1961, p. 3; it is not recorded in Higginson's bibliography of Graves.

19. Cf., e.g., items C 341, 349, 434, 538a.

20. See H. F. O'Brien, "'The House Beautiful': A Reconstruction of Oscar Wilde's American Lecture," *Victorian Studies*, 17 (1974), 395–418, based on a collation of "over 100 newspaper reports of Wilde's three lectures" (397).

21. R. Toole Stott, *A Bibliography of the Works of W. Somerset Maugham* (London: Kay & Ward, 1973), item D 177. "Mr. Maugham's speech at the Royal Academy Banquet reported verbatim [in *News Chronicle*, 3 May 1951].

22. Higginson, included C 679 among Graves's writings, but not item E 66.

The Society for Textual Scholarship

The Society for Textual Scholarship, founded in 1979, is an organization devoted to the interdisciplinary discussion of textual theory and practice. The Society's members are scholars from many different fields, including English, American, French, Spanish, Italian, German, Slavic, and Oriental Languages and Literatures, Classics, Biblical Studies, History, Linguistics, Musicology, Folklore, Art History, Theater History, Legal History, Cinema Studies, Epigraphy, Palaeography, Codicology, Enumerative, Analytical, and Descriptive Bibliography, Textual Criticism, and Computer Science. The Society convenes at a biennial conference (usually three or four days, with seventy-five to one hundred speakers), where members and invited guests present papers in plenary or special sessions. Members may also organize discussion groups at the conferences. Each conference features a special address by the current president of the Society, the first two presidents being G. Thomas Tanselle and Paul Oskar Kristeller. The last two conferences held in New York City in 1981 and 1983, attracted scholars from several countries, including (in addition to the U.S.A. and Canada) England, Scotland, Ireland, France, Germany, Sweden, Saudi Arabia, and Australia. The next conference of STS will be held in April 1985, again in New York City. The Society also meets periodically under the auspices of the various professional conventions (e.g., the Modern Language Association of America).

The Society publishes an annual hardback volume of contributions, *TEXT*, which contains articles selected from papers given at the biennial conferences, together with articles submitted independently.

The Editors welcome contributions for future volumes of *TEXT* from scholars concerned with any aspect of the enumeration, description, transcription, editing, or annotation of texts in any discipline. Submissions are read and evaluated by selected representatives of the STS Advisory Board. The Society also publishes periodic Bulletins, and a Newsletter, which contains correspondence, reviews, and bibliographies of interest to scholars in various disciplines.

The Society for Textual Scholarship welcomes applications for membership. All inquiries, or submissions to *TEXT*, should be sent to:

D.C. GREETHAM, *STS Executive Director*
Ph.D. Program in English
Graduate Center
The City University of New York
33 West 42nd Street, New York, N.Y. 10036

OFFICERS

President	PAUL OSKAR KRISTELLER, Columbia University (1983–85)
Executive Director	D.C. GREETHAM, Queensborough Community College and Graduate Center, CUNY (1983–85)
Secretary	KEITH WALTERS, Graduate Center, CUNY (1983–85)
Treasurer	W. SPEED HILL, Herbert H. Lehman College and Graduate Center, CUNY (1983–85)
Executive Committee	ALLAN ATLAS, Brooklyn College and Graduate Center, CUNY (1984)
	JOHN MOYNE, Queens College and Graduate Center, CUNY (1984)
	MARY B. SPEER, Rutgers University (1984)
	BARBARA OBERG, Baruch College, CUNY (1985)
	THOMAS G. PALAIMA, Fordham University (1985)
	MARTIN STEVENS, Baruch College and Graduate Center, CUNY (1985)
	DONALD H. REIMAN, The Carl H. Pforzheimer Library (1986)
	G. THOMAS TANSELLE, The John Simon Guggenheim Memorial Foundation (1986)
	JOHN VAN SICKLE, Brooklyn College and Graduate Center, CUNY (1986)
Past President	G. THOMAS TANSELLE, The John Simon Guggenheim Memorial Foundation (1981–83)